THE IRON RHINE (*IJZEREN RIJN*) ARBITRATION
(BELGIUM–NETHERLANDS)
AWARD OF 2005

―――

L'ARBITRAGE DU « RHIN DE FER »
(BELGIQUE–PAYS-BAS)
SENTENCE DE 2005

PERMANENT COURT OF ARBITRATION AWARD SERIES

THE IRON RHINE (*IJZEREN RIJN*) ARBITRATION (BELGIUM–NETHERLANDS) AWARD OF 2005

With an Introduction by Colin Warbrick

———————

L'ARBITRAGE DU « RHIN DE FER » (BELGIQUE–PAYS-BAS) SENTENCE DE 2005

Avec une Introduction de Colin Warbrick

Series Editor

BELINDA MACMAHON

Legal Counsel/Chief Editor
Permanent Court of Arbitration

Responsable de série

BELINDA MACMAHON

Conseillere juridique/Rédactrice en chef
Court permanente d'arbitrage

T·M·C·ASSER PRESS

Published by T·M·C·ASSER PRESS
P.O. Box 16163, 2500 BD The Hague, The Netherlands
<www.asserpress.nl>

T·M·C·ASSER PRESS' English language books are distributed exclusively by:

Cambridge University Press, The Edinburgh Building, Shaftesbury Road,
Cambridge CB2 2RU, UK,
or
for customers in the USA, Canada and Mexico:
Cambridge University Press, 100 Brook Hill Drive, West Nyack, NY 10994-2133, USA
<www.cambridge.org>

ISBN 13: 978-90-6704-235-2

The Permanent Court of Arbitration (PCA) is an intergovernmental organization, founded at the first Hague Peace Conference in 1899, and based in the Peace Palace in The Hague. It provides a wide range of dispute resolution mechanisms – including arbitration, conciliation and fact finding – in disputes involving various combinations of states, private parties and intergovernmental organizations. The PCA is committed to meeting the rapidly evolving dispute resolution needs of its member states and the international community.

International Bureau
Permanent Court of Arbitration
Peace Palace
Carnegieplein 2
2517 KJ The Hague
The Netherlands
Telephone: +31 70 302 4165
Facsimile: +31 70 302 4167
Email: bureau@pca-cpa.org
Website: www.pca-cpa.org

CONTENTS–SUMMARY
SOMMAIRE

FOREWORD

This volume contains the Award of the Arbitral Tribunal established to decide the dispute between the Kingdom of Belgium and the Kingdom of the Netherlands concerning the reactivation of the Iron Rhine (or "IJzeren Rijn" as it is known in Dutch) railway linking the port of Antwerp, Belgium, to the Rhine basin in Germany, via the Netherlands' provinces of North-Brabant and Limburg. The Iron Rhine railway traces its legal origins to a right of transit across Dutch territory which was conferred on Belgium and later elaborated through several treaties concluded in the nineteenth century.

The Parties agreed to arbitrate their differences, *inter alia*, over the entitlement of Belgium, on the one hand, to embark on plans for the reactivation of the railway, and the entitlement of the Netherlands, on the other, to impose conditions specified under Dutch law – particularly with respect to environmental protection – for such a reactivation. A distinguished arbitral tribunal, comprised of Judge Bruno Simma, Judge Peter Tomka (both of the International Court of Justice), Professor Alfred A.H.A. Soons and Professor Guy Schrans, and presided over by Judge Rosalyn Higgins (now President of the ICJ), was established by reference to the Arbitration Agreement between the Parties. The Permanent Court of Arbitration served as Registry for the arbitration. Under the terms of their Arbitration Agreement, the Parties jointly posed specific questions to the Tribunal regarding the nature and extent of their respective rights under international law, "including European law if necessary", to determine the parameters of the reactivation of the Iron Rhine railway, as well as the allocation of related costs. The Tribunal dealt with issues such as jurisdictional conflicts, the balance between the rights of one State over the territory of another and the latter's residual sovereignty, and treaty interpretation.

The PCA would like to express its immense gratitude to Colin Warbrick, Professor of Public International Law at the University of Birmingham, for writing his perceptive introduction on the contribution of the Iron Rhine Award to international law. As Professor Warbrick remarks, "[i]t is the combination of the Tribunal's treatment of treaty interpretation with the 'fragmentation' [of international law] considerations which give the Award its significance beyond the precise concerns of the Parties." Professor Warbrick further notes that the Award will be of interest to far more States than Belgium and the Netherlands, not least because of the significance of the international and European Union law issues which arose in the case.

The Award has been translated into French specifically for this edition, to make the text of the Award more easily accessible to the francophone community worldwide. It does not, however, constitute an official French version of the Award.

The Award as reproduced here contains one official correction. In September 2005 the Arbitral Tribunal agreed to a correction of paragraph 65 of its Award so that, in the final phrase of that paragraph, the word "works" replaced the word "plan". The correction is printed in italics and accompanied by a footnote. At Belgium's request, the Arbitral Tribunal also issued an Interpretation of the Award in September 2005. This is also included in the volume. A map, which was agreed by the governments, is annexed to the Award.

Special mention must be made of Anne Joyce, who served as Registrar to the Tribunal, and to Belinda Macmahon, who assisted Ms. Joyce and edited this volume. Thanks are also due to Dominique Stern, who translated both the Award and Professor Warbrick's Introduction into French, and to Guillaume Tattevin and Samuel Moss, who assisted with the French translations.

The Hague, June 2007   Tjaco T. van den Hout
                                        Secretary-General
                                        Permanent Court of Arbitration

AVANT-PROPOS

Cet ouvrage contient la sentence rendue par le tribunal arbitral institue pour se prononcer sur le différend entre le Royaume de Belgique et les Pays-Bas concernant la ré-activation du Rhin-de-fer (ou « IJzeren Rijn » en néerlandais), une ligne ferroviaire reliant le port d'Anvers, en Belgique, au bassin de la Rhur, en Allemagne, via les provinces néerlandaises du Nord-Brabant et du Limbourg. Le Rhin-de-fer a son origine dans un droit de passage à travers le territoire néerlandais, qui avait été concédé à la Belgique et précisé par plusieurs traités conclus au dix-neuvième siècle.

Les différends que les parties étaient convenues d'arbitrer portaient, notamment, sur le droit pour la Belgique d'une part, de mettre en œuvre les plans de réactivation de la ligne ferroviaire et pour les Pays-Bas d'autre part, d'assortir cette réactivation de conditions spécifiées par le droit néerlandais – notamment en matière de protection de l'environnement. En application du compromis d'arbitrage entre les parties, un tribunal arbitral éminent fut mis en place, composé du juge Bruno Simma, du juge Peter Tomka (tous deux membres de la Cour internationale de justice), du professeur Alfred A.H.A. Soons et du professeur Guy Schrans. Le tribunal était présidé par Madame le juge Rosalyn Higgins (qui préside aujourd'hui la CIJ). La Cour permanente d'arbitrage a servi de greffe dans cet arbitrage. Conformément au compromis, les parties ont posé conjointement au tribunal des questions relatives à la nature et l'étendue de leurs obligations respectives aux termes du droit international, « y compris le droit communautaire si nécessaire », afin de déterminer les paramètres de réactivation du Rhin-de-fer, ainsi que la question de la répartition des coûts associés. Le tribunal s'est prononcé sur des questions telles que les conflits de compétence, l'équilibre entre les droits d'un Etat sur le territoire d'un autre et la souveraineté résiduelle de ce dernier, ainsi que sur l'interprétation des traités.

La CPA exprime toute sa gratitude à Colin Warbrick, professeur de droit international public à l'Université de Birmingham, pour sa pertinente introduction consacrée à l'apport de la sentence du Rhin-de-fer au droit international. Comme le professeur Warbrick le souligne, « [c]'est la combinaison du traitement par le Tribunal de l'interprétation des traités et des considérations de « fragmentation » [du droit international] qui confère à la Sentence une signification allant au-delà des préoccupations précises des Parties. » Le professeur Warbrick souligne également que la sentence intéressera beaucoup plus d'Etats que les seuls Belgique et Pays-Bas, notamment en raison de l'importance des questions juridiques de droit communautaire et de droit international qui ont été soulevées dans cette affaire.

La sentence a été spécialement traduite en français pour cette publication, afin de rendre le texte accessible à la communauté francophone dans le monde. Le texte traduit ne constitue cependant pas une version authentique de la sentence.

La sentence reproduite ici contient une correction officielle. En septembre 2005, le tribunal arbitra a accepté de corriger le paragraphe 65 de la sentence afin qu'à la dernière phrase, le mot « travaux » remplace le mot « plan ». La correction est imprimée en italique et accompagnée d'une note de bas de page. A la demande de la Belgique, le tribunal arbitral a également émis une interprétation de la sentence en septembre 2005. Cette interprétation figure dans le présent volume. Une carte, dont le tracé a été réalisé avec l'accord des deux gouvernements, est annexée à la sentence.

Il faut mentionner également Anne Joyce, qui était la greffière du tribunal, ainsi que Belinda Macmahon, qui assistait Madame Joyce et qui a publié le présent ouvrage. Des remerciements sont dus aussi au Dominique Stern (Paris), qui a assuré la traduction en français de la sentence et de l'introduction du professeur Warbrick. Guillaume Tattevin et Samuel Moss ont collaboré à la traduction.

La Haye, juin 2007

Tjaco T. van den Hout
Secrétaire général
Cour permanente d'arbitrage

x

THE "IRON RHINE" ("IJZEREN RIJN") ARBITRATION (BELGIUM–NETHERLANDS)

Its Contribution to International Law

by

Colin Warbrick*

I. THE IRON RHINE[1]

The "Iron Rhine" is the name given to the railway line which ran from Antwerp across the Netherlands to what is now Moenchengladbach in Germany, where it connected to the important terminus at Duisburg in the Rhur. The line was built in the interest of Belgium and its legal origins go back to the Congress of Vienna. The conditions for the independence of Belgium were not agreed at Vienna but were set out in the Treaty between Belgium and the Netherlands relative to the Separation of their Respective Territories ("Treaty of Separation"; "Treaty of 1839").[2] Because of the territorial settlements in the Treaty, Antwerp was cut off from direct access to the German Empire by land which became territory of the Netherlands. So, the Treaty provided in Article XII:

> In the case that in Belgium a new road would have been built or a new canal dug, which would lead to the Maas facing the Dutch canton of Sittard, then Belgium would be at liberty to ask Holland, which in that hypothesis would not refuse it, that the said road, or the said canal be extended in accordance with the same plan, entirely at the cost and expense of Belgium, through the canton of Sittard, up to the borders of Germany. This road or canal, which could be used only for commercial communication, would be constructed, at the choice of Holland, either by engineers

---

* Professor of Public International Law, University of Birmingham.

[1] The text of the exchange of notes submitting the dispute to arbitration between Belgium and the Netherlands of 22/25 July 2003 is available on the website of the Permanent Court of Arbitration <http://www.pca-cpa.org>. The facts about the Iron Rhine and its history are largely taken from the Award.

[2] Treaty between Belgium and the Netherlands relative to the Separation of their Respective Territories, 88 C.T.S. 427 (1838–1839).

and workers whom Belgium would obtain authorisation to employ for this purpose in the canton of Sittard, or by engineers and workers whom Holland would supply, and who would execute the agreed works at the expense of Belgium, all without any burden to Holland, and without prejudice to the exclusive rights of sovereignty over the territory which would be crossed by the road or canal in question.

Eventually, under the terms of the "Iron Rhine" Treaty of 1873,[3] the two States agreed on the construction of a railway on a more northerly route through Limburg to what was by now the boundary with Prussia. The railway came into use in 1879. It became part of the Netherlands public railway network in 1897. The level of traffic on the Iron Rhine fluctuated. The line was destroyed during World War II and restored afterwards but its use was intermittent and declining. After 1991, there was no through traffic from Belgium to Germany, although parts of the "historic route" of the Iron Rhine did remain in use as part of the Netherlands railway system. In Belgium, interest in "reactivating" the route had arisen even before its eventual demise – the object was not just the restoration of the original track but its modernisation as a multi-track, electrified line capable of taking many more and longer trains than it had ever done.[4] The Netherlands had economic interests which would not have been served by the construction of such a route to such a specification, notably its own proposed freight route from Rotterdam to Germany. There is a railway line from Antwerp to Germany across Belgian territory but it is substantially longer (210 kilometres against 160 kilometres) than the route of the Iron Rhine. The decline of the port of Antwerp, perhaps especially relative to the prosperity of Rotterdam, was an element in approaches made by Belgium to the Netherlands about the future of the Iron Rhine during the 1990s.

In the 1990s, the Netherlands established a number of nature reserves along where the track of the Iron Rhine had run and when discussions about reactivation were going on between the two governments, they agreed on environmental impact studies of the effects of reactivation. The conditions were agreed in a memorandum of understanding in 2000, which envisaged a temporary restoration

---

[3] Convention between Belgium and the Netherlands relative to the Payment of the Belgian Debt, the Abolition of the Surtax on Netherlands Spirits, and the Passing of a Railway Line from Antwerp to Germany across Limburg, 145 C.T.S. 447 (1872–1873). This Treaty and the Treaty of Separation, *supra* note 2, will be referred to as "the Treaties". The map of the route of the Iron Rhine used by the Tribunal is at p. 313 .

[4] The Parties used the term "reactivation" of the railway, without prejudice as to whether this referred to the restoration of the line in its final condition before removal or the proposed modernised railway envisaged by Belgium.

of the line and then its operation in a permanent form. In the discussions, the issue of the conditions for reactivation and the allocation of costs could not be resolved. In 2003, an agreement between Belgium and the Netherlands submitted the dispute to arbitration under the auspices of the Permanent Court of Arbitration ("PCA").[5] The Parties were agreed that the Treaty of 1839 was still in force and, with other agreements, it provided a right of rail transit passage for Belgium along the historic route over Netherlands' territory. The core of the dispute between them had two elements: what was the extent of the unilateral power of the Netherlands to impose conditions on the reactivation of the line, especially to do with environmental protection, and who should pay for the building of the railway to satisfy any conditions upon which the Netherlands might be entitled to insist.

II. THE ARBITRAL TRIBUNAL

The Tribunal was established by agreement between Belgium and the Netherlands. Belgium appointed Professor Guy Schrans and Judge Bruno Simma as arbitrators; the Netherlands, Professor Alfred Soons and Judge Peter Tomka. These arbitrators appointed Judge Rosalyn Higgins, now the President of the International Court of Justice, as the President of the Tribunal. The distinction of the Tribunal, including three judges of the International Court of Justice, is of importance, given the potential significance of certain aspects of the Award for international law in general.

The arbitral agreement took advantage of the facilities of the Permanent Court of Arbitration, proceeding in large part according to the PCA's rules of procedure. In principle, the Tribunal was to proceed by written argument, although provision was made for oral hearings. In the event, neither State nor the Tribunal itself asked for an oral stage. Both sides kept to the time limits established by the Tribunal. Belgium submitted a memorial ("BM") and a reply ("BR"); the Netherlands, a counter-memorial ("NCM") and a rejoinder ("NR").[6] The Award was delivered on 24 May 2005.

---

[5] *Supra* note 1.
[6] The submissions of the Parties are available on the PCA's website, *supra* note 1.

III. THE AWARD

The Parties put three rather complicated questions to the Tribunal, to which it gave specific answers.[7] It is not proposed here to detail either the questions or the answers or the reasons given for them. The Award is a concentrated document, not easily summarised. For what is to follow in this note, it is enough to say that the Tribunal (which was unanimous):

confirmed the continuing right of Belgium to a right of rail transit across Netherlands' territory along the historic route of the Iron Rhine;[8]

decided that the operation of the route was subject to the application of Dutch legislation on matters such as construction standards, safety and environmental protection;[9]

held that the limit on the powers of the Netherlands was that its regulations should not render the exercise of the right of rail transit impossible or unreasonably difficult;[10]

concluded that, while Belgium had the right to upgrade the route, it could be done only on conditions acceptable to the Netherlands, subject to the same considerations of impossibility and unreasonableness;[11] and

decided that the historic route could be varied by the Netherlands only with the agreement of Belgium.[12]

The Tribunal laid down the principles upon which the costs and financial risks of any scheme should be allocated between the Parties, breaking the line into four sections to which different calculations would apply.[13] The Award recommended

---

[7] Award, para. 3. The final submissions of the Parties are at para. 26 (Belgium) and para. 27 (Netherlands) of the Award. The answers of the Tribunal are at paras. 238–244 of the Award. This note does not deal with all the legal issues and technical arguments put forward by the Parties and considered by the Tribunal. There are some interesting comments about the status of memoranda of understanding: see Award, paras. 142, 154–158.

[8] There is no specific finding to this effect but the Tribunal proceeds on the basis that it was to decide what limits on the sovereignty of the Netherlands arose from Belgium's right of transit under the Treaties. See Award, para. 56.

[9] Award, para. 239.

[10] Award, para. 239(c).

[11] Award, para. 241.

[12] Award, para. 241(c).

[13] Award, para. 244.

the setting up of a committee of independent experts to calculate various costs and quantify various benefits, so that the Parties could use the information to determine their respective shares of the upgrading of parts of the reactivated Iron Rhine, the use of which they would share.[14] Significantly, the Tribunal found that compliance with the environmental protection measures stipulated by the Netherlands rendered passage neither impossible nor unreasonable,[15] even though this would mean building a tunnel and carrying out other works to a sum of 500 million euros.

This simplified account of the decision might suggest that the arbitrators were little more than a firm of sophisticated accountants but that would be to disguise the number and importance of the international and European Union law issues which arose in the case. Their disposition was doubtless helped by the large measure of agreement on many of the fundamentals between the States and, even where they were not quite *ad idem*, by the Tribunal's capacity to see the differences as ones of emphasis rather than substance. However, underlying these detailed issues lie fundamental questions.

IV. "THE FRAGMENTATION OF INTERNATIONAL LAW"

It was rather a surprise when the International Law Commission ("ILC") took up the study of "The Fragmentation of International Law".[16] It was not that the practical importance of the subject was underestimated[17] but that it was hard to see how the ILC could deal with the topic in a way which would produce anything useful to States – imagining a treaty or code which could result from the study was difficult. "Fragmentation" is a description of several features of the modern international legal system. Although it suggests a process running counter to an ideal of coherence, seen as a virtue of a domestic legal order, "fragmentation" does not necessarily carry any judgment about its desirability or otherwise. The word is used to include various phenomena which generate incompatibilities in interna-

---

[14] Award, para. 235.

[15] Award, para. 244(e).

[16] Study Group to examine "Fragmentation of International Law: difficulties arising from the diversification and expansion of international law" in *Report of the International Law Commission: Fifty-fourth session*, UN GAOR, 57th Sess., Supp. No. 10, UN Doc. A/57/10 (2002), 267 at paras. 492–494. "Fragmentation" will be used in this note in the sense the word is understood by the ILC.

[17] Martii Koskenniemi & Paivi Leino, *Fragmentation of International Law? Postmodern Anxieties*, 15 Leiden Journal of International Law p. 553 (2002).

tional law. There are both procedural (or institutional) and substantive elements involved but they share the risk that States and other international persons may be faced with incompatible obligations arising because of the uncoordinated nature of the way international law is made and the processes by which it is determined. Equally, systemic incoherence will arise if the same legal concepts are regarded differently by different parts of the international legal system. The procedural face of fragmentation comes from the proliferation of authoritative dispute-settlement mechanisms and the willingness of States to use them.[18] So, the question of what constitutes genocide arises before the International Court of Justice ("ICJ") in the Bosnia Genocide case[19] and in cases decided by the International Criminal Tribunals for Yugoslavia ("ICTY")[20] and Rwanda ("ICTR");[21] or the same dispute is submitted to different tribunals, like the Chile/European Communities ("EC") Swordfish dispute, characterised as a trade dispute by the EC and sent to the World Trade Organisation ("WTO") Dispute Settlement Mechanism,[22] and as an environmental case by Chile and referred to settlement under Part XI of the United Nations Convention on the Law of the Sea ("UNCLOS").[23] Where these different processes produce different understandings of key terms, there will be substantive consequences for States. However, this kind of problem for States need not have an institutional origin – the resolution of conflicts of treaty obligations, the identification of the context in which treaties should be interpreted, and, more tentatively perhaps, the increasingly asserted claims for some hierarchy of rules of international law, create similar prospects of dissonance of obligations for States. Now, doubtless, some of these are what American conflicts lawyers would call "false" conflicts: when everything is inspected closely, it turns out that no inconsistency emerges. One alternative rule may not apply after all, or the meanings of standards derived from different legal regimes turn out to be the same, or the clash turns out to be between a power and a duty rather than between two conflicting duties. Nonetheless, it cannot be denied that some real conflicts do

---

[18] Yuval Shany, The Competing Jurisdictions of International Courts and Tribunals (2003).

[19] Application of the Convention on the Prevention and Punishment of the Crime of Genocide (Bosn. & Herz./Serb. & Mont.), Preliminary Objections of the Government of Serbia & Montenegro, 1996 I.C.J. 595.

[20] *Prosecutor v. Krstic*, ICTY (Appellate Chamber), Case No. IT-98-33-A (2004).

[21] *Prosecutor v. Akayesu*, ICTR (Appellate Chamber), Case No. ICTR-96-4-A (2001).

[22] Chile – Measures Affecting the Transit and Importing of Swordfish, complaint by European Communities, WT/DS193.

[23] Case concerning Conservation and Sustainable Exploitation of Swordfish Stocks in the South-East Pacific Ocean (Chile/European Community), International Tribunal for the Law of the Sea, Case No. 7 (2003).

exist. The *Iron Rhine* Tribunal faced two versions of "fragmentation", though one of them – an alleged incompatibility of the jurisdiction of the Tribunal and the obligations of the Parties under EC law – was not asserted by either Party but raised by the Tribunal itself.

The ILC has recently been considering the Report of its study group on "fragmentation", which has proposed a series of "conclusions" presented in schematic form as guidance to States and other decision-makers faced with a "fragmentation" question.[24] After describing what the "fragmentation" issues were for the *Iron Rhine* Tribunal, this note will look to see how the Tribunal's Award fits with the ILC study group's conclusions, for after the Award was handed down, the group was able to come up with a catalogue of principles for ameliorating differences emanating from "fragmentation" (see below).

V. JURISDICTION OF THE TRIBUNAL AND EUROPEAN COMMUNITY LAW

The Tribunal was asked to decide the case "on the basis of international law, including European law if necessary, while taking into account the Parties' obligations under Article 292 of the EC Treaty."[25]

Article 292 reads: "Member States undertake not to submit a dispute concerning the interpretation or application of this Treaty to any method of settlement other than those provided for therein."

The European Court of Justice ("ECJ") is provided with jurisdiction over the interpretation of the EC Treaty, both as against other international means of settlement and national judicial processes. This authority is seen as an essential part of maintaining the integrity and supremacy of EC law. The Commission of the European Communities has the power to start proceedings against a State or States which do refer differences about the meaning of the EC Treaty to extra-EC procedures. It did so in the *UNCLOS/MOX* case (see below).[26] Belgium and the

---

[24] Fragmentation of International Law: difficulties arising from the diversification and expansion of international law, A/CN.4/L.702 (2006) [ILC Report].

[25] Award, para. 4.

[26] Action brought on 30 October 2003 by the *Commission v. Ireland*, Case C-459/03, 2004 O.J. (C 7) 24.

Netherlands were conscious of this provision when they sent this case to the Arbitral Tribunal. They wrote to the Commission saying that it was their view that the dispute concerned only points of international law but, if it did turn out that issues of EC law arose they "commit[ted] themselves to take all necessary measures in order to comply with all the obligations resting on them under the EC Treaty, and in particular Article 292 thereof."[27]

Briefly, EC law was referred to by the Parties in three ways. It was contended by Belgium that the "Trans-European Networks" project for the railways of the EC States showed the importance of the reactivation of the Iron Rhine but the weight it put on this point gradually diminished, and the Tribunal was able to conclude that there was little between the positions of the two States on this question which was of "very limited relevance" to the case.[28] There was reference by Belgium to Article 10 of the EC Treaty but on this the Tribunal said that there was nothing between the Parties about its impact on their dispute.[29] Far more significant were references to European environmental law. It was noted above that the Netherlands had designated certain areas on the historic route of the Iron Rhine as environmentally protected. For the Tribunal, the now relevant EC legislation was the Habitats Directive.[30] It is to be noted that Article 175 of the EC Treaty specifically "shall not prevent any member State from maintaining or introducing more stringent protective measures".

So long as the Netherlands had not adopted national measures less protective of the interests falling within the Habitats Directive, then there would be no incompatibility with EC law. The Netherlands had identified one area, the Meinweg, through which the historic route ran, as a special conservation area under the Habitats Directive. It was concern for the preservation of this area for which the Dutch authorities specified that a tunnel would be necessary if the Iron Rhine were reactivated, this being the item of greatest expense in the project. Belgium responded by arguing that the Netherlands was obliged to harmonise any protection of the Meinweg with the international obligations it owed to Belgium under the Treaties – which meant, *inter alia*, adopting the least expensive protection option. On the face of it, this put squarely before the Tribunal the interpretation and application of the Habitats Directive, but the Netherlands

---

[27] Award, para. 15.
[28] Award, para. 117.
[29] Award, para. 141.
[30] Council Directive, 92/43/EEC, 21 May 1992, 1992 O.J. (L 206) 7.

8

maintained that the designation of the Meinweg was an act under domestic law (compatible with EC law but not driven by it).[31] Following this, the Tribunal said that it had concluded that whether or not the Habitats Directive existed had no impact on how it would determine whether the demand for the Meinweg Tunnel was lawful or not (and who should pay for it if it were). The Parties had "debated" EC law but it was not determinative for the Tribunal – "it is not necessary for the Tribunal to interpret the Habitats Directive in order to render its Award".[32]

Since the Tribunal had reached the same conclusion about all three of the EC law points – that they were not relevant to making the Award – it could proceed to exercise its jurisdiction without risking the Parties being in breach of their obligations under Article 292. It is not clear what would have happened if its conclusions had been different. The Tribunal had earlier made the curious remark that it was "in a position analogous to that of a domestic court within the EC . . .".[33] The claim of analogy appears to contradict directly the position under EC law.[34] Under Article 234 of the EC Treaty, domestic courts may, and in some cases must, refer a point of EC law to the ECJ. The Tribunal looked at the case law of the ECJ about how national courts should exercise their powers, relying on the *CILFIT* case,[35] in particular, on the emphasis that the point of EC law must be both decisive and conclusive for the case before the national court.[36] The Tribunal, of course, had neither power nor duty to send a case to the ECJ. It would, one presumes from the thrust of the decision, have declined to exercise its jurisdiction (perhaps by relying on its applicable law, which included EC law) and relied on the Parties to find a way of getting the contested point of EC law to the ECJ. Maybe even, given their undertaking, the Parties would have sought an adjournment of the proceedings to allow them to do this if the Tribunal indicated that a point of EC law had been necessary for its decision.

---

[31] NCM, para. 3.3.5.6. Anticipating this claim, Belgium argued that, since the Netherlands was not under any international obligation to adopt the contested environmental measures, it was under a duty to accommodate its national schemes to Belgium's rights under Article XII. See BM, paras. 73–74.

[32] Award, para. 137.

[33] Award, para. 103.

[34] Nikolas Lavranos, *The MOX Plant and IJzeren Rijn Disputes: Which Court is the Supreme Arbiter?*, 19 LEIDEN JOURNAL OF INTERNATIONAL LAW p. 223, at pp. 239–240 (2006).

[35] *Srl CILFIT and Lanificio di Gavardo SpA v. Ministerio della Santa*, Case 283/81 [1982] E.C.R. 3415.

[36] Award, para. 137.

There are other ways in which this matter might have been resolved. It does not seem to be the case that an agreement between EC member States to take a point of EC law to settlement outside the ECJ would render the agreement void, so much as that bodies bound by EC law should disapply it and that the individual States would be answerable to the ECJ or in national courts. Accordingly, a hierarchical relationship of the rules of the jurisdiction of the ECJ and the Tribunal was not in play as a matter of international law. Among the devices which may help to deal with "fragmentation" problems which were considered by the ILC, two have some purchase here – the rules which deal with priorities of treaties and the application of the maxim *lex specialis derogat lex generali*. On the first, the ILC refers to Article 30 of the Vienna Convention on the Law of Treaties ("Vienna Convention")[37] which, as between the same parties, subjects the earlier treaty obligations to the later ones.[38] Here though, there are other States with an interest in the EC Treaty, not to mention the Union itself. Article 30, paragraph 4, of the Vienna Convention accepts the position that here a State might be bound by incompatible obligations. In such a case, the State will encounter responsibility for violation of the obligation it does not fulfil, although it might be able to negotiate a solution with the parties to either or both of the treaties.[39] The promises by Belgium and the Netherlands not to proceed before the Tribunal if an EC law point became germane look like a pre-emptive solution to a possible incompatibility. If the Tribunal had found it necessary to determine a point of EC law and the Parties had been willing to argue the case before it, the *lex specialis* principle would appear *prima facie* to favour the Tribunal's jurisdiction but, as the ILC's Conclusions acknowledge, the principle is not one of automatic application but one to be decided "contextually".[40] The context here would include the terms of the Arbitral Agreement – its reference to "EC law" is not limited to EC substantive law and so could include Article 292 – and the statements of the Parties before the Tribunal about EC law could also be taken into account. From these factors put together, a better conclusion might be that the Parties did not intend the Tribunal to have jurisdiction over matters which would fall within the ambit of Article 292. The

---

[37] Vienna Convention on the Law of Treaties, 23 May 1969, 1155 U.N.T.S. 331 [VCLT].

[38] ILC Report, *supra* note 24, paras. 14(24–30).

[39] An example is the way the United Kingdom resolved the clash between its obligation to extradite a fugitive under its extradition treaty with the United States and its duty not to return him arising out of the interpretation of the European Convention on Human Rights by the European Court of Human Rights in *Soering v. U.K.*, EctHR, App. No. 14038188 (1989). Soering was returned to the U.S. on a warrant which did not specify an offence carrying a capital sentence.

[40] ILC Report, *supra* note 24, para. 14(6).

ways that they relied on EC law in their arguments show an almost painful attempt to refer to EC law but to minimise its dispositive consequences.[41]

Apart then from the Tribunal's analogy between itself and a national court, no harm might appear to have been done by its resolution of this matter – the jurisdictional clash was a false conflict. However, in a challenging article, the approach the Tribunal took has been roundly criticised by Dr Nikolas Lavranos.[42] He refers to the two *MOX* arbitrations, arising out of claims made by Ireland against the United Kingdom about the operation of the Sellafield nuclear installations.[43] He states his preference for the conclusion of the *UNCLOS* Tribunal, which, it will be recalled, adjourned its proceedings pending a judgment of the ECJ on the jurisdictional issue (see below). Dr Lavranos's position follows from his assertion of the "Supremacy of EC Law over International Law", which is probably a correct reflection of the position from the perspective of EC law.[44] From this, everything else follows. The demands of consistency and uniformity of EC law require that the ultimate repository of the meaning of the Treaty be the ECJ and Article 292 is just one of the elements securing the ECJ's authority. For Dr Lavranos, the "fragmentation" question is to be settled by recourse to both a notion of special regimes and of hierarchy – that EC law enjoys the same superiority over international law as it does over national law. This may seem a handy device – and doubtless to EC lawyers, a self-evident one – but, as we shall see in a moment, it is one which rejects the propriety of the way the Tribunal handled this problem and of the alternative suggestions canvassed in the preceding paragraphs. This is not the place to discuss in detail the matter of the superiority of EC law over international law – for an international lawyer, it is enough to note that the EC Treaty is an international treaty and should be interpreted according to the rules of the Vienna Convention. It is to be interpreted in the general context of international law as well as in consideration of its own special characteristics. The recent case

---

[41] There is hardly a reference to EC law in the answers by Belgium to the questions put to the Tribunal and none at all in the answers of the Netherlands. See BM, "Final Submissions" and NR, Chapter 4.

[42] *Supra* note 34. I am indebted to Dr Lavranos's article.

[43] UNCLOS Tribunal, *Ireland v. United Kingdom* [MOX Plant Case], Suspension of Proceedings on Jurisdiction and Merits: see PCA website, *supra* note 1; OSPAR Tribunal, *Ireland v. United Kingdom* [OSPAR Arbitration]: see PCA website, *supra* note 1.

[44] *Supra* note 34, at pp. 232–233. See Daniel Bethlehem, *Chapter 11*, *in* INTERNATIONAL LAW ASPECTS OF THE EUROPEAN UNION (Martti Koskenniemi ed., 1998).

law before the ECJ on the effect of Security Council resolutions in EC law[45] and of the relationship between the EC Treaty and the European Convention on Human Rights ("ECHR")[46] are vital examples to show that the automatic superiority of EC law over international law is not a proposition which can be taken for granted.

Dr Lavranos does, though, raise a crucial point which will inevitably complicate attempts to resolve jurisdictional conflicts. It is the threshold question for one tribunal as to whether or not the issue it needs to decide does in fact fall within the jurisdiction, even the ostensibly exclusive jurisdiction, of another body. As has been explained, the Tribunal was able to avoid any possible conflict with the ECJ by finding that there was no need for the Tribunal to reach a conclusion on a matter of EC law. Dr Lavranos disputes this finding. He argues that a finding on EC law was necessary to resolve the claims in the *Iron Rhine* case. Even in the absence of specific authority in EC law dealing with circumstances like the Meinweg, Dr Lavranos considers that there is a case that reactivating the Iron Rhine through the Meinweg would be incompatible with the Habitats Directive.[47] If the Tribunal had been a national court, it would have been obliged to seek a preliminary ruling from the ECJ. He writes: "since the arbitral tribunal could not request such a preliminary ruling, it was *obliged* to reject jurisdiction and refer the parties to the ECJ".[48]

This is the *UNCLOS/MOX* solution. At one level, nothing turns on whether or not Dr Lavranos is right or wrong about the position in EC law under the Habitats Directive. The question of whether or not a point of EC law was necessary to resolve the *Iron Rhine* arbitration is a matter of EC law if there is a *prima facie* case (I use this expression in a non-technical sense) that it is necessary to resolve the dispute. There is a sanction. If the Tribunal's decision about the necessity to look at EC law is wrong and if EC law had been examined the Award would have been different; depending upon the nature of the deficiency, there would be a range of possibilities, including individual actions in national courts or before the ECJ, to

---

[45] *Yusuf and Al Barakaat International Foundation v. Council and Commission*, Case T-306/01, 2005 O.J. (C 281) 17; *Kadi v. Council and Commission*, Case T-315/01, 2005 O.J. (C 281) 17; *Hassan v. Council and Commission*, Case T-49/04, 2006 O.J. (C 224) 36; *Chafiq Ayadi v. Council and Commission*, Case T-253/02, 2006 O.J. (C 224) 34.

[46] *Bosphorus Hora Yollari Turzim ve Ticaret AS v. Minister of Transport, Energy and Communications*, Ireland and Attorney-General, Case C-84/95, [1996] E.C.R. I-3953; see also, *Bosphorus Hora Yollari Turzim ve Ticaret Anonim Sirkati v. Ireland*, ECtHR (Grand Chamber), App. No. 45036/98 (2005).

[47] *Supra* note 34, at pp. 238–241. For the EC Commission's position, see BM, pp. 52–57.

[48] *Supra* note 34, at p. 240 (emphasis added).

challenge any action either of the States were taking to implement the Award. This seems to me to be an element in the legal context of this dispute which the Tribunal had to take into account. It would have been of no help in settling the dispute between Belgium and the Netherlands about the Iron Rhine reactivation if the effect of the Award could be challenged decisively in one forum or another. Indeed, any *ad hoc* tribunal could probably anticipate that the parties before it, as EC members, would be constrained to accept the judgment of the ECJ. There was nothing which prevented the Tribunal from adopting the approach it did. It did not, unlike the *OSPAR* Tribunal, act without regard to EC law. The conclusion that there was no need for the Tribunal to resolve a question of EC law is unlikely to be challenged by the Parties. Convinced that this was the case, there was no reason for the Tribunal to follow the *UNCLOS/MOX* Tribunal pattern and adjourn its proceedings pending an ECJ judgment with goodness knows what delay in being able to bring the Tribunal's proceedings to an end. Of course, the vulnerability of its conclusion to a case being brought by the Commission or by a private actor is there but, just as the Tribunal respected the competence of the ECJ, so the ECJ, if it were later called upon to consider the matter, ought to take into account the Tribunal's finding as part of the context in which it would reach a decision on whether or not the determination of the point of EC law really was necessary to decide the Award.

The *UNCLOS/MOX* case was decided by the ECJ after the *Iron Rhine* Award was rendered and after Dr Lavranos had written his article.[49] The judgment is a forthright assertion of ECJ jurisdiction, whether the matter of EC law is one of exclusive EC competence or one with which it shares competence with the member States, whether the EC has exercised its competence or not. The UNCLOS is a mixed agreement. Accordingly, its interpretation is a matter of EC law, a matter within the exclusive jurisdiction of the ECJ.[50] Doubtless, the ECJ was reinforced in this conclusion (reached entirely by reference to EC law and principle) by the terms of Article 282 of the UNCLOS, which allows States parties to the UNCLOS to submit disputes between them about its meaning or application to, *inter alia*, binding settlement through a regional agreement, and by the terms of Ireland's pleadings, which made frequent reference to EC law in any event. Not only does it follow that the ECJ has exclusive competence over the matters of EC law, it will (necessarily) have competence over any relevant issues of international law which

---

[49] *Commission v. Ireland* (30 May 2006), Case C-459/03, O. J. (C 165) 2 [ECJ Judgment].
[50] ECJ Judgment, *supra* note 49, para. 84.

fall for decision and, crucially, over the threshold question of whether or not there is a significant point of EC law to be decided.[51] The ECJ said that the provisions of the UNCLOS relied on by Ireland come within the area of Community competence and "clearly cover a significant part of the dispute".[52] Further, the ECJ said that it was for the Court to "identify the elements of the dispute which relate to provisions of the [UNCLOS] which fall outside its jurisdiction".[53] Unless there is an "*acte clair*" doctrine (i.e., where there is no question of EC competence) which allows member States to take a case to another tribunal and the facts of a particular dispute fall unequivocally within its terms, as Dr Lavranos argues those in the *Iron Rhine* case did not, the uncompromising terms of the *UNCLOS/MOX* judgment raise the question about whether or not, as a matter of EC law, the Tribunal was correct to proceed to exercise its jurisdiction without allowing (or even requiring) the Parties to go to the ECJ first. From the perspective of international law generally, it is much less clear that that would have been required, so long as the Tribunal made a proper assessment of the threshold question of the relevance of EC law to its Award, an alternative the ECJ dismisses.[54] The European Commission has no authority to concede jurisdiction to another tribunal, although its acquiescence in a claim by States that there is no point of EC law decisive to their dispute might reassure those States that the prospect of proceedings against them before the ECJ is remote. It should be noted that the ECJ's position on exclusivity is driven by principle – the need to maintain the superiority and uniformity of European law.[55] There is no room for anything like a *forum non conveniens* doctrine which might persuade the ECJ to defer to the better claims of another jurisdiction. In the *Iron Rhine* case, the States felt no need to press any EC law arguments: indeed, we could say that they were agreed that there were no issues which *might* involve the determination of points of EC law. The Tribunal endorsed these positions. It was doubtless reinforced in its conclusion by the attitudes of the Parties and will have since been reassured because their stances did not change after the Award was handed down and because no objection to the Award was taken by the ECJ in the *Commission v. Ireland* case. On the substance of the criticism which Dr Lavranos raises against the Award, it might well be that

---

[51] ECJ Judgment, *supra* note 49, para. 86.

[52] ECJ Judgment, *supra* note 49, para. 120.

[53] ECJ Judgment, *supra* note 49, para. 135.

[54] ECJ Judgment, *supra* note 49, para. 156.

[55] ECJ Judgment, *supra* note 49, para. 169. There were three parts to the Commission's application. The ECJ held Ireland to be in violation of Articles 10 and 292 of the EC Treaty and Articles 192 and 193 of the Euratom Agreement.

the disposal of the possible Article 292 argument by the Tribunal was correct but his identification of the threshold question about conflicting jurisdictions is of great importance.

VI. TREATY INTERPRETATION[56]

Before we get to the relationship of treaty interpretation to "fragmentation", it is necessary to consider some more orthodox but equally important issues of treaty interpretation which concerned the Tribunal. It is the combination of the Tribunal's treatment of treaty interpretation with the "fragmentation" considerations which give the Award its significance beyond the precise concerns of the Parties.

Belgium and the Netherlands are parties to the Vienna Convention but the Tribunal reaffirmed the customary law status of parts of the Convention, including those articles which govern the interpretation of treaties, Articles 31–33.[57] The Tribunal described its task thus: "[it] must interpret various provisions in the governing instruments, as well as apply the relevant rules of international law".[58]

The principal item for consideration was Article XII of the Treaty of 1839, as it had been affected by the 1873 Treaty (they were among the "governing instruments") and, therefore, the reference to "the relevant rules of international law" indicated that the Tribunal did not regard itself as confined to the text and its immediate treaty context of Article XII (see below).

While the provisions on interpretation in the Vienna Convention are widely understood to represent customary international law as it was in 1969, the formulation of them reduced the weight of two previously well-established principles of interpretation – that treaties are to be interpreted in the light of law and conditions at the time of their conclusion (which here will be called the principle of "original" contemporaneity)[59] and that restrictions on the sovereignty

---

[56] All the major textbooks have sections on the interpretation of treaties. For a helpful treatment, see MALCOLM SHAW, INTERNATIONAL LAW pp. 838–844 (5th ed. 2003).

[57] Award, para. 45.

[58] Award, para. 44.

[59] For discussion, see DONALD W. GREIG, INTERTEMPORALITY AND THE LAW OF TREATIES pp. 2–10 (2001). IAN BROWNLIE, PRINCIPLES OF INTERNATIONAL LAW p. 604 (6th ed. 2003) puts the obligation to take into account "original" contemporaneity as part of the search for the "natural and ordinary meaning" of words.

of the parties are not to be presumed.[60] It hardly needs saying that interpretation of treaties, like the interpretation of any texts in any legal system, has more characteristics of a craft than of a rule-based science. In any system of law, the principles of interpretation are the paradigm of Dworkin's concept of "principles", to be differentiated from "rules" by the need for appreciation of their application and consequences.[61] Besides, a search for the intention of the parties may in many cases be to look for a non-existent needle in a very large haystack of text and supporting materials. The Vienna Convention brings the text of the treaty to the fore – it is in the words chosen by the parties that their intention is understood to be expressed and thus where it is to be discovered. However, the text does not stand alone. Article 31, paragraph 1, says: "A treaty shall be interpreted in good faith in accordance with the ordinary meaning to be given to the terms of the treaty in their context in the light of their object and purpose."

The documentary context of a treaty is set out in Article 31, paragraph 2, while Article 31, paragraph 3 – which will be discussed below – provides for a number of kinds of other material to be taken into account. Article 32, which has its congeners in all legal systems, allows for recourse to "supplementary means of interpretation" where, relying on Article 31, either (a) leaves the meaning ambiguous or obscure, or (b) leads to a result which is manifestly absurd or unreasonable.

It is always worth stressing that any tribunal charged with treaty interpretation will have heard the arguments that an Article 31 meaning falls within one of the four Article 32 categories before the judges have to commit themselves to a final decision about what the treaty means.

If the principles of "original" contemporaneity and sovereignty have been suffering an eclipse, the principle of effectiveness has enjoyed the favour of interpretative institutions in recent times, the line being taken that it is the intention of the parties that the object and purpose of their treaties is to be given effective realisation, rather than be diminished by narrow and crabbed meanings.[62] It needs

---

[60] See Lord McNair, *Treaties and Sovereignty, reproduced in* THE LAW OF TREATIES pp. 754–768 (1961), in which he said that the sovereignty principle was connected with a restrictive approach to the interpretation of treaties, an approach which was (in 1958) of "declining importance", at p. 765.

[61] Ronald Dworkin, Taking Rights Seriously (1977), Chapter 3.

[62] Award, para. 49. ANTHONY AUST, MODERN TREATY LAW AND PRACTICE p. 188 (2000), suggests that the object and purpose of the treaty are more often used to confirm a meaning reached

emphasising that what is understood here is that the Parties intended a particular approach to interpretation, not that they necessarily intended any particular result of that approach in a discrete set of circumstances. The principle of effectiveness has enjoyed particular prominence in the interpretation of two broad categories of treaty – those which establish international organisations[63] and those which are for protection of human rights.[64]

Belgium's claim about the right of transit in Article XII of the Treaty of Separation was that the right was clearly established and, although it conceded residuary rights of sovereignty over the route (there was no assertion of extraterritorial status to the Iron Rhine), those rights could not be exercised to thwart or to impose unreasonable conditions on the exercise of Belgium's right of passage.[65] The Netherlands, conceding Belgium's fundamental point, nonetheless argued that its rights of sovereignty remained intact except where they had been clearly surrendered in the 1839 and 1873 Treaties.[66]

While nodding to the now rather ancient authority from the Permanent Court of International Justice ("PCIJ") which supports the presumption of sovereignty,[67] the Tribunal noted that the principle had never had a hierarchically superior status and that it was not referred to in the Vienna Convention, and concluded that "its contemporary relevance is to be doubted".[68] Instead, the Tribunal relied on the *Lac Lanoux* arbitration,[69] another case which involved finding the balance between the rights of one State on the territory of another and the residual sovereignty of that other State. One sees how the principle of effectiveness takes over – the Tribunal said that the conflict was not to be decided

---

on the text itself than as an independent basis for interpretation. Manifestly, that is not the case where the principle of effectiveness is relied upon.

[63] Elihu Lauterpacht, The Development of the Law of International Organisations by the Decisions of International Tribunals, 52 RECEUIL DE COURS p. 377, at pp. 416–420 (1976).

[64] Rudolf Bernhardt, Evolutive Treaty Interpretation, Especially of the European Convention on Human Rights, 42 GERMAN YEARBOOK OF INTERNATIONAL LAW p. 11 (1999).

[65] BM, para. 76, submission no. 6.

[66] NR, para. 3.2.

[67] Award, paras. 51–53, referring, *inter alia*, to the Case of the Free Zones of Upper Savoy and the District of Gex, 1932 P.C.I.J. (ser. A/B) No. 46.

[68] Award, para. 53. The Tribunal does not address a supplementary problem of original contemporaneity (which in this case might well have given more weight to the sovereignty principle), that is, whether or not a tribunal should apply the rules of interpretation as they were at the time of the creation of the treaty.

[69] *France v. Spain*, 16 Nov. 1957, 24 INTERNATIONAL LAW REPORTS p. 101 (1957).

by invoking a restrictive theory of interpretation but, by identifying Belgium's rights granted by the Treaties, the rights of the Netherlands which remain were any but those which "would conflict with the treaty rights granted to Belgium, or rights which Belgium may hold under general international law, or constraints imposed by EC law".[70]

This looks like a truism rather than a useful guide to treaty interpretation. Only if the delineation of sovereignty on the one hand and the treaty right of the other State on the other were precisely determinable does this statement in paragraph 56 of the Award make sense. But of course they are not – that is what the process of interpretation is about, even if the result of it, an award itself, pretends to a precision which was not there. Interpretation is often not about drawing bright lines between clear categories but of resolving conflicts between opposing claims, each of which has something to say for it. For all the simplicity of the statement from paragraph 56 just quoted, what is at stake is a conflict between the presumption in favour of sovereignty, maintained by the Netherlands, and the claim of a right to an effective railway, asserted by Belgium. By "effective", Belgium meant "cost effective" or even "least costly" as well as operationally effective, namely that trains could run in a commercially competitive way.[71]

VII. THE *LOTUS* PRINCIPLE, TREATY INTERPRETATION AND THE PRINCIPLE OF EFFECTIVENESS

The presumption in favour of sovereignty often appears in a modified form, as an aspect of the "*Lotus* principle", which derives its force from the notion of what it means to be a State – that within a State's territory, it has the exclusive right to exercise jurisdiction of all kinds – to make and enforce laws or to leave matters unregulated.[72] These otherwise unlimited powers are subject to international obligations of the State, an example being the rules on State immunity which affect the enforcement of a State's laws even within its territory against certain classes of persons. Thus, to limit the territorial State, it is necessary to show that there is a rule of international law which constrains its choices. This will often mean

---

[70] Award, para. 56.

[71] BR, para. 70.

[72] JAMES CRAWFORD, THE CREATION OF STATES IN INTERNATIONAL LAW pp. 41–43 (2nd ed. 2006). The principle takes its name from the judgment in the Case of the SS Lotus (Turk./Fr.), 1927 P.C.I.J. (ser. A) No. 9.

18

interpreting the international legal rule alleged to restrict the State's internal sovereignty. The strong presumption of treaty interpretation which would give the fullest effect to the *Lotus* principle would be one that provided that express words alone were sufficient to impose an obligation on the territorial State – any gap or ambiguity should be resolved in its favour.[73] Any strict rule or presumption of this kind has fallen from favour, not least because the rule of interpretation in Article 31 of the Vienna Convention not only makes no reference to it but because Article 31 is formulated in such a way as to minimise its impact. Article 31 puts the emphasis on the text – its "ordinary" meaning but also its meaning "in the light of [the treaty's] object and purpose". These latter words allow space for consider-ations of the effective interpretation of a treaty, without the principle of effective-ness being expressly referred to. The principle of effectiveness suggests that treaties be read in such a way as to make the treaty work to achieve its purposes to the fullest extent, save where express language of the treaty pre-empts such a conclusion. In the face of the way this possibility may be realised, the caution of States is understandable. Effectiveness not only stands against language capable of protecting the rights of a State party in the interests of a more expansive interpretation of the treaty but it also allows the implication into the treaty of terms which are not there, to the same end, that they are necessary for the effective implementation of the object and purpose of the treaty. We have become used to this approach to treaty interpretation, particularly for the constitutional treaties of international organisations and for human rights treaties. The interpreters pay what may seem like lip service to the *Lotus* principle by saying that the State parties intended the effective operation of their treaties (and, especially where they established machinery for interpretation, anticipated that that would be the approach these bodies would take). The shift of power from the States to the authoritative interpreter has been extensive because many modern, multilateral treaties contain within their preambular paragraphs wide statements of the purposes of the organisation or strong statements of the objective of protecting human rights. Those supporting the principle of effectiveness have always conceded that it is not the function of the interpreter to rewrite the treaty for the States[74] but the temptation to do so can be high. In a recent judgment of the European Court of Human Rights ("ECtHR"),[75] perhaps the most vigorous proponent of the principle of effectiveness as an element in treaty interpretation,

---

[73] See McNair, *supra* note 60.

[74] Award, para. 49.

[75] *Mamatkulov and Askarov v. Turkey*, ECtHR (Grand Chamber), App. Nos. 46827, 46951/99 (2005).

19

the undoubtedly laudable pursuit of the most effective interpretation on the matter of the binding effect on States of interim orders of the Court does appear to be at odds with the text, the context and the background of the European Convention on Human Rights. The dissenting minority had a more orthodox approach.[76] So far, the parties to the ECHR have shown little disposition to reject the ECtHR's technique[77] but there are examples from the law of international organisations, notably the long-running dispute about the legitimacy of certain peace-keeping operations,[78] which show that recourse to effectiveness as a free-standing principle of treaty interpretation has its limits.

While the importance of the *Lotus* principle to treaty interpretation may have diminished, it has not disappeared, particularly in cases like the *Iron Rhine* where a treaty grants to one State or its nationals certain rights on the territory of another. Belgium had two lines of argument against too great a weight to the *Lotus* principle. First, it claimed that as a matter of international law, State jurisdiction must be exercised in good faith and in accordance with the principle of reasonableness and these standards applied to the treaty rights of other States.[79] Then, Belgium argued that Article XII was not a "derogation" from the sovereignty of the Netherlands but was compensation to Belgium for loss of its direct access to Germany as a result of the territorial adjustments elsewhere in the 1839 Treaty.[80] Claims made by the beneficiary State that treaty concessions of rights over its territory are absolute and so exclude all regulation by the territorial State on the exercise of the treaty right go back to the *North Atlantic Fisheries* arbitration.[81] If the treaty is silent on the matter of regulation, as it often will be, then "sovereignty" is all the territorial State has to rely on, that is to say, by invoking its sovereignty it does not need to find a justifying source in the treaty for the regulation to which it proposes to subject the exercise of the right – it may be for safety, for security, for environmental protection, whatever policy end the State chooses to pursue. What decline of the *Lotus* principle means, though, is that the identification of a source of the power (that is to say, by relying on the *Lotus* principle) will not be decisive for the legality of any *use* of the power. The test proposed by Belgium and

---

[76] *Id.*, Judges Caflisch, Turmen and Kovler (dissenting).

[77] But see *Olachea Cahuas v. Spain*, ECtHR, App. No. 24668/03 (2006).

[78] Certain Expenses of the United Nations, Advisory Opinion, 1962 I.C.J. 151.

[79] BM, para. 56; BR, paras. 21–22.

[80] BR, para. 20, although Belgium made no claim for an extraterritorial status for the Iron Rhine: BR, para. 28.

[81] North Atlantic Coast Fisheries (*Great Britain v. United States*), HAGUE COURT REPORTS (Scott) pp. 141, 170 (Permanent Court of Arbitration 1910)), available at the PCA's website, *supra* note 1.

endorsed by the Tribunal is that the regulation must not prevent the exercise of the extraterritorial right nor must it impose unreasonable burdens on its use and in some cases at least, deciding what are the rights of the other State will take into account the principle of effectiveness.[82] The Tribunal resolved the conflict between the opposing claims using the metaphor of balance, which seems to rule out the conclusive presumptive value of either the right under the treaty or the right of regulation deriving from sovereignty.[83]

VIII. "PRESENT" CONTEMPORARY INTERPRETATION OF TREATIES

The implication from the paragraphs above is that the approach to treaty interpretation has changed over the years, even if it has not changed much since 1969. The question then arises as to how treaties concluded under different, earlier dispensations should be interpreted today. It is an element of a much broader issue – how should the terms of old treaties be understood now and how should the injunction in the Vienna Convention that an interpreter should take into account "any relevant rules of international law applicable in the relations between the parties" be applied with respect to rules which have emerged since the treaty was concluded. I shall use the term "present" contemporaneity to describe the principle of interpretation which would take into account changes in the law (and possibly also the facts) since the treaty was concluded up to the time of interpretation. It is sometimes written that these questions require application of the "intertemporal law", with the implication that the treaty must be read in the light of the understandings at the time of its conclusion.[84] The "intertemporal law" is an expression with different meanings in international law and it is important that it be used precisely when recourse is had to the term.

IX. THE INTERTEMPORAL LAW[85]

The rule on interpretation in the Vienna Convention was widely understood at the time of its adoption to be a statement of customary law; practice since then,

---

[82] Award, paras. 49, 82–84.

[83] Award, para. 83.

[84] BROWNLIE, *supra* note 59.

[85] THE INTERTEMPORAL PROBLEM IN PUBLIC INTERNATIONAL LAW (Institute of International Law, Weisbaden 1975); Rosalyn Higgins, *Time and the Law: International Perspectives on an Old Problem*, 46 INTERNATIONAL AND COMPARATIVE LAW QUARTERLY p. 501, at pp. 515–520 (1997).

including practice of international courts and tribunals (of which the *Iron Rhine* Award is one more example), has consolidated this position. However, it is never suggested that the adoption of the Vienna Convention rule simplifies the process of treaty interpretation. Not only does the rule have several elements to it but each of them involves a greater or lesser degree of appreciation and, though there is some indication of priorities in Articles 31 and 32, the resolution of conflicts of meaning depending upon the use of this or that part of a rule is a further exercise of the interpreter's judgment. There is no specific reference to intertemporality in the provisions on interpretation in the Vienna Convention but it is obvious that some decision has to be made on time questions, if only to decide whether the proper temporal frame of reference is the date of conclusion of the treaty or the date of interpretation itself. The reference to "subsequent" agreements and practice in Article 31, paragraph 3, shows that there is scope for events after the conclusion of the treaty to be taken into account and, if the reference to "relevant rules of international law" in Article 31, paragraph 3, sub-paragraph (c) is also taken to include developments after the conclusion of the treaty, the range of materials potentially relevant to the interpretation of a treaty right up to the time the interpretation is made may be very wide indeed.

There can be very serious problems with the application of Article 31, paragraph 3, sub-paragraph (c) and the jurisdiction of international courts, as was shown by the *Oil Platforms* case.[86] The jurisdictional basis was Article XXI, paragraph 2, in the United States–Iran Treaty of Amity, Economic Relations and Consular Rights which provided:

> Any dispute between the High Contracting parties as to the interpretation or application of the present Treaty, not satisfactorily adjusted by diplomacy, shall be submitted to the International Court of Justice unless the High Contracting parties agree to settlement by some other pacific means.

After the United States had sought to rely on the national security exception in Article XX, paragraph 1, of the Treaty to explain its use of force against Iran, Iran sought to raise matters to do with the legality of this use of force. The ICJ dealt with this question over the objections of the United States, which argued that the Court

---

[86] Oil Platforms (*Islamic Republic of Iran v. U.S.*), 2003 I.C.J. 161. For an illuminating discussion of the issues in the case relevant to this note, see Campbell McClachlan, *The Principle of Systemic Integration and Article 31(3)(c) of the Vienna Convention*, 54 INTERNATIONAL AND COMPARATIVE LAW QUARTERLY p. 279 (2005).

had no jurisdiction to do so; it was a matter outside the jurisdictional clause of the Treaty.[87] The possible limitation of the applicable law was not a consideration germane to the Tribunal in the *Iron Rhine* case because it was charged with applying "international law" and so had authority to examine any question of international law which it deemed pertinent to the resolution of the dispute before it. The Tribunal was not given any instructions about the intertemporal law aspects of the international law which it was to apply. In fact, the Tribunal took a generous view of its competence here, looking at the text of nineteenth century treaties in the light of contemporary developments in international environmental law (see below).

X. THE "INTERTEMPORAL LAW" AND THE INTERPRETATION OF TREATIES[88]

The "intertemporal law" is a familiar concept of international law, although it is not always appreciated that it carries different meanings in different contexts.[89] Primarily, it is an aspect of the law of title to territory, requiring that the relevance and weight of factual matters contributing to title be assessed against the international law contemporaneous with their occurrence.[90] It is driven by a search for certainty and stability in territorial title by seeking to avoid the unpicking of settled arrangements in the light of subsequent developments in the law. As such, it seems an almost inevitable rule. In the law of treaties, the need to apply an equivalent approach, that is to say, that treaties should be interpreted in the light of the law and context prevailing at the time of the conclusion of the treaty ("original" contemporaneity), is not so compelling, though it is a conceivable position and one that has some support from the older authorities.[91] Its weight, however, has been diminishing, especially with respect to certain classes of treaty.

---

[87] For criticism of the approach of the ICJ, see Frank Berman, *Treaty "Interpretation" in a Judicial Context*, 29 YALE JOURNAL OF INTERNATIONAL LAW p. 315 (2004), arguing that the meaning of the various terms of the Treaty, especially Article X(1), was "readily discoverable".

[88] See GREIG, *supra* note 59.

[89] See Higgins, *supra* note 85.

[90] Island of Palmas case (*Neth. v. U.S.*), II REPORTS ON INTERNATIONAL ARBITRAL AWARDS pp. 829, 845 (Permanent Court of Arbitration 1928), available at the PCA's website, *supra* note 1.

[91] BROWNLIE, *supra* note 59, cites the Grisbadarna Arbitration, XI REPORTS ON INTERNATIONAL ARBITRAL AWARDS 147 (Permanent Court of Arbitration 1909), available at the PCA's website, *supra* note 1, which is a boundary case and which GREIG, *supra* note 59, at p. 41, says is "something of an exception".

The Tribunal found the authority to resolve the problem of intertemporality in the *Iron Rhine* case in Article 31, paragraph 3, sub-paragraph (c) of the Vienna Convention, which makes reference to "any relevant rules of international law applicable in the relations between the parties."[92] There is neither subject-matter nor time-limitation in this provision. It has a value in the "fragmentation" debate because it allows the integration of States' obligations deriving from a specific treaty with their wider obligations, reducing the risk of incompatibilities. An important example of this practice is the judgment of the European Court of Human Rights in the *Al-Adsani* case.[93] The United Kingdom said that it had the (implied) power to impose restrictions on the (implied) right of access to a court for a person bringing a civil action in the UK for torture by a foreign State in order to give effect to the rules of State immunity which imposed a duty on the UK not to allow such an action to proceed. The ECtHR, saying that the Convention was to be interpreted "so far as possible in harmony with other rules of international law", accepted this as a "reasonable" limitation on the right of access under Article 6, paragraph 1 of the ECHR,[94] and this despite the strong value the ECtHR gives to the effective protection of human rights (and which is the justification for the implied right of access itself).[95] The ECtHR said that the Convention had to be interpreted in its international legal context. In this instance, there was no difficulty about relying on the rules of international law against the UK, which had introduced them into the case itself (nor possibly against any other of the parties to the ECHR, since it is likely that they shared the UK's position on the reach of State immunity). However, where there is more doubt about the rule, especially where there is doubt about its application to a State affected by the interpretation, a tribunal should move carefully – Article 31, paragraph 3, sub-paragraph (c) refers only to rules of international law "applicable in relations between the parties". The whole-scale importation of swathes of human rights law or environmental law into the interpretation of a treaty without regard to the bindingness of those rules on the parties cannot be justified by reference to Article 31, paragraph 3, sub-paragraph (c).

An approach analogous to those taken to the interpretation of international constitutions and human rights treaties can be found in the judgment of the ICJ with respect to environmental law in the *Gabčíkovo* case.[96] First, the Court was not

---

[92] Award, para. 58.

[93] *Al-Adsani v. United Kingdom*, ECtHR, App. No. 35763/97 (2002).

[94] *Id.* at paras. 55–56, 66.

[95] *Golder v. United Kingdom*, ECtHR, App. No. 4451/70 (1975).

[96] Case Concerning the Gabčíkovo-Nagymaros Project (Hung./Slovk.), 1997 I.C.J. 7.

prepared to accept Hungary's argument that its treaty with Czechoslovakia of 1977 for development of the Danube was invalid because of an unforeseen and fundamental change of circumstances, to wit the developments in environmental science and law. One of the reasons why the changes were not unforeseeable, according to the ICJ, was that the 1977 Treaty contained provisions which could be interpreted to accommodate changes in the environmental context.[97] So, when it came to the interpretation of the treaty, the ICJ said

> It is clear that the [development] Project's impact upon, and its implications for, the environment are of necessity a key issue . . .

> In order to evaluate the environmental risks, current standards must be taken into consideration. This is not only allowed by the wording of Articles 15 and 19, but even prescribed, to the extent that these articles impose a continuing – and thus necessarily evolving – obligation on the parties to maintain the quality of the water of the Danube and to protect nature.

> . . . new [environmental] norms have to be taken into consideration, and such new standards given proper weight, not only when States contemplate new activities but also when continuing with activities begun in the past. This need to reconcile economic development with the protection of the environment is aptly expressed in the concept of sustainable development.[98]

There is not much by way of explanation about why this should be the case – the customary law status of a rule on sustainable development was not explicitly established, and no reason was adduced as to why the States could not have agreed by their treaty to create a *lex specialis*, even if there were a customary rule on sustainable development. Rather, it was the nature of the terms used in the treaty, one which was held to create continuing obligations of environmental reassessment of their operations, which provided the basis for the interpretation adopted by the Court. Without such limitation, it could have been argued after the *Gabčíkovo* judgment that all treaty obligations of States, the performance of which had sufficiently substantial environmental consequences, should have been read, if at all possible, to take contemporary environmental law (that is, "present"

---

[97] *Id.* at para. 104.

[98] *Id.* at para. 140. For a valuable comment on the intertemporal aspects of the case, see Afshin A-Khavari, *The Passage of Time in International Environmental Disputes*, 10 Murdoch University Electronic Journal of Law (Dec. 2003), paras. 32–66, available at <http://www.murdochedu.au/elaw/issues/v104/akhavari104_text. html>.

contemporaneity) into account. There are echoes of the *Palmas* arbitration here and the actual use of the intertemporal law made by the arbitrator. Arbitrator Huber determined that even if title had been lawfully established according to the "original" contemporary law, it remained incumbent on a State to keep that title up if the law changed to require more, not merely to establish title but to sustain it.[99] He was criticised for introducing an element of uncertainty into an area of the law where stability was a primary virtue[100] but, read carefully, his opinion did not do that. If the interpretative approach in *Gabčíkovo* were not to be confined to the provisions of the kind which faced the Court, a similar aura of uncertainty would be introduced into treaty relations, a constant need to re-assess what all and any of a State's agreements require as international law on the environment developed or knowledge progressed.

A question *Gabčíkovo* leaves open is whether the principle of "present" contemporaneity is confined to certain classes of treaty, these classes now including environmental agreements, or whether the principle is applicable to any exercise of treaty interpretation. The benefit from any uncertainty which would result would be the better integration of international obligations, that the effects of "fragmentation" would be reduced. There may be another price: in his note on the *Oil Platforms* case, Professor Franklin Berman suggested that States would now be looking carefully at the jurisdictional clauses in their treaties to see to what risks of litigation they might now be exposed, though he did not anticipate much change in drafting practice.[101]

XI. THE 1839 TREATY OF SEPARATION, ARTICLE XII AND THE INTERTEMPORAL LAW

This was the point reached by the *Iron Rhine* Tribunal. Did Article XII have to be interpreted in the light of, *inter alia*, modern environmental law? However, the Treaty of 1839 was not an environmental treaty, nor were there any provisions in it like those which were held to impose continuing obligations in the 1977 Treaty considered in *Gabčíkovo*. The Tribunal drew attention to Article 31, paragraph 3, sub-paragraph (c) of the Vienna Convention and said "international environmental

---

[99] *Supra* note 90.

[100] Philip Jessup, *The Palmas Arbitration*, 22 AMERICAN JOURNAL OF INTERNATIONAL LAW p. 735 (1928).

[101] *Supra* note 87, at pp. 321–322.

law has relevance to the relations between the Parties", but noted "there is considerable debate as to what, within the field of environmental law, constitutes 'rules' or 'principles'; what is 'soft law'; and which environmental treaty law or principles have contributed to the development of customary international law."[102]

Although the Tribunal does not labour the point, if it or any other tribunal were to rely on Article 31, paragraph 3, sub-paragraph (c), it must identify "relevant rules of international law" to be taken into account for interpretative purposes, not simply refer to a rag-bag of non-binding standards and aspirations.

The first matter for the Tribunal was whether Belgium's request for the restoration of the Iron Rhine was for the reactivation of the original scheme or whether it was for a wholly new right of transit, given the modifications which it sought. Belgium's right to transit was to a route constructed "according to the same plan" as the route in Belgium. Looking at Article XII as a whole, the Tribunal rejected a plain meaning solution if that would have meant that "plan" covered the entire venture in all its particularities. Because the Belgian line would be continued over Netherlands' territory where the Netherlands had sovereign rights except to the extent reduced by Article XII, the Netherlands enjoyed "a right of decision-making".[103] As to whether a "new" railway was envisaged, the Tribunal rather ran the question together with the matter of who was to pay. It identified a distinction between "maintenance" and "modernisation". The Treaties were silent on financial responsibility once the line was built. The Netherlands had paid for the upkeep of the Iron Rhine in the past and it conceded responsibility to reinstate the line to its previous, relatively modest standards. Article 31, paragraph 3, sub-paragraph (c) was called in aid by the Tribunal. The "intertemporal rule" was one of the rules of international law which applied between the Parties.[104] What was at stake here was the difference between the "limited and relatively modest" cost of the project envisaged in 1839 and the great advances in rail transport and concomitant costs which "could not have been foreseen by the Parties."[105] The Tribunal said: "It has long been established that the understanding of conceptual or generic terms in a treaty may be seen as 'an essentially relative question: it depends upon the development of international relations'."[106]

---

[102] Award, para. 58.
[103] Award, para. 67.
[104] Award, para. 79.
[105] Award, para. 79.
[106] Award, para. 79.

Patently, this is a reasonable and indeed necessary way of understanding legal terms like "nationality" or "continental shelf". But, as the Tribunal acknowledged, it was not faced with finding the understanding of a generic term but of accommodating the language of an old treaty to the technical developments in railway construction and operation over a long period of years. Here too, the Tribunal decided, "an evolutive interpretation . . . will be preferred to the strict application of the intertemporal rule."[107] This was not reliance on Article 31, paragraph 3, sub-paragraph (c) but was justified by the Tribunal because it would ensure that the Treaty was applied in a way which would be effective to realise its object and purpose. The Tribunal alluded to *Gabčíkovo*, without acknowledging, still less disposing of, any differences between the treaties involved in the two cases. Also, it is worth repeating that an "evolutive" or "dynamic" approach to interpretation is not exactly the same thing as applying Article 31, paragraph 3, sub-paragraph (c) to take account of contemporary international law. For the European Court of Human Rights, for example, an "evolutive" approach is primarily designed to allow the Court to take into account changes in the relevant factual elements of a case then and a case now (with changes in national law being "facts" for these purposes).[108]

The considerations just referred to affected the understanding of the Treaties as follows:

(a) The Iron Rhine Treaty was not intended as a treaty of fixed duration.[109]

(b) The object and purpose of Article XII was to provide a "commercial communication" between Belgium and Germany over Netherlands' territory, so that what was required to secure "present" contemporary commerciality would develop over time.[110]

(c) "[A]n interpretation compatible with the principle of effectiveness leads to . . . the continued applicability of Article XII . . . to upgrading and improvements . . ." so, applying "this dynamic and evolutive approach" means that the reactivation of the line to considerably increased specifications would not be the creation of a "new" line.[111]

---

[107] Award, para. 80.
[108] For example, *Christine Goodwin v. United Kingdom*, ECtHR, App. No. 28957/95 (2002).
[109] Award, para. 82.
[110] Award, para. 83.
[111] Award, para. 84.

(d) In the light of (c), it might be necessary to read into Article XII elements of international law "as they apply today" on matters of cost allocation.[112]

The Tribunal then turned to the precise legal position of the railroad which comprised the means for the exercise of Belgium's right of transit. Article XII said that its construction was "without prejudice to the exclusive rights of sovereignty [of the Netherlands] over the territory which would be crossed by the road or canal in question", now a railway by virtue of the 1873 Treaty. While the "ordinary meaning" of "without prejudice" might suggest without any intrusion at all into Netherlands' sovereignty, the Tribunal said that the phrase had to be read in good faith and in the light of the context and object and purpose of the Treaty.[113]

The context of Article XII established that the sovereignty of the Netherlands had been derogated from to the extent that was necessary to construct the right of transit but that the Netherlands retained the "police power" over the area of the track, including, *inter alia*, the power to establish environmental standards.[114] Noting that the object and purpose of the 1839 Treaty was to be the grand end of securing the satisfactory separation of the Netherlands and Belgium, the Tribunal concluded that, applied to Article XII, this required the "careful balancing of the rights allowed to each party".[115] The precise difference between the Parties about environmental matters turned upon Belgium's claim that, while the Netherlands retained the power of environmental regulation, it could exercise this power only in consultation with Belgium.[116] The Netherlands stood on the position that, since environmental matters, and the designation of the Meinweg specifically, did not impinge on the operational right of transit, it was free to proceed with its measures unilaterally.[117] While the Tribunal preferred the contention of the Netherlands, it noted that the action taken by the Netherlands was not necessarily without financial consequences for Belgium's right of transit.[118]

The Tribunal then turned to the application of its understanding of the meaning of Article XII. Its conclusion was that the obligations of the Netherlands under

---

[112] Award, para. 84.
[113] Award, para. 85.
[114] Award, paras. 89, 202–206.
[115] Award, para. 91.
[116] BM, para. 82.
[117] NCM, paras. 3.3.5.5 and 3.3.6.3.
[118] Award, para. 96.

Article XII did not require the application of its national law and policy to the reactivation of the Iron Rhine in any way more favourable to Belgium than with respect to other railways in the Netherlands' system, unless to do so would amount to a denial of Belgium's transit right or render it unreasonably difficult, which, in the Tribunal's view, the present measures would not.[119]

There remained the matter of the allocation of costs of reactivation, which itself had a bearing on the reasonableness of the Netherlands' regulations.[120] Belgium had taken a very forthright position on this question, maintaining that reactivation was not a "new road" but the necessary modification of the historic route in order to maintain its commerciality in modern conditions. Accordingly, all costs fell to the Netherlands.[121] The Netherlands, arguing that reactivation was a "new" railway, contended that it was to be constructed entirely at Belgium's expense and subject to compliance with the Netherlands' regulatory regimes. The Tribunal accepted neither claim. The answer was to be found in Article XII and the relevant rules of international law. Except where Article XII provided otherwise, the Netherlands retained its sovereignty but, to the extent that adaptation and modernisation were necessary, they had to take into account the rules of international law, which included environmental law. This enabled the Tribunal to give some structure to the balancing exercise between Belgium's transit right and the Netherlands' power of regulation.

Belgium's right of transit was now expressed as a right of transit "in a way which corresponds to its current economic needs", thus interpreting Belgium's rights in a contemporary context, here a factual one.[122] The Netherlands' need to impose environmental measures in response to the upgrading was "legitimate", taking into account the development of environmental law, so a "present" contemporary element was introduced into its claim.[123] The Tribunal moved by analogy from the obligation of States to conduct their activities in such a way as

---

[119] Award, paras. 204–205.

[120] The Tribunal noted that the matter of financial risk associated with the project was a matter quite outside the terms of the Treaty and the contemplation of the Parties. It decided that the financial risk would lie with the Party responsible for the costs of each part of the project. Award, para. 209.

[121] In fact, Belgium had made a concession, offering a contribution to the costs of reactivation. Award, para. 215.

[122] Award, para. 221 – this "evolutive" interpretation, rather than recourse to Article 31(3)(c), VCLT.

[123] Award, para. 221 – not expressly but this is recourse to Article 31(3)(c), VCLT.

to respect the environment of other States to the Iron Rhine – where one State using a treaty-based right across the territory of another State was obliged to respect the environment of the territorial State. So, "[t]he reactivation of the Iron Rhine railway cannot be viewed in isolation from the environmental protection measures necessitated by the intended use of the railway line. The measures are to be fully integrated into the project and its costs."[124]

Belgium's responsibility for the costs of the environmental measures arose because they were indispensable to the operation of the railway envisaged by reactivation.[125] The exception was the Meinweg Tunnel. The Tribunal was of the view that both States had some responsibility for the situation which had arisen – Belgium had not in a timely manner kept the Netherlands aware of the scale of its plans for reactivation of the Iron Rhine; the Netherlands had not taken into account that the historic route of the railway crossed the designated area of the Meinweg. The Tribunal said that the costs of the Tunnel should be shared.[126] There is no consideration of Belgium's position that the environmental concerns could have been met by a less expensive means than building the Tunnel. The reason is that the Tribunal was of the view that there was no obligation of "most cost-effectiveness" (read, "cheapest") on the Netherlands in selecting measures for environmental protection: the limitation on the Netherlands' power was the general one, that it could not make demands which unreasonably interfered with Belgium's right of transit, and the Tribunal felt that the costs of the Tunnel were not so great as to do this. These parts of the Award, though clear in what they require, are opaque as to why the outcomes are required. The trouble was that there was not much by way of detailed guidance to be obtained about responsibility for environmental measures arising out of the running of the railroad from the analogy to customary law obligations about extraterritorial environmental damage. Recourse to the detailed law which might have helped, the EC Habitats Directive, was ruled out, in order to allow the Tribunal to side-step any jurisdictional objection which might have been made on the basis of Article 292 of the EC Treaty if the Tribunal had taken on the application of the Habitats Directive. Although it is nowhere made explicit, the result is that the cost-allocation mechanism is driven by the residual power of sovereignty. So long as the Netherlands remained within the powers left by Article XII, Belgium had to pay for what measures the Netherlands specified, save where there were also benefits to the Netherlands,

---

[124] Award, para. 223.
[125] Award, para. 226.
[126] Award, para. 234.

31

mainly from shared use of the track, and, for the Tunnel, where the Netherlands shared a degree of responsibility for the situation which required a particularly expensive solution.

There runs through the Award a consistent methodology – interpreting the Treaties in the light of their object and purpose and in their legal context. Further, where Belgium had a right, that right was to be effective. The Tribunal finds a way of incorporating changes in both the rules of international law and in the notion of commerciality, allowing it to discern an understanding of the Treaty of Separation which keeps it useful as a framework for the operation of a railway in contemporary conditions (and, if it were to become necessary, in future ones). However, for all the elaborate attention given to the principles of interpretation, in the end the most important element in the Award is that the object and purpose of the Treaty of Separation is served by striking a balance between the transit right of Belgium and the regulatory powers of the Netherlands. The invocation of "reasonableness" for guidance as to where the balance should be struck, a very lawyerly device (and, for the avoidance of doubt, not one which I deprecate), avoids the possibility of *non liquets* resulting from the Parties' failure to provide for what they could not possibly have foreseen. It seems to me that what the detailed principles of interpretation do is condition the limits of reasonableness, narrowing down the margin of decision for the Tribunal, though ultimately, not removing it altogether.

XII.   CONCLUSION

The Award is far from self-executing. The Parties have announced that they intend to constitute the panel of independent experts to provide the information necessary for the allocation of costs on shared parts of the line.[127] It will be important to the panel that the Award give it sufficient guidance to carry out its task. The States, in the meantime, are addressing provision of finance over the longer-term for the whole project. Ultimately, what divided the two States was a question of money. The Award provides a means for resolving it which has a legal

---

[127] Award, para. 235. The Award recommended that the panel be constituted within four months of the Award. The announcement of their intention to do so was made by the Parties more than twelve months after the Award was published, Joint Press Release, Minister of Transport, the Netherlands, and Secretary of State, Belgium, 6 July 2006. I am grateful to Belinda Macmahon of the PCA for providing an English translation of the Press Release and for other information about the Iron Rhine.

basis and which is not simply a decision *ex aequo et bono* (however much the actual outcome might correspond to an untethered "fair" proportionality).

If the Iron Rhine railway is reactivated, the Parties will doubtless think that the Tribunal has played its part. But this Award will be of interest to far more States than Belgium and the Netherlands. From the perspective of international lawyers, the most important aspect of the Award is the affirmation of the principle of interpretation of old treaties in the light of present international law and their factual context. Although the Tribunal makes frequent reference to Article 31, paragraph 3, sub-paragraph (c) of the Vienna Convention as part of the explanation of why this is a proper thing to do, the accommodation of changes of circumstance cannot be brought within this provision, which speaks solely of rules of international law. Rather, the Award is also an extension of processes hitherto confined to certain classes of treaty said to require "constitutional", "dynamic" or "evolutive" interpretation. It has been possible to explain these phenomena by maintaining that it is the intention of the parties that such "regime" treaties be kept up to date. The 1839 Treaty and the Iron Rhine Treaty do not belong to any established class of treaty to which this approach has so far been applied. The Tribunal invokes the object and purpose of the Treaties as the justification for extending the principle. In doing so, it raises an interesting prospect: any treaty, the application of which has consequences for other obligations of the parties – human rights, the environment, international peace and security and so on – should be interpreted in the light of these "background" rules, even if they have arisen since the conclusion of the treaty the meaning of which is being looked for. This may be so – the interpretation of the EC Treaty to take into account human rights standards before there was specific mention of them in the Treaty itself might be an early example. In the light of this move against "fragmentation", the protection for States, which may have reservations about the development, ought to be twofold:

(a) as far as developing rules are concerned, a tribunal should be at pains to show what the rule is, that it is binding on the respective States and that its application supports the line of the award;

(b) as far as changing circumstances go, a tribunal should indicate the evidence on which it bases its conclusion that there has been a change, while noting that on many matters, there may be room for quite considerable disagreement between States.

In either case, the tribunal should also be aware that there may be other bodies charged with interpretation of the laws which are relevant to the award or which have addressed the same claims of changing circumstances. There may be no binding obligation on one tribunal to give way to the decision of another but the development of a culture of respect between tribunals would alleviate some of the problems resulting from procedural "fragmentation". Other States may have intense interests or even legal interests: for instance, where a multilateral treaty to which they are parties is the "other rule of international law". The *Iron Rhine* Award is part of a process which might – perhaps should – see international courts regarding themselves as actors within the international legal system and owing responsibilities to its coherent development, as well as being dispute-settlement mechanisms of concern only to the parties before them. What the *Iron Rhine* case shows above all is that international litigation is not likely to get any easier. States need to be aware not only of the precise details of each dispute, but of the whole context which tribunals might feel necessary to take into account in order to arrive at the proper award.

Finally, I refer back to the Report of the ILC's study group on "fragmentation". The Report has two premises – first, that international law is a legal system, not a random collection of norms and second, that it is a generally accepted principle that when several norms bear on a single issue, they should, so far as is possible, be interpreted to give rise to a single set of compatible obligations.[128] The Report sets out a number of techniques for pursuing the objective of harmonisation, though it gives no guidance about how these techniques relate one to another. The ILC was concerned only with substantive "fragmentation" and so has nothing to say about jurisdictional clashes of the kind affecting the *Iron Rhine* Tribunal. However, both as a matter of principle and pragmatically, there is an indication in the Award that the exclusive jurisdiction of the ECJ under Article 292 of the EC Treaty does have a hierarchical authority, at least so far as all parties to litigation are also members of the EU. Identifying whether or not there is a conflict of jurisdictions might in many cases, as Dr Lavranos argues there was in the *Iron Rhine* case,[129] be a more difficult question than appears at first sight. The central issue of substantive "fragmentation" for the *Iron Rhine* Tribunal was the application (or not) of the intertemporal rule to the Treaties. The ILC refers to Article 31, paragraph 3, sub-paragraph (c) of the Vienna Convention as an important element

---

[128] ILC Report, *supra* note 24, para. 14(1 & 2).
[129] *Supra* note 34.

in integrating the particularities of obligations under a treaty with the broader duties of the parties in international law. International law, the ILC says, is a "dynamic" legal system. Accordingly, the meaning of a treaty provision "might be affected" by subsequent developments in the law.[130] I should have liked to see more emphasis on the need to demonstrate the changes in the law and their binding effect on the relevant States. The ILC goes beyond Article 31, paragraph 3, sub-paragraph (c) to endorse an evolutive approach to treaty interpretation to take account of, *inter alia*, "subsequent technical, economic or legal developments", citing the *Iron Rhine* Award as an example.[131] As Professor McClachlan notes in his article, Article 31, paragraph 3, sub-paragraph (c) is not a panacea to resolve the dilemmas of "fragmentation" in the treaty context (and, indeed, cannot do so where there is a genuine incompatibility of obligations).[132] Here, it is the job of politics – but there is a job for international law first, to try to avoid these conflicts by a sensitive use of the techniques set out by the ILC. It may be judicial politics, but it is still a task for judges.

*****

---

[130] ILC Report, *supra* note 24, para. 14(22).
[131] ILC Report, *supra* note 24, para. 14(23), referring to paras. 82 and 83 of the Award.
[132] *Supra* note 86, at p. 318.

IN THE ARBITRATION

REGARDING THE IRON RHINE ("IJZEREN RIJN") RAILWAY

BETWEEN:

THE KINGDOM OF BELGIUM

- AND -

THE KINGDOM OF THE NETHERLANDS

AWARD OF THE ARBITRAL TRIBUNAL

The Arbitral Tribunal:

Judge Rosalyn Higgins, President

Professor Guy Schrans

Judge Bruno Simma

Professor Alfred H.A. Soons

Judge Peter Tomka

The Hague, 24 May 2005

AWARD OF THE ARBITRAL TRIBUNAL

TABLE OF CONTENTS

CHAPTER I – PROCEDURAL HISTORY, BACKGROUND, AND SUBMISSIONS OF THE PARTIES

A.   Procedural History

1.   This Award is rendered pursuant to an Arbitration Agreement ("Arbitration Agreement") between the Kingdom of Belgium ("Belgium") and the Kingdom of the Netherlands ("the Netherlands") ("the Parties"). Its terms were agreed through an exchange of diplomatic notes dated 22 and 23 July 2003, which provided that the Arbitration Agreement would be provisionally applied pending completion of the constitutional formalities in both countries.

2.   Under the Arbitration Agreement, the Parties agreed "to submit [their] dispute concerning the reactivation of the Iron Rhine to an arbitral tribunal they are to set up under the auspices of the Permanent Court of Arbitration in The Hague" and "to execute the Arbitral Tribunal's decision as soon as possible."

3.   The Arbitration Agreement further posed specific Questions for the Arbitral Tribunal as follows:

> 1.   To what extent is Dutch legislation and the decision-making power based thereon in respect of the use, restoration, adaptation and modernisation of railway lines on Dutch territory applicable, in the same way, to the use, restoration, adaptation and modernisation of the historical route of the Iron Rhine on Dutch territory?
>
> 2.   To what extent does Belgium have the right to perform or commission work with a view to the use, restoration, adaptation and modernisation of the historical route of the Iron Rhine on Dutch territory, and to establish plans, specifications and procedures related to it according to Belgian law and the decision-making power based thereon? Should a distinction be drawn between the requirements, standards, plans, specifications and procedures related to, on the one hand, the functionality of the rail infrastructure in itself, and, on the other hand, the land use planning and the integration of the rail infrastructure, and, if so, what are the implications of this? Can the Netherlands unilaterally impose the building of underground and above-ground tunnels, diversions and the like, as well as the proposed associated construction and safety standards?
>
> 3.   In the light of the answers to the previous questions, to what extent should the cost items and financial risks associated with the use, restoration, adaptation and modernisation of the historical route of the Iron Rhine on

Dutch territory be borne by Belgium or by the Netherlands? Is Belgium obliged to fund investments over and above those that are necessary for the functionality of the historical route of the railway line?

4.   In the Arbitration Agreement, the Parties requested that the Arbitral Tribunal "render its decision on the basis of international law, including European law if necessary, while taking into account the Parties' obligations under article 292 of the EC Treaty."

5.   In accordance with the Arbitration Agreement, the Parties subsequently agreed upon Rules of Procedure for the arbitration ("Rules of Procedure"),[1] which were based on the "Permanent Court of Arbitration Optional Rules for Arbitrating Disputes between Two States."

6.   In conformity with Article 5, paragraph 1 of the Rules of Procedure, Belgium appointed as arbitrators Professor Guy Schrans and Judge Bruno Simma, and the Netherlands appointed Professor Alfred H.A. Soons and Judge Peter Tomka. The four arbitrators met on 22 September 2003, and, pursuant to Article 5, paragraph 2 of the Rules of Procedure, appointed Judge Rosalyn Higgins as President of the Arbitral Tribunal ("Tribunal").

7.   Consistent with the Arbitration Agreement and the designation of the Permanent Court of Arbitration ("PCA") as Registry under Article 1, paragraph 3 of the Rules of Procedure, the Secretary-General of the PCA appointed Ms. Anne Joyce, Deputy General Counsel, to serve as Registrar to the Tribunal.

8.   By letters dated 3 September 2003 and 9 September 2003, respectively, the Netherlands and Belgium each designated their Agents. The Agent appointed by the Netherlands was Professor Johan G. Lammers, and the Agent appointed by Belgium was Mr. Jan Devadder.

9.   The Tribunal held a meeting with the Agents on 29 September 2003. At the meeting, the Tribunal and the Agents reached certain understandings regarding implementation of the Rules of Procedure and discussed other practical matters relating to the arbitration

---

[1] The Rules of Procedure, as well as other documents related to the arbitration, are available at http://www.pca-cpa.org.

proceedings. The Rules of Procedure provide for the possibility of oral proceedings only in the event of a specific request of a Party (Article 13). However, it was agreed that should the Tribunal wish to seek additional information from the Parties following receipt of the written pleadings, the Tribunal would notify the Parties and consult with them as to whether such information would best be obtained through further written pleadings or through an oral proceeding. It was further agreed that, in the event of a hearing or an additional round of written pleadings, the time limits for issuance of the Award would commence following the date of the last submission or the closure of hearings, as the case may be.

10. The Parties filed their written pleadings in accordance with the timetable set forth in the Rules of Procedure. The pleadings consisted of Belgium's Memorial filed on 1 October 2003 ("BM"), the Netherlands' Counter-Memorial filed on 30 January 2004 ("NCM"), Belgium's Reply filed on 30 March 2004 ("BR"), and the Netherlands' Rejoinder filed on 1 June 2004 ("NR").

11. No request for an oral hearing was made by either Party or sought by the Tribunal.

12. In June 2004, it came to the attention of the Tribunal that approval of the Arbitration Agreement by the Netherlands Parliament was taking longer than anticipated, and that ratification was unlikely prior to the date envisaged under Article 18 of the Rules of Procedure (29 September 2004) for rendering the Tribunal's Award. In light of these developments, the Tribunal decided that it would not render the Award before completion by both Parties of their respective constitutional procedures required for the entry into force of the Arbitration Agreement. On 6 and 13 July 2004, the Tribunal received from Belgium copies of the relevant documents indicating that the constitutional procedures required in Belgium for the entry into force of the Arbitration Agreement had been completed. On 20 May 2005, the Tribunal was notified by the Netherlands that the constitutional procedures required in the Netherlands for entry into force of the Arbitration Agreement had been completed and copies of the relevant documents were provided. On 20 May 2005, the Parties informed the Tribunal that, although the Arbitration Agreement, on its terms, would not enter into force until 1 July 2005, the necessary ratification procedures in each country and the mutual notification thereof had been completed. They both wished to request that the Tribunal render its

Award "as soon as possible prior to its formal entry into force." The Tribunal acceded to the Parties' request, and the Award has been rendered accordingly.

* * *

13. Neither Party has challenged the jurisdiction of the Tribunal to decide the dispute. Nevertheless, Belgium, in a section of its Reply with the heading "Jurisdiction," cites the requirement under Article 292 of the Treaty Establishing the European Community (1997 Official Journal of the European Communities ("O.J.") (C 340) 3) ("EC Treaty") pursuant to which "Member States undertake not to submit a dispute concerning the interpretation or application of this treaty to any method of settlement other than those provided therein," and states that, although both Belgium and the Netherlands had referred to EC law in their pleadings, such references do not constitute sufficient reason to conclude that Article 292 had been violated (BR, pp. 2, 4, paras. 3, 5).

14. In support of its view, Belgium distinguishes the ongoing *MOX Plant* case,[2] wherein Ireland has brought a dispute with the United Kingdom before an arbitral tribunal established pursuant to Annex VII to the United Nations Convention on the Law of the Sea (which proceedings that tribunal suspended), and the Commission of the European Communities ("European Commission") has instituted proceedings against Ireland before the Court of Justice of the European Communities ("European Court of Justice") for an alleged violation of Article 292 of the EC Treaty. Belgium states that, unlike the United Kingdom in the *MOX Plant* case, the Netherlands had not objected to Belgium's references to EC law in its Memorial. Belgium further argues that neither Party was contending that the other had violated EC law. Moreover, Belgium states, "issues where Community law comes into play in the present cases [sic] really boil down to the apportionment of costs, which is not a matter of Community law" (BR, p. 4, para. 6).

15. The Parties elaborated further on their view of applicable law and its relationship to EC law in a letter addressed to the Secretary-General of the European Commission, which was dated 26 August 2003, a copy being sent to the PCA. In the letter, the Parties stated:

---

[2] For a description of the case and other related information, *see* http://www.pca-cpa.org/ENGLISH/ RPC/#Ireland v. United Kingdom ("MOX Plant Case").

For both parties the core of the dispute relates to the interpretation of the bilateral Separation Treaty of 1839 and the interpretation of the obligations laid down in this treaty, i.e., questions of international law.

The letter concluded:

Should the eventuality of an application or interpretation of community law arise in the course of the procedure, the Kingdom of Belgium and the Kingdom of the Netherlands commit themselves to take all necessary measures in order to comply with all the obligations resting with them under the EC Treaty, and in particular Article 292 thereof.

B. Background

16. The Iron Rhine, or "*IJzeren Rijn*" as it is known in Dutch, is a railway linking the port of Antwerp, Belgium, to the Rhine basin in Germany, via the Netherlands provinces of Noord-Brabant and Limburg.[3] The Iron Rhine has its origins in the negotiations surrounding the separation of Belgium from the Netherlands in the 1830s, and in particular in the Treaty between Belgium and the Netherlands relative to the Separation of their Respective Territories ("1839 Treaty of Separation") (Consolidated Treaty Series ("C.T.S."), 1838–1839, Vol. 88, p. 427).

17. Among other matters treated in the 1839 Treaty of Separation was the question of a communication link between Antwerp and Germany. In this connection, Article XII of the 1839 Treaty of Separation provides as follows:

> *Dans le cas où il aurait été construit en Belgique une nouvelle route, ou creusé un nouveau canal, qui aboutirait à la Meuse vis-à-vis le canton hollandais de Sittard, alors il serait loisible à la Belgique de demander à la Hollande, qui ne s'y refuserait pas dans cette supposition, que la dite route ou le dit canal fussent prolongés d'après le même plan, entièrement aux frais et dépens de la Belgique, par le canton de Sittard, jusqu'aux frontières de l'Allemagne.[4] Cette route ou ce canal, qui ne pourraient servir que de communication commerciale, seraient construits, au choix de la Hollande, soit par des ingénieurs et ouvriers que la Belgique obtiendrait l'autorisation d'employer à cet effet dans le canton de Sittard, soit par des ingénieurs et ouvriers que la Hollande fournirait, et qui exécuteraient,*

---

[3] For a map of the Iron Rhine railway provided jointly by the Parties, *see* Annex.

[4] The Tribunal notes that Article XII speaks of "*l'Allemagne*" even though in 1839 Germany did not exist as a state under international law, but as a mere confederation ("*Deutscher Bund*"). The new road or canal envisaged in the Treaty would thus have reached the borders of Prussia. At the time of the conclusion of the Iron Rhine Treaty in 1873 (*see* paragraph 18), Prussia and other German states had been united in the German Empire.

> *aux frais de la Belgique, les travaux convenus, le tout sans charge aucune pour la Hollande, et sans préjudice de ses droits de souveraineté exclusifs sur le territoire que traverserait la route ou le canal en question. Les deux parties fixeraient, d'un commun accord, le montant et le mode de perception des droits et péages qui seraient prélevés sur cette même route ou canal.*[5]

18.   The transit right conferred on Belgium by Article XII of the 1839 Treaty of Separation was further specified through treaties concluded in the nineteenth century, culminating in the Convention between Belgium and the Netherlands relative to the Payment of the Belgian Debt, the Abolition of the Surtax on Netherlands Spirits, and the Passing of a Railway Line from Antwerp to Germany across Limburg of 1873 ("Iron Rhine Treaty") (C.T.S., 1872–1873, Vol. 145, p. 447), pursuant to which the Iron Rhine railway was constructed across Netherlands territory. It was completed in 1879.

19.   From 1879 until World War I, the Iron Rhine railway was used continuously. During this period, the legal status of the Iron Rhine railway remained essentially unchanged with one exception – namely, ownership of the track was transferred from the Belgian concessionnaire "*Grand Central Belge*" to the Government of Belgium, and thence to the Government of the Netherlands pursuant to the Railway Convention between Belgium and the Netherlands of 23 April 1897 ("1897 Railway Convention") (C.T.S., 1896–1897, Vol. 184, p. 374). Use of the line then varied in intensity during the period 1914–1991. It is common ground that all commercial transit traffic was halted during World War I. Belgium states that thereafter "twelve international freight trains a day travelled in both directions between Antwerp and the Ruhr area, between Rotterdam and the Ruhr area" (BM, p. 22, para. 18); whereas the Netherlands specifies the line was little used, with eight freight trains per 24-hour period passing in 1920, nine in 1921, and since 1922, only 1 or 2 per 24-hour period (and only rarely over the entire track) (NCM, p. 19, para. 2.11; NR, p. 29, paras. 115–117). The Netherlands explains this by referring to the access had by Belgium to the then recently constructed Hasselt-Montzen-Aken line and its economic advantages. Both agree that during World War II, the Iron Rhine track was destroyed and it was necessary to rebuild it. For a period thereafter it was used for military transportation. During the ensuing forty years only

---

[5] *See* paragraph 32 below for the Tribunal's translation of Article XII. The text of the 1839 Treaty of Separation provided by the Netherlands to the Tribunal uses, in the French and English versions, Roman numerals; the text provided by Belgium uses Roman numerals in the English version and Arabic numerals in the French version. The Tribunal will use Roman numerals when referring to the 1839 Treaty of Separation.

light use was made of the line. Since 1991, the Iron Rhine railway has not been used for through traffic between Belgium and Germany, although use of certain sections of the line in the Netherlands has continued (which use is not in issue between the Parties).

20. During the 1990s, a number of legal steps were taken by the Government of the Netherlands with respect to designation of nature reserves in the provinces of Noord-Brabant and Limburg, some of which lie across the route of the Iron Rhine railway. In 1987 and during the 1990s (thus beginning even prior to the cessation of through traffic in 1991), there were a number of communications, both oral and written, between government officials of Belgium and the Netherlands concerning possible reactivation of the Iron Rhine railway.

21. Formal inter-governmental discussions on the issue of use, restoration, adaptation and modernisation of the Iron Rhine railway were initiated by the Prime Minister of Belgium on 12 June 1998. (Hereinafter, the term "reactivation" will be used to denote the just-mentioned various activities.) These discussions led to the adoption, on 28 March 2000, of a Memorandum of Understanding ("March 2000 MoU") between the two Governments, which, among other things, provided for completion of certain environmental impact studies of the reactivation, as well as a timetable for phasing in renewed use of the line.

22. The environmental impact studies envisaged by the March 2000 MoU were completed in May 2001. However, further implementation of the March 2000 MoU, particularly with respect to the plans for so-called "temporary use" of the Iron Rhine railway, foundered on disagreements between the Parties concerning conditions to be attached to such use and allocation of costs necessary for making the line suitable for long-term use as requested by Belgium. The Parties have further disagreed as to whether this temporary use can occur in the absence of agreement on long-term use. Discussion between the Parties then turned to the possibility of submitting their dispute to arbitration and led to the Arbitration Agreement concluded between the Parties in July 2003.

23. In general, Belgium argues that the exercise of jurisdiction by the Netherlands over the Iron Rhine railway is limited by the Netherlands' obligations under international law

and in particular the obligations of good faith and reasonableness. As applied to the transit right granted under the 1839 Treaty of Separation, Belgium argues, the Netherlands is obliged at a minimum to allow immediate – albeit modest – "temporary" use of the historic track and, for the long term, a major reactivation of the track. Exercise of its rights, Belgium asserts, must not be rendered "unreasonably difficult" by, among other things, the various "highly expensive" environmental protection measures the Netherlands seeks to impose in relation to any such reactivation.

24. Belgium also argues that, alternatively, and if such measures are nonetheless to be imposed, the Netherlands must ensure that Belgium's use of the Iron Rhine railway is not adversely affected by the resulting construction works, and bear the costs and financial risks. In support of this view, Belgium emphasizes that its obligations to bear costs under Article XII relate to the *construction* of the road or canal, and not to the exercise of Belgium's right of passage (BR, p. 98, para. 104). Belgium also looks to the language of Article XI of the 1839 Treaty of Separation – including the term "*entretien*," which appears therein – and argues further that the Netherlands has a responsibility to maintain the track of the Iron Rhine railway "in a good state and prone to facilitating trade." The question of what constitutes "a good state and prone to facilitating trade," Belgium asserts, must be viewed in light of current circumstances and what is considered commercially viable (BR, p. 113, para. 122). If the Tribunal determines that Belgium should bear any of the costs, such costs should, in Belgium's view, be limited to those needed to meet only minimum requirements consistent with Netherlands legislation, for example with respect to noise abatement. Moreover, if Belgium is to bear the costs of measures resulting from other international obligations (such as EC law), the Netherlands must require only the least costly and/or onerous options available to meet these obligations.

25. In general, the Netherlands, for its part, argues that while it does not contest Belgium's right of transit across Netherlands territory, that right is circumscribed by the requirements set forth in Article XII of the 1839 Treaty of Separation, and that, as a limitation of Netherlands territorial sovereignty, the transit right must be interpreted restrictively. The Netherlands cites in particular the reservation of its sovereignty in Article XII and the requirements that Belgium bear the costs of the "*travaux*" envisaged under that article. Environmental measures and other requirements putatively imposed

by the Netherlands on reactivation of the Iron Rhine railway, the Netherlands maintains, constitute the legitimate exercise of its sovereignty under Article XII, leaving Belgium's obligation to pay the costs of complying with the Netherlands' requirements intact. Further, nothing in Article XI of the 1839 Treaty of Separation, the 1897 Railway Convention, or subsequent practice of the Parties, the Netherlands asserts, leads to a different conclusion (NCM, p. 57, paras. 3.3.8.2–3.3.8.4; NR, pp. 33–35, paras. 133–139). Belgium employs too broad a definition of the term "*entretien*," the Netherlands argues, and it cannot be stretched to cover the costs associated with reactivation (NR, p. 33, para. 135).

C. Final Submissions of the Parties

1. Belgium

26. The final submissions of Belgium, made in the Reply, were as follows:

> **ON QUESTION NO. 1**
>
> Dutch legislation and the decision-making power based thereon in respect of the use, restoration, adaptation and modernisation of railway lines on Dutch territory do not apply in the same way to the use, restoration, adaptation and modernisation of the historical route of the Iron Rhine on Dutch territory, in that:
>
> - The Netherlands shall, if Belgium decides to construct a "*new road or canal*" on Belgian territory, as described in Article XII of the Separation Treaty of 19 April 1839, allow for the prolongation of this road or canal on Dutch territory "*according to the same plan*" as on Belgian territory, without the Netherlands' agreement as to the plan.
>
> - If, in the hypothesis just-mentioned, the Netherlands takes the option to perform the works by itself, such works can only be at the expense of Belgium if they have been agreed upon by both Governments. Conversely, if the Netherlands chooses to have these works performed by Belgium, no agreement is necessary as to the works. In the latter hypothesis, Belgium has the right to benefit from a treatment not less favourable than the one accorded to other operators in this respect.
>
> - Without prejudice to European law, the Netherlands have the obligation to allow for the use of the Iron Rhine route provided that it "*only serve[s] as commercial communication*" and to take all the measures necessary to permit this use.
>
> - The height and mode of collection of toll rights shall be determined by a common agreement between the Netherlands and Belgium. Such agreement must be taken in conformity with international law and European law.

- No re-routings deviating from the historical route shall be decided upon by the Netherlands without the agreement of Belgium.

- The Netherlands is under the obligation to exercise its legislative and decision-making power in good faith and in a reasonable manner, and so as not to deprive Belgium's rights to have the Iron Rhine prolonged on Dutch territory according to the same plan as on Belgian territory to use the historical route of the Iron Rhine, of their substance, and so as not to render the exercise of these rights unreasonably difficult. The Netherlands shall take all necessary measures so as to allow for such a use.

- If the Netherlands has several possibilities of complying with an international obligation, one of which allows it to comply with its obligation towards Belgium as concerns the Iron Rhine, while the others does or did not, the Netherlands are under the obligation to take the possibility which makes it possible for it to comply with both obligations.

- If the Netherlands has conflicting obligations as concerns the reactivation of the Iron Rhine, it shall reduce the effect of such a conflict by taking measures, which are the least onerous for Belgium.

- Without prejudice to Belgium's right to an immediate use of the historical route of the Iron Rhine at full capacity and on a long-term basis, when Belgium makes a demand for provisional driving on the historical route of the Iron Rhine, by 15 trains per natural day (both directions summed up), including at limited speed in evening hours and at night, for a period of 5 years at least, the Netherlands shall immediately accept that demand, and immediately take all decisions necessary to effectively allow for such driving within the shortest time materially feasible, which shall not be more than one month.

- The Netherlands shall take all necessary measures so as to prevent any interruption of the use of the Iron Rhine between "temporary driving" and "long-term" driving, and to effectively allow for the latter within the shortest time feasible.

- Without prejudice to Belgium's position under Question No. 3, the measures foreseen in ProRail's "*IJzeren Rijn Concept Ontwerp-tracébesluit versie 1.4*" of July 2003 with respect to parts A2, B and C of the track as identified therein, may not be required as a prior condition to Belgium's exercise of its rights on the Iron Rhine, unless such measures do not render the exercise of Belgium's right to the use of the Iron Rhine unreasonably difficult and:

  o In primary order, unless the costs and financial risks associated with these measures shall be borne in whole by the Netherlands.

  o In subsidiary order, unless the costs and financial risks associated with such measures be borne by the Netherlands at the least in proportion to its forecasted use of the railway line by 2020, which is at least 77,889 percent, and by Belgium in a proportion of maximum 22,111 percent, under the further proviso that the Netherlands may not charge to Belgium costs which are charged on the users of the line in accordance with Article XII of the 1839 Separation Treaty and European Community rules, nor charge to Belgium costs unrelated to the reactivation, which includes, but is not limited to, costs for the abatement of road traffic noise.

- Without prejudice to Belgium's position under Question No. 3, the measures foreseen in ProRail's "*IJzeren Rijn Concept Ontwerp-tracébesluit versie 1.4*" of July 2003 with respect to noise abatement which are not necessary so as to reach the maximal exemption limit of 70 dB(A) or 73 dB(A) provided by law, unless if such measures do not render the exercise of Belgium's right to the use of the Iron Rhine unreasonably difficult, and unless if the costs and financial risks associated with such abatement measures are borne in whole by the Netherlands.

- Without prejudice to Question No. 3, the Netherlands may not require the building of a tunnel in the Meinweg area nor other wildlife and nature protection measures including compensatory measures in areas passed through by the historical route of the Iron Rhine, unless if such requirement does not render the exercise of Belgium's right to the use of the Iron Rhine unreasonably difficult and if the costs and financial risks associated with these measures are borne in whole by the Netherlands.

- In subsidiary order to the last submission, if the Tribunal esteems that the former point is outside its jurisdiction, the Netherlands may not require the building of a tunnel in the Meinweg area nor other wildlife and nature protection measures including compensatory measures in areas passed through by the historical route of the Iron Rhine, unless if such requirement does not render the exercise of Belgium's right to the use of the Iron Rhine unreasonably difficult and if the costs and financial risks associated with these measures are borne in whole by the Netherlands, safe to the extent that the Netherlands had no other possibilities to meet its obligations under EC law, and to the extent that the measures required are the least costly for allowing the Netherlands to meet its EC obligations.

ON QUESTION NO. 2

- Belgium does not have the right to perform or commission work with a view to the use, restoration, adaptation and modernisation of the historical route of the Iron Rhine on Dutch territory, unless Belgium requests to have a new road on Belgian territory prolonged according to the same plan on Dutch territory, and the Netherlands takes the option of having that prolongation according to the new plan built by Belgium in accordance with Article XII of the Separation Treaty of 19 April 1839.

- Belgium has the right according to Article XII of the 1839 Separation Treaty to have a new road on Belgian territory prolonged on Dutch territory according to the same plan. This is subject to Dutch jurisdiction within the limits set forth under Question No. 1. The right of Belgium to establish plans, specifications and procedures for such works according to Belgian law and the decision-making power based thereon, is limited accordingly.

- The "plan" within the meaning of Article XII of the 1839 Separation Treaty shall be determined by Belgium without the agreement of the Netherlands, however, Belgium shall inform and consult the Netherlands in accordance with the principles of good faith and reasonableness, all of this without prejudice to European Community law.

- The word "plan" in Article XII of the Separation Treaty must be interpreted on the basis of its ordinary meaning, according to which it refers to all the technical characteristics and particularities of the railway.

- Belgium's present request for reactivation does not amount to a request for a "*new road or canal*" within the meaning of Article XII of the Separation Treaty with the consequence that the Netherlands does not have the option provided by Article 12 of the 1839 Separation Treaty to require that Belgium performs work on Dutch territory.

- Works on Dutch territory performed by the Netherlands shall be agreed upon between Belgium and the Netherlands. As the present request of Belgium to reactivate the Iron Rhine is not a request to have the Iron Rhine prolonged on Dutch territory according to the same plan as on Belgian territory, such limitation is not at stake at present. The same is true of Belgium's right to benefit from a treatment not less favourable than that accorded to other operators with respect to other railways on Dutch territory, as concerns the freedom to establish plans, specifications and procedures.

  Further, Dutch regulatory powers to establish plans, specifications and procedures remains limited by the principles set out under Question No. 1.

- The distinction between the requirements, standards, plans, specifications and procedures related to, on the one hand, the functionality of the railway infrastructure in itself, and, on the other hand, the land use planning and the integration of the rail infrastructure, is irrelevant, as such, as concerns the extent to which Belgium has the right to perform or commission work on Dutch territory. The distinction is also irrelevant, as such, with respect to the extent to which Belgium has the right to establish plans, specifications and procedures related to it according to Belgian law and the decision-making power based thereon. This does not affect the relevance of the said distinction for determining the reasonableness of Dutch requirements for the building of infrastructure to be paid for by Belgium.

- The right of the Netherlands to unilaterally require the building of underground and above-ground tunnels, as well as the proposed associated construction and safety standards, is limited by the abovementioned rights of Belgium in case it requests that the railway on Belgian territory be prolonged on Dutch territory according to the same plan, which is not the case at present. It is further limited by the obligations of the Netherlands to cooperate with Belgium as well as by the principles stated under Question No. 1.

Therefore, the Netherlands may not impose the construction of underground and above-ground tunnels at the expense of Belgium, if such a requirement is contrary to the principles set under Question No. 1, which notably include the standards of normality and of proportionality, as well of non-arbitrariness and non-discrimination.

The Netherlands is under the obligation to inform and to consult in good faith with Belgium as concerns such requirements, in accordance with its obligation to cooperate and the principle of reasonableness and good faith.

The 'pacta sunt servanda' principle, and its corollaries the principles of good faith and of reasonableness, also applies in the hypothesis that the Netherlands wishes to build underground and above-ground tunnels on the Iron Rhine on Dutch territory at its own expenses, and not at the expenses of Belgium. As a consequence, the Netherlands may not, notably, decide to build a tunnel at their expenses, if such a construction infringes in an unreasonable manner on the right to passage of Belgium conferred to it by Article XII of the Separation Treaty.

- Diversions and the like may not unilaterally be imposed by the Netherlands, in that they require the consent of Belgium.

ON QUESTION NO. 3

In primary order:

- That, in application of the Iron Rhine's conventional regime, Belgium shall bear the costs and financial risks associated with the Iron Rhine on Dutch territory, only to the extent that Belgium requests that a new route on Belgian territory be prolonged on Dutch territory according to the same plan, and, if the Netherlands would then take the option of having the route constructed by engineers and workers which the Netherlands would employ, to the further condition that the works be agreed upon.

- That Belgium's present request for the reactivation of the Iron Rhine does not amount to a request that a new route on Belgian territory be prolonged on Dutch territory according to the same plan, with the consequence that Belgium is not under the obligation to bear the costs and financial risks associated with this reactivation.

- That, in application of the Iron Rhine's conventional regime, the Netherlands shall be responsible for all cost items and financial risks associated with the restoration, adaptation and modernization of the historical route of the Iron Rhine on Dutch territory, so as to make it in a good state and prone to facilitating trade.

- That the reactivation of the Iron Rhine as it is presently envisaged does not exceed what is necessary for the line to be in a good state and prone to facilitating trade, with the consequence that the Netherlands shall be responsible for all costs and financial risks associated with the envisaged restoration, adaptation and modernization.

In subsidiary order:

- That all costs items and financial risks related to restoration of the historical route, caused by the Netherlands' dismantling part of the infrastructure of the historical track, making it unfit for use or failing to provide maintenance, shall be borne by the Netherlands.

- That the Netherlands shall be responsible for all costs and financial risks associated with (a) of measures related to tracks which are in present or future use for Dutch railway transports, (b) of measures required to meet objectives over and above Dutch legislative requirements, (c) of building a loop around Roermond, and (d) of building a tunnel in the Meinweg and similar nature protection devices and compensatory measures, within the limits set under Question No. 1.

2. Netherlands

27. The final submissions of the Netherlands, made in the Rejoinder, were as follows:

ON QUESTION NO. 1

The Netherlands submits that it has retained the right to exercise in full its legislative, executive and judicial authority in respect of the reactivation of the Iron Rhine, so that the Dutch legislation in force and the decision-making power based thereon in respect of the use, the restoration, the adaptation and the modernisation of railway lines on Dutch territory is applicable in the same way to the use, restoration, adaptation and modernisation of the historical route of the Iron Rhine on Dutch territory.

Other than Article XII of the Separation Treaty, as supplemented by the Iron Rhine Treaty, there is no agreement obliging the Netherlands to permit Belgium the right to the use, the restoration, the adaptation and the modernisation of the Iron Rhine on Dutch territory.

Article XII of the Separation Treaty forms a special agreement. It contains a restriction on the territorial sovereignty of the Netherlands involving the right of Belgium to the use, the restoration, the adaptation and the modernisation of the Iron Rhine. However, Article XII of the Separation Treaty should, in so far as it contains a restriction to the territorial sovereignty of the Netherlands, in accordance with international law, be construed restrictively.

ON QUESTION NO. 2

In view of the answer given to Question 1 the Netherlands submits that Belgium does not have the right to perform or commission work with a view to the use, the restoration, the adaptation and the modernisation of the historical route of the Iron Rhine on Dutch territory and to establish plans, specifications and procedures related to it according to Belgian law and the decision-making power based thereon.

As to the right of Belgium to perform or commission work with a view to the use, the restoration, the adaptation and the modernisation of the Iron Rhine on Dutch territory, the Netherlands refers to the text of Article XII of the Separation Treaty, which specifically states "*Cette route ... seraient construits,* aux choix de la Hollande, *soit par des ingénieurs et ouvriers, que la Belgique obtiendrait l'autorisation d'employer à cet effet dans le canton de Sittard, soit par des ingénieurs et ouvriers, que la Hollande fournirait ....*"

No distinction may be drawn between the requirements, standards, plans, specifications and procedures related to, on the one hand, the functionality of the rail infrastructure in itself, and, on the other hand, the land use planning and the integration of the rail infrastructure.

The Netherlands may unilaterally impose the building of underground and above-ground tunnels, diversions and the like, as well as the proposed associated construction and safety standards, as long as these are not contrary to applicable rules of international law.

ON QUESTION NO. 3

The Netherlands submits that in view of the passages of Article XII of the Separation Treaty reading "*entièrement aux frais et dépens de la Belgique*," and "*qui exécuteraient aux frais de la Belgique*," all cost items and financial risks associated with the use, restoration, adaptation and modernisation of the historical route of the Iron Rhine on Dutch territory subject to the requirements of Dutch legislation and decision-making power based thereon in respect of the functionality of the rail infrastructure and the protection of the residential and lived environment should be borne by Belgium.

CHAPTER II – LEGAL BASIS AND SCOPE OF BELGIUM'S TRANSIT RIGHT

A.   The Applicable Legal Provisions

28.   The Arbitral Tribunal has been asked to render an Award, answering Questions jointly put to it by the Parties, "on the basis of international law, including European law if necessary, while taking into account the Parties' obligations under Article 292 of the EC Treaty."

29.   Various treaties have a relevance to this dispute and have been brought to the Tribunal's attention by the Parties. In addition, the Parties have each invoked various rules and principles of international law.

30.   As noted above (*see* paragraph 16), a key treaty relevant to this dispute is the 1839 Treaty of Separation. By this treaty, Belgium and the Netherlands settled the allocation of territory, and also dealt with various other matters. This was achieved after prolonged diplomatic multilateral negotiations, which had begun in 1830, in which other Powers were involved ("the Conference of London").

31.   The 1839 Treaty of Separation determined the territory of Belgium and the Netherlands and specified their borders (Articles I, II and VI). Articles II and V deal with the cession by Willem I of part of the Grand Duchy of Luxembourg. Articles III and IV attribute part of Limburg to the Netherlands. Article VII affirms the continued neutrality of Belgium. Article XIII distributes debts between the two countries. Various transit rights are guaranteed to Belgium by virtue of Articles IX, X, XI and XII. It is Article XII which has been most at issue in the pleadings of the Parties in the present arbitration.

32.   The Treaty was concluded in Dutch and in French. There is no dispute between the Parties about such small distinctions as exist in the two languages. The Parties have used the French text (Martens, *Nouveau Recueil des Traités*, Vol. XVI, p. 773) in their pleadings. They have each provided for the benefit of the Tribunal a translation in English of the particular articles. These translations differ from each other in several

respects. For this and other technical reasons the Tribunal has prepared its own translation of Article XII, which is as follows:

> In the case that in Belgium a new road would have been built or a new canal dug, which would lead to the Maas facing the Dutch canton of Sittard, then Belgium would be at liberty to ask Holland, which in that hypothesis would not refuse it, that the said road, or the said canal be extended in accordance with the same plan, entirely at the cost and expense of Belgium, through the canton of Sittard, up to the borders of Germany. This road or canal, which could be used only for commercial communication, would be constructed, at the choice of Holland, either by engineers and workers whom Belgium would obtain authorization to employ for this purpose in the canton of Sittard, or by engineers and workers whom Holland would supply, and who would execute the agreed works at the expense of Belgium, all without any burden to Holland, and without prejudice to the exclusive rights of sovereignty over the territory which would be crossed by the road or canal in question.
>
> The two Parties would set, by common agreement, the amount and the method of collection of the duties and tolls which would be levied on the said road or canal.

The French text of which this is a translation is reproduced above (*see* paragraph 17).

33. On the very same day as the 1839 Treaty of Separation was concluded, two further treaties were concluded at the Conference of London, one being a treaty by Belgium with Austria, France, Great Britain, Prussia, and Russia, and the other being a treaty by the Netherlands with the same parties (C.T.S., 1838–1839, Vol. 88, p. 411 ff). These treaties each referred to the provisions of the 1839 Treaty of Separation (the articles of which were annexed thereto), and provided that they "*sont considérés comme ayant la même force et valeur que s'ils étaient textuellement insérés dans le présent Acte, et qu'ils se trouvent ainsi placés sous la garantie de Leursdites Majestés.*"

34. It was thus clear from the outset that the provisions of the 1839 Treaty of Separation, including Article XII thereof, were of more than bilateral interest. That has remained the case until today. In the current era there is a certain interest of the EC in the railway that was in due course to be established by reference, *inter alia*, to Article XII of the 1839 Treaty of Separation. That interest, and the legal implications for this arbitration, are further examined below (*see* paragraphs 145 and 146).

35. Article XII of the 1839 Treaty of Separation referred to a road which might have been built or a canal which might have been dug. In 1842, the Boundary Treaty between

Belgium and the Netherlands was concluded in The Hague (C.T.S., 1842–1843, Vol. 94, p. 37 ff). Its purpose, as stated in the preamble, was to clarify a number of issues arising from the 1839 Treaty of Separation. In particular, Article III made clear that the road or canal across the Netherlands referred to in Article XII of the 1839 Treaty of Separation could be constructed by a concessionnaire. (In 1869, Belgium provided for such a concession for a railway (BM, p. 9, para. 9).) The second paragraph of Article III of the Boundary Treaty envisaged the possibility of expropriation by the Netherlands, on the basis of its legislation and for a public utility purpose, of the necessary land for the project that had been envisaged under Article XII. There was immediately added to Article III of the Boundary Treaty the phrase "*et ce de la même manière que si le Gouvernement Belge procédait par lui-même aux travaux d'exécution et d'exploitation de la route ou du canal*," thus maintaining the careful balance between the Parties that had been struck in Article XII of the 1839 Treaty of Separation.

36. In the event, the Boundary Treaty did not resolve all the outstanding difficulties between the Netherlands and Belgium. The Parties were in dispute about whether, for purposes of the extension envisaged in Article XII of the 1839 Treaty of Separation, the road or canal would have had to have been built or merely planned. This problem has since been resolved, as is explained below (*see* paragraph 62). The Parties were also in dispute as to whether Article XII of the 1839 Treaty of Separation envisaged a railway line extension, in contradistinction to the extension of a road or canal. That Belgium could extend a railway line was eventually agreed to by the Netherlands in a letter dated 12 August 1868 (BM, Exhibit No. 15, Letter of the Dutch Government to the Belgian Ambassador at The Hague, dated 12 August 1868).

37. In 1873, Belgium and the Netherlands entered into a further treaty, the Iron Rhine Treaty. Under Article IV of that treaty the Netherlands acknowledges the *Compagnie du Nord de la Belgique* as the concessionnaire of the railway line on Netherlands territory. It was also agreed that the Antwerp-Gladbach section would be built by either that company or by the *Grand Central Belge*, on conditions echoing the requirements of Article XII of the 1839 Treaty of Separation, namely "*sans charge aucune pour le Gouvernement des Pays-Bas, et sans préjudice de ses droits de souveraineté sur le territoire traversé.*" Agreement was also reached on matters relating to the bridge that in 1873 the Netherlands had agreed would be built over the Maas, near Roermond.

38. Importantly, in the context of this arbitration, a modification to the original route as specified in the 1839 Treaty of Separation was also agreed in the Iron Rhine Treaty: it would now not pass through Sittard after all. Article IV, paragraph 4[6] provides as follows (in the Tribunal's English translation):

> The line will enter the territory of the Duchy of Limburg passing to the south of Hamont (Belgium); it will head towards Weert, pass to the south of that locality as well as of Haelen, traverse the Maas on a fixed bridge in the right part upstream of the bend at Buggenum, between the markers 83 and 84, rejoin the Maastricht line to Venlo north of the station of Roermond, follow part of this line, leave it south of that station to go to reach the Prussian frontier in a direction to be agreed upon with the Government of the German Empire.

39. The Parties thus varied the provision in Article XII of the 1839 Treaty of Separation whereby the road or canal was intended to pass through Sittard. To make clear that this amendment did not amount to an additional line to the one envisaged in 1839, the Belgian and Netherlands representatives jointly confirmed, in a document appended to the treaty at the moment of ratification, that as provided in the statements of the two Governments to their legislative chambers,

> *la concession de l'établissement d'un chemin de fer d'Anvers à Gladbach par le Duché de Limbourg, en passant à Ruremonde, comme elle est stipulée par le Traité du 13 janvier, 1873, constitue l'exécution pleine et entière de l'article XII du Traité du 19 avril, 1839* [C.T.S., 1872–1873, Vol. 145, p. 447].

There was no suggestion voiced during these ratification procedures that the "*exécution pleine*" was to be understood as meaning that the right of transit had expired or that Belgian rights in relation to what today is termed the "historic route" had lapsed. Rather, the intention was to show an agreed amendment to the location of the track that had originally been designated at Sittard; Belgium's right of transit would henceforth be along a track that now incorporates the variation agreed in Article IV, paragraph 4 of the Iron Rhine Treaty (the "historic track"). The agreed statement made clear that this was a final decision, in the sense that no future claim made by Belgium for a canal, road, or railway through Sittard would be entertained.

---

[6] The Netherlands uses Arabic numerals in the Dutch text provided to the Tribunal and Belgium uses Roman numerals in referring to the French text of the Iron Rhine Treaty. The Tribunal will use Roman numerals.

40. To affirm the continued existence of an "historic route" and Belgian rights in relation thereto, does not, of course, answer the question as to whether Belgium's current requests do amount to a *further* "new track"; or whether, if not, Article XII has any role to play. These questions, of great importance for this arbitration, are distinct, and will be addressed by the Tribunal below (*see* paragraphs 74 ff).

41. The Iron Rhine railway, on the revised route stipulated in Article IV, paragraph 4 of the Iron Rhine Treaty, came into use from 1879, the concessionnaire on both Belgian and Netherlands territory being, in the event, the *Grand Central Belge*.

42. At the end of the nineteenth century, railway lines on Belgian territory were nationalised by that Government. The Netherlands purchased the railway interests of *Grand Central Belge* on its own territory, under an arrangement whereby Belgium was allowed in the first place to buy from *Grand Central Belge* the concession "*[d']Anvers à la frontière Prussienne vers Gladbach*," and then sell it on to the Netherlands (the 1897 Railway Convention). A further arrangement was made between the Netherlands Government and the *Maatschappij tot Exploitatie van Staatsspoorwegen* ("*Maatschappij tot Exploitatie*") to run the railway lines on Netherlands territory which had been passed by the 1897 Railway Convention to the Netherlands. This further arrangement of 1897, which contained detailed financial provisions to apply as between the *Maatschappij tot Exploitatie* and the Government, was annexed to the Netherlands legislation of 2 April 1898, applying the 1897 Railway Convention (BM, Exhibit No. 25, Agreement between the State of the Netherlands and the *Maatschappij tot Exploitatie*, 29 October 1897, annexed to the Act of 2 April 1898 approving the Railway Convention of 23 April 1897). It stipulated, *inter alia*, that the provisions of an earlier agreement between the Netherlands Government and the *Maatschappij tot Exploitatie* as regards maintenance, would apply to the recent transfers.

43. As has been explained above (*see* paragraphs 16–22), there has arisen, against the background of a certain long pattern and level of use of the Iron Rhine railway, and the Belgian interest in reactivation as initiated and developed between 1987 and 2003, a dispute between Belgium and the Netherlands as to their legal rights and obligations in respect of the Iron Rhine railway, entailing Belgian proposals and Netherlands counter-proposals. It will be necessary for the Tribunal both to interpret some

60

provisions of the above-mentioned treaties and to comment upon the legal significance of certain terms.

B.   The Principles of Interpretation to be Applied by the Tribunal

44.   It is clear that, in order to respond to the Questions put to it by the Parties, the Tribunal must interpret various provisions in the governing instruments, as well as apply the relevant rules of international law.

45.   Belgium and the Netherlands are both parties to the Vienna Convention on the Law of Treaties of 23 May 1969 ("Vienna Convention") (United Nations Treaty Series ("U.N.T.S."), Vol. 1155, p. 331). It is precisely because some terms in that Convention reflected customary law, and some were new, that Article 4 provided generally for non-retroactivity of the Convention, but "without prejudice to the application of any rules set forth in the present Convention to which treaties would be subject under international law independently of the Convention." It is now well established that the provisions on interpretation of treaties contained in Articles 31 and 32 of the Convention reflect pre-existing customary international law, and thus may be (unless there are particular indications to the contrary) applied to treaties concluded before the entering into force of the Vienna Convention in 1980. The International Court of Justice has applied customary rules of interpretation, now reflected in Articles 31 and 32 of the Vienna Convention, to a treaty concluded in 1955 (*Territorial Dispute (Libyan Arab Jamahiriya/Chad), Judgment, I.C.J. Reports 1994*, p. 6 at pp. 21–22, para. 41); and to a treaty concluded in 1890, bearing on rights of States that even on the day of the Judgment were still not parties to the Vienna Convention (*Kasikili/Sedudu Island (Botswana/Namibia), Judgment, I.C.J. Reports 1999 (II)*, p. 1045 at p. 1059, para. 18). In the *Sovereignty over Pulau Ligitan and Pulau Sipadan* case, the Court noted that Indonesia was not a party to the Vienna Convention, but nevertheless applied the rules as formulated in Articles 31 and 32 of that Convention to a treaty concluded in 1891. Indonesia did not dispute that the rules codified in these articles were applicable (*Sovereignty over Pulau Ligitan and Pulau Sipadan (Indonesia/Malaysia), Judgment, I.C.J. Reports 2002*, p. 625 at pp. 645–646, paras. 37–38). There is no case after the adoption of the Vienna Convention in 1969 in which the International Court of Justice or any other leading tribunal has failed so to act.

46. These articles provide as follows:

Article 31
General rule of interpretation
1. A treaty shall be interpreted in good faith in accordance with the ordinary meaning to be given to the terms of the treaty in their context and in the light of its object and purpose.
2. The context for the purpose of the interpretation of a treaty shall comprise, in addition to the text, including its preamble and annexes:
   (a) any agreement relating to the treaty which was made between all the parties in connection with the conclusion of the treaty;
   (b) any instrument which was made by one or more parties in connection with the conclusion of the treaty and accepted by the other parties as an instrument related to the treaty.
3. There shall be taken into account, together with the context:
   (a) any subsequent agreement between the parties regarding the interpretation of the treaty or the application of its provisions;
   (b) any subsequent practice in the application of the treaty which establishes the agreement of the parties regarding its interpretation;
   (c) any relevant rules of international law applicable in the relations between the parties.
4. A special meaning shall be given to a term if it is established that the parties so intended.

Article 32
Supplementary means of interpretation
Recourse may be had to supplementary means of interpretation, including the preparatory work of the treaty and the circumstances of its conclusion, in order to confirm the meaning resulting from the application of article 31, or to determine the meaning when the interpretation according to article 31:
   (a) leaves the meaning ambiguous or obscure; or
   (b) leads to a result which is manifestly absurd or unreasonable.

47. Although the clauses contained within Article 31 are not hierarchical, there is no doubt that the starting point for interpretation is the ordinary meaning to be given to the terms, taking them in context, and having regard also to the object and purpose of the treaty. The Tribunal will pay particular attention to these factors in carrying out its tasks of interpretation, along with the other principles of interpretation as appropriate. Its elaboration on the application of the various principles of interpretation will be made in the paragraphs dealing with the various phrases contained within Article XII of the 1839 Treaty of Separation whose meaning is disputed.

48. At the same time, it is convenient for the Tribunal to make certain more general observations at the outset. Although the Parties have provided it with extracts from the prolonged diplomatic negotiations leading up to the conclusion of the 1839 Treaty of

Separation, these do not, in the view of the Tribunal, have the character of *travaux préparatoires* on which it may safely rely as a supplementary means of interpretation under Article 32 of the Vienna Convention. These extracts may show the desire or understanding of one or other of the Parties at particular moments in the extended negotiations, but do not serve the purpose of illuminating a common understanding as to the meaning of the various provisions of Article XII. This observation is relevant, in particular, to the question of whether the right of transit afforded to Belgium is to be read as a *quid pro quo* for the agreement that subsequent to the separation, the territory that now constitutes the Netherlands province of Limburg should be part of the Netherlands (the view of Belgium); or whether the obtaining of Limburg by the Netherlands was a *quid pro quo* for the obtaining by Belgium of a part of Luxembourg (the view of the Netherlands). In the absence of *travaux préparatoires* reflecting a common understanding, the answer cannot be certain, but the Tribunal is of the view that there were very many elements in play (and not one or other of these alone) that contributed to the balance struck in the text of Article XII. At the same time, the Tribunal will remain mindful of the circumstances of the conclusion of each of the applicable treaties, as required in Article 32 of the Vienna Convention. The Tribunal notes also that good faith is both a specific element in Article 31, paragraph 1 of the Vienna Convention and a general principle of international law that relates to the conduct of parties *vis-à-vis* each other.

49. The Tribunal further observes that there exist other well-established principles relevant to the process of interpretation. Of particular importance is the principle of effectiveness: *ut res magis valeat quam pereat*. The relevance of effectiveness is in relation to the object and purpose of a treaty; at the same time this does not entitle a Tribunal to revise a treaty.

50. The Netherlands has placed emphasis on the fact that a right of transit by one country across the territory of another can only arise as a matter of specific agreement. This proposition of law is undoubtedly correct and is not challenged by Belgium. The Netherlands further contends that the transit right as such is to be construed restrictively, citing various cases in support. This latter proposition *is* challenged by Belgium.

51.   In the *Case of Free Zones of Upper Savoy and the District of Gex* (*P.C.I.J., Series A/B, No. 46 (1932)* at p. 166) the Permanent Court of International Justice ("Permanent Court") said, of the stated rights in the case, France's "sovereignty . . . is to be respected in so far as it is not limited by her international obligations, and . . . by her obligations under the treaties . . ." and that "no restriction exceeding these ensuing from those instruments can be imposed on France without her consent." In the *Interpretation of the Statute of the Memel Territory* case (*P.C.I.J., Series A/B, No. 49 (1932)* at pp. 313–314) the Permanent Court stated that in the absence of provisions in the treaty providing for the autonomy of Memel, "the rights ensuing from the sovereignty of Lithuania must apply." Nor can it be doubted in the present case that, beyond what rights of Belgium are provided for in Article XII of the 1839 Treaty of Separation, Netherlands sovereignty remains intact.

52.   It is true that in both the *Free Zones* case and in *Case of the S.S. Wimbledon* (*P.C.I.J. Series A, No. 1 (1923)* at p. 24) the Permanent Court said that in case of doubt about a limitation on sovereignty that limitation is to be interpreted restrictively. In the latter case, the Permanent Court did caution, however, that it would nonetheless "feel obliged to stop at the point where the so-called restrictive interpretation would be contrary to the plain terms of the article and would destroy what has been clearly granted."

53.   The doctrine of restrictive interpretation never had a hierarchical supremacy, but was a technique to ensure a proper balance of the distribution of rights within a treaty system. The principle of restrictive interpretation, whereby treaties are to be interpreted in favour of state sovereignty in case of doubt, is not in fact mentioned in the provisions of the Vienna Convention. The object and purpose of a treaty, taken together with the intentions of the parties, are the prevailing elements for interpretation. Indeed, it has also been noted in the literature that a too rigorous application of the principle of restrictive interpretation might be inconsistent with the primary purpose of the treaty (*see* Jennings and Watts, *Oppenheim's International Law*, 9th Edition (1992), at p. 1279). Restrictive interpretation thus has particularly little role to play in certain categories of treaties – such as, for example, human rights treaties. Indeed, some authors note that the principle has not been relied upon in any recent jurisprudence of international courts and tribunals and that its contemporary relevance is to be doubted

(Bernhardt "Evolutive Treaty Interpretation, Especially of the European Convention on Human Rights," 42 *German Yearbook of International Law* (1999), p. 11, at p. 14).

54. The Award in the *Lac Lanoux Arbitration* (24 *International Law Reports* (1957), p. 101) remains to this day a very useful guide to the present type of inevitable tension between rights on one's own territory given under a treaty, and reservations as to sovereignty. The relevant clause in the treaty provision for the utilization of the waters of Lac Lanoux referred to territorial sovereignty "except for the modifications agreed upon between the two Governments" (p. 120). Article XII of the 1839 Treaty of Separation has the converse structure, whereby the rights of Belgium are specified and the general reservation as to sovereignty then follows. In the view of the Tribunal, this makes no difference – each is a balancing of special rights granted by a state to another on its own territory, and a general affirmation of territorial sovereignty. As the *Lac Lanoux* tribunal held,

> [i]t has been contended before the Tribunal that these modifications should be strictly construed because they are in derogation of sovereignty. The Tribunal could not recognize such an absolute rule of construction. Territorial sovereignty plays the part of a presumption. It must bend before all international obligations, whatever their origin, but only before such obligations [*Ibid.*].

The *Lac Lanoux* tribunal observed that in the application of this observation "the question is therefore to determine the obligations of the French Government in this case . . . ." (*Ibid.*).

55. In precisely that same way, the sovereignty reserved to the Netherlands under Article XII of the 1839 Treaty of Separation cannot be understood save by first determining Belgium's rights, and the Netherlands' obligations in relation thereto. This is to be done not by invocation of the principle of restrictive interpretation, but rather by examining – using the normal rules of interpretation identified in Articles 31 and 32 of the Vienna Convention – exactly what rights have been afforded to Belgium. All else falls within the Netherlands' sovereignty. And indeed, the correctness of this methodology seems in the final analysis to be recognized by the Netherlands (NR, p. 7, para. 24).

56. Put differently, the Netherlands may exercise its rights of sovereignty in relation to the territory over which the Iron Rhine railway passes, unless this would conflict with the treaty rights granted to Belgium, or rights that Belgium may hold under general international law, or constraints imposed by EC law.

57. Finally, the Tribunal wishes to draw attention to a matter which in its view is of great importance in this case: the problem of intertemporality in the interpretation of treaty provisions. This idea will have considerable relevance in the ensuing interpretation of certain phrases contained in Article XII of the 1839 Treaty of Separation.

58. It is to be recalled that Article 31, paragraph 3, subparagraph (c) of the Vienna Convention on the Law of Treaties makes reference to "any relevant rules of international law applicable in the relations between the parties." For this reason – as well as for reasons relating to its own jurisdiction – the Tribunal has examined any provisions of European law that might be considered of possible relevance in this case (*see* Chapter III below). Provisions of general international law are also applicable to the relations between the Parties, and thus should be taken into account in interpreting Article XII of the 1839 Treaty of Separation and Article IV of the Iron Rhine Treaty. Further, international environmental law has relevance to the relations between the Parties. There is considerable debate as to what, within the field of environmental law, constitutes "rules" or "principles"; what is "soft law"; and which environmental treaty law or principles have contributed to the development of customary international law. Without entering further into those controversies, the Tribunal notes that in all of these categories "environment" is broadly referred to as including air, water, land, flora and fauna, natural ecosystems and sites, human health and safety, and climate. The emerging principles, whatever their current status, make reference to conservation, management, notions of prevention and of sustainable development, and protection for future generations.

59. Since the Stockholm Conference on the Environment in 1972 there has been a marked development of international law relating to the protection of the environment. Today, both international and EC law require the integration of appropriate environmental measures in the design and implementation of economic development activities. Principle 4 of the Rio Declaration on Environment and Development, adopted in 1992

(31 I.L.M. p. 874, at p. 877), which reflects this trend, provides that "environmental protection shall constitute an integral part of the development process and cannot be considered in isolation from it." Importantly, these emerging principles now integrate environmental protection into the development process. Environmental law and the law on development stand not as alternatives but as mutually reinforcing, integral concepts, which require that where development may cause significant harm to the environment there is a duty to prevent, or at least mitigate, such harm (*see* paragraph 222). This duty, in the opinion of the Tribunal, has now become a principle of general international law. This principle applies not only in autonomous activities but also in activities undertaken in implementation of specific treaties between the Parties. The Tribunal would recall the observation of the International Court of Justice in the *Gabčikovo-Nagymaros* case that "[t]his need to reconcile economic development with protection of the environment is aptly expressed in the concept of sustainable development" (*Gabčikovo-Nagymaros (Hungary/Slovakia), Judgment, I.C.J. Reports 1997*, p. 7 at p. 78, para. 140). And in that context the Court further clarified that "new norms have to be taken into consideration, and . . . new standards given proper weight, not only when States contemplate new activities but also when continuing with activities begun in the past" (*Ibid.*). In the view of the Tribunal this dictum applies equally to the Iron Rhine railway.

60. The mere invocation of such matters does not, of course, provide the answers in this arbitration to what may or may not be done, where, by whom and at whose costs. However, the Tribunal notes that, as regards the Questions put to it, neither Party denies that environmental norms are relevant to the relations between the Parties. To that extent, they may be relevant to the interpretation of those treaties in which the answers to the Questions may primarily be sought.

61. The Tribunal now turns to the application of the principles of interpretation to the relevant treaty provisions.

C. The Interpretation of Disputed Elements in Article XII of the 1839 Treaty of Separation

1. "Would have been built"

62. As early as 1864, differences had arisen over the meaning of "would have been built" – differences which did not disappear with the agreement in 1873 to replace the references in the 1839 Treaty of Separation to "road" and "canal" with "railway." The Netherlands informed Belgium in 1864 that what had been agreed to in the 1839 Treaty of Separation was the extension of a route that had already been built in Belgium and not the extension to a route whose status was still that of a project (BM, Exhibit No. 13, Letter of the Dutch Government to the Belgian Ambassador at The Hague, dated 7 March 1864). In 1868, an extension to a projected route was agreed to "*en principe*," for the sake of "*des bonnes et cordiales relations*" (BM, Exhibit No. 15, Letter of the Dutch Government to the Belgian Ambassador at The Hague, dated 12 August 1868). The legal issues regarding "would have been built/*aurait été construit*" remained unresolved, but no longer of importance. Article IV of the Iron Rhine Treaty of 1873 provided that the *Compagnie du Nord de la Belgique*, which was the concessionnaire of the Antwerp to Gladbach railway line would become concessionnaire "*de cette même ligne qui est située sur le territoire du Duché de Limbourg*." Notwithstanding the present tense, that sector was yet to be built. But Article IV provided that the Netherlands section "will be constructed and exploited" either by the *Compagnie du Nord de la Belgique* or by the *Grand Central Belge*.

2. "That the said road, or the said canal be extended in accordance with the same plan"

63. The dispute between the Parties as to the meaning of the term "plan" is easy to comprehend. In the opinion of the Netherlands, the word "plan" refers to the works that physically allow cross-border transit to be possible – for a railway to be "extended" from Belgium into and across the Netherlands (NR, p. 31, para. 126). Belgium, invoking the "plain meaning" of that term, and also the meaning to be given to the term in the context of construction projects, insists that "plan" is to be understood as relating to the proposals for and descriptions of the project in its entirety.

64.   The Parties are also in dispute as to the rights arising for each of them consequent upon these different views of "the same plan." The Netherlands' position is straightforward: It believes the Belgian request constitutes a demand for a "new railway," which is therefore to be extended "in accordance with the same plan." The reservation of "exclusive rights of sovereignty over the territory which would be crossed" means, in the view of the Netherlands, that "the same plan" cannot entail specifications for the entire project. It can at most be a reference to trans-border functionality. The "same plan" refers to the physical continuity that the Netherlands is obliged to undertake, but not more. The Netherlands finds its view supported by the reference in Article XII to the execution of "the agreed works" – this term affirming that a plan for the line as a whole cannot therefore be unilaterally imposed by Belgium. The Netherlands also contends that Article V of the Iron Rhine Treaty, taken with Article 3 of the 1867 Convention between Belgium and the Netherlands *"pour le jonction de quatre chemins de fer"* (Convention Between Belgium and the Netherlands for the Junction of Railways, The Hague, 9 November 1967, C.T.S. 1866–1867, Vol. 135, p. 467), suggest that agreement is needed upon "the plan."

65.   Belgium finds these last provisions irrelevant. Belgium contends that no request is being made for a railway to be extended under Article XII; but it regards the developments and upgrading of the railway as also subject to the "same plan" provisions in Article XII. As the "same plan" refers to the plan that Belgium alone was entitled to make for Belgian territory, it cannot be subject to negotiations for its application on Netherlands territory. The unilateral determination of the plan is, in the eyes of Belgium, also a "logical corollary of the fact that pursuant to Article XII of the Treaty, the costs of building the new route in the Netherlands were to be borne by Belgium" (BR, p. 77, para. 77). Acknowledging that the Netherlands is entitled to exercise jurisdiction within its own territory (the example of establishment of crossings is given), Belgium argues that it may not do so in a manner that denies Belgian rights recognized under international law. It differentiates, however, its claimed entitlement unilaterally to establish the plan when *it* is to perform the work, from the provision when the Netherlands would opt to perform the work. In the former hypothesis agreement may be desirable, but is not in Belgium's view legally necessary; Belgium accepts that in the

latter hypothesis the agreement of the Netherlands to the *works* is legally necessary (BR, p. 82, para. 81).[*]

66. The Tribunal finds that the functionality of continuation of the line in Belgium through the Netherlands is to be in accordance with track specifications, the dimensions and character of which may indeed have found their origin in Belgian decision-making. But, whether as regards extension or reactivation, the overall plan for the line is subject to mutual agreement. The ensuing works are "agreed works." Naturally, agreement shall not be withheld by the Netherlands, were that to amount to a denial of Belgium's transit right. The Tribunal sees nothing in Article XII of the 1839 Treaty of Separation or in the Iron Rhine Treaty which draws a distinction in this regard between works which may be done legally by Belgium or works which the Netherlands will cause to be done. It cannot accept the contentions of Belgium on this point.

67. The phrase "according to the same plan" is to be read as to give an interpretation that reconciles Belgium's specific rights and the Netherlands' reservation of sovereignty. Although the term "plan" is commonly understood in the construction industry, and in some dictionary references, as comprising the depiction of the entire venture, various provisions in Article XII suggest that this is not the meaning to be accorded in this case. In particular, the reference to "agreed works" and the reservation of Netherlands' sovereignty suggest otherwise. The reservation of Netherlands' sovereignty ensures for it that, apart from the elements specified in terms in favour of Belgium, no further limitations of sovereignty are to be implied. But at the same time, the reservation of sovereignty cannot serve the converse purpose of detracting from the rights given to Belgium under Article XII. Applying these observations, the Tribunal notes that the plan referred to in the phrase "according to the same plan," insofar as it relates to continuity at the border, is a matter for Belgium. That follows from the fact that under Article XII a Belgian line will have been built, and it may or may not be the subject of a later request for extension. Beyond that, specifications for use of the entirety of the line are to be jointly agreed. Matters reserved to the sovereignty of the Netherlands, on which it has the right of decision-making, includes, *inter alia*, all safety elements of the whole work and safety conditions under which the work is carried out.

---

[*] The text in italics represents a Correction to the Award agreed upon by the Arbitral Tribunal in September, 2005, following a Request for Correction of the Award submitted by Belgium, to which the Netherlands agreed.

3. "The said road, or the said canal [would] be extended . . . entirely at the cost and expense of Belgium . . . ."
"Engineers and workers . . . would execute the agreed works at the expense of Belgium, all without any burden to Holland . . . ."

68. The Tribunal first observes that the introduction of the adjective "agreed" before the noun "works" clearly suggests, as a matter of ordinary meaning, that both Parties envisaged that although the Netherlands would not refuse a request for a railway to be extended across its territory, the works therefore would be a matter for them both. In this way the reserved sovereign rights of the Netherlands and the entitlement of transit of Belgium could be reconciled.

69. Beyond that, it is clear that the works for a railway to be extended from Belgium up to the borders of Germany were to be paid for by Belgium alone.

70. The dispute that arises is as to whether the specific request of Belgium for the upgrading and restoration of the line beyond its previous capacity is "an extension" within the meaning of Article XII (a question discussed by the Tribunal in paragraphs 82–84 below); and, more particularly, whether the costs and expenses to be incurred by Belgium should include the costs and expenses incurred should the works ultimately agreed upon entail the environmental protection measures required by Netherlands law. Belgium denies such a duty, on the ground that these measures are not measures necessitated by the physical extension of the line – they are measures unilaterally undertaken by the Netherlands in the exercise of its sovereignty. Belgium further claims that it should have been consulted before the various areas were declared protected nature reserves. It observes that the Netherlands has affirmed (NR, p. 23, para. 93) that these specific measures are not as such required of it under EC law. Further, Belgium asserts that the proposed measures for noise protection, in particular tunnelling, are not the least costly available to mitigate any environmental harm.

71. The Netherlands asserts that it has the sovereign right to assess the appropriate means to protect the environment to EC and its own domestic standards; that it has sought to identify objectively, through expert reports, those means; and that the measures would

not otherwise have been necessary save for Belgium's request for a restoration and significant upgrading of the capacity of the Iron Rhine railway.

72.   There is merit in both arguments. The Tribunal finds it necessary, in order to answer this matter, first to ascertain whether the project is one which would attract the cost-allocation provisions of Article XII, and second, if so, to see if the costs and expenses of the measures envisaged by the Netherlands are integral to the extension of the Iron Rhine line.

73.   The Tribunal will later return to these questions.

4.   A "new road" or a "new canal" to "be extended"?

74.   The Belgian request for reactivation is both immediate and over the longer term. It is understood that Belgium wishes to achieve by 2020 use in both directions by 43 trains of 700 metres length per day, able to travel at 100 kilometres per hour. The work needed for this is, in the Netherlands' view, so substantial that it "amounts . . . to a request within the meaning of Article XII for the extension of a railway on Belgian territory on Netherlands territory. This railway is *new* to the extent that considerable adaptation and modernization is necessary in many ways in order to achieve the desired use." (NCM, para. 3.3.4.5). For the Netherlands, therefore, the Article XII provisions on the costs (beyond restoration to the 1991 level of maintenance, which costs it will bear) apply. This new work is, as regards functionality, to be "entirely at the cost and expense of Belgium" and "without any burden to the Netherlands." Belgium, by contrast, asserts that its request for reactivation is not a demand for "extension" – "[t]he Iron Rhine was prolonged on Netherlands territory in the 1870's and still exists at present." To that extent, in Belgium's view its current claims are outside of Article XII of the 1839 Treaty of Separation.

75.   The question thus arises as to whether the Belgian request is a request for a new road or canal or railway line to be extended across the Netherlands within the meaning of Article XII; or whether it is a request for the adaptation of a transit right already in existence under Article XII. The Tribunal is called upon to state whether or not the costs of the reactivation are to be borne by Belgium. In this context it notes that the positions

taken by the Parties are not wholly identical to what they were each prepared to contemplate during negotiations, before resort to arbitration. Belgium assimilates its request to the maintenance of an existing line, such costs to be borne by the Netherlands. It invokes Article XI of the 1839 Treaty of Separation to that end. The Netherlands assimilates Belgium's request to one for a new railway line, with the costs all to be borne by Belgium. In any event, neither Party wholly excludes the relevance of Article XII. Each of these possibilities is not without its difficulties.

76. The Tribunal observes that Article XII of the 1839 Treaty of Separation addresses neither the question of maintenance nor of "adaptation and modernization" (the description jointly agreed in the Questions put to the Tribunal by the Parties). The former has been resolved by a Netherlands practice assuming physical and financial responsibility for maintenance (no doubt perceived by it as an element of its territorial sovereignty) and is accepted by both Parties. Neither Article XII nor the detailed financial arrangements, elaborated in the 1897 Railway Convention, made specific reference to maintenance costs of the lines on Netherlands territory (including the Iron Rhine railway) and now owned by the Netherlands. Article IX of the 1897 Railway Convention spoke of future agreements for the "*exploitation internationale des chemins de fer rachetés*," but never seems to have been applied to maintenance. And the related agreement between the Netherlands and the *Maatschappij tot Exploitatie* (which Netherlands company was henceforth to exploit the Iron Rhine railway on Netherlands territory) clearly presupposes Netherlands Government responsibility for repairs and renovations (BM, Exhibit No. 25, Agreement between the State of the Netherlands and the *Maatschappij tot Exploitatie*, 29 October 1897, annexed to the Act of 2 April 1898 approving the Railway Convention of 23 April 1897, Articles 2 and 8). The Explanatory Statement associated with the Netherlands' ratification of the 1897 Railway Convention observes that "the State has the obligation to provide, on its own account, a sufficient level of maintenance for the railways to be taken over by the Exploitatie-Maatschappij" (BM, Exhibit No. 22, Approval of the agreement between the Netherlands and Belgium signed at Brussels on 23 April 1897 – Explanatory Statement, pp. 12–13). At the same time, this does not necessarily lead to the conclusion that "renovation" to meet standards needed for previously unanticipated levels of activity under the current Belgian request is thereby part of the maintenance and renovation obligation assumed by the Netherlands at the end of the nineteenth century. In the view of the Tribunal, the

Netherlands (as it accepts) is under an obligation to bring the Iron Rhine railway back to the levels maintained during the regular (albeit light) use of the line prior to discontinuation of such use in 1991; but these maintenance and repair obligations do not cover the significant upgrading costs now involved in Belgium's request. Whether these are for Belgium's account under Article XII of the 1839 Treaty of Separation depends on further questions.

77. The question of significant adaptation and modernisation is a more complex, and as yet uncharted, problem. The application of international law principles of treaty interpretation may assist in its resolution.

78. The provision that Belgium will bear all the costs and expenses of the "new road" or "new canal" (railway) is clear, as a matter of "plain meaning." But in deciding what is or is not a "new road" or "new canal" (railway), or rather a reactivation of an existing one, and the related questions of whether, and the extent to which, Article XII is applicable, other principles of interpretation must be borne in mind.

79. Article 31, paragraph 3, subparagraph (c) of the Vienna Convention also requires there to be taken into account "any relevant rules of international law applicable in the relations between the parties." The intertemporal rule would seem to be one such "relevant rule." By this, regard should be had in interpreting Article XII to juridical facts as they stood in 1839. In particular, it is certainly the case that, in 1839, it was envisaged that the costs for any extension of a new road or canal that Belgium might ask for would be limited and relatively modest. The great advances that were later to be made in electrification, track design and specification, freight stock, and so forth – and the concomitant costs – could not have been foreseen by the Parties. At the same time, this rule does not require the Tribunal to be oblivious either to later facts that bear on the effective application of the treaty, nor indeed to all later legal developments. It has long been established that the understanding of conceptual or generic terms in a treaty may be seen as "an essentially relative question; it depends upon the development of international relations" (*Nationality Decrees Issued in Tunis and Morocco, P.C.I.J. Series B, No. 4 (1923)*, p. 24). Some terms are "not static, but were by definition evolutionary . . . . The parties to the Covenant must consequently be deemed to have accepted them as such" (*Namibia (SW Africa) Advisory Opinion, I.C.J. Reports 1971*,

p. 16 at p. 31). Where a term can be classified as generic "the presumption necessarily arises that its meaning was intended to follow the evolution of the law and to correspond with the meaning attached to the expression by the law in force at any given time" (*Aegean Sea Continental Shelf (Greece/Turkey), Judgment, I.C.J. Reports 1978*, p. 3 at p. 32, para. 77). A similar finding was made by the WTO Appellate Body when it had to interpret the term "natural resources" in Article XX, paragraph (g) of the WTO Agreement (*United States – Import Prohibition of Certain Shrimp and Shrimp Products*, WT/DS58/AB/R, 12 October 1998, para. 130).

80.   In the present case it is not a conceptual or generic term that is in issue, but rather new technical developments relating to the operation and capacity of the railway. But here, too, it seems that an evolutive interpretation, which would ensure an application of the treaty that would be effective in terms of its object and purpose, will be preferred to a strict application of the intertemporal rule. Thus in the *Gabčíkovo-Nagymaros* case, the International Court was prepared to accept, in interpreting a treaty that predated certain recent norms of environmental law, that "the Treaty is not static, and is open to adapt to emerging norms of international law" (*I.C.J. Reports 1997*, p. 7 at pp. 67–68, para. 112). The Netherlands District Court of Rotterdam was faced with the question of whether a provision that referred to telegraph cables could be interpreted as to include telephone cables, even though these had not yet been developed at the time that the 1884 Convention on the Protection of Submarine Cables was concluded. The Court thought that it was "reasonable" to include the later telephone cables in the interpretation of what was protected under the Convention (*The Netherlands (PTT) and the Post Office (London) v. Ned Lloyd*, 74 *International Law Reports*, p. 212).

81.   Finally, the Tribunal notes a general support among the leading writers today for evolutive interpretation of treaties. The editors of the 9th Edition of *Oppenheim* agree that, notwithstanding the intertemporal rule, "in some respects the interpretation of a treaty's provisions cannot be divorced from developments in the law subsequent to its adoption . . . the concepts embodied in a treaty may be not static but evolutionary . . . ." (Jennings and Watts, *Oppenheim's International Law*, Vol. 1, p. 1282). *See further* Jiménez de Aréchaga "International Law in the Past Third of a Century," 159 *Recueil des Cours* (1978-1), at p. 49). Rudolf Bernhardt explains it thus: "The object and purpose of a treaty plays . . . a central role in treaty interpretation. This reference to

object and purpose can be understood as entry into a certain dynamism. If it is the purpose of a treaty to create longer lasting and solid relations between the parties . . . , it is hardly compatible with this purpose to eliminate new developments in the process of treaty interpretation" (42 *German Yearbook of International Law* (1999) at pp. 16–17).

82. The Iron Rhine Treaty was not intended as a treaty of limited or fixed duration. The Parties probably did not think beyond an "extension" of a Belgian railway across the Netherlands, to take place at one moment of time. Indeed, the statements made by the Parties when ratifying the Iron Rhine Treaty, in which, *inter alia*, Article XII of the 1839 Treaty of Separation had been amended, provided that this "constitutes the full and complete execution of Article XII of the Treaty of 19 April, 1839." However, the Tribunal believes that it would be incompatible with the object and purpose of the earlier treaty to read those declarations as stating that further work and requests were to be regarded as *en dehors* Article XII. The declarations are to be understood as referring rather to the amended routing of the Iron Rhine track that they had agreed.

83. The object and purpose of the 1839 Treaty of Separation was to resolve the many difficult problems complicating a stable separation of Belgium and the Netherlands: that of Article XII was to provide for transport links from Belgium to Germany, across a route designated by the 1842 Boundary Treaty. This object was not for a fixed duration and its purpose was "commercial communication." It necessarily follows, even in the absence of specific wording, that such works, going beyond restoration to previous functionality, as might from time to time be necessary or desirable for contemporary commerciality, would remain a concomitant of the right of transit that Belgium would be able to request. That being so, the entirety of Article XII, with its careful balance of the rights and obligations of the Parties, remains in principle applicable to the adaptation and modernisation requested by Belgium.

84. Further, it is reasonable to interpret Article XII as envisaging future work occurring – beyond necessary maintenance – on the line. No separate provisions for the allocation of such future costs and rights over the line and the territory which it traversed were provided for in Article XII. However, an interpretation compatible with the principle of effectiveness leads the Tribunal to determine the continued applicability of Article XII of the 1839 Treaty of Separation to upgrading and improvements (save for the path of

the route, which remains governed by the amendments of the Iron Rhine Treaty). Applying this dynamic and evolutive approach to a treaty that was meant to guarantee a right of commercial transit through time, the Tribunal concludes that a request for a reactivation of a line long dormant, with a freight capacity and the means to achieve that considerably surpassing what had existed before for nearly 130 years, is still not to be regarded as a request for a "new line." At the same time, the conditions attaching to this request (that is, for a revival of and considerable upgrading and modernisation of an existing "extension") remain governed by the provisions of Article XII of the 1839 Treaty of Separation. It must be acknowledged that the wording as drafted was directed to the construction of a new road, canal or track, rather than a periodic upgrading inherent in a right of commercial transit. It may therefore be necessary to read into Article XII, so far as the allocation of contemporary costs for upgrading is concerned, the provisions of international law as they apply today (*see* paragraph 59). The Tribunal will have regard to the concept of reasonableness in the light of all the circumstances and to the fairness and balance embodied in Article XII.

5. **"Without prejudice to the exclusive rights of sovereignty over the territory which would be crossed by the road or the canal in question."**

85. Applying that element in Article 31, paragraph 1 of the Vienna Convention, whereby a treaty is to be interpreted in accordance with the ordinary meaning to be given to the terms, it might be thought that the phrase "without prejudice" suggests that any intrusion at all into Netherlands' sovereignty, beyond the acceptance of an extension of a new railway across Limburg, is contrary to Article XII. However, Article 31, paragraph 1 requires that that "ordinary meaning" be read not only in good faith, but also in context and in the light of the object and purpose of the treaty.

86. The Parties have in their pleadings contested whether good faith constitutes a distinct source of international law. Belgium alludes to an absence of good faith in a series of both acts and omissions of the Netherlands, whereas the Netherlands alludes to an abuse of rights in connection with various demands being made by Belgium as regards the reactivation of the Iron Rhine railway. The Tribunal finds rather that there have been important different perceptions by the Parties as to the scope of their respective rights and obligations under international law, and under Article XII of the 1839 Treaty of

Separation in particular, and that it is these different perceptions that have occasioned the ancillary contentions of absence of good faith and abuse of rights. The task of the Tribunal is to clarify the rights and obligations held by each, and then to be able to answer the Questions the Parties have jointly put to it.

87.   As for the injunction in Article 31, paragraph 1 of the Vienna Convention that a term be read "in context" for its correct interpretation, the Tribunal notes that the relevant context of the phrase "without prejudice to the exclusive rights of sovereignty" is its location in a paragraph which also includes rights given to Belgium. The Netherlands has necessarily already derogated from its territorial sovereignty in allowing a railway to be built, at the request of another state, over its territory. The sovereignty reserved is over the territory over which the track runs. The Netherlands has forfeited no more sovereignty than that which is necessary for the track to be built and to operate to allow a commercial connection from Belgium to Germany across Limburg. It thus retains the police power throughout that area, the power to establish health and safety standards for work being done on the track, and the power to establish environmental standards in that area.

88.   In this context, the Tribunal has noted that Netherlands law provides for maintenance of railways not at a fixed level, but rather in relation to the level of traffic occurring at a particular time. With the passing of the Iron Rhine track into disuse after 1991, only minimum upkeep occurred. In 1996, the level crossings on the Roermond-Vlodrop section on the line were removed. Also in accordance with Netherlands legislation, so too, more generally, were flashing signals removed. It has been explained to the Tribunal that "[t]his policy is pursued to prevent road-users from becoming accustomed to level crossings that are no longer in use, so that they would create a risk that they would not expect trains even at crossings that are in use" (NCM, p. 10, para 2.5.4).

89.   The Tribunal finds this policy, and the lowering of the maintenance levels thereunder, not to violate Belgium's rights under Article XII of the 1839 Treaty of Separation, and thus to fall within the reservation of Netherlands' sovereignty in that provision. This is the more so as the Netherlands fully accepts its obligation to restore, at its own expense, the maintenance and safety features of the line to the 1991 condition upon a Belgian demand for reactivation.

90. It may thus be said that only if retained sovereignty would be exercised in such a manner that it is inconsistent with Belgium's right to have a railway extended across Limburg, or in violation of other international obligations, would the Netherlands be acting other than in conformity with Article XII. The Tribunal examines below (*see* paragraphs 202–206) whether this is the case.

91. Article 31, paragraph 1 of the Vienna Convention also requires the terms of a treaty to be interpreted "in the light of its object and purpose." It may be queried as to whether any great illumination will follow in this case from the application of this very important principle, because the object and purpose of the 1839 Treaty of Separation was so broad – namely the separation of Belgium and the Netherlands on terms that could satisfy the participants in the Conference of London. It is clear that a Belgian claim to what is now the Netherlands province of Limburg was forfeited and at the same time the commercial proximity that Belgium would otherwise have had to Germany was retained by the road and canal prolongation provisions. In this way (among others) was the overall object and purpose of the 1839 Treaty to be achieved. What may certainly be said is that this object and purpose requires the careful balancing of the rights allowed to each party in Article XII.

92. There requires also to be addressed the question of whether the clause reserving Netherlands sovereignty did or did not require consultation with Belgium before designating any territory over which the historic route runs as a nature reserve.

93. Belgium has not denied the Netherlands' sovereign right to designate reserved nature areas; but it has implied (BM, p. 42, para. 31) that the right of transit which it holds under the 1839 Treaty of Separation and the Iron Rhine treaty was such that the Netherlands should have consulted it before designating the Meinweg as such an area (*see* paragraph 189). Belgium furthermore points to Article 9 of the Treaty of 21 December 1996 concerning the construction of a railway connection for high-speed trains between Rotterdam and Antwerp, which makes reference to the Iron Rhine railway:

The cases concerning the extension of the No. 11 freight line to the railway line between Goes and Bergen-op-Zoom and the opening up of the port of Antwerp through the so-called "IJzeren Rijn" ["Iron Rhine"] to Germany shall be judged on their own merits, after close consultation and as befits good neighbours. In the first case, efforts shall be made to decide on a route before 1 January 2000. In the second case, the Netherlands shall actively participate in the feasibility study, also in connection with the development of alternative routes near Roermond and the border between the Netherlands and Germany. Depending on the results of that study, the Parties shall jointly hold consultations with the competent authorities of the Federal Republic of Germany [2054 U.N.T.S. p. 293 (1999)].

94. On 12 June 1998, the Prime Minister of Belgium made clear to the Prime Minister of the Netherlands the preference of Belgium for the historic route of the Iron Rhine railway, claiming "a right of public international law on this historic track." Diversions were either too long or could "only be realised in the long run" (BM, Exhibit No. 67, Letter of Belgian Prime Minister Dehaene to Dutch Minister-President Kok of the Netherlands, dated 12 June 1998). Under the seventh and eighth paragraphs of the March 2000 MoU (*see also* paragraph 155 of this Award), it was provided as follows:

If it is decided that the definitive route shall be another route than that passing through the Meinweg (as the Netherlands assumes, but not Belgium), this route will be considered the complete fulfilment of the obligations under public international law arising from the Separation Treaty of 1839 and the Belgian-Dutch Iron Rhine Treaty of 1873. These arrangements will be laid down in a Treaty.

Until the definitive route has been selected, Belgium reserves all its rights under the Separation Treaty of 1839 and the Dutch-Belgian Iron Rhine Treaty of 1873.[7]

95. The Tribunal notes that the Netherlands has on several occasions acknowledged Belgium's right of transit under international law (BM, p. 46, para. 34). This right of transit was not, *per se*, affected by the designation of the Meinweg as a nature reserve: the relationship between Belgium's right of transit and the Netherlands' rights of sovereignty remained in balance as intended under Article XII. Had the Netherlands at the time of the designation of the Meinweg supposed that Belgium would soon propose a major reactivation programme, it might have been desirable on the basis of "good neighbourliness" to consult with it before the designation. The measures relating to the Meinweg were taken in 1994, after the Belgian communication of 1987. However, against the background of minimal use – and a recent period of non-use – of the line by Belgium, and only periodic reservations of its transit right, it was not unreasonable for

---

[7] The Netherlands and Belgium offer slightly different English translations of these provisions (BM, para. 34; NCM, para. 2.12.1). The Tribunal here uses the Netherlands' version.

the Netherlands to assume that that situation would possibly continue into the foreseeable future. In any event, as the designation of the Meinweg did not in theory constitute a limitation of the right of transit, there was no legal obligation for the Netherlands to have consulted Belgium. If later, the designation of the Meinweg as a nature reserve would have implications for any unforeseen demands for reactivation at a level previously unknown, that is a different matter, and one which clearly requires resolution initially by consultations between the Parties. On this particular point, therefore, the Tribunal finds the Netherlands' contention to be preferred.

96. That being said, the legitimate exercise of the Netherlands' sovereign right to designate the Meinweg as a nature reserve, in the particular circumstances described above, is not necessarily without financial consequences so far as the exercise by Belgium of its right of transit is concerned.

CHAPTER III – THE ROLE OF EUROPEAN LAW IN THE PRESENT ARBITRATION

A. **Obligations Arising under Article 292 of the EC Treaty**

97. The Arbitration Agreement between the Parties requests the Tribunal "to render its decision on the basis of international law, *including European law if necessary, while taking into account the Parties' obligations under article 292 of the EC Treaty*" (emphasis added).

98. The Tribunal has already (*see* paragraph 15 above) referred to the letter sent by the Parties to the European Commission on 26 August 2003, in which they stated their common position that, although the core of the present dispute related to questions not of EC law but international law, they would, if necessary, take all measures required to comply with their obligations under EC law, in particular under Article 292 of the EC Treaty.

99. According to Article 292 of the EC Treaty, "Member States undertake not to submit a dispute concerning the interpretation or application of this Treaty to any method of settlement other than those provided therein" (*see* paragraph 13 above).

100. This provision is to be seen in connection with Articles 227 and 239 of the EC Treaty. Pursuant to Article 227, a Member State that considers that another Member State has failed to fulfil an obligation under the EC Treaty may bring the matter before the European Court of Justice, while Article 239 provides the means for Member States of the EC in any dispute which relates to the subject matter of the Treaty, to submit this dispute to the European Court of Justice on the basis of a special agreement.

101. The combined effect of the EC Treaty articles thus referred to (together with Article 234 on preliminary rulings, on which *see* paragraph 102 below) is to establish the exclusive competence of the European Court of Justice "to ensure that in the interpretation and application of this Treaty the law is observed" (Article 220 of the EC Treaty). Hence, within the EC legal system, following a division of competences among the courts of

EC Member States and the European Court of Justice, only the European Court of Justice ultimately has the power to decide authoritatively questions of the interpretation or application of EC law. If Member States submit to a "non-EC" tribunal a legal dispute that requires that tribunal to interpret or apply provisions of EC law, proceedings may be instituted against them by the Commission for violation of Article 292 of the EC Treaty.[8]

102. With regard to the obligation to refer questions of EC law to authoritative adjudication by the European Court of Justice, the EC Treaty expressly addresses the domestic courts of Member States in Article 234. Pursuant to this article, a national court faced with the interpretation of EC law may, and in certain cases shall,[9] request the Court to give a preliminary ruling "if it considers that a decision on the question [of the interpretation of EC law] is necessary to enable it to give judgment." According to the settled jurisprudence of the European Court of Justice (*see, e.g., Case C-373/95 Maso, Gazzetta et al. v. Istituto Nazionale della Previdenza Sociale (INPS)*, Judgment of 10 July 1997, para. 26),

> it is solely for the national courts before which actions are brought, and which must bear the responsibility for the subsequent judicial decision, to determine in the light of the particular facts of each case both the need for a preliminary ruling in order to enable them to deliver judgment and the relevance of the questions which they submit to the Court.

The Court has further held that "[a] request from a national court may be rejected only if it is quite obvious that the interpretation of Community law . . . sought bears no relation to the actual nature of the case or to the subject-matter of the main action" (*Case C-186/90 Durighello v. Istituto Nazionale della Previdenza Sociale (INPS)*, Judgment of 28 November 1991, para. 9).

103. In rendering its Award, the Tribunal has carefully considered these elements. The Tribunal is of the view that, with regard to the determination of the limits drawn to its jurisdiction by the reference to Article 292 of the EC Treaty in the Arbitral Agreement, it finds itself in a position analogous to that of a domestic court within the EC, described

---

[8] *Cf.* Application of the European Commission to the European Court of Justice against Ireland in the *Mox Plant* case (BR, Exhibit No. 1, pp. 1 ff).

[9] The distinction between a national court having a right of referral or a duty to do so is irrelevant in the present context, as are other issues of the application of Article 234.

in the preceding paragraphs. In other words, if the Tribunal arrived at the conclusion that it could not decide the case brought before it without engaging in the interpretation of rules of EC law which constitute neither *actes clairs* nor *actes éclairés*, the Parties' obligations under Article 292 would be triggered in the sense that the relevant questions of EC law would need to be submitted to the European Court of Justice (in the present instance not *qua* Article 234 but presumably by means of Article 239 of the EC Treaty).

104. As to the necessity *vel non* of the Tribunal having to decide issues of EC law in order to enable it to render its Award, the criteria elaborated in the application of Article 234 of the EC Treaty by national courts and the European Court of Justice will also apply by analogy. In this regard, not all mention of EC law brings with it the duty to refer. The European Court of Justice clarified this matter in *Case 283/81, Srl CILFIT and Lanificio di Gavardo SpA v. Ministero della Sanità* [1982] ECR 3415 ("*CILFIT* case") by stating that domestic courts or tribunals faced with the interpretation of EC law and obliged to submit this question to the Court of Justice in accordance with Article 234 of the EC Treaty,

> have the same discretion as any other national court or tribunal to ascertain whether a decision on a question of Community law is necessary to enable them to give judgment. Accordingly, those courts or tribunals are not obliged to refer to the Court of Justice a question concerning the interpretation of Community law raised before them if that question is not relevant, that is to say, if the answer to that question, regardless of what it may be, can in no way affect the outcome of the case.
> . . . If, however, those courts or tribunals consider that recourse to Community law is necessary to enable them to decide a case, Article 177 [now 234] imposes an obligation on them to refer to the Court of Justice any question of interpretation which may arise [*CILFIT* case at 3429, paras 10–11].

105. From the perspective of a domestic court, the same point was explained with characteristic lucidity by Lord Denning in the case of *H.P. Bulmer Ltd. v. J. Bollinger SA*, [1974] 2 C.M.L.R. 91, [1974] 2 All E.R. 1226. As he emphasised,

> *The point must be conclusive.*
> The [domestic] court has to consider whether 'a decision of the question is *necessary* to enable it to give *judgment.*' That means judgment in the very case which is before the court. The judge must have got to the stage when he says to himself: 'This clause of the Treaty is capable of two or more meanings. If it means *this*, I give judgment for the plaintiff. If it means *that*, I give judgment for the defendant.' In short, the point must be such that, whichever way the point is decided, it is conclusive of the case. Nothing more remains but to give judgment. . .

106. It is on the basis thus described that the Tribunal will consider the issues of EC law put forward by the Parties. In their submissions the Parties refer repeatedly to provisions of secondary EC law in two areas, namely that of trans-European rail networks and that of protection of the environment (*see* paragraphs 121–137 below). Further, Article 10 of the EC Treaty is referred to by Belgium. At the same time Belgium states that this is not determinative. The Tribunal will now decide whether these references have the effect that the dispute that has arisen between the Parties requires the "interpretation" of EC law in the sense of conclusiveness, or relevance, described immediately above.

B. Issues Concerning Trans-European Networks

107. As both Parties note, the Iron Rhine railway has been earmarked as a priority project within the system of "trans-European networks" ("TEN") provided for in Articles 154–156 of the EC Treaty. Although the Parties do not appear actually to be in dispute concerning the "interpretation or application" of the relevant provisions of EC law (and thus it seems that in this regard a "dispute" within the meaning of Article 292 of the EC Treaty has not arisen at all), a brief review of the provisions of the EC Treaty on the TEN system and of the relevant secondary EC law, as well as of the respective arguments of the Parties, is necessary.

108. According to Article 154 of the EC Treaty, the EC "shall contribute to the establishment and development of the TEN system in the areas of transport, telecommunications and energy infrastructures" (paragraph 1). Action by the EC "shall aim at promoting the interconnection and interoperability" of national networks as well as access to them (paragraph 2).

109. In order to achieve these aims, Article 155 provides for the establishment of "a series of guidelines covering the objectives, priorities and broad lines of measures envisaged in the sphere of trans-European networks." These guidelines shall identify projects of common interest. Article 155 further calls for EC measures to ensure the interoperability of the networks, authorizes EC support for projects of common interest identified in the framework of TEN guidelines, and mentions the possibility of contributing through the EC Cohesion Fund to the financing of specific projects in the

area of transport infrastructure (paragraph 1). Article 155 then stipulates a duty of EC Member States to coordinate among themselves national policies that may have a significant impact on the achievement of the TEN objectives (paragraph 2).

110. Article 156 contains procedural provisions to the effect that the guidelines and other measures referred to in Article 155, paragraph 1 shall be adopted by the Council by way of the co-decision procedure established by Article 251, with the proviso, however, that guidelines and projects of common interest that relate to the territory of a Member State shall require the approval of the Member State concerned.

111. The program set out in Articles 154 and 155 has been implemented by various instruments of EC legislation, foremost among them Decision No. 1692/96/EC of 23 July 1996 ("Decision No. 1692/96") (1996 O.J. (L 228) 1) of the European Parliament and of the Council relating to Community guidelines for the development of the trans-European transport network. The purpose of Decision No. 1692/96 is to lay down the guidelines referred to in the title as "a general reference framework intended to encourage the Member States and, where appropriate, the Community in carrying out projects of common interest" (Article 1, paragraph 2). Section 3 of Decision No. 1692/96 is devoted to the development of a trans-European rail network, comprising both high-speed and conventional lines. It has been concretised by a number of further legislative acts of a more technical nature. Concerning the costs of developing TEN projects, Article 155 of the EC Treaty has been implemented by Council Regulation (EC) No. 2236/95 of 18 September 1995 (1995 O.J. (L 228) 1), as substantially amended by Regulation (EC) No. 807/2004 of the European Parliament and of the Council of 21 April 2004 (2004 O.J. (L 143) 46), in which the rules for the granting of Community financial aid – generally up to a ceiling of 10% of total investment cost – to the TEN system, are laid down.

112. Annex II of Decision No. 884/2004/EC of the European Parliament and of the Council of 29 April 2004 (2004 O.J. (L 167) 1), amending Decision No. 1692/96, lists the "priority projects on which work is due to start before 2010," including (as part of project No. 24) the "'Iron Rhine' Rheidt-Antwerpen, cross-border section."

113. It is to this set of EC legislation, as far as it is devoted to the development of a trans-European railway network, that the Parties refer in their pleadings, albeit arriving at different conclusions and employing different degrees of emphasis.

114. Belgium takes the view that the reactivation of the Iron Rhine railway is governed not only by Article XII of the 1839 Treaty of Separation but also by EC law (BR, p. 23, para. 25), namely the TEN system just described as well as EC environmental law to which the Tribunal will turn later (*see* paragraphs 121–137 below). More specifically, regarding the trans-European railway network, Belgium points to the "high European value added" through the inclusion of the Iron Rhine railway among the TEN priority projects on all sections of which work is to begin at the latest in 2010 so that they can be made operational at the latest in 2020 (BM, p. 29, para. 22). Belgium views the upgrading of the Iron Rhine railway also as a significant step towards the realization of the policy of so-called "modal shift" from road to rail transportation advocated by the EC and thus towards sustainable development. The need for this modal shift, Belgium argues, will help reduce greenhouse gas emissions and is recognized and supported in various EC official documents, as well as in statements of the Netherlands Government itself (BM, p. 26, para. 20). Belgium further refers to its position expressed in a joint note of the Belgian, Netherlands and German administrations of 20 August 2001, in which the three countries listed their respective viewpoints with regard to the repartition of costs for the definitive track of the Iron Rhine. According to the view of Belgium, the obligations flowing from Decision No. 1692/96 "comprise that each Member State involved has the responsibility of realising the required infrastructure on its territory . . . and bears the burden of financing the works on its own territory" (BM, p. 64, para. 47).[10] However, the Tribunal notes that in its Reply, in the last instance in which it refers to the set of EC rules on the TEN system, Belgium states that it

> does not . . . rely on these provisions for the purpose of interpreting the conventional regime of the Iron Rhine in the light of Community law or otherwise. It only seeks to draw the Tribunal's attention to the existence of European Community rules in the field presently discussed for jurisdictional purposes [BR, p. 112, para. 119].

---

[10] The fact that the TEN decisions relevant to the upgrading of the Iron Rhine railway were adopted with the approval of the Netherlands, appears to indicate that the Netherlands did not consider that it would have to finance the development of the Iron Rhine within the TEN system on Dutch territory in its entirety.

115. With this concluding assessment, the Belgian view on the relevance of the TEN system in EC law for the present case appears essentially to reconcile itself with that of the Netherlands. Thus, regarding Belgium's arguments in support of reactivation of the Iron Rhine railway arising from its inclusion as a priority project in the TEN system, the Netherlands states:

> This classification signifies that the EU attaches importance to the link in question and that any improvements to the link will in principle be eligible for limited EU co-financing (10 percent of the investment at most). Other than that, it has no specific meaning or effect [NCM, p. 17, para. 2.9.3].

116. In addition, the Netherlands cites Article 8 of Decision No. 1692/96 pursuant to which TEN projects must take environmental protection into account. With respect to the environmental advantages cited by Belgium of modal shift (*see also* paragraph 114 above) the Netherlands maintains that the extent of the benefits from modal shift is controversial, and that, in any event, "the Netherlands does not pursue an active modal shift policy" (NR, p. 25, para. 105). Moreover, the Netherlands argues, Belgium has not stated what the specific consequences of reactivation of the Iron Rhine railway, in terms of emissions, would be for the areas in need of environmental protection along the route of the Iron Rhine railway (NCM, p. 15, para. 2.9.1).

117. The Tribunal concurs with the Netherlands' assessment of the – very limited – relevance of the TEN system for the case at hand. The Belgian view according to which the reactivation of the Iron Rhine railway is governed not only by the 1839 Treaty of Separation but also by EC law (and in particular EC secondary law on the TEN system) is in principle correct. However, nowhere does Belgium argue that the inclusion of the Iron Rhine railway in the TEN system of the Community results in any rights in its favour going beyond the right of transit claimed by it on the basis of Article XII of the 1839 Treaty of Separation. Rather, the purpose of Belgium's reliance on the EC law constituting the legal basis for the trans-European rail network seems to be merely that of emphasizing the general desirability of an upgraded Iron Rhine railway from the perspective of fostering both EC transport policy and the modal shift from road transport to railways. As far as the specific issues are concerned on which Belgium and the Netherlands are actually in dispute, the development of the Iron Rhine railway within the TEN system in EC law thus provides no more than a background in policy

and in law in front of which the Tribunal has to interpret Article XII of the 1839 Treaty of Separation. In this regard, what is relevant in the specific context of the present case is of a purely programmatic nature. The inclusion of the Iron Rhine railway in the EC list of priority projects in the sphere of trans-European transport networks is a situation the existence of which the Tribunal acknowledges but from which there flow no legal consequences at issue in the present arbitration.

118. While the Netherlands may have a different view on the modal shift policy to which Belgium subscribes, it does not contest Belgium's transit right derived (exclusively, in its view) from Article XII of the 1839 Treaty of Separation, even with the sense given to Article XII in Belgium's pleadings. However, the Netherlands subjects the exercise of this right to what it considers to be measures of environmental protection, adequate under EC law and required under its own law on Netherlands territory, affected by the reactivation of the Iron Rhine railway. Such claims, however, do not generate any conflict with the TEN system which expressly bows to environmental requirements by stating in Article 8, paragraph 1 of Decision No. 1692/96:

> When projects are developed and carried out, environmental protection must be taken into account by the Member States through execution of environmental impact assessments of projects of common interest which are to be implemented, pursuant to Directive 85/337/EEC and through the application of Directive 92/43/EEC.

(The Tribunal will turn shortly to the Directives mentioned; *see* paragraph 123 below).

119. In summary of this point, the fact of the inclusion of the Iron Rhine railway in the EC list of priority projects in the sphere of the trans-European rail network does not give rise to the necessity for the Tribunal to engage in the interpretation of EC (*i.e.* TEN) law in the sense set out above (*see* paragraphs 99–105), because this inclusion has not created any rights, or obligations, for the Parties that go beyond what Article XII of the 1839 Treaty of Separation already provides. Thus, the points of EC law put forward by the Parties are not conclusive for the task of the Tribunal.

120. Even had it been the case that EC law on the TEN system afforded a right to Belgium for a renovated and modernised Iron Rhine railway, this would not be determinative of the Tribunal's decision. It is sufficient for the task of the Tribunal that this right derives

from Article XII of the 1839 Treaty of Separation, a point on which both Parties are agreed. As a result, to use the terms of Article 234 of the EC Treaty, in the context of the TEN system it is not necessary for the Tribunal to decide on any question of interpretation of EC law. Thus, the obligation under Article 292 of the EC Treaty does not come into play.

C.   Issues Concerning EC Environmental Legislation

121. The legal consequences for the reactivation of the Iron Rhine railway, particularly with respect to the allocation of the costs involved, resulting from the subjection of certain areas along the historic route to the regime, *inter alia*, of Council Directive No. 92/43/EEC of 21 May 1992 on the conservation of natural habitats and of wild fauna and flora (1992 O.J. (L 206) 7) ("Habitats Directive") have also been discussed by the Parties. From the viewpoint of Article 292 of the EC Treaty the question thus faced by the Tribunal is the same as that posed with regard to the law of the trans-European rail network: does the Tribunal have to engage in the interpretation of the Habitats Directive in order to enable it to decide the issue of the reactivation of the Iron Rhine railway and the costs involved?

122. In order to answer this question, the Tribunal will proceed as it did in the case of the TEN issue. It will first briefly sketch the legal regime of the Habitats Directive. Following this, it will set out the arguments of the Parties with respect to this Directive, before deciding about the relevance, from the point of view of their being determinative, of the EC law issues for its own decision.

123. The Tribunal notes that in their pleadings the Parties refer not only to the Habitats Directive but also to an earlier act of EC legislation in a more narrow field, namely Council Directive No. 79/409/EEC of 2 April 1979 on conservation of wild birds (1979 O.J. (L 103) 1) ("Birds Directive"). However, as was made clear by its Preamble and Article 7, the Habitats Directive superseded the regime established 13 years earlier by the Birds Directive for the purposes of the present case. Consequently, the Tribunal finds it unnecessary to treat the Birds Directive separately; its findings as to the question of the conclusive nature of the Habitats Directive *vel non* also apply to the earlier EC legislation.

124. The Habitats Directive finds its legal basis in Articles 174 and 175 of the EC Treaty which spell out the EC policy of environmental protection and which were originally introduced by the Single European Act of 1986 (1987 O.J. (L 169) 1). While Article 174 decrees the objective and basic principles of EC environmental policy, Article 175 regulates decision- and law-making in this area. More recently, the Treaty of Amsterdam (1997 O.J. (C 340) 1) amended the EC Treaty to include a new Article 6, which integrates EC environmental considerations into the definition and implementation of all EC policies and activities.

125. The EC Treaty provisions thus mentioned are supplemented by Article 176, according to which, and subject to certain conditions, protective measures adopted pursuant to Article 175 "shall not prevent any Member State from maintaining or introducing more stringent protective measures."

126. The Habitats Directive aims at reconciling the maintenance of biodiversity with sustainable development by developing a coherent European ecological network ("Natura 2000"). This is to be effected by the designation of special areas of conservation, as "sites of Community importance," in accordance with a specified timetable. Sites eligible for such designation are proposed by the EC Member States (Article 4). In exceptional cases, and after consultation with the Member State concerned, the European Commission may propose to the Council the selection of additional sites. The areas thus chosen are subjected to an elaborate conservation regime securing a high level of protection (*cf.* Article 174, paragraph 2, subparagraph 1 of the EC Treaty), the maintenance of which is to be monitored by the European Commission.

127. The provisions of the Habitats Directive most frequently relied on by the Parties are paragraphs 2–4 of Article 6, which read as follows:

> 2. Member States shall take appropriate steps to avoid, in the special areas of conservation, the deterioration of natural habitats and the habitats of species as well as disturbance of the species for which the areas have been designated, in so far as such disturbance could be significant in relation to the objectives of this Directive.

91

3.   Any plan or project not directly connected with or necessary to the management of the site but likely to have a significant effect thereon, either individually or in combination with other plans or projects, shall be subject to appropriate assessment of its implications for the site in view of the site's conservation objectives. In the light of the conclusions of the assessment of the implications for the site and subject to the provisions of paragraph 4, the competent national authorities shall agree to the plan or project only after having ascertained that it will not adversely affect the integrity of the site concerned and, if appropriate, after having obtained the opinion of the general public.

4.   If, in spite of a negative assessment of the implications for the site and in the absence of alternative solutions, a plan or project must nevertheless be carried out for imperative reasons of overriding public interest, including those of a social or economic nature, the Member State shall take all compensatory measures necessary to ensure that the overall coherence of Natura 2000 is protected. It shall inform the Commission of the compensatory measures adopted.

Where the site concerned hosts a priority natural habitat type and/or a priority species, the only considerations which may be raised are those relating to human health or public safety, to beneficial consequences of primary importance for the environment or, further to an opinion from the Commission, to other imperative reasons of overriding public interest.

128. The second EC law aspect of the present case thus turns on the fact that the Netherlands has designated the Meinweg area, through which the historic track of the Iron Rhine railway runs, as a special area of conservation according to the Habitats Directive, besides identifying it as a national park and as a "Silent Area" under its domestic legislation (*see* paragraph 189 below). The Netherlands had in 1994 also identified the Meinweg as a special protection area in accordance with the Birds Directive mentioned above in paragraph 123, but, as already mentioned, the provisions of the Birds Directive that are pertinent in the present dispute were amended, and for all practical purposes superseded, by the Habitats Directive.

129. As to the Parties' arguments developing the issues of EC environmental law thus described, Belgium's position regarding the submission of the Meinweg to the regime of the Habitats Directive *per se* is not wholly clear. However, Belgium does claim that the Netherlands should have done (and should still do) more to harmonise the obligations arising for it under EC law on the one hand and Article XII of the 1839 Treaty of Separation on the other (BR, pp. 64–65, para. 67). According to Belgium, this harmonisation would be feasible because the Netherlands has a certain margin of discretion with respect to the scope of the designation of the Meinweg and the

consequences flowing therefrom. For instance, Belgium claims, the Netherlands should, for the Meinweg, have followed the approach taken by the European Court of Justice in the so-called *Poitevin Marsh* case (C-96/98 *Commission v. French Republic,* Judgment of 25 November 1999), in which a strip of land was exempted from a designated conservation area in France for the development of a motorway (BM, pp. 85 ff, paras. 70 ff; BR, pp. 65–66, para. 68). Belgium further argues that the Netherlands retained some discretion in determining the type of protection required under EC law. In particular, the Netherlands could have considered the possibility of compensatory measures under Article 6, paragraph 4 of the Habitats Directive, pursuant to which such measures are to be adopted in the designated areas if a project, although conflicting with the conservation regime established in accordance with the Habitats Directive, must nevertheless be carried out for "imperative reasons of overriding public interest" (BM, p. 87, para. 72). In any event, Belgium is not convinced that the environmental measures envisaged by the Netherlands in the area designated in accordance with the Habitats Directive, and in particular the building of a tunnel under the Meinweg, are the least costly and onerous options that could have been chosen consistent with the Netherlands' obligations under EC law. In Belgium's view, even if the extremely costly measures envisaged by the Netherlands to protect the environment of the Meinweg would have been the only means at the disposal of the Netherlands to meet its obligations under EC law, this would, according to EC law, still not imply that such measures would have to be financed by Belgium (BM, p. 88, para. 75). In any case, Belgium insists, a tunnel under the Meinweg cannot be the only possible solution for the Netherlands to meet environmental obligations (BM, p. 87, para. 73; BR, pp. 61–62, para. 62).

130. Belgium further refers to a discussion in July of 2001 that took place between the Netherlands, Belgium, and Germany with the European Commission, as a result of which the European Commission stated that the benchmark conservation value according to the Habitat Directive was to be based on the environmental situation prevailing in 1994; that is, at a time when, according to the European Commission, the Meinweg area was still crossed by railway traffic[11] (the respective benchmark according to the earlier Birds Directive was to be the situation in 1981) (BM, pp. 52–56,

---

[11] The Tribunal notes that the Parties agree that as far as trans-border traffic between Belgium and Germany, crossing Limburg, was concerned, use of the Iron Rhine railway ceased after 1991.

paras. 39–42). Belgium also reminds the Tribunal that in the Commission's 2001 opinion the modal shift from road to train transportation to which the Iron Rhine railway will contribute might eventually imply beneficial consequences of primary importance for the environment in the sense of Article 6 of the Habitats Directive (BM, pp. 54–56, para. 42).

131. At other points in its pleadings, however, Belgium itself detracts from the import of the Habitats Directive for the case at hand by referring to (without in any way disputing) Netherlands statements (*see* paragraphs 132–136 below) as confirming that the designation of the Meinweg and the measures flowing from it were decided by the Netherlands by its own free will, rather than pursuant to obligations under EC law in the sense that these measures would have been the only possible means for the Netherlands to comply with obligations under the Habitats Directive). Thus, according to the observations of Belgium, the environmental requirements decreed by the Netherlands are acknowledged as made necessary not by EC law but by the Netherlands' domestic norms governing the status of nature protection zones, which the Netherlands decided to create in the areas crossed by the historic route of the Iron Rhine railway (BM, p. 87, para. 73; BR, p. 51, para. 56). Further, it is not suggested by Belgium that these Netherlands measures are inconsistent with the Netherlands' obligations under EC law.

132. An analysis of the Netherlands' pleadings concerning the relevance of the Habitats Directive for the case at hand indeed confirms that Belgium has read these arguments correctly.

133. On the one hand, the Netherlands is ready to discuss the arguments put forward by Belgium on the impact of the Habitats Directive on the measures it took concerning the natural environment surrounding the route of the Iron Rhine railway. It thus disputes the Belgian contention as to the degree of discretion left to it regarding the choice of the Meinweg as a conservation area; rather, according to the Netherlands, the designations made according to the Directive(s)[12] are to be determined by ecological criteria which leave little freedom to Member States (NR, p. 23, paras. 95–97) and were made pursuant to consultations with the European Commission.

---

[12] The Meinweg was first identified as a special protection area according to the Birds Directive before, more recently, being subjected to the regime of the Habitats Directive; *cf.* BM, pp. 38–40, para. 29.

134. Further, the Netherlands denies the applicability of the *Poitevin Marsh* jurisprudence to the Iron Rhine railway (NR, pp. 24–25, para. 102). It distinguishes the facts of this case from the situation at hand and argues that an analogous approach to the Iron Rhine railway would be inappropriate and would not be accepted in Netherlands courts or by the European Commission.

135. So far as the relevant measures consequent upon designation are concerned, Belgium argues that compensatory measures could have been taken according to Article 6, paragraph 4 of the Habitats Directive. However, in the Netherlands' view, such measures may be taken only if and to the extent that a significant negative impact on the environment cannot be mitigated, and alternative solutions cannot be found (NCM, p. 51, para. 3.3.5.6). The Netherlands regards the building of a tunnel under the Meinweg as precisely such a mitigating measure, so that as a consequence, the necessity of taking compensatory steps within the meaning of Article 6, paragraph 4 of the Habitats Directive does not arise. The Netherlands argues further that it would be doubtful whether its national courts or the European Court of Justice would accept the obligation on the Netherlands deriving from Belgium's transit right as providing an "imperative reason of overriding public interests" within the meaning of Article 6, paragraph 4 (NCM, p. 51, para. 3.3.5.6). In any case, the Netherlands argues, the designation of the Meinweg area as a protected zone under the Directive(s)[13] took place in accordance with EC case law and objective criteria (NR, p. 26, para. 107).

136. What is ultimately more significant in the present context, however, is the Netherlands' repeated and unequivocal assertion that while it has taken EC law fully into account,

> it is not necessary – in view of the legislative power based on the Netherlands' exclusive territorial sovereignty – for the measures required by Dutch legislation for the protection of nature and the environment to be based on or justified by the Birds and Habitats Directives, in any event in so far as such measures are not contrary to EU law [NCM, p. 49, para. 3.3.5.6].

Thus, the Netherlands' decisions as to the appropriate environmental protection measures to take in the context of the reactivation of the Iron Rhine railway, were taken

---

[13] *See* preceding note.

by reference to Netherlands environmental law and administrative procedures, albeit in a way consistent with the relevant EC Directives.

The Netherlands continues:

> The Netherlands is *not* saying: 'The European Commission is telling us we must construct a tunnel in the Meinweg, because that is an automatic consequence of the Habitats Directives [*sic*].'
>
> The Netherlands has *itself* decided on the basis of the Flora and Fauna Act (Flora en Faunawet) and the ecological values which it protects, that the construction of a tunnel is necessary in order to protect the ecological values in the Meinweg because it considers it to be the only way to adequately protect those values [NCM, p. 49, para. 3.3.5.6].

Finally, the Netherlands refers to the principle embodied in Article 176 of the EC Treaty, according to which EC Member States have the right to impose more stringent environmental framework conditions and conservation measures than what is required by EC Directives. In sum, for the Netherlands, the application of these Directives "is not a decisive factor for the construction of a tunnel in the Meinweg" (NR, p. 23, para. 93). Rather, what is decisive is Netherlands environmental law; provided always that it is in conformity with EC law. According to the Netherlands, it is fully entitled to take these measures, not only under EC law but also by virtue of Article XII of the 1839 Treaty of Separation, due to the reservation of sovereignty embodied therein. In the Netherlands' view it thus necessarily follows that it is for Belgium to bear the costs involved.

127. It is precisely this issue upon which the Tribunal has later to pronounce. But the Tribunal will first have to decide whether it must interpret the Habitats Directive in order to render its Award. Applying the test enunciated at paragraphs 102–105 above, the Tribunal has examined whether it would arrive at different conclusions on the application of Article XII to the Meinweg tunnel project and its costs if the Habitats Directive did not exist. The Tribunal answers this question in the negative, as its decision would be the same on the basis of Article XII and of Netherlands environmental legislation alone. Hence, the questions of EC law debated by the Parties are not determinative, or conclusive for the Tribunal; it is not necessary for the Tribunal to interpret the Habitats Directive in order to render its Award. Therefore, as in the case

of the TEN, the questions of EC law involved in the case do not trigger any obligations under Article 292 of the EC Treaty.

D.   Article 10 of the EC Treaty

138. Pursuant to Article 10 of the EC Treaty,

> Member States shall take all appropriate measures, . . . , to ensure fulfilment of the obligations arising out of this Treaty or resulting from action taken by the institutions of the Community. They shall facilitate the achievement of the Community's tasks.
>
> They shall abstain from any measure which could jeopardise the attainment of the objectives of this Treaty.

139. Belgium refers to this basic tenet of EC law by arguing that pursuant to Article 10 it does find itself under an obligation to facilitate the application of the environmental rules of EC law discussed above and, to that end, assist the Netherlands which is bound to apply these rules on its territory (BM, p. 90, para. 75). In Belgium's view, however, its duty arising under Article 10 could never go as far as obliging it to finance EC implementation measures on Netherlands territory. Belgium then points to various aspects of the position it has taken over the years with regard to the modernisation of the Iron Rhine railway, which it wants to be understood as acts of assistance to the Netherlands in complying with Article 10.

140. The Netherlands' pleadings, on their part, nowhere contest this point. Thus, there exists no dispute between the Parties concerning Article 10.

141. The Tribunal therefore finds that the question of obligations arising under Article 10 in the context of the dispute about the Iron Rhine railway does not have to be decided by the Tribunal; it is not determinative or conclusive in the sense of bringing Article 292 of the EC Treaty into play.

CHAPTER IV – THE BELGIAN REQUEST FOR REACTIVATION AND THE MEMORANDUM OF UNDERSTANDING OF MARCH 2000

142. On 28 March 2000 the Belgian and the Netherlands Ministers of Transport signed a Memorandum of Understanding concerning the Iron Rhine railway "in accordance with the arrangement between the Ministers of 29 February 2000" ("March 2000 MoU"). The main aspects of this instrument were confirmed in a trilateral meeting of the Belgian and Netherlands Ministers of Transport and the German Secretary of State for Transport held on 5 April 2001 (BM, Exhibit No. 86, Report of the discussions between the Belgian and Dutch Ministers and the German Secretary of State for Transport on the reactivation of the Iron Rhine, held in Luxembourg on 5 April 2001). Normally, a Memorandum of Understanding is "an instrument concluded between states which is not legally binding" (A. Aust, *Modern Treaty Law and Practice*, Cambridge University Press (2000), p. 26, at p. 31). A key factor in distinguishing a "non-legally binding instrument" from a treaty is the intention of the parties. To ascertain this intention, the Tribunal will, first, review the circumstances that preceded the signature of the March 2000 MoU. It will then set out the content and determine the legal significance of this particular instrument. Finally, it will summarize the circumstances that followed the signature of the March 2000 MoU, and that ultimately led to the present arbitration between the Parties.

A.   Circumstances Preceding the Signature of the Memorandum of Understanding

143. As noted in paragraph 19 above, use of the Iron Rhine railway line varied in intensity during the period 1914–1991. It is common ground between the Parties that there was no further transit use of the Iron Rhine railway between Belgium and Germany after 31 May 1991 (BM, p. 23, para. 18; NCM, pp. 9–10, para. 2.5.4).

144. Of interest for the present arbitration is the fact that even before May 1991, various Belgian officials had affirmed Belgium's interest in the future use of the Iron Rhine railway (BM, pp. 32–38, paras. 24–28). The most striking expression of that interest is the letter of 23 February 1987 which the Belgian Minister of Transport addressed to his colleague the Minister of Transport of the Netherlands (original Dutch text in BM, Exhibit No. 59, Letter of the Belgian Minister of Transport to the Dutch Minister of

Transport and Waterstaat, dated 23 February 1987; unofficial translation in BM, p. 33, para. 24). This letter already refers to the forthcoming difficulties of reconciling the future use of the Iron Rhine railway with the protection of the environment. The Tribunal now reproduces that translation of certain passages of the Belgian Minister's letter:

> I have the honour of asking your attention for the transboundary railway Antwerp-Roermond-Mönchen Gladbach, also called the Iron Rhine.
> In Belgian circles,[14] there is strong interest for a modern direct railway link between Antwerp and the Ruhr area, with the consequence that I consider it necessary that an in-depth cost-benefits analysis be made of such a linkage.
> The NMBS [Belgian railways] has been instructed to study this issue. However such a study could not be finalised without the cooperation of the NS [Dutch railways] and DB [German railways].[15]
> I would be highly appreciative if you could request the NS to cooperate in this study with the NMBS.
> [. . .]
> To conclude, I refer to plans existing in The Netherlands, to create a natural park between Roermond and Erkenbosch alongside the Iron Rhine, which would limit the railway exploitation on that line.
> In my view, such a limitation would go against the rights accorded to Belgium by Article 12 of the Treaty of London of 19 April 1839 between Belgium and the Netherlands, which was executed through the Treaty of 13 January 1873 regulating the passage of the railway Antwerp-Gladbach through the territory of Limburg.
> In the above context, it is beyond doubt that Belgium will hold firm to its right of free transport through the Iron Rhine.

In her response of 26 October 1987 the Netherlands Minister of Transport did not address the relationship between the Iron Rhine railway and the designation of an area in the vicinity of the railway line as a nature reserve, but simply acknowledged Belgium's right of transit.

145. In May 1991 an economic study commissioned by the European Commission was published. This study recommended that the existing route of the Iron Rhine railway be preserved, and concluded that "the economics for rehabilitating the Iron Rhine are generally positive" (BM, Exhibit No. S2, Prognos, *The Iron Rhine Railway Link between Antwerp and the Rhine-Ruhr Area*, Final Report, May 1991). This study was

---

[14] The Tribunal notes that the Netherlands, in its Counter-Memorial, states that the correct English translation of "*in sommige Belgische middens*" is "in *certain* Belgian circles" (see NCM, p. 12, para. 2.7.1.2. and note 19). The Tribunal interprets this phrase to mean "in *some* Belgian circles."
[15] See also the Belgian Minister of Transport's letter of 9 November 1987 to his German colleague: BM, Exhibit No. 60, Letter of the Belgian Minister of Transport to the German Minister of Transport, dated 9 November 1987.

discussed at the meeting of the Benelux Economic Union, Commission for Transport, on 11 December 1991, during which the Belgian representative stated that "the possible reactivation of the Iron Rhine must remain guaranteed in the light of an increase of transport in the future" (BM, Exhibit No. 63, Benelux Economic Union, Commission for Transport, Sub-Commission "Railway Transports," Report of the meeting held in Luxembourg on 11 December 1991). A similar statement was made at the meeting of the Benelux Economic Union, Commission for Transport on 20 April 1993 (BM, Exhibit No. 64, Benelux Economic Union, Commission for Transport, Sub-Commission "Railway Transport," Report of the meeting held at The Hague on 20 April 1993).

146. In 1994 the European Commission approved a Belgian request to fund a feasibility study into the modernisation of the Iron Rhine railway. Such a study was subsequently provided for in Article 9 of the Treaty concerning the construction of a railway connection for high-speed trains between Rotterdam and Antwerp in 1996. The study (the Tractebel Report) was commenced in December 1996 and concluded in January-February 1997.

147. On 12 June 1998 the Prime Minister of Belgium wrote to his colleague, the Prime Minister of the Netherlands, as follows (BM, Exhibit No. 67, Letter of Belgian Prime Minister Dehaene to Dutch Minister-President Kok of the Netherlands, dated 12 June 1998, unofficial translation: BM, p. 38, para. 28):

> I accord great importance to a rapid realisation of the Iron Rhine. Therewith, the preference is given to the currently existing historic track. This historic track is the flattest, the shortest and the most economical. Furthermore, Belgium can claim a right of public international law on this historic track. Alternative connections (the Brabant-route, the diversion via Venlo) are either a too long roundabout route or necessitate the installation of new lines which can only be realised in the long run.

148. Whether any legal consequences flow from discontinuation in 1991 may now be addressed.

149. In the view of the Netherlands, this history evidenced an inconsistent position on the part of Belgium regarding the reactivation of the Iron Rhine railway.

150. Be that as it may, it is the view of the Tribunal that the Netherlands knew that it was possible that, notwithstanding what had happened before, a formal demand for reactivation at a significantly higher level of use might be forthcoming in the foreseeable future. And Belgium had reserved its right of "free transit" – which right the Netherlands has always acknowledged and continues to acknowledge.

151. The Tribunal observes that the reaction of the Netherlands to these developments has consistently been based on two principles: (i) the Netherlands does not contest Belgium's right of transit with respect to the Iron Rhine railway; and (ii) pursuant to the Netherlands' sovereignty over its territory, any reactivation of the Iron Rhine railway must comply with Netherlands legislation, in particular legislation concerning the protection of the environment. This is clear from, *inter alia*, the answer of 10 July 1998 of the Prime Minister of the Netherlands to the letter of the Prime Minister of Belgium cited above:

> [T]he Netherlands will participate in the consultations in a neighbourly spirit, as it has stated on many occasions. It speaks for itself that reactivating the historical line – or any other line – within Dutch territory is subject to Dutch environmental legislation and EC legislation on the conservation of natural habitats (Habitats Directive) [NCM, Exhibit No. 19, Letter of 10 July 1998 from the Dutch Prime Minister Wim Kok to the Belgian Prime Minister Jean-Luc Dehaene].

152. In the same period the Netherlands made an inventory of its national legislation relevant to the reactivation of the Iron Rhine railway (*see* NCM, p. 21, para. 2.12.2). On the basis of this inventory Belgium agreed with the proposal of the Netherlands to submit the entire railway line to the procedure set out in the Netherlands Transport Infrastructure (Planning Procedures) Act. In addition, the Meinweg area was designated by the Netherlands on 20 May 1994 as a "special protection area" within the meaning of the Birds Directive, later superseded by the Habitats Directive. In the years 1994–1995 the Netherlands also identified the Meinweg area as a national park and as a "Silent Area" under its domestic legislation (*see* discussion below at paragraph 189).

153. It soon became evident that the reactivation of the Iron Rhine railway under the prevailing environmental legislation of the Netherlands would give rise to substantial infrastructure costs (including the envisaged tunnel in the Meinweg area). At a meeting of the Netherlands and Belgian Ministers of Transport and the German Secretary of

State for Transport, held in Brussels on 9 December 1999, no overall agreement could be reached on the allocation of the costs between the countries concerned. While it was agreed that the costs for the temporary reactivation of the historic track would be borne by Belgium, no agreement appeared possible on the allocation of costs for a definitive solution. Belgium and Germany based their view on the territoriality principle: each country must bear the investments in infrastructure on its own territory. The Netherlands relied on Article XII of the 1839 Treaty of Separation to contend that such costs on Netherlands territory should be borne by Belgium (BM, Exhibit No. 96, Report of the meeting between Belgian and Dutch Ministers and the German Secretary of State for Transport on the reactivation of the Iron Rhine, held in Brussels on 9 December 1999).

B. **The Contents and Legal Significance of the Memorandum of Understanding**

154. The text of the Memorandum of Understanding of 28 March 2000 between Minister Durant and Minister Netelenbos concerning the Iron Rhine reads as follows:[16]

> Belgium and the Netherlands emphasise the importance of being able to swiftly transport freight by rail from the Belgian and Dutch ports to the hinterland, and back again, in an ever-expanding internal market. Access to the infrastructure that is available for this purpose will be open to all railway companies.
>
> Both countries will closely cooperate with Germany on an international study of the positive and negative consequences of the reactivation of the Iron Rhine and of the possible alternative routes. This study will assess the situation "as if there were no border." The results of this study must be available in March 2001, so that at that time the international decision-making can take place.
>
> Given the relationship between the international study and the Dutch EIA,[17] the Netherlands will do its utmost to have the results of the EIA for the part of the Iron Rhine that is located on Dutch territory, ready in March 2001. In the EIA the following will be investigated:
> - For the short term the possible[18] temporary, limited reactivation of the complete historic route, this temporary reactivation being applicable until the definitive route is being put to use.
> - For the definitive solution all relevant routes shall be studied; possibilities for the transportation of passengers will also be examined.

---

[16] For the authentic Dutch text of the March 2000 MoU, see BM, Exhibit No. 82 and NCM, Exhibit No. 22. Unofficial English translations of selected paragraphs are in BM, pp. 44–47, para. 34 and NCM, pp. 20–21, para. 2.12.1. Except as noted below, the Netherlands' translation is reproduced here.

[17] EIA = Environmental Impact Assessment.

[18] The Tribunal here has used the word "possible" (from Belgium's translation) rather than "possibility," which appears in the Netherlands' version.

The Netherlands and Belgium will propose to Germany that they discuss the progress of the EIA regularly on a trilateral basis. The Netherlands will invite Belgium to designate an official to monitor the day-to-day progress of the EIA.

The decisions on temporary use and the definitive route will be taken simultaneously.

If, when decisions are taken on the temporary and definitive route in mid 2001 at the latest, the EIA-study concludes that a temporary, limited use will not cause irreversible environmental damage, then, from the end of 2001 onwards a few trains a day will be allowed to use the whole historic route at limited speed between 7 AM and 7 PM. Under these same conditions of timely decision-making and of absence of irreversible environmental damage, trains could, from the end of 2002 onwards, also use temporarily at limited speed the whole historic route in evening hours and at night, up to a maximum of fifteen per 24-hour period (combined total in both directions). The possible loss of ecological value will be compensated for.

If it is decided that the definitive route will be another route than that passing through the Meinweg (as the Netherlands assumes, but not Belgium), this route will be considered the complete fulfilment of the obligations under public international law arising from the Separation Treaty of 1839 and the Belgian-Dutch Iron Rhine Treaty of 1873. These arrangements will be laid down in a Treaty.

Until the definitive route has been selected, Belgium reserves all its rights under the Separation Treaty of 1839 and the Dutch-Belgian Iron Rhine Treaty of 1873.

The costs for the temporary use of the historic route will be met by Belgium.

If the Belgian railways company (NMBS) so wishes, it may undertake these works either by itself or by a third party, always taking account of the European public procurement rules and of the Dutch legal requirement that such works are undertaken by a contractor who is recognized in The Netherlands. This contractor could be Belgian.[19]

For the construction of the definitive route The Netherlands is willing to bear part of the costs related thereto. Further arrangements will be made in this respect after the definitive route has been chosen.

155. The Tribunal observes that the intentions contained in the March 2000 MoU can be summarized as follows.

(1) An "international study" is to be carried out (jointly with Germany) on the consequences of the reactivation of the Iron Rhine railway and of possible alternative routes. The results of this study must be available in March 2001.

---

[19] The translation of this paragraph is that prepared by the Tribunal (neither Party having offered a translation).

(2)   The Netherlands "will do its utmost" to have ready, also in March 2001, the results of its Environmental Impact Assessment ("EIA") procedure for the part of the Iron Rhine railway that is located on Netherlands territory. The EIA procedure will include an investigation of both the temporary use of the Iron Rhine railway and the relevant routes for a definitive solution.

(3)   The decisions on the temporary use and on the definitive route are to be taken simultaneously ("dual decision"), in mid-2001 at the latest. The decision concerning temporary use has been made contingent on the decision concerning long-term use, because otherwise there would be no guarantee that this use would be temporary.

(4)   During the negotiations between the Parties, several meanings have been advanced for the notion of "temporary use" of the Iron Rhine railway. Under the MoU, temporary use is a "limited reactivation of the complete historic route" until the definitive route is being put to use. (If the definitive route coincides with the historic route, it may be expected that upgrading the historic route will have negative consequences for the temporary use of the route.) The MoU does not address this issue, but its terms perhaps suggest likely agreement on a definitive use that does not wholly follow the historic route. The temporary use is to be allowed if, at the time the Parties take the dual decision, the EIA procedure concludes that a temporary limited use will not cause irreversible environmental damage. If so, from the end of 2001 onwards, a few trains a day will be allowed to use the whole historic route at limited speed between 7 am and 7 pm. From the end of 2002 onwards, trains could, under the same conditions, use the whole historic route at limited speed in the evening hours and at night, up to a maximum of 15 trains per 24-hour period (combined total in both directions). The costs for the temporary use of the historic route would be borne by Belgium.

(5)   For the definitive solution, all relevant routes will be examined. Until the definitive route has been selected, Belgium will reserve all its rights under the 1839 Treaty of Separation and the Iron Rhine Treaty of 1873. If it is decided that the definitive route will be another route than that passing through the Meinweg, this other route will be considered the complete implementation of Article XII of

the 1839 Treaty of Separation and of the Iron Rhine Treaty of 1873, and the relevant arrangements will be laid down in a treaty. The Netherlands would be willing to bear part of the costs relating to the construction costs of the definitive route.

156. The Parties agree that, as a matter of international law, the March 2000 MoU is not a binding instrument (BR, p. 29, para. 32; NR, p. 7, para. 26). At the same time, it was clearly not regarded as being without legal relevance. The Parties have in fact given effect to a number of provisions of the March 2000 MoU (*see* paragraph 159 below). Further, Belgium has spoken of it as "lapsing" when the date envisaged therein for the dual decision – "mid 2001 at the latest" – was not met. Belgium concludes that, as a consequence, "Belgium's undertaking to finance costs of temporary activation has equally lapsed."

157. The Tribunal notes that, in the arguments that the Parties advance in respect of certain of the Questions put to the Tribunal, the March 2000 MoU is equally not treated as legally irrelevant. Principles of good faith and reasonableness lead to the conclusion that the principles and procedures laid down in the March 2000 MoU remain to be interpreted and implemented in good faith and will provide useful guidelines to what the Parties have been prepared to consider as compatible with their rights under Article XII of the 1839 Treaty of Separation and the Iron Rhine Treaty. The respective allocation of costs for temporary use will depend not upon any undertakings given in the March 2000 MoU, but on other legal considerations (including what the Parties have thought reasonable during their negotiations in connection with the March 2000 MoU). The putative definitive route will – insofar as it may entail a short deviation from the historic route – require agreement; and the March 2000 MoU suggests that such an option was not *per se* considered as unreasonable by the Parties.

158. The Tribunal also finds it of continuing relevance that it was envisaged that the short term and definitive decisions were to be taken simultaneously. Just as Belgium cannot be said to have agreed to the financing of the temporary solution in the absence of agreement on a definitive solution, so the Netherlands cannot be held to have agreed to put the short term solution envisaged immediately into effect, without agreement on the definitive solution having been reached. Further, while at no time did Belgium's right of

transit lapse, the long period of minimal use or absence of use, coupled with the technical complexities entailed in reactivation of the Iron Rhine railway, suggests that provision for Belgium's desired short term use may not reasonably be expected in the immediate future. The Netherlands has made clear it would prefer no temporary use, but it has also stated that any temporary use could not continue for more than five years (NCM p. 25, para. 2.12.4; NR p. 9, para. 35).

C.   Acts Taken Subsequent to the Adoption of the Memorandum of Understanding

159. The international study referred to in the March 2000 MoU was delivered in May 2001 (BM, Exhibit No. S3, Arcadis, *Comparative Cross-Border Study on the Iron Rhine*, Final Report, 14 May 2001). In the same month the results of the Netherlands' EIA procedure, referred to as the "Route Assessment/Environmental Impact Statement" ("EIS"), was delivered (BM, Exhibit No. S4, *Railinfrabeheer/Directoraat-Generaal Rijkswaterstaat, Trajectnota/MER*). Both the international study and the Netherlands Route Assessment/EIS involved detailed examinations of various options for the routes of a reactivated Iron Rhine railway, all starting at the historic entry point into the Netherlands at the border with Belgium. One series of options involved routes through Venlo; the other series of options involved routes through or near Roermond. The routes through or near Roermond included the historic track, with several variations. All options, with their required works, were evaluated on the basis of comprehensive criteria that included costs and environmental effects. Both studies concluded that the preferred option would be the historic route. The Route Assessment/EIS determined that the "most environmentally friendly" option would be the historic route, with modifications including a tunnel in the Meinweg and a diversion around Roermond. On 21 September 2001, the Belgian, Netherlands and German Ministers of Transport decided that an overall decision would be taken, including the dual decision as to the temporary and long term use (*see* paragraph 155, subparagraph 4 above) and a decision on the allocation of costs (BM, Exhibit No. 89, Memo of the informal discussions between the Belgian, Dutch and German Ministers of Transport on the reactivation of the Iron Rhine, held at The Hague on 21 September 2001). During the same period, the three countries concerned met with the Directorate General Environment of the European Commission, which meeting led to a provisional and a final statement of the Commission concerning questions of interpretation of the Habitats Directive. When it

appeared that the reactivation of the Iron Rhine railway could not be properly realised on the sole basis of negotiations, the Parties agreed to have a number of issues resolved through arbitration.

CHAPTER V – THE MEASURES ENVISAGED BY THE NETHERLANDS IN THE LIGHT OF ARTICLE XII OF THE 1839 TREATY OF SEPARATION

A.   Introduction

160. The Tribunal has concluded above (*see* paragraph 56) that, as a consequence of the reservation of sovereignty in Article XII of the 1839 Treaty of Separation, the Netherlands may exercise its rights of sovereignty in relation to the territory over which the Iron Rhine railway passes, unless this would conflict with the treaty rights granted to Belgium, or rights that Belgium may hold under general international law, or constraints imposed by EC law.

161. The question of constraints posed by EC law is discussed separately, in Chapter III above and paragraph 206 below.

162. In the view of Belgium, the limitations flowing from Article XII entail that the Netherlands is under the obligation to exercise its legislative and decision-making power in good faith and in a reasonable manner and so as not to deprive Belgium's transit right of its substance or to render the exercise of the right unreasonably difficult (BR, p. 69, para. 70). The Netherlands does not contest these limitations, but contends that its actions fully comply with these requirements.

163. In the view of the Tribunal, the first and obvious limitation flowing from Article XII is that the entitlement of the Netherlands to apply its national legislation to the reactivation of the Iron Rhine may not amount to a denial of the right of transit by Belgium over the historic route. The second limitation flows from the generally accepted principles of good faith and reasonableness: any measures to be prescribed by the Netherlands on the basis of its national legislation for the reactivation of the Iron Rhine railway may not render unreasonably difficult the exercise of Belgium's transit right.

164. In this context, the Tribunal notes that Belgium takes the position that the works envisaged by the Netherlands as necessary for the reactivation of the Iron Rhine "do not curtail Belgium's rights *per se*, provided that measures are taken to ensure the

uninterrupted use of the railway during and notwithstanding these works, so that (1) temporary driving is followed directly by long-term use [*see* paragraph 155, subparagraphs 3 and 4 above] and (2) neither of these 'regimes' is affected by construction works" (BR, p. 34, para. 37).

165. Belgium submits that the requirement of the Netherlands for such works is not *per se* an unreasonable exercise of the Netherlands' rights. However, when this requirement is combined with the further insistence that the works be financed by Belgium, and not by the Netherlands, it does, according to Belgium, become such an unreasonable exercise. Thus, Belgium considers that its transit right could be denied through the imposition of financial obligations (BR, p. 34, para. 37). The measures to be prescribed for the reactivation of the Iron Rhine railway, and the allocation of costs therefor, are closely intertwined issues. The former is addressed in this chapter and the latter is addressed in Chapter VI.

166. In the present chapter the Tribunal will examine the measures envisaged by the Netherlands for the reactivation of the Iron Rhine railway in the light of their compatibility with the treaty obligations of the Netherlands. For this purpose it is first necessary to devote some attention to the Netherlands legislation which forms the basis for the envisaged measures.

B.   The Applicable Legislation and Decision-making Procedures of the Netherlands

167. In its pleadings the Netherlands has made a distinction between two categories of legislation that are applicable to the reactivation of the Iron Rhine railway: so-called "sector-specific" legislation; and general rules of administrative law. The Netherlands has only provided fragmentary information on the content of its national legislation, and Belgium has only commented on specific elements. Nevertheless the Tribunal deems it useful to provide an overview of the information provided by the Parties.

1.   Sector-specific legislation

168. Various Netherlands acts and decrees apply to the reactivation of the Iron Rhine railway. Of particular importance are those dealing with technical and safety issues, such as the technical specifications for the track and railroad crossings, and those dealing with environmental issues (land-use planning, health and soil protection, and nature preservation). The technical and safety issues are mainly covered by the Railways Act (*Spoorwegwet*). The dispute between the Parties about the consequences of the implementation of Netherlands legislation focuses in particular on the environmental legislation. The legislation considered most relevant by the Parties in their pleadings includes the following.

169. The Noise Abatement Act (*Wet Geluidhinder*) lays down the allowable noise level standards to be applied with respect to various categories of buildings and activities. Where dwellings and similar structures are affected, a distinction is made between maximum exemption levels and so-called "preferential levels" of noise. The maximum permitted noise impact of a modified railway is 73 dB(A); for a new railway it is 70 dB(A). The preferential level is 57 dB(A). Section 106, paragraph (d), subparagraph (4) of the Act prescribes the measures to be taken when the preferential level is exceeded. Measures are to be taken in the following order: (1) measures at the source (*e.g.*, using quieter infrastructure and/or quieter trains); (2) measures related to the transfer of noise (*e.g.*, noise barriers); and (3) measures at the point of impact (*e.g.*, façade insulation). Where such measures are insufficient to ensure that the noise will not exceed the preferential level an exemption can be granted under certain conditions. When the noise nuisance is allowed to exceed the maximum exemption level, the relevant dwellings lose their residential function (which may result in compensated expropriation) (BR, pp. 44–46, paras. 48–50; NR, pp. 18–19, paras. 74–77).

170. The Railway Noise Abatement Decree (*Besluit Geluidhinder Spoorwegen*) provides the basis for imposing requirements (for the purpose of abating noise caused by the use of railways)

> on the nature, composition or method of construction and the alteration of a railway line. Alteration refers, among other things, to a significant increase in the number

110

of trains and/or the speed of transit. Certain measures are required in such cases. The railway management company must present these measures to the municipalities concerned. Construction or adaptation can only commence after a final decision has been reached [NCM, p. 21, n. 44].

171. The Flora and Fauna Act (*Flora en Fauna Wet*) protects plant and animal species. It entails

> a ban on the destruction or disruption of the species it protects, as well as of their nests, reproduction, resting and living environments. The stipulations of the bans in the Flora and Fauna Act do not feature the term 'significant.' As a consequence, *any* disruption and/or destruction occurring as a result of the laying of the route represents a violation of the ban stipulations. For the varieties suffering such effects due to the construction of the route, the implementation of a project can only be undertaken if an exemption is obtained on the basis of article 75 of the Flora and Fauna Act [NCM, Annex A, p. 1].

172. The Environmental Management Act (*Wet Milieubeheer*): as explained in paragraph 82 of the Netherlands' Rejoinder, Section 4, paragraph 9 of this Act requires provinces

> to adopt a Provincial Environmental Policy Plan every four years, in which they identify areas that require special protection to preserve the environment or certain aspects thereof (such as quiet). A silent area is an area where the noise nuisance should be so low that the sounds that occur there naturally are hardly disturbed, if at all (stand still principle). The preferential noise value in silent areas can vary from province to province. Both the province of North Brabant and the province of Limburg employ a value of 40 dB(A) during the daytime in their Environmental Policy Plans.

173. The Environmental Impact Assessment ("EIA") Decree (*Besluit Milieueffect-rapportage*) requires the preparation of an EIS for the adoption of a plan for a new railway or the reactivation of an existing railway line that passes for a distance of at least five kilometres through a buffer zone or a sensitive area delimited in a zoning plan or a regional plan (NCM, p. 21, n. 45).

174. The Netherlands also implements international guidelines adopted in 1969 with respect to the establishment of national parks, within the framework of the International Union for Nature Conservation and the Conservation of Natural Resources ("IUCN"). A National Park is defined as

> a consecutive area of at least 1000 hectares consisting of natural land, water and/or woodland, with special landscape features and plant and animal life. The area offers good possibilities for recreational use. In a National Park, nature

conservation and nature development are intensified, nature and environmental education is heavily encouraged and forms of nature-oriented recreation and research are promoted [NCM, Annex A, p. 2].

175. At the provincial level also a number of regulations and policies implementing national legislation are relevant. In addition to the Provincial Environmental Policy Plan required by the Environmental Management Act already mentioned in paragraph 172, provinces can designate areas as part of their "Ecological Main Structure" (Limburg) or "Green Main Structure" (Noord-Brabant). These consist of core areas, nature development areas and linking zones for the conservation of which basic protection applies. In addition, areas can be designated for their landscape values under the Provincial Development Plan for the province of Limburg (NCM, Annex A, pp. 1–2).

176. Finally, at the provincial level the Provincial Environmental Regulation for Limburg provides for the possibility of designation as "Silent Area." This provincial regulation includes a general protection stipulation for environmental protection areas, including "Silent Areas" (Article 5.4) which reads as follows:

> Any party carrying out actions in an environmental protection area, who knows or could reasonably have suspected that through those actions in that area the special importance on the basis of which the area is designated a protected area will be or could be damaged, is required to take all measures which can reasonably be demanded with a view to preventing such damage or, if such damage occurs, as far as possible to limit that damage and as far as possible to limit and to reverse the consequences of the actions.

In the Provincial Environmental Regulations, no quantitative noise standards are laid down for "Silent Areas." However, the Provincial Environment Plan for Limburg specifies that the Province of Limburg has set a maximum value of 40 dB(A) for noise, and that the Province intends to include this value in the Provincial Environmental Regulation (NCM, Annex A, p. 3).

2. General rules of administrative law

177. In the application of sector-specific legislation the Netherlands Government is also required to comply with the general norms for governmental action, in particular the general principles of sound administration as codified in the General Administrative Law Act (*Algemene Wet Bestuursrecht*). The Netherlands refers in particular to the "general principles of sound administration" codified in sections 3.2 and 3.4 of the General Administrative Law Act, which read as follows:

> When preparing an order an administrative authority shall gather the necessary information concerning the relevant facts and the interests to be weighed.
>
> The administrative authority shall weigh the interests directly involved in so far as no limitation on this duty derives from a statutory regulation or the nature of the power being exercised [NR, p.17, para. 69].

According to the Netherlands, these principles can influence the interpretation and application of statutory provisions and the implementation of policy and can also serve as administrative policy in cases where a statutory regulation leaves a certain amount of freedom or is entirely lacking. The Netherlands explains that such principles will be applied in any judicial review proceedings (NR, p. 17, paras. 69–70).

3. The Transport Infrastructure (Planning Procedures) Act

178. In principle, each sector-specific law has its own decision-making procedures (including judicial review) to be followed for the implementation of its substantive provisions. In case of significant transport infrastructure projects a separate law applies, replacing the sector-specific decision-making procedures: the Transport Infrastructure (Planning Procedures) Act (*Tracéwet*) (NCM, p. 21, para. 2.12.2). This procedure incorporates reviews of compliance with all the relevant specific legislation and includes an EIA. Only the final Planning Procedure Order issued under this procedure will be open to judicial review. The Netherlands explains that the Transport Infrastructure (Planning Procedures) Act must be applied to the reactivation of the part of the Iron Rhine between Roermond and the German border (NCM, p. 21, para 2.12.2). The Netherlands, with the agreement of Belgium, has chosen to apply the Act for the purpose of the reactivation of the Iron Rhine railway in its entirety.

113

179. The decision-making procedure under the Transport Infrastructure (Planning Procedures) Act (including the EIA) consists of six stages which are described in the Netherlands' Counter-Memorial (p. 22, para. 2.12.3.1) as follows (footnotes omitted):

> 1. A *Notification of Intent* (*Startnotitie*) marks the formal beginning of the procedure. It specifies the plans of the initiator, what alternatives to the planned activity will be examined and the potential consequences for the environment of each alternative.
> 2. The results of the study of the alternatives and their consequences are recorded in the *Route Assessment/EIS* (*Trajectnota/MER*), taking into consideration the results of public input regarding the Notification of Intent. The purpose of the Route Assessment/EIS is to describe the anticipated consequences for the environment, so that the environment receives proper attention in the decision-making concerning the planned activity.
> 3. On the basis of the Route Assessment/EIS, and with due regard to the results of public input and the advisory report of the independent Committee for Environmental Impact Assessment established pursuant to statute, the competent authorities select a preferred option, which is published in an *Official Position* (*Standpuntbepaling*).
> 4. The preferred alternative is worked out in detail (this involves specification of the position of the railway line that is accurate to within one meter) and the result is recorded in a *Draft Planning Procedure Order* (*Ontwerp-Tracébesluit*), which is published.
> 5. After public input on the Draft Planning Procedure Order, the competent ministers adopt a *Planning Procedure Order* (*Tracébesluit*), which forms the basis for issuing building permits, expropriation procedures and the like. A Planning Procedure Order is open to judicial review, which can lead to the annulment of all or part of the Order.
> 6. Once the Planning Procedure Order has become final and conclusive, the construction stage of the project can begin.

180. Stage 1 (the Notification of Intent) was completed in November 1999. Stage 2 (the Route Assessment/EIS) was completed in May 2001. This document analysed and evaluated a series of options for the reactivation of the Iron Rhine railway. At the same time the international study (sponsored by the three Governments involved in the planning for the reactivation of the Iron Rhine railway, i.e. Belgium, Germany and the Netherlands) was completed (*see* paragraph 159 above). The Governments involved ultimately agreed on the preferred option of the historic track (with a diversion around Roermond).

181. Stage 3 of the decision-making procedure (the issuing of the Official Position) could not be completed because agreement could not be reached with Belgium in the negotiations regarding the costs and their allocation in relation to the preferred option. Stating that its

intention was to prevent delays in the execution of the project, the Netherlands Government decided to continue the procedure on an informal basis (NCM, p. 23, para. 2.12.3.2). The Government approved a preliminary Official Position in November 2001 (which has not been published) and on that basis a preliminary version of a Draft Planning Procedure Order (*IJzeren Rijn, Concept ontwerp-tracébesluit*) was finalised by the Netherlands infrastructure manager ProRail in July 2003. This preliminary version was informally communicated to the Belgian railway company NMBS, and was used by Belgium in the preparation of its Reply (which fact was objected to by the Netherlands (NR, p.13, para. 52)).

182. According to the Netherlands, the application of its legislation would result in a series of measures required for the long-term reactivation of the Iron Rhine railway as listed in the preliminary version of the Draft Planning Procedure Order. The Tribunal notes that this document has an informal and provisional status, as explained in paragraph 181 above. The Netherlands has observed that, in a formal sense, the measures proposed in this preliminary version cannot be regarded as the definitive ones which will have to be implemented. Even after the issuance of the definitive version of the Order there will still be the possibility of judicial review. Thus, there is still uncertainty about the exact measures to be prescribed for the reactivation of the Iron Rhine railway on Netherlands territory. However, since the arguments of the parties have specifically focused on the measures proposed in the preliminary version, the Tribunal will deal with them in more detail. The Tribunal notes that Belgium, in its Reply (p. 35, para. 38), states that, in referring to this document, Belgium does not imply any acceptance of the contents of the document.

C. The Measures Envisaged in the Preliminary Version of the Draft Planning Procedure Order

183. The Tribunal observes that the preliminary version of the Draft Planning Procedure Order is based on the assumption by the Netherlands that it is Belgium's desire to reactivate the Iron Rhine railway in such a way that it can be used by 43 trains (combined total for both directions per working day) in 2020 (NR, p. 14, para. 54). The Tribunal notes that Belgium, in its pleadings, has not contested this assumption.

184. The route of the Iron Rhine railway over Netherlands territory is divided into four track segments (A to D, from west to east). Section 3 of the preliminary version of the Draft Planning Procedure Order describes the track segments in the following way (BR, pp. 35–38, para. 40):

(1)   Track segment A covers the municipalities of Cranendonck and Weert, and lies on the existing, historic track of the Iron Rhine railway between the Belgian border near Budel and the eastern limit of Weert. The preliminary version of the Draft Planning Procedure Order makes a further distinction between two parts of Track segment A. The first part is located between the Belgian-Netherlands border and the junction with the railway line Eindhoven-Weert, and is also referred to as A1. This part crosses the nature area "Weerter- en Budelerbergen." It is described as follows:

> The railway line is and remains single track between the Belgian-Dutch border and the junction with the railway line Eindhoven-Weert. This railway is not electrified. Currently, the line is used by two freight trains per 24 hours, the two directions combined. Reactivating the Iron Rhine involves an intensification of the railway traffic up to 45 freight trains per 24 hours, both directions combined.
> As far as norm setting is concerned, this is a matter of an existing situation. For security on crossings use is made of the national average collision risk. The collision risk on the track must not go beyond the national average as a consequence of reactivation.

The second part of Track segment A is located east of the junction with the railway line Eindhoven-Weert, and is also referred to as A2. It is described as follows:

> East of the junction the existing railway is and remains double track and electrified. Currently the line is used by 104 trains per 24 hours, the two directions combined, 92 of which are passenger trains. This concerns both freight and passenger trains. In 2020, the 43 "Iron Rhine" trains will be added thereto. Including the autonomous development of railway transports, the line will then be used according to the prognosis by 199 trains per 24 hours, the two directions combined, 152 of which are passenger trains. The norm setting is also based on an existing situation. With respect to collision risks, this means that application is made of the stand-still principle. The incident risk will thus remain below the national average.

(2) Track segment B covers the municipalities of Nederweert, Heythuysen and Haelen. It passes next to the nature area "Leudal" and is described as follows:

> This part of the railway lies on the track, which already exists and is in use, between Weert and the eastern accesses to the bridges over the Maas near Roermond. The track is, like track A2, part of the railway line leading from Eindhoven via Weert to Roermond. Track B is and remains double track and electrified. The track is used by 92 trains per 24 hours in both directions combined. This concerns both freight and passenger trains.
> The norm setting is the same as for track segment A2, which is intensification of the existing train traffic up to 199 trains per 24 hours in both directions combined.

(3) Track segment C covers the municipalities of Roermond and Swalmen and is described as follows:

> For this track a new railway will be realised, which joins eastern of the Maas river near Roermond. The track consists of a loop north and east of Roermond. Near Herkenbosch it joins the part of the historic track which is out of use and which leads from the station of Roermond to the German border near Vlodrop. The new railway will insofar as possible be bound up with the National Road 73. The railway is single track and not electrified. The norm setting for this part of the track is based on the fact that a new situation is created locally.

(4) Track segment D covers the municipality of Roerdalen and is described as follows:

> This part of the track lies on the historical track, which is out of use since 1991. Track D lies between the Asenrayerweg and the German-Dutch border near Vlodrop. The track lies in the nature area De Meinweg. For the purpose of reactivation of the Iron Rhine, the track in De Meinweg will be built in part in a tunnel and in part in an embankment. This track is currently out of use. The norm setting for track D is based on the creation of a new situation as a consequence of the reactivation of the Iron Rhine.

185. For these different track segments the preliminary version of the Draft Planning Procedure Order describes in detail all the measures to be taken for the long-term reactivation of the Iron Rhine railway. The main sources of disagreement between the Parties are the measures for noise abatement and nature protection. The Tribunal will next focus on these measures.

1. Noise abatement measures for dwellings and similar objects

186. For the entire track, significant measures are envisaged in order to protect the inhabitants of the areas close to the railway from the increasing noise levels to be produced by the projected future use of the Iron Rhine railway. These measures, required by the Noise Abatement Act, further envisage compensated expropriation of dwellings where noise abatement measures will be insufficient to stay below the maximum exemption level.

187. According to Belgium, the Netherlands does not apply the maximum exemption level that is provided for by the Noise Abatement Act but applies the stricter preferential level. Application of the maximum exemption level would result in less extensive measures to be required. On this issue, and returning also to the financial implications thereof, Belgium concludes that

> it would be contrary to the principle of good faith and the principle of reasonableness to submit the reactivation of the Iron Rhine to the taking of noise abatement measures as contemplated in the Concept [the preliminary version of the Draft Planning Procedure Order] which are not necessary so as to reach the maximal exemption limit of 70 dB(A) (or 73 dB(A)), if such abatement measures are to be financed by Belgium or in any other way render the exercise of Belgium's rights on the Iron Rhine more difficult.

In Belgium's view, this would amount to an unnecessary interference with its right of transit (BR, p. 44–46, paras. 48–50).

188. The Netherlands agrees that the preliminary version of the Draft Planning Procedure Order applies the preferential level but argues that the noise abatement legislation, including the preferential level criteria, is applied in the same way as in other cases of railways, and sees no reason to deviate from the general policy to the disadvantage of the interested parties involved. In this context, the Netherlands additionally invokes the principles of sound administration on which the proposed measures are also based (NR, pp. 18–19, paras. 74–78).

2.   **Tunnel Meinweg**

189. The Meinweg is an area of approximately 1,600 hectares located adjacent to the eastern part of track segment D. On 18 February 1994 the Province of Limburg designated the area as a "Silent Area." By Ministerial Decree of 20 May 1994 the Meinweg was designated as a special protection area under Article 4, paragraph 1 of the Birds Directive. On 1 June 1995 the area was designated a national park by the Minister of Agriculture, Nature Management and Fisheries. On 18 February 2003 the Netherlands Government included the Meinweg on the proposed list of specially protected areas under the Habitats Directive. This proposal was accepted by the European Commission in July 2003. Belgium states that it was not consulted before any of these designations. The Netherlands says there was no requirement for it to consult.

190. According to Belgium, the Netherlands had the obligation to prevent any designations not flowing from its obligations under the EC Directives that would result in the requirement to take additional measures for noise abatement and nature protection.

191. For the passage of the Iron Rhine railway through the historic track in the Meinweg area the preliminary version of the Draft Planning Procedure Order envisages the construction of a tunnel of 6.5 kilometres in length with an aqueduct, and an embankment.

192. According to the Netherlands, these measures are a consequence of the designation of the Meinweg as a national park and as a "Silent Area," and not as a consequence of its designation under the EC Directives which would only require the building of noise barriers. EC law allows the Netherlands to apply stricter standards for environmental protection than those required by the relevant EC Directives. The designation of the area as a national park and "Silent Area" flow from the application of national legislation and policy, which the Netherlands has stated employ objective criteria. The measures envisaged are the result of careful studies and consideration of alternative options under the applicable decision-making procedures, including an EIA (NCM, p. 49, para. 3.3.5.6; NR, p. 23, paras. 93 ff).

119

193. Belgium does not in principle dispute that the Netherlands could make these designations, but disagrees as to the financial consequences for the Parties.

3. Weerter- en Budelerbergen

194. The Weerter- en Budelerbergen are a nature area located in Track segment A1. This area was designated as a special protection area under the Birds Directive on 24 March 2000 (both Parties assert this, but Belgium's Exhibit 77 to its Memorial – The Netherlands, Ministerial Decree of 24 March 2000 – does not include this area), and as a "Silent Area" by the province of Limburg on 18 February 1994 (the same date as the Meinweg), and apparently also by the province of Noord-Brabant.

195. The preliminary version of the Draft Planning Procedure Order envisages a number of measures for the area of the Weerter- en Budelerbergen. These involve the building of noise barriers, a partial deepening of the track, and the building of an ecoduct. In addition, loss of habitat area is to be compensated for.

196. According to the Netherlands, these measures flow from the application of its national legislation and policy; they are a consequence of the designation by it of the area as a "Silent Area" and as a specially protected area under the Birds Directive.

197. That this is so is not contested by Belgium, but it disagrees as to the financial consequences for the Parties.

4. Loop around Roermond

198. The proposed Track segment C involves a rerouting of the historic track of the Iron Rhine railway through the town of Roermond to a new track to the east and north of the town. This is the preferred option of the Netherlands Government for this part of the track. Although it would be possible to keep the historic track, under the current legislative requirements concerning safety and noise abatement, significant additional measures would be required for this purpose. Such measures would not be necessary in the case of a rerouted track staying beyond the town centre. Furthermore, in view of further developing norms on the safety of transport of dangerous goods, preventing the

passing through the town of Roermond of large numbers of freight trains in the future, is considered preferable by the Netherlands (NCM, pp. 28–29, para. 2.13.2).

199. Belgium insists that no rerouting deviating from the historic route may be decided upon by the Netherlands without the agreement of Belgium (BR, p. 69, para. 70).

200. The Netherlands essentially agrees with this position. Further, it is willing to pay the extra costs caused by the rerouting (NR, p. 21, para. 85).

201. The Tribunal concludes that the Parties concur that any decision by the Netherlands on the rerouting of the Iron Rhine railway would require the agreement of Belgium. It also notes that such agreement seems in principle to be forthcoming.

D. Conclusions

202. With respect to the measures envisaged by the Netherlands discussed above, Belgium argues that the Netherlands is under an obligation to apply its legislation in the way least unfavourable for Belgium; in not doing so the Netherlands would be acting contrary to the principles of reasonableness and good faith. Belgium regards some of the measures envisaged as an unnecessary interference with its transit right. They would constitute a breach by the Netherlands of its obligations towards Belgium (BR, pp. 32–33, 46, and 68–71, paras. 37, 50, and 70).

203. The Netherlands argues that it treats the reactivation of the Iron Rhine railway in the same way as other railways in the Netherlands. It accepts Belgium's right to reactivation, but it sees no reason why the Iron Rhine railway should be treated more favourably than regular Netherlands railways. In requiring the envisaged measures for the reactivation, the Netherlands claims that it is acting reasonably and in good faith. Its actions do not constitute an abuse of right, and are not arbitrary or discriminatory. In fact, it asserts that its legislative requirements are applied in the most favourable way for Belgium (NR, pp. 40–42, paras. 158–170).

204. In the view of the Tribunal, the obligations of the Netherlands under Article XII of the 1839 Treaty of Separation do not require it to apply its national legislation and policy

with respect to the reactivation of the Iron Rhine railway in a more favourable way than with respect to other railways in the Netherlands, unless such non-discriminatory application would amount to a denial of Belgium's transit right or render the exercise of that right unreasonably difficult.

205. The Tribunal concludes that the measures as such as presently envisaged by the Netherlands cannot be regarded as amounting to a denial of Belgium's transit right or render the exercise of the right unreasonably difficult. The related but distinct question as to whether the laying of the costs for any of these measures on Belgium would amount to a denial of Belgium's transit right or render the exercise of the right unreasonably difficult will be addressed by the Tribunal in Chapter VI.

206. Since the Netherlands insists that the envisaged measures flow exclusively from the application of its national legislation, and Belgium does not say otherwise, the Tribunal has not found it necessary to address any issue of constraints posed by EC law (*see* Chapter III above).

CHAPTER VI – ALLOCATION OF COSTS

207. The Tribunal will now turn to the issue of the allocation of costs which forms the subject-matter of the third Question put jointly by the Parties to the Tribunal. It is formulated in the following terms:

> In the light of the answers to the previous questions, to what extent should the cost items and financial risks associated with the use, restoration, adaptation and modernisation of the historical route of the Iron Rhine on Dutch territory be borne by Belgium or by the Netherlands? Is Belgium obliged to fund investments over and above those that are necessary for the functionality of the historical route of the railway line?

208. The Tribunal notes that under the Arbitration Agreement it is requested to render its decision on the basis of international law, including European law if necessary. It is not authorized to decide these matters *ex aequo et bono*. The introductory words of the third Question clearly indicate that the Tribunal's decision on the cost allocation shall be rendered in the light of the Tribunal's answers to the two previous Questions. The ensuing consideration by the Tribunal of the question of costs is thus based upon the reasoning in the previous chapters.

209. The Tribunal observes that the 1839 Treaty of Separation does not refer to "financial risks." The Parties use that term in the Questions they jointly put to the Tribunal, without specifying the meaning they give to it, nor in their pleadings does either Party explain its understanding of the term. The Tribunal understands that in the context of infrastructure projects such term refers to the covering of financial costs over and above those budgeted for the project, due to different factors, such as higher than projected inflation, underestimation of the costs, unforeseen events, and increases in the costs of materials used and of labour costs. The Tribunal notes that, whatever position on the question of allocation of risks and costs, respectively, the Parties may have taken from time to time in negotiations, the Parties, in their pleadings, have not made any distinction between the costs of the reactivation and financial risks associated with it, nor have they suggested that the financial risks should be borne by a Party other than that which would bear the costs themselves. The Tribunal is of the view that the financial risks are not to be severed from the costs. Thus, the Party which bears the

costs will also have to bear the financial risks, and, when the Tribunal refers in this chapter to the costs, it should be understood as including the financial risks as well.

A.   Arguments of the Parties

210. The Tribunal further notes that both Parties argue that the cost allocation falls within the ambit of the conventional regime for the Iron Rhine railway. They differ, however, in the identification of the relevant provisions and in their interpretation.

211. Article XII of the 1839 Treaty of Separation provides that the "agreed works" would be executed "at the expense of Belgium, all without any burden to Holland."

212. Belgium, however, contends that its obligation to bear expenses as provided in Article XII related to the *construction* of a railway on Netherlands territory as a prolongation of a new railway on Belgian territory, but not to the exercise of Belgium's right of transit (BR, p. 98, para. 104). Belgium refers to Article XI of the 1839 Treaty of Separation and what it terms the *"travaux préparatoires"* to support its contention that its obligation to bear expenses relates to the construction of a new railway prolonged on Netherlands territory, but not to the exercise of its right of passage (BR, pp. 99–100, para. 105). The exercise of the right of passage is, according to Belgium, subject only to moderate toll fees, to be paid by the users of the Iron Rhine railway, for the financing of its maintenance (BR, p. 99, para. 105).

213. Belgium, as a consequence of its view that its present request for reactivation does not amount to a request for a "new road" within the meaning of Article XII of the 1839 Treaty of Separation, maintains that it has no obligation to bear the costs and financial risks associated with the reactivation of the Iron Rhine. Belgium thus argues that in application of the conventional regime for the Iron Rhine all cost items and financial risks associated with the use, restoration, adaptation and modernisation of the historic route of the Iron Rhine railway on Netherlands territory shall be borne by the Netherlands and not by Belgium (BM, p. 101, para. 86; BR, pp. 103 ff and p. 127, paras. 110 ff and Submission on Question No. 3).

214. Belgium also contends that the Netherlands has rendered impossible the use of the railway by dismantling part of its infrastructure and making it unfit for use, by failing to provide for maintenance, and by deciding to interrupt works aimed at restoring the historic route to a standard necessary for temporary use. Thus, according to Belgium, the Netherlands violated Belgium's right to use the historic route of the Iron Rhine railway as well as the principle of due diligence. Belgium concludes that consequently the costs and financial risks related to the restoration of the historic route, which would not have arisen had the Netherlands not violated its obligations, shall be borne by the Netherlands (BM, p. 109, para. 96). Were the Tribunal to reject Belgium's submissions that all costs and financial risks shall be borne by the Netherlands, then Belgium contends, by way of a subsidiary argument ("in subsidiary order"), that it would still have no obligation to bear those costs and financial risks caused by the Netherlands' violation of its obligation towards Belgium. According to Belgium that would be a consequence of the obligation to make reparation for the prejudice caused by a violation of international law, as well as an application of the principle that no one shall benefit from his illegal acts (*nullus commodum capere de sua injuria propria*) (BM, p. 107, para. 95).

215. Belgium insists that all costs relating to reactivation, including environmental protection, are for the Netherlands. However, as a "subsidiary" argument, it maintains, with respect to the long-term use of the historic route of the Iron Rhine railway, that the Netherlands may not insist on Belgium paying for the following: (1) measures related to tracks in present or future use for Netherlands railway transport; (2) measures necessary to meet objectives over and above Netherlands legislative requirements; (3) a loop around Roermond; and (4) a tunnel in the Meinweg and similar nature protection structures and compensatory measures there and elsewhere along the route. Belgium concludes that, if the Netherlands imposes these requirements, the Netherlands will have the obligation to finance the measures necessary so as to ensure the exercise of Belgium's right of transit (BR, pp. 118–119, para. 131).

216. The Netherlands contends that Belgium is claiming the right of transit but is not prepared to respect the conditions and obligations inextricably linked to that right under Article XII of the 1839 Treaty of Separation (NCM, p. 43, para. 3.3.4.4).

217. The Netherlands further argues that the Belgian demand for reactivation of the Iron Rhine railway amounts to a request within the meaning of Article XII of the 1839 Treaty of Separation for the extension of a railway originating in Belgium into and over Netherlands territory. In the view of the Netherlands, this railway is new to the extent that a very considerable adaptation and modernisation is necessary in order to achieve the desired use (NCM, p. 43, para. 3.3.4.5). Consequently, the Netherlands, referring to Article XII, and in particular to the words "entirely at the cost and expense of Belgium" and "at the expense of Belgium, all without any burden to Holland, and without prejudice to the exclusive rights of sovereignty over the territory which would be crossed by the road or canal in question," maintains that the costs referred to in Article XII should be borne in full by Belgium (NCM, p. 56, para. 3.3.8.1).

218. The Netherlands thus interprets Article XII of the 1839 Treaty of Separation as requiring Belgium to bear the full costs incurred in connection with its request for adaptation and modernisation of the existing infrastructure, which is at present not suitable for the use desired by Belgium (NCM, p. 57, para. 3.3.8.2).

B. Consideration by the Tribunal

219. That the Parties should advance these arguments is understandable. But each of their positions finds its origins in divergent readings of Article XII of the 1839 Treaty of Separation, neither of which can be sustained. The Tribunal has explained above (*see* paragraphs 82–84) that although Article XII was directed towards the construction of, and regime for, the Iron Rhine, the right of transit there provided for also covers the reactivation of the track and its use through time. The specific financial provisions of Article XII were formulated in respect of the construction of a new road, canal or track. The real questions, so far as allocation of costs is concerned, are the following: what elements of Article XII relating to costs are applicable to a reactivation that is not a construction of a new railway but is nonetheless within the ambit of Article XII? And what other elements within Article XII, interpreted in accordance with the legal principles explained in Chapter II above, may illuminate the allocation of costs for the reactivation that Belgium seeks and is entitled to?

220. The Tribunal finds itself in the presence of three points of departure for its analysis of these questions. The first is that, in matters other than those specifically provided for in relation to the construction of a new line, the Netherlands retains its rights of sovereignty. The second is that a major adaptation and modernisation of an existing railway must today include necessary environmental protection measures as an integral component of such a project. It has been shown in paragraphs 58 and 59 that rules of international law on protection of the environment are applicable law between the Parties in the interpretation of the conventional regime for the Iron Rhine railway. As a third point, the Tribunal will remain mindful that the financial burdens associated with the reactivation must not fall in such a way as effectively to prevent or render unreasonably difficult the exercise of Belgium's right of transit under Article XII of the 1839 Treaty of Separation. These elements, taken together, suggest that the costs are not to be borne solely by Belgium as if it were "a new road"; but neither are they to be borne solely by the Netherlands. The financial obligations of the Parties must therefore be subjected to careful balancing. Such balancing requires a variety of factors to be taken into account. That the Parties did not consider such a balancing unreasonable is demonstrated by their offers, during the negotiations, to contribute to the costs of the reactivation: the Netherlands offered, in October 2001, to pay 25% (€140 million) of the then estimated costs (NR, p. 15, para. 60), with an additional contribution of €40 million if Belgium waived temporary use of the line (NR, p. 16, para. 65), and Belgium was willing to contribute €100 million (BM, pp. 66–67, para. 48).

221. The Tribunal considers that Belgium is in principle entitled to exercise its right of transit in a way which corresponds to its current economic needs. At the same time, the concern of the Netherlands for its environment and the impact thereon of the intended, much more intensive, use of the railway line is to be viewed as legitimate. Such exercise of Belgium's right of transit and the Netherlands' legitimate environmental concerns are to be, as far as possible, reconciled. The Tribunal notes that such a reconciliation of rights echoes the balancing of interests reflected in Article XII of the 1839 Treaty of Separation. The Tribunal has found that the restoration and upgrading of the line as requested by Belgium falls to be analysed by reference of Article XII of the 1839 Treaty of Separation – not because it amounts to a "new line" (the Netherlands' view) but rather because the object and purpose of the Treaty suggests an interpretation that would include within the ambit of the balance there struck new needs and developments

relating to operation and capacity (*see* paragraph 84 above). As the Tribunal has already observed above (*see* paragraph 59), economic development is to be reconciled with the protection of the environment, and, in so doing, new norms have to be taken into consideration, including when activities begun in the past are now expanded and upgraded.

222. The use of the Iron Rhine railway started some 120 years ago and it is now envisaged and requested by Belgium at a substantially increased and intensified level. Such new use is susceptible of having an adverse impact on the environment and causing harm to it. Today, in international environmental law, a growing emphasis is being put on the duty of prevention. Much of international environmental law has been formulated by reference to the impact that activities in one territory may have on the territory of another. The International Court of Justice expressed the view that "[t]he existence of the general obligation of States to ensure that activities within their jurisdiction and control respect the environment of other States or of areas beyond national control is now part of the corpus of international law relating to the environment" (*Legality of the Threat or Use of Nuclear Weapons, Advisory Opinion, I.C.J. Reports 1996 (I)*, p. 226 at pp. 241–242, para. 29).

223. Applying the principles of international environmental law, the Tribunal observes that it is faced, in the instant case, not with a situation of a transboundary effect of the economic activity in the territory of one state on the territory of another state, but with the effect of the exercise of a treaty-guaranteed right of one state in the territory of another state and a possible impact of such exercise on the territory of the latter state. The Tribunal is of the view that, by analogy, where a state exercises a right under international law within the territory of another state, considerations of environmental protection also apply. The exercise of Belgium's right of transit, as it has formulated its request, thus may well necessitate measures by the Netherlands to protect the environment to which Belgium will have to contribute as an integral element of its request. The reactivation of the Iron Rhine railway cannot be viewed in isolation from the environmental protection measures necessitated by the intended use of the railway line. These measures are to be fully integrated into the project and its costs.

224. The Tribunal is not asked to, nor could it, determine which particular measures are to be taken. What the Tribunal is asked to do is to pronounce on the allocation of costs in respect of such measures as are to be specified. The Tribunal notes that it was the intention under the March 2000 MoU that these measures would be laid down in a treaty. The Tribunal will not specify in monetary terms the allocation of costs but will, on the basis of the law applicable to this issue, indicate relevant criteria and principles that the Parties should apply to this question.

225. The Tribunal starts by recalling that it is for the Netherlands at its expense to bring the Iron Rhine railway line back to the state in 1991 (*see* paragraphs 76 and 89 above). This is the case for the entire historic line. This conclusion is not dependent upon any violation by the Netherlands as regards maintenance of the line since the early 1990s. The Tribunal further recalls that the Netherlands recognizes that it will be responsible for the maintenance of a reactivated line (NR, p. 34, para. 136).

226. The Belgian obligation to fund the environmental element of the overall costs of the reactivation is integral to its exercise of its right of transit. At the same time, an interpretation, based on reasonableness, of the financial provisions of Article XII also requires that the Netherlands' use of parts of the line be acknowledged. On those parts of the line, both expenditures attributable to autonomous development, and benefits to the Netherlands may be envisaged. This has particular relevance where the line is so significantly adapted and modernised. On those parts of the line where both Iron Rhine trains and Netherlands trains will pass, Belgium will only be obliged to fund the expenditures associated with the measures attributable to the use of the line by Iron Rhine trains. The Netherlands will have to contribute to the total cost to the extent that those measures represent particular, quantifiable benefits to the Netherlands.

227. The application of these principles will depend upon the information given to the Tribunal as regards the particular segments of the line. These segments and their planned future use are described in paragraph 184 above. Relevant information was provided by the Parties, with no distinction being made by them between freight trains and passenger trains as far as the measures necessitated by their use is concerned.

228. Segment A is divided into two parts. The first part between the Belgian-Netherlands border and the junction with the railway line Eindhoven-Weert (referred to also as segment A1) (*see* paragraph 184 above) is currently used by just two trains per 24-hour period. These are local trains and are not to be viewed as trains being used in the exercise of the transit right of Belgium over the Iron Rhine. The costs of work needed for the reactivation (that is, the use, restoration, adaptation and modernisation, including necessary environmental protection measures) of this part of the track are, in the view of the Tribunal, due to the Belgian request to allow in the future up to 43 freight trains in addition per 24-hour period. Accordingly, the Tribunal concludes that the costs for the reactivation of this part of segment A are to be borne by Belgium.

229. The second part of segment A (also referred to as segment A2) (*see* paragraph 184 above) is located east of the junction with the railway line Eindhoven-Weert up to the municipality of Nederweert. Currently, the line is used by 104 trains per 24-hour period. It is envisaged in the preliminary version of the Draft Planning Procedure Order that in 2020 it will be used by 199 trains including the 43 Iron Rhine trains. It cannot be ruled out that the development of the Netherlands railway transport ("autonomous development") envisaged for 2020 amounting to the addition of 52 trains to the current level of use by 104 trains per 24-hour period would also entail a certain expenditure. Therefore, in the view of the Tribunal, the costs for the reactivation of this segment A2 shall be apportioned between the Parties: the Belgian obligation to fund the costs associated with the reactivation is to be diminished by a financial factor that includes the costs which would otherwise have been required for the autonomous development had the Iron Rhine not been reactivated, so far as both track and environmental factors are concerned. The Tribunal here refers to and bases itself upon the envisaged autonomous development which the Netherlands has itself taken into account when preparing the preliminary version of the Draft Planning Procedure Order.

230. While the overall financial obligation remains that of Belgium, the Tribunal is further of the view that an element that may represent particular, quantifiable benefits to the Netherlands – resulting from, in particular, improved road traffic circulation, enhanced road safety, reduced noise, and potential beyond the currently anticipated development for additional use of the track by Netherlands trains – are also to be taken into account in the apportioning of costs between the Parties. In fact, during the trilateral negotiations

with Belgium and Germany in early 1999, the Netherlands advocated that the distribution of the benefits (both from the perspective of business economics and socio-economics) should be a point of departure for the distribution of the costs of the reactivation between the Parties (BM, Exhibit 78, Flemish-Dutch Administrative Steering Group, Draft Report "Iron Rhine" for the Ministers of Transport of Belgium, the Netherlands and Germany, p. 25).

231. Segment B (*see* paragraph 184 above) covers the line between the municipalities of Nederweert and Haelen. The current and the planned use of this segment is similar to the segment A2, save that the current use is 92 trains per 24-hour period, rather than 104 trains per 24-hour period (notwithstanding that by 2020 the comparable figure of 199 trains per 24-hour period is envisaged). The Tribunal is therefore of the view that the costs of the reactivation of the railway line shall also be apportioned between the Parties according to the principle set out in paragraphs 229 and 230 above.

232. Segment C (*see* paragraph 184 above) covers the municipalities of Swalmen and Roermond. From the material before it, the Tribunal understands that this segment will be used solely for the railway connection between Belgium and Germany (BR, Exhibit No. 10, as corrected, Preliminary Version 1.4 of the Draft Planning Procedure Order, p. 98, para. 6.1 ff). The track is envisaged as a loop north and east of Roermond proposed by the Netherlands which, during the negotiations, expressed its willingness to pay the extra costs for a such diversion around Roermond. The loop constitutes a deviation from the route agreed on in Article IV of the Iron Rhine Treaty. Such a deviation cannot be executed without the consent of Belgium, *i.e.,* it must be done by agreement, thus modifying the agreed historic route. Belgium is therefore entitled to request that the Netherlands undertake to bear the extra financial costs of such a deviation over and above those which would otherwise be involved had the historic route through Roermond been adapted and modernised. On the other hand, if the Netherlands is willing to bear these extra costs, Belgium cannot reasonably withhold its consent to a deviation. If a loop around Roermond is agreed, then the costs would be distributed between the Parties in the following manner: Belgium would be obliged to fund the amount which would have been required for the reactivation of the historic route in its current location, while the Netherlands would be obliged to bear costs incurred above that amount due to the relocation of the line to the north and east of Roermond.

233. Segment D (*see* paragraph 184 above) runs through the municipality of Roerdalen. It lies between the Asenrayerweg and the German-Netherlands border. The railway line in this segment has been out of use since 1991 and in the future, as the Tribunal understands, will be used solely for the connection between Belgium and Germany (BR, Exhibit No. 10, as corrected, Preliminary Version 1.4 of the Draft Planning Procedure Order, p. 117, para. 7.1 ff). The reactivation is required because of the Belgian request. Belgium will, for the reasons given above, have to bear the cost of the reactivation of the track.

234. Specifically, Belgium will have to bear costs for noise barriers to be built near dwellings and compensatory conservation measures in this segment. The Tribunal is aware that the major cost factor not only in this segment but in relation to the whole project of the reactivation of the Iron Rhine is attributable to the envisaged tunnel in the Meinweg. Belgium contended that the costs of various environmental measures, in particular of the tunnel in the Meinweg, were "too costly" (BM, p. 82, para. 66), "highly expensive" (BM, p. 88, para. 74), and even "prohibitive" (BM, p. 81, para. 66). The construction of such a tunnel is envisaged in light of the fact that the track lies in the Meinweg area designated as a national park by the Netherlands Minister of Agriculture, Nature Management and Fisheries on 1 June 1995 and as a "Silent Area" by the Province of Limburg. When the Netherlands took that decision it already knew that the historic route crossed that area and that Belgium, despite not exercising since 1991 its right of transit, had reserved its right to the use of the line in the future. The Tribunal is of the view that the Netherlands' decision to declare the Meinweg a national park in an area over which Belgium was entitled under treaty to a right of transit, though a permitted act of Netherlands' sovereignty, cannot remain without financial consequence for the Netherlands. On the other hand, the Belgian Government reserved its right only in abstract terms, and did not specify the parameters of its future use of the line before the decisions of the Netherlands were taken. The construction of the tunnel is required not only in view of the intensive use envisaged by Belgium, of which nevertheless the Netherlands was not fully informed in a timely fashion, but also arises out of the Netherlands' decision to establish a national park in the area which was already crossed by the historic route. The Tribunal considers that both Parties contributed to the occurrence of the situation which now requires much more costly measures. The

Tribunal is therefore of the view that the costs for the tunnel in the Meinweg are to be apportioned equally between the Parties.

235. The Tribunal has in paragraphs 228–234 identified the principles of apportionment of costs in the various segments that it sees as flowing from Article XII of the 1839 Treaty of Separation, taking into account the applicable provisions of international law. The Tribunal has not been asked to calculate precisely the overall costs of reactivation, the costs of autonomous development, and the benefits of the reactivated Iron Rhine railway to the Netherlands. Moreover, it understands that the Draft Planning Procedure Order is of a preliminary character and its content may be subject to further changes. Nor is it the task of this Tribunal to investigate questions of considerable scientific complexity as to which measures will be sufficient to achieve compliance with the required levels of environmental protection. These issues are appropriately left to technical experts. To that effect, the Tribunal recommends that the Parties promptly, and in any case not later than 4 months from the date of this Award, put into effect the conditions necessary for a committee of independent experts to be set up within the same time frame, unless the Parties agree otherwise, to engage in the task of determining:

1. the costs of the reactivation of the Iron Rhine railway;

2. the costs of the autonomous development; and

3. the particular, quantifiable benefits to the Netherlands – in financial terms – of the reactivation resulting from, in particular, improved road traffic circulation, enhanced road safety, reduced noise and the potential beyond currently anticipated autonomous development for additional use of the track by Netherlands trains.

This committee of independent experts should conclude its findings as soon as possible, and in any case not later than 6 months from the date of its establishment.

The findings of this committee of independent experts are to be used by the Parties in determining their respective share for the costs and risks associated with the upgrading of the Iron Rhine railway in segments A2 and B. The Netherlands will have to contribute to the costs of and financial risks associated with the reactivation of the Iron Rhine in segments A2 and B in the amount which comprises the costs of the autonomous development (point 2 above) and the financial equivalent of the benefits for it (point 3), as determined by the committee of independent experts. Belgium will have

133

to bear all the remaining costs of and financial risks associated with the reactivation of the Iron Rhine in segments A2 and B.

236. The Tribunal thus concludes that the costs and financial risks associated with the long-term use of the Iron Rhine railway are to be borne by the Parties in the following way:

1. Belgium alone will be obliged to bear the costs and financial risks of the reactivation of segment A1 and segment D with the exception of the tunnel in the Meinweg;

2. Belgium and the Netherlands will have to share the costs and financial risks of the reactivation of segments A2, B, C and the Meinweg tunnel in segment D in accordance with the formulas specified in paragraphs 229–231 (for segments A2 and B), 232 (for segment C) and 234 (for the Meinweg tunnel).

237. Within the Parties' pleadings there was debate, not only about the separation of temporary use from agreement on long-term use, but also how long any temporary use might last, whether it could be interrupted by work for the long-term reactivation, and the financing of such temporary use. In the March 2000 MoU, the Parties had agreed that Belgium would pay the costs for such temporary use. However, Belgium has since claimed that this undertaking has lapsed, as no timely agreement has been reached on long-term use. The Tribunal notes that the financing of temporary use is not, in terms, among the formal Questions put to it. Nor has the Tribunal understood the Questions it is asked concerning the "use, restoration, adaptation and modernization of the historic route" as being related to the above issues regarding temporary use.

AWARD OF THE ARBITRAL TRIBUNAL

CHAPTER VII – REPLIES OF THE TRIBUNAL TO THE QUESTIONS PUT BY THE PARTIES

A.   Question 1

238. The first specific Question for the Arbitral Tribunal posed in the Arbitration Agreement reads as follows:

> To what extent is Dutch legislation and the decision-making power based thereon in respect of the use, restoration, adaptation and modernisation of railway lines on Dutch territory applicable, in the same way, to the use, restoration, adaptation and modernisation of the historical route of the Iron Rhine on Dutch territory?

239. The Tribunal responds as follows:

(a)   The Tribunal understands the phrase "in the same way" to refer to an application of Dutch legislation, and the decision-making power based thereon, in respect of the use, restoration, adaptation and modernisation of the historic route of the Iron Rhine as would be the case in respect of the use, restoration, adaptation and modernisation of any other railway on Dutch territory.[20]

(b)   Dutch legislation and the decision-making power based thereon in respect of the use, restoration, adaptation and modernisation of railway lines on Dutch territory are applicable in the same way to the use, restoration, adaptation and modernisation of the historic route of the Iron Rhine on Dutch territory to the extent specified in subparagraphs (c) and (d) following.

(c)   Such application of Dutch legislation and the decision-making power based thereon may not conflict with the treaty rights granted to Belgium, or the rights and obligations of the Parties under general international law, or constraints imposed by EU law (*see* paragraph 56). Thus, the application of Dutch legislation and of the decision-making power based thereon may not amount to a denial of Belgium's right of transit (*see* paragraph 66), nor render unreasonably difficult the exercise by Belgium of its right of transit (*see* paragraph 163).

---

[20] The Tribunal has used the formal adjective "Netherlands" throughout this Award, but in answering the Questions it has used the adjective "Dutch," as this is the terminology there employed by the Parties.

(d)   The Tribunal further finds that:

(i)   Dutch legislation and the decision-making power based thereon may not be applied unilaterally to order a deviation from the historic route;

(ii)   the application of such Dutch legislation and the decision-making power based thereon is not dependent upon whether the relevant works are to be performed by the Netherlands itself or by Belgium;

(iii) Dutch legislation and the decision-making power based thereon may not unilaterally fix the level and rate of toll collection; and

(iv)   the measures resulting from the application of Dutch legislation and the decision-making power based thereon must allow for the reactivation of the Iron Rhine railway to be executed in accordance with "the same plan" (understood in the sense of functionality: *see* paragraph 67 above).

B.   Question 2

240. The second specific Question for the Arbitral Tribunal posed in the Arbitration Agreement reads as follows:

> To what extent does Belgium have the right to perform or commission work with a view to the use, restoration, adaptation and modernisation of the historical route of the Iron Rhine on Dutch territory, and to establish plans, specifications and procedures related to it according to Belgian law and the decision-making power based thereon? Should a distinction be drawn between the requirements, standards, plans, specifications and procedures related to, on the one hand, the functionality of the rail infrastructure in itself, and, on the other hand, the land use planning and the integration of the rail infrastructure, and, if so, what are the implications of this? Can the Netherlands unilaterally impose the building of underground and above-ground tunnels, diversions and the like, as well as the proposed associated construction and safety standards?

241. The Tribunal responds as follows:

(a)   Belgium has the right to make a plan to establish track specifications relevant for the functionality of the continuation of the line through the Netherlands. The works consequential upon the requested use, restoration, adaptation and modernisation of the historic route of the Iron Rhine are to be "agreed works." Belgium may not engage in works on Dutch territory that have not been agreed to. The Netherlands may not withhold its agreement to any proposal by Belgium should such withholding of agreement amount to a denial of Belgium's transit rights, or render unreasonably difficult the exercise by Belgium of its right of transit.

(b)   This is the case whether the Netherlands chooses itself to carry out the agreed works on its territory, or asks Belgium to do so.

(c)   The Tribunal observes, however, that the Netherlands may not unilaterally impose a diversion from the historic route.

(d)   The Netherlands was entitled to have designated areas along the historic route as protected areas as this did not *per se* constitute a limitation to Belgium's right of transit and the circumstances examined by the Tribunal do not suggest that there was a legal obligation to have consulted Belgium before doing so.

(e)   The Netherlands is in principle entitled unilaterally to impose the building of underground and above-ground tunnels "and the like." However, any such measures that it seeks to impose may not amount to a denial of Belgium's right of transit over the historic route, nor render unreasonably difficult the exercise by Belgium of its right of transit.

C.   Question 3

242. The third specific Question for the Arbitral Tribunal posed in the Arbitration Agreement reads as follows:

> In the light of the answers to the previous questions, to what extent should the cost items and financial risks associated with the use, restoration, adaptation and modernisation of the historical route of the Iron Rhine on Dutch territory be borne by Belgium or by the Netherlands? Is Belgium obliged to fund investments over and above those that are necessary for the functionality of the historical route of the railway line?

243. The Tribunal responds as follows, taking the second element of the Question first:

The Tribunal recalls that Belgian obligations other than those associated with functionality flow from the fact that the requested reactivation represents an economic development on the territory of the Netherlands, with which the prevention and minimalisation of environmental harm is to be integrated. The Tribunal has further found that the costs of environmental protection measures and other safety measures cannot be severed from the costs necessary for the functionality of the historic route.

The costs and financial risks associated with the right of transit on which the use, restoration, adaptation and modernisation ("reactivation") requested by Belgium is based are to reflect the balance between the Parties inherent in Article XII of the 1839 Treaty of Separation, interpreted by reference to the applicable principles of international law. Accordingly, Belgium's obligations to fund investments are not limited to those necessary for the functionality of the historic route of the railway line.

244. The Tribunal further finds that the cost items and financial risks associated with the reactivation of the historic route of the Iron Rhine on Dutch territory are:

   (a)   As to the sector between the Belgian-Netherlands border and the junction with the railway line Eindhoven-Weert ("segment A1"), to be borne by Belgium.

   (b)   As to the sector located east of the junction with the railway line Eindhoven-Weert up to the municipality of Nederweert ("segment A2"), to be apportioned between the Parties as follows: Belgium has the obligation to bear the costs and financial risks associated with the reactivation, such obligation being diminished by a financial factor that represents the costs which would have been required for the autonomous development envisaged for Dutch railway transport by 2020, were the Iron Rhine not to be reactivated. This remaining obligation of Belgium is further to be diminished by a financial factor representing particular, quantifiable benefits to the Netherlands (other than as regards autonomous development) resulting from, in particular: improved road traffic circulation, enhanced road safety, reduced noise, and potential beyond the autonomous development plans.

   (c)   As to the sector between the municipalities of Nederweert and Haelen ("segment B"), to be apportioned between the Parties as follows: Belgium has the obligation to bear the costs and financial risks associated with the reactivation, such obligation being diminished by a financial factor that represents the costs which would have been required for the autonomous development envisaged for Dutch railway transport by 2020, were the Iron Rhine not to be reactivated. This remaining obligation of Belgium is further to be diminished by a financial factor representing particular, quantifiable benefits to the Netherlands (other than as regards autonomous development) resulting from, in particular: improved road traffic circulation, enhanced road safety, reduced noise, and potential beyond the autonomous development plans.

(d)   As to the sector covering the municipalities of Swalmen and Roermond ("segment C"), to be apportioned between the Parties as follows: if a loop around Roermond is agreed, Belgium has the obligation to bear the costs and financial risks associated with the reactivation of the historic route had that reactivation been in the current location of the historic line; while the Netherlands has the obligation to bear the costs and risks over and above that sum due in respect of the relocated line agreed to the north and east of Roermond.

(e)   As to the sector running through the municipality of Roerdalen ("segment D"), to be apportioned between the Parties as follows: Belgium has the obligation to bear the costs and financial risks of reactivation of the railway line, which is to be used solely for the connection between Belgium and Germany, including the costs and financial risks associated with noise barriers to be built near dwellings and compensatory conservation measures in this segment. However, as regards any tunnel that may be built in the Meinweg area designated as a national park by the Netherlands Minister of Agriculture, Nature Management and Fisheries on 1 June 1995 and as a "Silent Area" by the Province of Limburg, the need for this being attributable to the past conduct of both of the Parties, they shall share the obligation to bear the costs and financial risks associated therewith in equal parts.

Done at the Peace Palace, The Hague, this **24** th day of **May**   2005,

Rosalyn Higgins
Judge Rosalyn Higgins
President

Schrans
Professor Guy Schrans

Bruno Simma
Judge Bruno Simma

Alfred Soons
Professor Alfred H.A. Soons

Peter Tomka
Judge Peter Tomka

THE IRON RHINE RAILWAY*

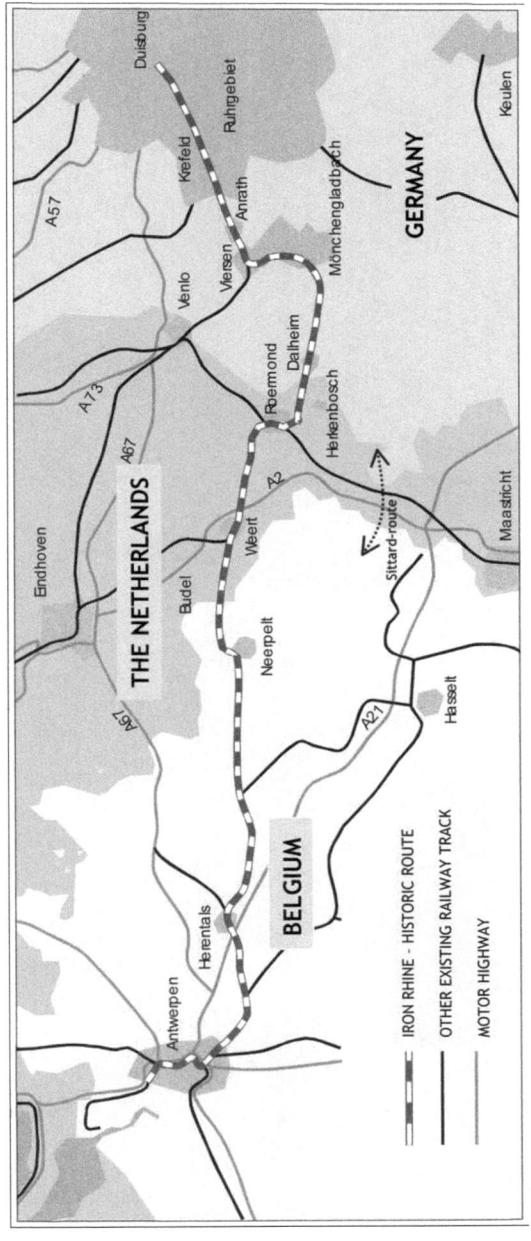

* For a full colour version of this map see page 313.

IN THE ARBITRATION
REGARDING THE IRON RHINE ("IJZEREN RIJN") RAILWAY

BETWEEN:

THE KINGDOM OF BELGIUM

- AND -

THE KINGDOM OF THE NETHERLANDS

———————————————

INTERPRETATION OF THE AWARD OF THE ARBITRAL TRIBUNAL

———————————————

The Arbitral Tribunal:

Judge Rosalyn Higgins, President

Professor Guy Schrans

Judge Bruno Simma

Professor Alfred H.A. Soons

Judge Peter Tomka

The Hague, 20 September 2005

INTERPRETATION OF THE AWARD OF THE ARBITRAL TRIBUNAL

1. On 25 July 2005, Belgium, pursuant to Article 23(1) of the Rules of Procedure for the Arbitration Regarding the Iron Rhine ("IJzeren Rijn") Railway between the Kingdom of Belgium and the Kingdom of the Netherlands, requested an Interpretation of the Award rendered by the Arbitral Tribunal on 24 May 2005.

2. The application of Belgium comprised three Requests, which were each accompanied by explanations and contentions, and by Exhibits.

3. By letter dated 25 July 2005, the Netherlands was invited to comment on Belgium's Requests. Comments of the Netherlands on each of the Belgian Requests for Interpretation of the Award were received by the Tribunal on 15 August 2005.

4. The Tribunal has examined carefully the contentions of each of the Parties. At the same time, it notes that it is for the Tribunal to interpret how the Award is to be understood, in the light of its own intentions at the time of rendering the Award. The ensuing paragraphs thus do not respond to the various observations and comments of the Parties but rather constitute an authoritative interpretation by the Tribunal of its own Award under Article 23(1) of the Rules of Procedure.

*   *   *

5. First Request:

    > Should the Award be interpreted as meaning that the Netherlands is under the obligation to bring at its own expenses the Iron Rhine railway back to a level allowing for a use of the Iron Rhine comparable to the one that prevailed during the regular albeit light use of the line prior to discontinuation of such use in 1991?

6. The Tribunal responds as follows.

7. At paragraph 76, the Award states: "In the view of the Tribunal, the Netherlands (as it accepts) is under an obligation to bring the Iron Rhine railway back to the levels

maintained during the regular (albeit light) use of the line prior to discontinuation of such use in 1991; but these maintenance and repair obligations do not cover the significant upgrading costs now involved in Belgium's request."

8. At paragraph 89, the Tribunal found that the Netherlands law which provides for the maintenance of railways by reference to the level of traffic occurring at a particular time did not violate Belgium's rights under Article XII of the 1839 Treaty of Separation. The Tribunal observed that "[t]his is the more so as the Netherlands fully accepts its obligation to restore, at its own expense, the maintenance and safety features of the line to the 1991 condition upon a Belgian demand for reactivation."

9. In the chapter of the Award on the allocation of costs (paragraph 225), the Tribunal recalled that "it is for the Netherlands at its expense to bring the Iron Rhine Railway line back to the state in 1991 (*see* paragraphs 76 and 89 above). This is the case for the entire historic line."

10. While this finding is not repeated in the Tribunal's Replies to the specific Questions put to it, at paragraphs 238–244 of the Award, the finding was a necessary step to the formulation of those Replies.

11. The Tribunal first observes that the reference to the Netherlands' obligation to restore the line to its 1991 condition is to be understood as a reference to financial obligations (rather than construction obligations) incumbent upon the Netherlands as regards outstanding maintenance in the event of a reactivation of the line. That is clear from the reference to cost allocation in each of the paragraphs of the Award cited above.

12. If a decision is taken by the Parties to reactivate the Iron Rhine Railway and if the Parties have agreed on the modalities of its future use, the allocation of costs for its reactivation (as specified in the Award in the Reply to Question 3) shall include as an element the obligation of the Netherlands to bear that portion of the costs that

represents the expenses that would have been incurred for outstanding maintenance of the track, including its safety features, to permit use comparable to the one that existed in 1991. The Tribunal recalled at paragraph 225 of its Award that the Netherlands had recognized that it would be "responsible for the maintenance of a reactivated line."

13.   The findings of the Tribunal cited above are to be understood as meaning that the financial obligations of the Netherlands (arising in the eventuality described in the preceding paragraph) would relate to safety standards (as an element of maintenance) as current Netherlands legislation would require and not as they may have been applicable in 1991.

*   *   *

14.   Second Request:

> Should the Award be interpreted as meaning that Belgium has no right to temporary use of the Iron Rhine line?
>
> Should the finding that the Netherlands' requirements may not amount to a denial of Belgium's right of transit nor render unreasonably difficult the exercise by Belgium of its right of transit (§§ 239(c) and 241(e)) be interpreted as applying to the issue of temporary use of the Iron Rhine, together with the Tribunal's findings on the principles and procedures laid down in the March 2000 MoU, contained in paragraphs 157 and 158 of the Award?

15.   Belgium in its Request states that "it is beyond doubt that the Tribunal decided not to uphold Belgium's submission" regarding immediate provisional driving and that "[i]t is also beyond doubt that the Tribunal did not rule on issues regarding temporary use." Belgium continues that: "However, this does not mean that the Award may be interpreted as meaning that Belgium has no right to temporary use, nor that temporary use is not governed by principles contained in the Award, notably the principles of reasonableness and good faith referred to in paragraphs 239(c), 241(e) and 157." Belgium seeks an interpretation as to these matters.

16. The Netherlands has observed to the Tribunal "that it believes that the decision-making on any actual use of the Iron Rhine is reserved to the Parties."

17. The Tribunal responds as follows.

18. The Award may not be interpreted as meaning that Belgium has no right to temporary use. Nor is the Award to be interpreted as containing any pronouncement by the Tribunal upon the circumstances in which any such right may be exercised.

19. At paragraph 237 of its Award, the Tribunal noted "that the financing of temporary use is not, in terms, among the formal Questions put to it." Accordingly, the Replies to the Questions do not include any findings concerning allocation of costs for any temporary use.

20. The Tribunal has made no findings as to the legal validity or correct interpretation of the Memorandum of Understanding signed on 28 March 2000 by the Belgian and the Netherlands Ministers of Transport, these not being asked of it in the Questions put. The Tribunal has confined itself to stating that "the principles and procedures laid down in the March 2000 MoU ... will prove useful guidelines to what the Parties have been prepared to consider as compatible with their rights under Article XII of the 1839 Treaty of Separation and the Iron Rhine Treaty" (Award, paragraph 157).

21. The Tribunal has found that the application of Dutch legislation and the decision-making powers based thereon may not amount to a denial of Belgium's right of transit over the historic route, nor render unreasonably difficult the exercise by Belgium of its right of transit. These findings, as others in the Award, are applicable to any use of the Iron Rhine.

*   *   *

22.   Third Request:

> Should the Tribunal's ruling on the apportionment of costs in segment C if a loop around Roermond is agreed, be interpreted as laying with Belgium the costs of a reactivation of the historic route through Roermond, when such costs result from measures required by the Netherlands after the award had been rendered, over and above those included in the figures presented to the Tribunal, the Dutch legislation of general application remaining unchanged?

23.   The Tribunal responds as follows.

24.   The pleadings of the Parties and the Annexes thereto suggested that both Parties envisaged that any reactivation of the Iron Rhine would be likely to entail a deviation from the historic route by means of a loop around the town of Roermond. The Tribunal had before it no other scenario for segment C.

25.   When it formulated its Replies to Question 3, at paragraph 244(d), and the principles there stated, the Tribunal did not suppose that the projected estimates for the contemplated works it had before it, provided by the Parties, would remain unchanged through time. At the same time, the Tribunal has made clear in its Award that the application of Dutch legislation and the decision-making powers based thereon may not amount to a denial of Belgium's right of transit over the historic route, nor render unreasonably difficult the exercise by Belgium of its right of transit.

26.   The Tribunal's ruling on the apportionment of costs in segment C, if a loop around Roermond is agreed, is to be interpreted as applicable to the scenario before it and not to any other hypothetical alternative.

Done at the Peace Palace, The Hague, this 20th day of September 2005,

_____

Judge Rosalyn Higgins
President

_____

Professor Guy Schrans

_____

Judge Bruno Simma

_____

Professor Alfred H.A. Soons

_____

Judge Peter Tomka

FRENCH TRANSLATION

TRADUCTION FRANÇAISE

L'ARBITRAGE DU « RHIN DE FER » (« IJZEREN RIJN ») (BELGIQUE–PAYS-BAS)

Sa contribution au droit international

par

Colin Warbrick*

I.   LE RHIN DE FER[1]

Le « Rhin de Fer » est le nom donné à la ligne de chemin de fer qui reliait Anvers à ce qui est maintenant Münchengladbach (Allemagne) en passant par les Pays-Bas, puis Münchengladbach à un terminus important à Duisbourg dans la Ruhr. La ligne fut construite dans l'intérêt de la Belgique et son origine juridique remonte au Congrès de Vienne. Les conditions de l'indépendance de la Belgique n'ayant pas fait l'objet d'un accord à Vienne, elles furent énoncées dans le Traité entre la Belgique et les Pays-Bas relatif à la séparation de leurs territoires respectifs (le « Traité de Séparation » ou le « Traité de 1839 »).[2] Du fait des répartitions territoriales dans le Traité de 1839, Anvers fut coupée de son accès terrestre direct à l'Empire germanique par l'interposition d'un territoire néerlandais. Dans ce contexte, l'article XII du Traité disposait que :

> Dans le cas où il aurait été construit en Belgique une nouvelle route, ou creusé un nouveau canal, qui aboutirait à la Meuse vis-à-vis le canton néerlandais de Sittard, alors il serait loisible à la Belgique de demander à la Hollande, qui ne s'y refuserait pas dans cette supposition, que la dite route ou le dit canal fussent prolongés d'après le même plan, entièrement aux frais et dépens de la Belgique, par le canton de Sittard, jusqu'aux frontières de l'Allemagne· Cette route ou ce canal, qui ne

---

* Professeur de droit international public à l'Université de Birmingham.

[1] Le texte de l'échange de notes soumettant le différend à un arbitrage entre la Belgique et les Pays-Bas des 22/25 juillet 2003 est disponible sur le site Internet de la Cour permanente d'arbitrage <http://www.pca-cpa.org>. Les faits relatifs au Rhin de fer et à son histoire sont en grande partie repris de la sentence.

[2] Traité entre la Belgique et les Pays-Bas relatif à la séparation de leurs territoires respectifs, et Série des Traités Consolidés [C.T.S.], vol. 88 (1838–1839), p. 427.

pourraient servir que de communication commerciale, seraient construits, au choix de la Hollande, soit par des ingénieurs et ouvriers que la Belgique obtiendrait l'autorisation d'employer à cet effet dans le canton de Sittard, soit par des ingénieurs et ouvriers que la Hollande fournirait, et qui exécuteraient, aux frais de la Belgique, les travaux convenus, le tout sans charge aucune pour la Hollande, et sans préjudice de ses droits de souveraineté exclusifs sur le territoire que traverserait la route ou le canal en question.

Ultérieurement, aux termes du Traité du Rhin de fer de 1873,[3] les deux États convinrent de construire une ligne de chemin de fer, sur un tracé situé plus au nord passant par le Limbourg, vers ce qui était alors devenu la frontière avec la Prusse. Le chemin de fer fut mis en service en 1879 et intégré au réseau public de chemins de fer néerlandais en 1897. Le volume de trafic transitant par le Rhin de fer a été fluctuant. La ligne fut détruite au cours de la seconde guerre mondiale, puis restaurée, mais son utilisation était devenue intermittente et sur le déclin. Après 1991, plus aucun trafic ne subsistait entre la Belgique et l'Allemagne bien que des tronçons du « tracé historique » du Rhin de Fer soient toujours utilisés dans le cadre du système ferroviaire néerlandais. En Belgique, un certain intérêt pour la « réactivation » du tracé était né avant même son abandon – l'objet étant non pas une simple réfection de la ligne originale mais sa modernisation en une ligne à voies multiples, électrifiée, capable de supporter des trains plus nombreux et plus longs que ceux qu'elle avait connus jusqu'à présent.[4] Les intérêts économiques des Pays-Bas étaient, quant à eux, contrariés par la construction d'un tel projet avec de telles spécifications, notamment du fait de leur propre projet de fret ferroviaire entre Rotterdam et l'Allemagne. Il existe par ailleurs une ligne de chemin de fer entre Anvers et l'Allemagne qui traverse le territoire belge, mais celle-ci est substantiellement plus longue que celle du Rhin de fer (210 kilomètres contre 160 kilomètres). Le déclin du port d'Anvers, en particulier par rapport à la prospérité de Rotterdam, fut un élément qui eut son importance dans les

---

[3] Convention entre la Belgique and les Pays-Bas relative relative au paiement de la dette belge, à l'abolition de la surtaxe sur les eaux de vie néerlandaises et au passage d'une ligne de chemin de fer entre Anvers et l'Allemagne à travers le Duché de Limbourg, C.T.S. vol. 145 (1872–1873), p. 447. Ce Traité et le Traité de Séparation, voir *supra* note 2, seront désignés sous l'appellation « les Traités ». La carte du tracé du Rhin de fer sur laquelle s'est fondé le Tribunal est à la page 314.

[4] Les parties ont utilisé le terme « réactivation » de la ligne de chemin de fer, sans préjuger de si ce terme désignait la réfection de la ligne dans son état final avant d'être déposée ou bien la proposition de modernisation du chemin de fer envisagée par la Belgique.

approches menées par la Belgique envers les Pays-Bas au sujet de l'avenir du Rhin de fer au cours des années 1990.

Dans les années 1990, les Pays-Bas créèrent un certain nombre de réserves naturelles le long de l'ancienne voie du Rhin de fer et, au cours des discussions qui eurent lieu entre les deux Gouvernements, ils se mirent d'accord pour commander des études d'impact environnemental concernant les effets de la réactivation. Les modalités de celles-ci firent l'objet d'un protocole d'accord, signé en 2000, qui envisageait une réfection temporaire de la ligne, ainsi que, dans un deuxième temps, son exploitation sous une forme permanente. La question des modalités de la réactivation et de la répartition du coût ne put être résolue lors des discussions. En 2003, la Belgique et les Pays-Bas acceptèrent de soumettre le différend à un arbitrage sous les auspices de la Cour permanente d'arbitrage (la « CPA »).[5] Les Parties convinrent du fait que le Traité de 1839 était toujours en vigueur et que, avec d'autres accords, il accordait à la Belgique un droit de passage ferroviaire sur le tracé historique situé en territoire néerlandais. Le cœur du différend entre les deux États était constitué de deux éléments : quelle était l'étendue du pouvoir unilatéral des Pays-Bas d'imposer des conditions à la réactivation de la ligne, notamment en ce qui concerne la protection de l'environnement; et qui devait payer le coût de la construction de la ligne de chemin de fer répondant aux conditions souhaitées par les Pays-Bas ?

II. LE TRIBUNAL ARBITRAL

Le Tribunal fut constitué en vertu d'un accord entre la Belgique et les Pays-Bas. La Belgique désigna le professeur Guy Schrans et le juge Bruno Simma en qualité d'arbitres, et les Pays-Bas désignèrent le professeur Alfred Soons et le juge Peter Tomka. Ces arbitres nommèrent à leur tour le juge Rosalyn Higgins, actuellement Présidente de la Cour internationale de justice. L'éminence des membres du Tribunal, qui comprenait trois juges de la Cour internationale de justice, a son importance, au vu des conséquences potentielles de certains aspects de la sentence pour le droit international en général.

---

[5] *Supra* note 1.

Le compromis d'arbitrage permettait de s'appuyer sur la Cour permanente d'arbitrage et de recourir en grande partie au règlement de procédure de la CPA. En principe, la procédure devant le Tribunal devait être écrite, mais il était prévu que des audiences puissent avoir lieu. En l'espèce, aucune des Parties, ni le Tribunal, n'a demandé d'audiences de plaidoirie. Les deux parties respectèrent les délais fixés par le Tribunal. La Belgique soumit un mémoire (« le MB ») et une réplique (la « RB ») et les Pays-Bas un contre-mémoire (le « CMPB »), ainsi qu'une duplique (la « DPB »).[6] La sentence fut rendue le 24 mai 2005.

III. LA SENTENCE

Les Parties soumirent trois questions assez compliquées au Tribunal auxquelles celui-ci répondit en détail.[7] Il n'est pas notre propos de rendre compte en détail des questions ou des réponses données. La sentence est un document dense qui n'est pas aisé à résumer. Pour ce qui doit suivre dans la présente introduction, il suffira de dire que le Tribunal (à l'unanimité) :

confirma le fait que le droit de passage ferroviaire de la Belgique sur le territoire néerlandais le long du tracé historique du Rhin de fer perdurait ;[8]

jugea que l'exploitation de la ligne était soumise à l'application du droit néerlandais pour des questions telles que les normes de construction, de sécurité ou de protection de l'environnement ;[9]

jugea que l'autorité des Pays-Bas était limitée par le fait que la réglementation ne devait pas rendre l'exercice du droit de passage ferroviaire impossible ou anormalement difficile ;[10]

---

[6] Les écritures des Parties sont disponibles sur le site de la CPA, *supra* note 1.

[7] Sentence, para. 3. Les soumissions finales des Parties se trouvent au para. 26 (Belgique) et au para. 27 (Pays-Bas) de la sentence. Les réponses du Tribunal se trouvent aux paras. 238–244 de la sentence. La présente introduction ne traite pas de toutes les questions juridiques et arguments techniques avancés par les Parties et examinés par le Tribunal. Pour quelques commentaires intéressants sur le statut du protocole d'accord : voir sentence, paras. 142, 154–158.

[8] Il n'existe pas de jugement spécifique à cet effet, mais le Tribunal procéda sur le fondement qu'il devait se prononcer sur quelles étaient les limites de la souveraineté des Pays-Bas découlant du droit de passage de la Belgique en vertu des Traités. Voir sentence, para. 56.

[9] Sentence, para. 239.

[10] Sentence, para. 239(c).

conclut que, bien que la Belgique soit en droit de moderniser le tracé, cette modernisation ne devait avoir lieu que dans des conditions acceptables pour les Pays-Bas, sous réserve des mêmes conditions d'impossibilité et d'absence de caractère raisonnable ;[11] et

décida que le tracé historique ne pouvait être modifié par les Pays-Bas qu'avec l'accord de la Belgique.[12]

Le Tribunal énonça des principes de répartition des coûts et des risques financiers du projet entre les Parties, en proposant un traitement différent pour chacun des quatre tronçons du Rhin de fer auxquels différents calculs seraient ainsi applicables.[13] La sentence recommandait la mise en place d'un comité d'experts indépendants pour calculer les différents coûts et avantages, de manière à ce que les Parties puissent utiliser ces informations afin de déterminer leur part respective dans la réfection et la réactivation de tronçons du Rhin de fer dont elles partageraient l'utilisation.[14] De manière remarquable, le Tribunal estima que la conformité avec les mesures de protection environnementales stipulées par les Pays-Bas ne rendaient le passage ni impossible ni déraisonnable,[15] même si cela impliquait de construire un tunnel et d'exécuter des travaux d'un montant de 500 millions d'euros.

Ce compte-rendu simplifié de la sentence pourrait suggérer que les arbitres se sont quasiment comportés comme des experts comptables sophistiqués mais ce serait masquer le nombre et l'importance des questions juridiques de droit communautaire et de droit international qui ont été soulevées dans cette affaire. La décision des arbitres était sans aucun doute facilitée par l'ampleur des accords entre les États s'agissant de nombreuses questions interétatiques fondamentales, et même s'ils n'étaient pas tout à fait *ad idem*, par la capacité du Tribunal à percevoir les désaccords comme relevant de la forme plutôt que du fond. Néanmoins, des questions fondamentales peuvent être dégagées des questions particulières nées dans le cadre de cette affaire.

---

[11] Sentence, para. 241.
[12] Sentence, para. 241(c).
[13] Sentence, para. 244.
[14] Sentence, para. 235.
[15] Sentence, para. 244(e).

IV. LA FRAGMENTATION DU DROIT INTERNATIONAL

Le fait que la Commission du droit international (la « CDI ») se soit lancée dans l'examen de la « fragmentation du droit international » fut une réelle surprise,[16] non pas tant du fait que l'importance pratique du sujet était sous-estimée,[17] mais qu'il était difficile de voir comment la CDI pourrait traiter ce sujet d'une manière telle que les États pourraient ensuite en tirer utilement parti ; il semblait en effet assez difficile d'imaginer que l'analyse de la CDI puisse déboucher sur un traité ou un code sur le sujet. La « fragmentation » englobe plusieurs caractéristiques du système moderne de droit international. Bien qu'elle suggère un procédé allant à l'opposé d'un idéal de cohérence – lui-même perçu comme une vertu au sein des ordres juridiques nationaux – la « fragmentation » n'implique pas nécessairement un quelconque jugement de valeur. Ce terme est utilisé pour recouvrir divers phénomènes générant des incompatibilités en droit international. Des éléments procéduraux (ou institutionnels) sont en jeu, ainsi que des éléments de fond, mais ils créent tous deux un risque que les États et d'autres sujets de droit international soient confrontés à des obligations incompatibles nées de l'absence de coordination lors de l'élaboration du droit international et des procédés par lequel il est déterminé. De même, des incohérences systémiques apparaîtront si les mêmes concepts juridiques sont envisagés de manière différente par les différentes parties du système juridique international. La face procédurale de la fragmentation provient de la prolifération de mécanismes de règlement des différends qui font autorité et du souhait des États à avoir recours à ces derniers.[18] Ainsi, par exemple, la question de ce que constitue un génocide est-elle soulevée devant la Cour internationale de justice (la « CIJ ») dans l'affaire du génocide de la Bosnie,[19] dans des affaires tranchées par le Tribunal pénal

---

[16] Groupe d'étude de « La fragmentation du droit international : difficultés découlant de la diversification et de l'expansion du droit international », *Rapport de la Commission du droit international : Cinquante-quatrième session*, Doc. off. AG NU, 57ème sess., supp. no. 1, Doc. NU A/57/10, 267 aux paras. 492–494. Le terme « fragmentation » sera utilisé dans la présente introduction au sens où il est entendu par la CDI.

[17] Martii Koskenniemi & Paivi Leino, *Fragmentation of International Law? Postmodern Anxieties*, 15 Leiden Journal of International Law p. 553 (2002).

[18] Yuval Shany, The Competing Jurisdictions of International Courts and Tribunals (2003).

[19] Affaire relative à l'Application de la Convention pour la prévention et la répression du crime du génocide (*Bosnie-Herzégovine c. Yougoslavie*), Exceptions préliminaires, CIJ Recueil 1996, p. 595.

international pour l'ex-Yougoslavie (le « TPIY »)[20] et par le Tribunal pénal international pour le Rwanda (le « TPIR ») ;[21] ou encore un même différend est parfois soumis à plusieurs tribunaux, comme le différend opposant le Chili aux Communautés européennes au sujet de l'espadon, considéré comme un différend commercial par la Communauté européenne et renvoyé à l'Organisation mondiale du commerce (l'« OMC ») en vertu de son mécanisme de règlement des différends,[22] alors qu'il est traité comme une affaire relevant du droit de l'environnement par le Chili et soumis pour règlement au titre de la partie XI de la Convention des Nations Unies sur le droit de la mer (la « CNUDM »).[23] Lorsque ces différentes procédures suscitent des lectures différentes de termes clefs, les conséquences en seront importantes pour les États. Néanmoins, ce genre de problème pour les États n'a pas nécessairement une origine institutionnelle : en effet, la résolution des obligations en cas de conflit de conventions, l'identification du contexte dans lequel les traités devraient être interprétés et, de manière plus hasardeuse peut-être, la demande croissante d'une certaine hiérarchie au sein des normes de droit international, créent pour les États des perspectives similaires de dissonance des obligations. Certaines de ces dissonances ou incompatibilités seraient sans aucun doute qualifiées par les juristes américains de « faux » conflits (*false conflicts*), c'est-à-dire qu'un examen attentif révèlerait qu'il n'existe en fait aucune incohérence. Ainsi, une règle alternative peut en fin de compte se révéler non applicable, le sens de critères pourtant dérivés de régimes juridiques différents peut s'avérer être en fin de compte identique, ou encore un conflit entre deux obligations contradictoires s'avérer en être un en fin de compte entre un pouvoir et une obligation. Néanmoins, il ne peut être nié que certains conflits existent bel et bien. Ce fut ainsi le cas pour le Tribunal arbitral du Rhin de fer qui fut confronté à deux versions de la « fragmentation », même si l'une d'elles – une incompatibilité alléguée entre la compétence du Tribunal et les obligations des Parties en vertu du droit communautaire – ne fut pas invoquée par les Parties, mais par le Tribunal lui-même.

---

[20] *Procureur c. Krstic*, IT-98-33-A, Arrêt (19 avril 2004) (Tribunal pénal international pour l'ex-Yougoslavie, Chambre d'appel).

[21] *Procureur c. Akayesu*, ICTR-96-4-A, Arrêt (1 juin 2001) (Tribunal pénal international pour le Rwanda, Chambre d'appel).

[22] Chili – Mesures concernant le transport en transit et l'importation d'espadons (Plainte des Communautés européennes), OMC Affaire WT/DS193.

[23] Affaire concernant la conservation et l'exploitation durable des stocks d'espadon dans l'océan Pacifique Sud-Est (Chili / Communauté européenne), Tribunal international du droit de la mer, Affaire No. 7 (2003).

La CDI a récemment étudié le Rapport de son groupe de travail sur la « fragmentation ». Ce rapport propose un certain nombre de « conclusions » présentées sous forme schématique pour guider les États et autres pouvoirs décisionnels confrontés à une question de « fragmentation ».[24] Après avoir décrit les questions de « fragmentation » auxquelles était confronté le Tribunal arbitral du Rhin de fer, la présente introduction examinera la manière dont la sentence rendue par ce Tribunal peut être appréciée au regard des conclusions du groupe de travail de la CDI, car ce dernier est, alors que la sentence avait déjà été rendue, parvenu à établir un catalogue de principes visant à atténuer les conflits ou incompatibilités nés de la « fragmentation » (voir ci-dessous).

V. COMPÉTENCE DU TRIBUNAL ET DROIT COMMUNAUTAIRE

Dans le cadre de l'arbitrage du Rhin de fer, il était demandé au Tribunal de se prononcer « sur le fondement du droit international, y compris du droit communautaire le cas échéant, en tenant compte des obligations des Parties en vertu de l'article 292 du Traité CE ».[25]

L'article 292 du Traité CE dispose : « [l]es États membres s'engagent à ne pas soumettre un différend relatif à l'interprétation ou à l'application du présent traité à un mode de règlement autre que ceux prévus par celui-ci ».

La Cour de justice des Communautés européennes (la « CJCE ») est dotée d'une compétence d'interprétation du Traité CE qui prévaut sur tout autre moyen de règlement international, ainsi que sur les procédures judiciaires nationales. Cette compétence de la CJCE est considérée comme un élément essentiel du maintien de l'intégrité et de la primauté du droit communautaire. La Commission a le pouvoir d'engager une procédure à l'encontre d'un État ou d'États qui lui soumettent des différends au sujet de l'interprétation du Traité CE dans le cadre de procédures externes à la Communauté. Ce fut notamment le cas dans l'affaire MOX/CNUDM (voir ci-dessous).[26] Dans le cadre de l'arbitrage du Rhin de fer, la Belgique et les Pays-Bas étaient conscients de

---

[24] *Fragmentation du droit international : difficultés découlant de la diversification et de l'expansion du droit international : Rapport du Groupe d'étude de la Commission du droit international*, Doc. off. AG NU, Doc. NU A/CN.4/L.702 (2006) [Rapport de la CDI].

[25] Sentence, para. 4.

[26] CJCE, *Commission c. Irlande*, arrêt du 30 mai 2006, C-459/03, *Rec.* p. I-4635.

cette disposition lorsqu'ils soumirent leur différend au Tribunal arbitral. Aussi, ils écrivirent à la Commission pour lui indiquer que, selon eux, le différend concernait uniquement des points de droit international mais que, s'il s'avérait que des questions de droit communautaire étaient soulevées, ils « s'engage[aie]nt à prendre toutes mesures nécessaires aux fins de se conformer aux obligations qui leur incombent en vertu du Traité CE et, en particulier, de son article 292 ».[27]

En résumé, les Parties renvoyaient au droit communautaire de trois manières. En premier lieu, la Belgique soutenait que le projet de « réseau transeuropéen » (en ce qui concerne les réseaux ferroviaires des États membres) démontrait l'importance de la réactivation du Rhin de fer ; cependant, le poids de cet argument déclina avec le temps et le Tribunal fut à même de conclure que la position des États était proche sur cette question qui avait un rapport très limité avec l'affaire.[28] En deuxième lieu, la Belgique renvoyait à l'article 10 du Traité CE mais le Tribunal a estimé que ce point n'était ni concluant ni déterminant dans le cadre du différend.[29] En troisième lieu, et de manière plus significative, intervenaient les références au droit communautaire de l'environnement. Nous avons indiqué ci-dessus que les Pays-Bas avaient classé certaines zones le long du tracé historique du Rhin de fer en réserves naturelles. Selon le Tribunal, le droit pertinent était à ce titre la Directive Habitats.[30] Il convient de noter que l'article 175 du Traité CE « ne doit pas empêcher un État membre de maintenir en vigueur ou d'introduire des mesures de protection plus rigoureuses ».

Tant que les Pays-Bas n'avaient pas adopté de mesures nationales moins protectrices des intérêts relevant de la Directive Habitats, aucune incompatibilité avec le droit communautaire ne pouvait exister. Les Pays-Bas avaient classé un secteur, le site du Meinweg, que traversait le tracé historique du Rhin de fer, en zone de protection spéciale au titre de la Directive Habitats. C'est le souci de préservation de cette zone qui a mené les autorités néerlandaises à spécifier qu'un tunnel serait nécessaire si le Rhin de fer était réactivé, ce tunnel représentant l'élément le plus coûteux du projet. La

---

[27] Sentence, para. 15.
[28] Sentence, para. 117.
[29] Sentence, para. 141.
[30] CE, *Directive 92/43/CEE du Conseil du 21 mai 1992 concernant la conservation des habitats naturels ainsi que de la faune et de la flore sauvages*, J.O. L 206/7 du 22 juillet 1992.

Belgique a répondu en soutenant que les Pays-Bas étaient tenus d'harmoniser toutes les mesures de protection du secteur du Meinweg avec les obligations internationales qu'ils avaient envers la Belgique en vertu des Traités, ce qui signifiait notamment adopter l'option de protection de l'environnement la moins onéreuse. A première vue, ceci revenait à soumettre au Tribunal l'interprétation de la Directive Habitats, mais les Pays-Bas soutenaient que le classement du secteur du Meinweg était un acte relevant de leur droit national (compatible avec le droit communautaire mais non prescrit par celui-ci).[31] Le Tribunal, quant à lui, conclut que le fait que la Directive Habitats existe ou n'existe pas n'avait aucun effet sur la manière dont il se prononcerait sur le fait de déterminer si l'exigence d'un tunnel dans le secteur du Meinweg était ou non licite (et qui devrait payer le coût de celui-ci s'il était effectivement licite). Ainsi, bien que les Parties aient en fait « débattu » du droit communautaire, celui-ci n'était pas déterminant car « il n'[était] pas nécessaire que le Tribunal interprète la Directive habitats pour rendre sa sentence ».[32]

Dans la mesure où le Tribunal était parvenu à la même conclusion au sujet des trois points de droit communautaire, à savoir qu'ils n'étaient pas pertinents dans le cadre de la sentence, le Tribunal pouvait exercer sa compétence sans encourir le risque que les Parties soient en situation de manquement à leurs obligations au titre de l'article 292 du Traité CE. Ce qui aurait pu se passer si les conclusions du Tribunal avaient été différentes n'est pas clair. Celui-ci avait fait un peu plus tôt la curieuse remarque selon laquelle il se trouvait dans une « dans une situation analogue à celle d'une juridiction nationale d'un État membre ... ».[33] L'assertion d'analogie semble contredire directement la position adoptée au regard du droit communautaire.[34] En vertu de l'article 234 du Traité CE, les tribunaux étatiques peuvent – et dans certains cas doivent – soumettre une question préjudicielle à la CJCE. Le Tribunal a étudié la jurisprudence de la CJCE au sujet de la manière dont les tribunaux étatiques

---

[31] CMPB, para. 3.3.5.6. Anticipant cet argument, la Belgique a soutenu que, dans la mesure où les Pays-Bas n'étaient tenus à aucune obligation d'adopter les mesures environnementales contestées en vertu du droit international, ils étaient tenus dès lors de faire en sorte que leurs systèmes nationaux puissent accueillir utilement les droits de la Belgique en vertu de l'article XII. Voir MB, paras. 73–74.

[32] Sentence, para. 137.

[33] Sentence, para. 103.

[34] Nikolas Lavranos, *The MOX Plant and IJzeren Rijn Disputes : Which Court is the Supreme Arbiter?*, 19 LEIDEN JOURNAL OF INTERNATIONAL LAW p. 223 (2006), aux pp. 239–240.

devraient exercer leurs compétences, se fondant sur l'affaire CILFIT,[35] en particulier concernant l'importance du point de droit communautaire, qui doit être à la fois déterminant et concluant pour l'affaire soumise au tribunal étatique.[36] Bien entendu, le Tribunal n'avait ni le pouvoir ni l'obligation de soumettre une affaire à la CJCE. On pourrait présumer, à partir de l'essentiel de la décision, qu'il aurait refusé d'exercer sa compétence (peut-être en se fondant sur son droit applicable, lequel comprenait le droit communautaire) et aurait attendu des Parties qu'elles trouvent le moyen de soumettre les points litigieux de droit communautaire à la CJCE. Peut-être même que les Parties, afin de satisfaire à leurs engagements, auraient tenté d'obtenir une suspension de la procédure dans le cas où le Tribunal aurait conclu qu'un point de droit communautaire s'avérait nécessaire pour rendre sa sentence.

Cette question aurait pu être résolue différemment. Il ne semble pas que le fait que des États membres conviennent de soumettre un point de droit communautaire à un règlement en dehors de la CJCE rende un tel contrat nul, si bien que des entités liées par le droit communautaire devraient ne pas l'appliquer et que les États membres seraient justiciables de ce fait devant la CJCE ou un tribunal étatique. En conséquence, une relation hiérarchique entre les règles de compétence de la CJCE et celles du Tribunal n'était pas en jeu en tant que point de droit international. Parmi les dispositifs permettant de traiter des problèmes de « fragmentation » qui ont été envisagés par la CDI, deux ont un impact dans la présente affaire, à savoir les règles traitant de la priorité des traités, ainsi que l'application de la maxime *lex specialis derogat lex generali*. S'agissant de la première, la CDI renvoie à l'article 30 de la Convention de Vienne sur le droit des traités (la « Convention de Vienne »)[37] qui, entre les mêmes parties, soumet les obligations nées antérieurement en vertu de traités à celles nées ultérieurement.[38] Dans la présente affaire, cependant, les intérêts, au titre du Traité CE, d'autres États sont en jeu, sans oublier de l'Union européenne elle-même. L'article 30, paragraphe 4, de la Convention de Vienne accepte la position selon laquelle, dans une telle situation, un État pourrait être lié par des obligations incompatibles. Dans un tel cas, l'État pourra être tenu

---

[35] CJCE, *Srl CILFIT et Lanificio di Gavardo SpA c. Ministère de la santé*, arrêt du 6 octobre 1982, C-283/81, *Rec.* p. 3415.

[36] Sentence, para. 137.

[37] *Convention de Vienne sur le droit des traités,* 23 mai 1969, R.T.N.U. vol. 1155, p. 331 [« CVDT »].

[38] Rapport de la CDI, *supra* note 24, aux paras. 14(24–30).

responsable de la violation de l'obligation qu'il n'a pas respectée, bien qu'il lui soit possible de négocier une solution avec les parties à l'un des traités ou aux deux.[39] Les promesses de la Belgique et des Pays-Bas de ne pas poursuivre leur action devant le Tribunal si un point de droit communautaire devenait pertinent semblent représenter une solution préalable à une possible incompatibilité. Si le Tribunal avait estimé qu'il était nécessaire de se prononcer sur un point de droit communautaire et que les Parties avaient été disposées à argumenter ce point devant lui, le principe de *lex specialis* aurait, à première vue, semblé favoriser la compétence du Tribunal mais, ainsi que le reconnaissent les Conclusions de la CDI, le principe n'est pas celui d'une application automatique mais, au contraire, doit être décidé « en fonction du contexte ».[40] En l'occurrence, le contexte inclurait les stipulations du compromis d'arbitrage, dont la référence au « droit communautaire » n'est pas limitée au droit communautaire matériel et pourrait donc inclure l'article 292, ainsi que les déclarations des Parties au sujet du droit communautaire faites devant le Tribunal. En prenant tous ces facteurs en compte, une conclusion plus appropriée pourrait être que les Parties n'entendaient pas conférer au Tribunal une compétence sur des questions relevant de l'article 292. La manière dont elles se sont fondées sur le droit communautaire dans leurs arguments atteste d'une tentative presque douloureuse de faire référence au droit communautaire mais d'en minimiser les conséquences sur le fond.[41]

En dehors de l'analogie évoquée par le Tribunal entre lui-même et un tribunal étatique, il semble qu'aucun préjudice ne soit né de sa résolution de la question – le conflit de compétences étant en fait un faux conflit. Toutefois, dans un article la mettant en cause, l'approche adoptée par le Tribunal a été vivement critiquée par le Docteur Nikolas Lavranos.[42] Celui-ci renvoie aux deux arbitrages MOX nés de demandes de l'Irlande à l'encontre du Royaume-

---

[39] Ce point est notamment illustré par la manière dont le Royaume-Uni a résolu le conflit existant entre, d'une part, son obligation d'extrader un fugitif en vertu de son traité d'extradition avec les États-Unis et, d'autre part, son obligation de ne pas le renvoyer en vertu de l'interprétation faite par la Cour de Strasbourg de la CEDH dans l'affaire *Soering* c. *Royaume-Uni*, A/161, 7 juillet 1989. Soering fut renvoyé aux États-Unis sur le fondement d'un mandat d'extradition portant sur un délit non passible de la peine de mort. *Soering* c. *Royaume-Uni*, No. 14038/88, Cour européenne des Droits de l'Homme (7 juillet 1989).

[40] Rapport de la CDI, *supra* note 24, para. 14(6).

[41] Il n'y a quasiment aucune référence au droit communautaire dans les réponses de la Belgique aux questions posées au Tribunal et aucun dans les réponses des Pays-Bas. Voir MB « soumissions finales » et DPB, chapitre 4.

[42] *Supra* note 34. Je remercie ici le Dr Lavranos pour son article.

Uni au sujet de l'exploitation des installations nucléaires de Sellafield.[43] Il y affirme sa préférence pour la conclusion à laquelle est parvenu le Tribunal dans l'affaire MOX qui, rappelons le, a sursis à statuer dans l'attente d'une décision de la CJCE sur la question de la compétence (voir ci-dessous). La position du Dr Lavranos découle de son affirmation selon laquelle il existe une « suprématie du droit communautaire sur le droit international », ce qui reflète probablement fidèlement la position du point de vue du droit communautaire.[44] Tout le reste découle de ce postulat. Les exigences de cohérence et d'uniformité du droit communautaire exigent que le dépositaire ultime du sens du Traité soit la CJCE et l'article 292 n'est que l'un des éléments garantissant l'autorité de la CJCE. Selon le Dr Lavranos, la question de la « fragmentation » doit être tranchée en ayant recours à la fois à la notion de régimes spéciaux et à celle de hiérarchie, selon lesquelles le droit communautaire jouit de la même supériorité par rapport au droit international que par rapport au droit national. Ceci peut sembler un procédé bien commode et, sans aucun doute pour les juristes de droit communautaire un procédé qui va de soi, mais, comme nous le verrons dans un instant, c'est un procédé qui va à l'encontre de la manière dont le Tribunal a traité ce problème, ainsi que des alternatives exposées aux paragraphes précédents. La présente introduction n'est pas le lieu pour discuter en détail de la question de la supériorité du droit communautaire sur le droit international ; pour un juriste international, il suffira d'observer que le Traité CE est un traité international et qu'il devrait en conséquence être interprété en vertu de la Convention de Vienne. Il doit être interprété dans le contexte général du droit international, ainsi qu'en fonction de ses propres caractéristiques spécifiques. La jurisprudence récente de la CJCE sur l'effet des résolutions du Conseil de sécurité de l'ONU sur le droit communautaire[45] et de la relation entre le Traité CE et la Convention européenne des droits de l'homme (la « CEDH »)[46] sont des exemples fondamentaux attestant du fait

---

[43] Tribunal CNUDM, *Irlande c. Royaume-Uni* [Affaire de l'Usine de Mox], suspension de la procédure sur la compétence et au fond : voir site Internet de la CPA, *supra* note 1 ; Tribunal OSPAR, *Irlande c. Royaume-Uni* [Arbitrage OSPAR] : voir site Internet de la CPA, *supra* note 1.

[44] *Supra* note 34, aux pp. 232–233. Voir Daniel Bethlehem, *Chapter 11*, INTERNATIONAL LAW ASPECTS OF THE EUROPEAN UNION (Martti Koskenniemi ed., 1998).

[45] TPICE, *Yusuf et Al Barakaat International Foundation c. Conseil et Commission*, T- 306/01, J.O.C.E. 2005, C 281 p. 17 ; TPICE, *Kadi c. Conseil et Commission*, T-315/01, J.O.C.E. 2005, C 281 p.17 ; TPICE, *Hassan c. Conseil et Commission*, T-49/04, J.O.C.E. 2006, C 224 p. 36 ; TPICE, *Chafiq Ayadi c. Conseil*, T-253/02, J.O.C.E. 2006, C 224 p. 34.

[46] CJCE, *Bosphorus Hora Yollari Turzim ve Ticaret AS c. Minister for Transport, Energy and Communications*, Ireland and Attorney-General, C-84/95, *Rec.* 1996 p. I-3953 ; voir aussi CEDH (Grande Chambre), *Bosphorus Hora Yollari Turzim ve Ticaret Anonim Sirkati c. Irlande* (2005), Requête no. 45036/98.

que la supériorité automatique du droit communautaire sur le droit international n'est pas une proposition qui va de soi.

Le Dr Lavranos soulève toutefois une question cruciale qui va inévitablement compliquer les tentatives de régler les conflits de juridiction. Il s'agit de la question du seuil à partir duquel un tribunal doit déterminer si la question qu'il doit trancher relève ou non de la compétence, voire de la compétence ostensiblement exclusive, d'un autre for. Comme nous l'avons exposé, le Tribunal a pu éviter tout conflit potentiel avec la CJCE en estimant qu'il n'avait pas besoin de se prononcer sur une question de droit communautaire. Le Dr Lavranos conteste cette décision. Il soutient qu'il était nécessaire de se prononcer sur le droit communautaire aux fins de statuer sur les demandes soulevées dans le cadre de l'affaire du Rhin de fer. Même en l'absence de jurisprudence spécifique de droit communautaire traitant d'une situation similaire à la question du site du Meinweg, le Dr Lavranos considère que le fait de réactiver le Rhin de fer traversant le site du Meinweg aurait pu être considéré comme incompatible avec la Directive Habitats.[47] Si le Tribunal avait été un tribunal étatique, il aurait été dans l'obligation de soumettre une question préjudicielle à la CJCE. Il écrit ainsi « dans la mesure où le tribunal arbitral ne pouvait pas soumettre une telle question préjudicielle, il était *tenu* de rejeter sa compétence et de renvoyer les parties devant la CJCE ».[48]

C'est la solution adoptée dans l'affaire MOX. Dans une certaine mesure, aucune conséquence ne peut être tirée du fait que le Dr Lavranos ait raison ou tort au sujet de la position du droit communautaire au titre de la Directive Habitats. La question de déterminer si un point de droit communautaire était ou non nécessaire pour résoudre l'arbitrage du Rhin de fer relève du droit communautaire si une telle question se pose *prima facie* (j'utilise le terme dans un sens commun) dans le cadre du différend. Il existe une sanction. Dans l'hypothèse où la décision du Tribunal au sujet de la nécessité de prendre en compte le droit communautaire serait erronée et où le droit communautaire aurait dû être examiné, à savoir que la sentence aurait été différente et que, en fonction de la nature du défaut, il y aurait toute une gamme de possibilités, pour contester toute action que l'un ou l'autre État aurait entreprise aux fins d'exécuter la sentence, qu'il s'agisse d'actions individuelles devant les

---

[47] *Supra* note 34, aux pp. 238–241. Pour la position de la Commission européenne, voir MB, pp. 52–57.

[48] *Supra* note 34, au p. 240 (soulignement ajouté).

tribunaux étatiques ou devant la CJCE. Ceci me semble être un élément du contexte juridique de ce différend que le Tribunal devait prendre en compte. Si les effets de la sentence pouvaient être contestés de manière décisive devant une instance ou une autre, cela n'aurait pas aidé à résoudre le différend au sujet du Rhin de fer entre la Belgique et les Pays-Bas. En fait, tout tribunal *ad hoc* pourrait probablement anticiper que les parties l'ayant saisi, en tant que membres de l'UE, seraient obligées d'accepter toute décision de la CJCE. Rien n'empêchait le Tribunal d'adopter l'approche qui fut la sienne. Il n'a toutefois pas statué, contrairement au tribunal dans l'affaire OSPAR, sans prendre en compte le droit communautaire. La conclusion selon laquelle le Tribunal n'avait pas besoin de statuer sur une question de droit communautaire ne sera sans doute pas contestée par les Parties et le Tribunal, convaincu que ce serait le cas, n'avait aucune raison de suivre le système proposé par le tribunal dans l'affaire MOX et d'ajourner sa procédure dans l'attente d'une décision de la CJCE avec on ne sait quel délai avant de pouvoir mener à terme la procédure du Tribunal. Bien entendu, la vulnérabilité de sa conclusion à une éventuelle remise en cause par la Commission ou par un tiers privé existe bien mais, de même que le Tribunal a respecté la compétence de la CJCE, la CJCE, s'il était fait appel à elle plus tard pour statuer sur la question, devrait prendre en compte les jugements du Tribunal en tant qu'éléments du contexte dans lequel elle parviendrait à une décision sur la question de trancher s'il était vraiment nécessaire de statuer sur un point de droit communautaire aux fins de rendre la sentence.

La CJCE s'est prononcée sur l'affaire MOX après qu'a été rendue la sentence du Rhin de fer et que le Dr Lavranos a écrit son article.[49] L'arrêt affirme de manière très directe la compétence de la CJCE et ce, que la question de droit communautaire relève exclusivement de la compétence communautaire ou qu'elle puisse être partagée avec les États membres, que la Communauté ait exercé sa compétence ou non. La CNUDM est un accord mixte. En conséquence, son interprétation relève du droit communautaire, autrement dit de la compétence exclusive de la CJCE.[50] La CJCE était sans aucun doute confortée dans sa conclusion (à laquelle elle est parvenue en se référant exclusivement au droit et aux principes communautaires) par les termes de l'article 282 de la CNUDM qui permet aux États parties à la

---

[49] CJCE, *Commission c. Irlande*, C-459/03, J.O.C.E. 2006, C 165 p. 2.
[50] CJCE, *supra* note 49, para. 84.

CNDUM de soumettre des différends nés entre eux au sujet de sa signification ou de son application notamment à des règlements obligatoires par le biais d'accord régionaux et par les termes des écritures de l'Irlande, lesquels renvoyaient fréquemment au droit communautaire. Il s'ensuit non seulement que la CJCE a une compétence exclusive sur tous points de droit communautaire, mais qu'elle sera nécessairement compétente pour statuer sur tous points pertinents de droit international devant être tranchés et, de manière cruciale, sur la question du seuil à partir duquel un point important de droit communautaire doit ou non faire l'objet d'une décision.[51] La CJCE a jugé que les dispositions de la CNUDM sur lesquelles se fondait l'Irlande relèvent du champ de compétence communautaire et « couvrent manifestement une partie significative du différend ».[52] En outre, la CJCE a affirmé qu'il lui appartenait « d'identifier les éléments du différend relatifs à des dispositions [de la CNUDM] qui ne relèvent pas de sa compétence ».[53] A moins que la doctrine de l'« *acte clair* » (c'est-à-dire en l'absence d'une quelconque compétence communautaire) s'applique, permettant aux États membres de soumettre une affaire à un autre for et que les faits d'un différend particulier relèvent sans équivoque de cette catégorie, comme le Dr Lavranos affirme que ce ne fut pas le cas dans l'affaire du Rhin de fer, les termes sans compromission de l'arrêt MOX/CNUDM soulèvent la question de déterminer si – en droit communautaire – le Tribunal du Rhin de fer a eu raison de retenir sa compétence sans permettre (ni même demander) aux Parties d'aller d'abord devant la CJCE. Du point de vue du droit international en général, il est beaucoup moins clair que ceci aurait été requis, dans la mesure où le Tribunal avait procédé à une évaluation correcte de la question du seuil de pertinence du droit communautaire dans le cadre de sa sentence, alternative que la CJCE rejette.[54] La Commission européenne n'a pas le pouvoir de déléguer sa compétence à un autre for, bien que son accord dans le cadre d'une demande émanant d'États au fait que n'existe aucun point de droit communautaire décisif dans leur affaire soit susceptible de rassurer ces États sur l'improbabilité d'une procédure à leur encontre devant la CJCE. Il convient de noter que la position de la CJCE sur l'exclusivité est guidée par un principe, à savoir celui de la nécessité de maintenir la supériorité et l'uniformité du droit

---

[51] CJCE, *supra* note 49, para 86.
[52] CJCE, *supra* note 49, para 120.
[53] CJCE, *supra* note 49, para 135.
[54] CJCE, *supra* note 49, para 156.

communautaire.[55] Il n'existe aucune place pour quoi que ce soit telle qu'une doctrine de *forum non conveniens* susceptible de persuader la CJCE de s'en remettre à la compétence d'un autre for, dont la compétence serait plus justifiée.

Dans la présente affaire, les États n'ont pas jugé nécessaire de formuler des arguments de droit communautaire ; plus encore, on pourrait dire qu'ils étaient convenus qu'il n'existait aucun point qui *puisse* impliquer une décision sur des points de droit communautaire. Le Tribunal a adopté cette position. Il a sans doute été renforcé dans ses conclusions par l'attitude des parties et aura depuis été rassuré car leur position n'a pas évolué depuis la sentence et car la CJCE n'a pas émis d'objection à la sentence dans son arrêt *Commission c. Irlande*. Sur le fond des critiques du Dr Lavranos à l'encontre de la sentence, il se pourrait bien que le Tribunal ait eu raison de traiter comme il l'a fait l'argument potentiel touchant à l'article 292, mais son identification de la question du seuil en ce qui concerne les conflits de compétence est de la plus grande importance.

VI. INTERPRÉTATION DES TRAITÉS[56]

Avant d'examiner plus avant la relation entre la « fragmentation » et l'interprétation des traités, il convient d'examiner les questions plus classiques, quoique tout aussi importantes, relatives à l'interprétation des traités auxquelles le Tribunal fut confronté. C'est la combinaison du traitement par le Tribunal de l'interprétation des traités et des considérations de « fragmentation » qui confère à la sentence une signification allant au-delà des préoccupations particulières des Parties.

Bien que la Belgique et les Pays-Bas soient parties à la Convention de Vienne, le Tribunal a réaffirmé la nature coutumière de plusieurs sous-ensembles de cette Convention, au premier rang desquels les articles qui

---

[55] CJCE, *supra* note 49, para 169. Il y avait trois parties dans la demande de la Commission. La CJCE a statué en affirmant que l'Irlande avait violé les dispositions des articles 10 et 292 du Traité CE et les articles 192 et 193 du Traité Euratom.

[56] Tous les manuels les plus importants comportent des développements sur l'interprétation des traités. Consulter notamment MALCOLM SHAW, INTERNATIONAL LAW pp. 838–844 (5e édition, 2003).

régissent l'interprétation des traités, à savoir les articles 31 à 33.[57] Le Tribunal a ainsi décrit sa mission : « [le Tribunal] doit interpréter diverses dispositions des instruments fondamentaux tout en appliquant les règles du droit international pertinentes ».[58]

La disposition ayant fait l'objet de l'examen essentiel était l'article XII du Traité de 1839, tel qu'il avait été modifié par le Traité de 1873 (ces traités figuraient parmi les « instruments fondamentaux ») et, par conséquent, la référence aux « règles du droit international pertinentes » indiquait que le Tribunal ne se considérait pas restreint à appliquer le seul texte de l'article XII, et contexte immédiat du traité (voir ci-dessous).

Bien que les dispositions de la Convention de Vienne relatives à l'interprétation soient largement comprises comme représentant le droit international coutumier tel qu'il existait en 1969, leur formulation réduisait le poids de deux principes d'interprétation précédemment bien établis, à savoir, d'une part, que les traités doivent être interprétés à la lumière du droit et des conditions prévalant au moment de leur conclusion (ce qui sera appelé ici le principe de contemporanéité « initiale »)[59] et, d'autre part, que les restrictions à la souveraineté des Parties ne se présument pas.[60] Il est à peine besoin de préciser que l'interprétation des traités, tout comme l'interprétation de tout texte dans tout système juridique, relève davantage de l'artisanat que de la science exacte. Dans tout système juridique, les principes d'interprétation sont les paradigmes du concept de Dworkin : il s'agit de « principes », à distinguer des « règles », en fonction, d'une part, du besoin d'appréciation de leur application et, d'autre part, de leurs conséquences.[61] Par ailleurs, la recherche de l'intention des parties peut très souvent s'avérer être la recherche d'une

---

[57] Sentence, para. 45.

[58] Sentence, para. 44.

[59] Pour une discussion, voir DONALD W. GREIG, INTERTEMPORALITY AND THE LAW OF TREATIES pp. 2–10 (2001). IAN BROWNLIE, PRINCIPLES OF INTERNATIONAL LAW p. 604 (6e édition, 2003) place l'obligation de prendre en compte la contemporanéité « originelle » dans la recherche du sens « naturel et ordinaire » des mots.

[60] Voir Lord McNair, *Treaties and Sovereignty*, reproduit dans THE LAW OF TREATIES pp. 754–768 (1961), dans lequel il écrit (à la page 765) que le principe de souveraineté est lié à une approche restrictive de l'interprétation des traits, approche qui, en 1958, voyait son influence décliner.

[61] RONALD DWORKIN, TAKING RIGHTS SERIOUSLY (1977), Chapitre 3.

aiguille qui n'existe pas dans une très grosse botte de foin faite de textes et de documents. La Convention de Vienne met en avant le texte même du traité, considérant que l'intention des parties peut être mise à jour à partir des mots que les Parties ont elles-mêmes choisis. Le texte ne saurait toutefois être pris isolément. Ainsi, l'article 31, paragraphe 1, dispose qu'« un traité doit être interprété de bonne foi suivant le sens ordinaire à attribuer aux termes du traité dans leur contexte et à la lumière de son objet et de son but ».

Le contexte documentaire d'un traité est énoncé à l'article 31, paragraphe 2, tandis que l'article 31, paragraphe 3 – dont nous reparlerons ci-après de manière plus détaillée – prévoit un certain nombre d'autres éléments devant être pris en compte. L'article 32, qui a des parents dans tous les systèmes juridiques, permet le recours à des « moyens complémentaires d'interprétation » à condition qu'à l'issue de leur analyse, fondée uniquement sur l'article 31, (a) le sens demeure ambigu ou obscur ou (b) que cette analyse mène à un résultat manifestement absurde ou déraisonnable.

Rappelons qu'un tribunal chargé de l'interprétation d'un traité ne saurait ignorer que la signification de l'article 31 est généralement considérée comme relevant de l'une des quatre catégories de l'article 32 avant que les juges n'aient à s'engager dans une décision finale sur le sens d'un traité.

Si les principes de contemporanéité « initiale » et de souveraineté ont subi une éclipse, le principe d'effet utile a, quant à lui, joui ces derniers temps de la faveur des instances chargées de l'interprétation des traités, l'idée fondamentale étant que l'intention des parties est qu'elle doit donner à l'objet et au but de leurs traités une application effective, plutôt que d'être restreinte par des sens étroits et tortueux.[62] Il convient ici de souligner que si les Parties ont pu adopter une approche particulière d'interprétation, elles n'ont pas pour autant souhaité aboutir à un résultat particulier de cette approche dans le cadre d'un ensemble de circonstances particulières. Le principe d'effet utile a joui d'une prééminence notable dans l'interprétation de deux catégories

---

[62] Sentence, para. 49. ANTHONY AUST, MODERN TREATY LAW AND PRACTICE p. 188 (2000), suggère que l'objet et le but du traité sont le plus souvent utilisés pour confirmer le sens du texte lui-même que comme fondement indépendant d'interprétation. Manifestement, ce n'est pas le cas lorsqu'on se fonde sur le principe d'effectivité.

particulières de traités, ceux établissant des organisations internationales[63] et ceux destinés à protéger les droits de l'homme.[64]

Ce que la Belgique soutenait au sujet du droit de passage prévu à l'article XII du Traité de Séparation était que ce droit était clairement établi et que, bien que des droits résiduels de souveraineté sur le tracé aient subsisté au profit des Pays-Bas (il n'existait en effet aucune assertion de statut extraterritorial du Rhin de fer), ces droits ne pouvaient être exercés d'une manière qui contrarierait l'exercice du droit de passage de la Belgique ou qui imposerait à l'exercice de ce droit des conditions déraisonnables.[65] Les Pays-Bas, s'inclinant devant l'argument principal de la Belgique, arguèrent toutefois que leur droit de souveraineté demeurait intact à l'exception des restrictions clairement prévues par les Traités de 1839 et 1873.[66]

Bien que faisant référence à la jurisprudence, désormais ancienne, de la Cour permanente de justice internationale (la « CPJI »), en faveur de la présomption de souveraineté,[67] le Tribunal a indiqué que ce principe n'avait jamais joui d'un statut de supériorité hiérarchique et que la Convention de Vienne n'y faisait pas référence, pour conclure que « sa pertinence actuelle [pouvait] être mise en doute ».[68] En revanche, le Tribunal s'est fondé sur l'arbitrage du Lac Lanoux,[69] une autre affaire qui impliquait la recherche d'un équilibre entre les droits d'un État sur le territoire d'un autre et la souveraineté résiduelle de cet autre État. On voit comment le principe de l'effet utile prend le dessus – le Tribunal a affirmé que le conflit ne devait pas être tranché en invoquant une théorie restrictive d'interprétation mais, en identifiant les droits concédés à la Belgique par les Traités, les droits résiduels des Pays-Bas étant

---

[63] Elihu Lauterpacht, *The Development of the Law of International Organisations by the Decisions of International Tribunals*, 52 RECUEIL DES COURS p. 377, aux pp. 416–420 (1976).

[64] Rudolf Bernhardt, *Evolutive Treaty Interpretation, Especially of the European Convention on Human Rights*, 42 GERMAN YEARBOOK OF INTERNATIONAL LAW p. 11 (1999).

[65] MB, para. 76, soumission no. 6.

[66] RPB, para. 3.2.

[67] Sentence, paras. 51–53, faisant référence notamment à l'*Affaire des zones franches de la Haute-Savoie et du Pays de Gex (France c. Suisse)* (1932), C.P.J.I. (sér. A/B) no. 46.

[68] Sentence, para. 53. Le Tribunal n'aborde pas un problème supplémentaire lié à la contemporanéité initiale (qui, dans ce cas, aurait fort bien pu conférer davantage de poids au principe de souveraineté), c'est-à-dire la question de déterminer si un tribunal devrait ou non appliquer les règles d'interprétation telles qu'elles existaient à l'époque de la signature du traité.

[69] *France c. Espagne*, 16 novembre 1957, R.S.A., XII, p. 285.

tous les droits sauf ceux « en contradiction avec les droits accordés à la Belgique par le Traité ou avec les droits dont la Belgique pourrait jouir en vertu du droit international général ou des contraintes imposées par le droit communautaire ».[70]

Ceci ressemble davantage à un truisme qu'un guide utile pour l'interprétation des traités. La déclaration figurant au paragraphe 56 de la sentence ne signifie quelque chose que si l'identification à la fois des droits d'un État et des droits résiduels de souveraineté sont déterminables précisément. Ils ne le sont toutefois évidemment pas. C'est bien ce dont il s'agit en matière d'interprétation, même si le résultat de celle-ci, une sentence, prétend à une précision qui est cependant absente. L'interprétation, bien souvent, ne consiste pas à tracer des lignes claires mais à résoudre un conflit entre des demandes contradictoires, qui ont chacune des arguments à faire valoir. En dépit de la simplicité de l'affirmation du paragraphe 56 à laquelle nous venons de nous référer, ce qui est en jeu est un conflit entre la présomption en faveur de la souveraineté, soutenue par les Pays-Bas, et l'affirmation d'un droit à un chemin de fer effectif, soutenue par la Belgique. Par « effectif », la Belgique entendait « d'un bon rendement » ou même « le moins coûteux », ainsi que d'un fonctionnement efficace, en d'autres termes que les trains puissent rouler d'une manière satisfaisante d'un point de vue économique.[71]

VII. LE PRINCIPE DU *LOTUS*, L'INTERPRÉTATION DES TRAITÉS ET LE PRINCIPE DE L'EFFET UTILE

La présomption en faveur de la souveraineté apparaît souvent sous une forme modifiée, celle d'un des aspects du « principe du *Lotus* », qui tire sa force de la notion d'État elle-même, à savoir qu'au sein du territoire d'un État, celui-ci a le droit exclusif d'exercer ses compétences de toutes natures, de faire et d'appliquer les lois ou encore de s'abstenir de réglementer certains domaines.[72] Ces pouvoirs, a priori illimités, sont cependant soumis aux obligations internationales de l'État, un exemple de celles-ci étant constitué par

---

[70] Sentence, para. 56.

[71] RB, para. 70.

[72] James Crawford, The Creation of States in International Law pp. 41–43 (2e édition, 2006). Le principe tire son nom de l'arrêt rendu dans l'affaire du Lotus (*Turquie c. France*), C.P.J.I. 1927, série A, No. 9.

les règles en matière d'immunité des États, qui limitent les pouvoirs de l'État, y compris au sein de son propre territoire, concernant certaines catégories de personnes. Ainsi, pour limiter la territorialité d'un État, est-il nécessaire de démontrer qu'il existe une règle de droit international restreignant celle-ci. Pour ce faire, il conviendra souvent d'interpréter une règle juridique internationale dont il est allégué qu'elle restreint la souveraineté interne d'un État. La manière d'interpréter un traité qui permettrait de donner un effet utile optimal au principe du *Lotus* est celle qui ne reposerait que sur la formulation expresse du traité permettant d'imposer une obligation à l'État territorial ; à l'inverse, toute lacune ou ambiguïté doit être interprétée en faveur de l'État territorial.[73] Toute règle stricte ou présomption de cette nature n'est plus en cour et ce, non seulement du fait que la règle d'interprétation prévue à l'article 31 de la Convention de Vienne n'y fait pas référence mais également du fait que l'article 31 est rédigé de telle manière qu'il en minimise l'effet. L'article 31 insiste sur l'importance de la formulation du texte, à savoir son sens « ordinaire » vu « à la lumière de [son] objet et [de son] but ». Ces derniers mots laissent la place à des considérations d'interprétation efficaces d'un traité, sans qu'il soit explicitement fait référence au principe de l'effet utile. Le principe de l'effet utile suggère que les traités soient lus de manière à faire fonctionner le traité afin qu'il atteigne son but de façon optimale, sauf dans le cas où une formulation expresse du traité ferait obstacle à une telle conclusion. La prudence des États, confrontés à la manière dont peut se réaliser cette possibilité, est compréhensible – le principe de l'effet utile ne consiste pas seulement à opposer une formulation capable de protéger les droits d'un État aux intérêts d'une interprétation plus large du traité, mais il permet surtout d'intégrer dans le traité des termes qui n'y sont pas, pour peu que ces termes soient nécessaires à la mise en œuvre effective de l'objet et du but du traité. Nous nous sommes habitués à cette approche de l'interprétation des traités, en particulier pour les traités instituant des organisations internationales et pour les traités concernant les droits de l'homme. Les interprètes ne se réfèrent qu'en apparence au principe du *Lotus* lorsqu'ils affirment que l'intention des parties était de permettre l'application de leur traité (et en particulier lorsqu'ils ont mis en place des procédures détaillées pour l'interprétation, anticipant le fait que ces organes adopteraient une telle approche). Le transfert de compétence des États vers les interprètes ayant autorité a été important car de nombreux traités modernes et multilatéraux contiennent, au sein de leurs

---

[73] Voir McNair, *supra* note 60.

préambules, de larges déclarations concernant le but de l'organisation ou une affirmation forte des objectifs de protection des droits de l'homme. Ceux qui soutiennent le principe de l'effet utile ont toujours concédé qu'il n'appartient pas à l'interprète de réécrire le traité en lieu et place des États,[74] mais la tentation de le faire peut s'avérer puissante. Dans un arrêt récent de la Cour européenne des droits de l'homme,[75] qui est l'un des partisans les plus vigoureux du principe de l'effet utile comme élément d'interprétation des traités, la recherche – louable sans aucun doute – de l'interprétation la plus efficace sur la question de l'effet contraignant pour les États des mesures provisoires de la Cour semble être en désaccord avec le texte, le contexte et l'histoire de la CEDH. La minorité dissidente eut une approche plus orthodoxe.[76] Jusqu'à présent, les parties à la CEDH ont été peu disposées à rejeter la technique de la Cour de Strasbourg[77] mais il existe des exemples du droit des organisations internationales et, notamment, le très long différend au sujet de la légitimité de certaines opérations de maintien de la paix,[78] qui démontrent que le recours à l'effet utile comme principe autonome de l'interprétation des traités a ses limites.

Bien que l'importance du principe du *Lotus* pour l'interprétation des traités ait pu diminuer, il n'a pas disparu, en particulier pour des affaires telles que le Rhin de fer dans le cadre de laquelle un traité concède à un État ou à ses ressortissants certains droits sur le territoire d'un autre. La Belgique avait deux arguments fondamentaux pour s'opposer à ce que soit accordé un poids trop important au principe du *Lotus*. En premier lieu, elle affirmait qu'en droit international, la compétence d'un État doit être exercée de bonne foi et conformément au principe de caractère raisonnable et que ces normes s'appliquaient aux droits conventionnels d'autres États.[79] En deuxième lieu, la Belgique soutenait que l'article XII constituait non pas une « dérogation » à la souveraineté des Pays-Bas mais une compensation au profit de la Belgique pour la perte de son accès terrestre direct à l'Allemagne du fait des ajustements

---

[74] Sentence, para. 49.

[75] *Mamatkulov et Askarov c. Turquie* (2005), Requêtes nos. 46827 et 46951/99 (CEDH, Grande Chambre).

[76] *Ibid.*, opinion dissidente des juges Caflisch, Turmen et Kovler.

[77] Voir toutefois *Olaechea Cahuas c. Espagne* (2006), Requête no. 24668/03 (CEDH, Cinquième section).

[78] Certaines dépenses des Nations Unies, Avis consultatif, C.I.J. *Rec.* 1962 p. 151.

[79] MB, para. 56, RB, paras. 21–22.

territoriaux auxquels il avait été procédé par ailleurs dans le Traité de 1839.[80] Les prétentions de l'État bénéficiaire selon lesquelles les concessions de droits en vertu de traités sur un territoire sont absolues et excluent ainsi toute réglementation par l'État territorial sur l'exercice du droit issu d'un traité remontent à l'arbitrage des Pêcheries de l'Atlantique nord.[81] Si le traité est muet sur la question de la réglementation, comme ce sera souvent le cas, la « souveraineté » est alors le seul point sur lequel peut se fonder l'État territorial, c'est-à-dire qu'en faisant valoir sa souveraineté, il n'a pas besoin de justifier d'une source dans le traité pour la réglementation à laquelle il propose de soumettre l'exercice du droit – cela peut concerner la sécurité, la sûreté, la protection de l'environnement, ou toute autre politique que l'État entend poursuivre. Ce qu'il faut comprendre du déclin du principe du *Lotus* toutefois est que l'identification d'une source du pouvoir (c'est-à-dire en s'appuyant sur le principe du *Lotus*) ne sera pas décisive pour la légalité de toute *utilisation* du pouvoir. Le critère proposé par la Belgique et repris par le Tribunal est que la réglementation ne doit pas empêcher l'exercice d'un droit extraterritorial, ni ne doit imposer des charges non raisonnables sur l'utilisation de ce droit et que, dans certains cas au moins, afin de décider quels sont les droits de l'autre État, il convient de prendre en compte le principe de l'effet utile.[82] Le Tribunal a résolu le conflit entre des prétentions opposées en recourant à la métaphore de l'équilibre, qui semble exclure la présomption de valeur contraignante à la fois du droit issu du traité et du droit d'exercice de la puissance publique dérivé de la souveraineté.[83]

VIII. INTERPRÉTATION CONTEMPORAINE « ACTUELLE » DES TRAITÉS

Ce qui découle des paragraphes ci-dessus est que l'approche de l'interprétation des traités a évolué au cours des années, même si elle a peu changé depuis 1969. La question se pose alors de déterminer comment des

---

[80] RB, para. 20, bien que la Belgique n'affirme pas le GT statut extraterritorial du Rhin de fer : RB, para. 28.

[81] Pêcheries de l'Atlantique Nord (*Grande Bretagne c. États Unis*), Sentence du 7 septembre 1910 (Cour permanente d'arbitrage), *R.S.A.* vol. XI, p. 189, disponible (dans la version originale anglaise) sur le site Internet de la CPA, *supra* note 1.

[82] Sentence, paras. 49 et 82–84.

[83] Sentence, para. 83.

traités, conclus dans des contextes antérieurs et différents, devraient être interprétés aujourd'hui. Cette question s'intègre dans une problématique plus large : comment les termes des traités anciens doivent-ils être compris à l'heure actuelle et comment la disposition de la Convention de Vienne selon laquelle un interprète devrait prendre en compte « toute règle pertinente de droit international applicable dans les relations entre les parties » devrait-elle être interprétée au regard des règles qui ont émergé depuis la conclusion du traité ? J'utilise le terme de contemporanéité « actuelle » pour décrire le principe d'interprétation qui prend en compte les modifications du droit (et peut-être également des faits) entre le moment de la conclusion du traité et le moment de son interprétation. Ces questions sont parfois écartées car réclamant l'application du « droit intertemporel », avec l'implication que le traité doit être lu à la lumière de la manière dont il était compris à l'époque de sa conclusion.[84] Le « droit intertemporel » est une expression recouvrant différents sens en droit international et il est important de l'utiliser avec précision.

IX. LE DROIT INTERTEMPOREL[85]

A l'époque de leur adoption, les règles d'interprétation édictées par la Convention de Vienne étaient largement comprises comme formalisant le droit coutumier ; la pratique depuis lors, y compris celle des cours et tribunaux internationaux (dont la sentence du Rhin de fer est un exemple de plus), a consolidé cette position. Il n'est toutefois jamais suggéré que l'adoption des règles de la Convention de Vienne simplifie le processus d'interprétation des traités. Non seulement ces règles comportent-elles plusieurs éléments, mais chacune d'entre elles implique un degré d'appréciation plus ou moins important et, bien que les articles 31 et 32 fournissent des indications de priorité, la résolution des conflits de sens en fonction de l'utilisation d'une partie ou d'une autre de ces règles est un facteur supplémentaire de recours au jugement de l'interprète. Dans les dispositions relatives à l'interprétation prévues par la Convention de Vienne ne figure aucune mention spécifique de l'intertemporalité, mais il est évident que certaines décisions doivent être prises

---

[84] BROWNLIE, *supra* note 59.

[85] THE INTERTEMPORAL PROBLEM IN PUBLIC INTERNATIONAL LAW (Institute of International Law, Wiesbaden 1975); Rosalyn Higgins, *Time and the Law: International Perspectives on an Old Problem*, 46 INTERNATIONAL AND COMPARATIVE LAW QUARTERLY p. 501, aux pp. 515–520 (1997).

sur les questions de temps, ne serait-ce que pour déterminer si le cadre temporel de référence approprié est la date de la conclusion du traité ou bien la date de son interprétation. La référence à des accords et pratiques « ultérieur[s] » à l'article 31, paragraphe 3, démontre qu'existe bien une latitude pour prendre en compte les événements intervenus après la conclusion du traité et, si la référence aux « règles pertinentes de droit international » figurant à l'article 31, paragraphe 3, alinéa (c) est également comprise comme incluant les développements postérieurs à la conclusion du traité, l'éventail d'éléments susceptibles d'être pertinents dans le cadre de l'interprétation du traité jusqu'au moment où celui-ci fait l'objet d'une interprétation peut en réalité être très vaste.

L'application de l'article 31, paragraphe 3, alinéa (c) et la compétence des juridictions internationales peuvent soulever de sérieux problèmes, comme le démontra l'affaire des Plates-formes pétrolières.[86] La base légale en matière de compétence était l'article XXI, paragraphe 1, du Traité d'amitié, de commerce et de droits consulaires entre l'Iran et les États-Unis qui prévoyait :

> Tout différend qui pourra s'élever entre les Hautes Parties contractantes quant à l'interprétation ou à l'application du présent Traité et qui ne pourrait pas être réglé d'une manière satisfaisante par la voie diplomatique sera porté devant la Cour internationale de justice, à moins que les Hautes Parties contractantes ne conviennent de le régler par d'autres moyens pacifiques.

Après que les États-Unis ont tenté de se fonder sur une réserve au titre de la sécurité nationale prévue à l'article XX, paragraphe 1 du Traité aux fins de justifier leur recours à la force contre l'Iran, l'Iran a tenté de soulever des arguments au sujet de la légalité de ce recours à la force. La CIJ a traité cette question, en dépit des objections des États-Unis, lesquels soutenaient que la Cour n'avait aucune compétence à cette fin ; il s'agissait d'une question ne relevant pas de la clause de compétence du Traité.[87] La limitation éventuelle

---

[86] Affaire des plates-formes pétrolières (*République islamique d'Iran c. Etats-Unis d'Amérique*), [2003] C.I.J. rec. 161. Pour un exposé clair des questions en jeu dans cette affaire, voir Campbell McClachlan, *The Principle of Systemic Integration and Article 31(3)(c) of the Vienna Convention*, 54 INTERNATIONAL AND COMPARATIVE LAW QUARTERLY p. 279 (2005).

[87] Pour une critique de l'approche de la CIJ, voir Frank Berman, *Treaty "Interpretation" in a Judicial Context*, 29 YALE JOURNAL OF INTERNATIONAL LAW p. 315 (2004), dans lequel l'auteur soutient que le sens des différents termes du Traité, en particulier de l'article X(1), était « aisément identifiable ».

du droit applicable n'était pas une considération pertinente pour le Tribunal dans l'affaire du Rhin de fer car sa mission était d'appliquer le « droit international » et il avait ainsi le pouvoir d'examiner tout point de droit international qu'il estimait pertinent pour la résolution du différend qui lui était soumis. Le Tribunal n'a pas reçu d'instructions au sujet des aspects de droit intertemporel qu'il devait appliquer. En fait, le Tribunal a eu en l'occurrence une vue généreuse de sa compétence, considérant les traités du 19ème siècle à la lumière des développements contemporains du droit international de l'environnement (voir ci-dessous).

X. LE « DROIT INTERTEMPOREL » ET L'INTERPRÉTATION DES TRAITÉS[88]

Le « droit intertemporel » est un concept familier de droit international bien que le fait qu'il recouvre différents sens dans des contextes différents ne soit pas toujours apprécié.[89] En premier lieu, c'est un aspect du droit de souveraineté sur un territoire ; il exige que la pertinence et le poids des données factuelles contribuant à établir la souveraineté soient appréciés au regard du droit international contemporain à l'époque de leur survenance.[90] Il est motivé par une recherche de certitude et de stabilité en ce qui concerne la souveraineté sur un territoire en cherchant à éviter de défaire les arrangements acquis à la lumière des évolutions ultérieures du droit. En tant que tel, il semble constituer une règle quasi inévitable. En droit des traités, le besoin d'appliquer une approche équivalente, c'est-à-dire que les traités devraient être interprétés à la lumière du droit et du contexte prévalant à l'époque de la conclusion du traité (la contemporanéité « initiale ») n'est pas si contraignante, bien qu'elle représente une position concevable et qu'elle jouisse d'un certain soutien dans la doctrine ancienne.[91] Son poids est toutefois allé en diminuant, en particulier en ce qui concerne certaines catégories de traités.

---

[88] Voir GREIG, *supra* note 59.

[89] Voir Higgins, *supra* note 85.

[90] Affaire de l'Île des Palmes (*Pays-Bas c. États-Unis*), 4 avril 1928, RSA vol. II, p. 839 (Cour permanente d'arbitrage 1928) disponible (dans la version originale anglaise) sur le site Internet de la CPA, *supra* note 1.

[91] BROWNLIE, *supra* note 59, se référant à l'Affaire des Grisbadarna (*Norvège c. Suède*), R.S.A. vol. XI p. 147 (Cour permanente d'arbitrage 1909), disponible (dans la version originale anglaise) sur le site Internet de la CPA, *supra* note 1. Il s'agit d'une affaire de délimitation frontalière dont GREIG, *supra* note 59, à la p. 41, écrit qu'il s'agissait « quelque peu d'une exception ».

Pour résoudre le problème de l'intertemporalité dans l'affaire du Rhin du fer, le Tribunal a fondé sa décision sur l'article 31, paragraphe 3, alinéa (c) de la Convention de Vienne qui renvoie à « toute règle pertinente du droit international applicable aux relations entre les parties ».[92] Cette disposition ne contient aucune précision quant à l'objet ou la temporalité de ces règles. Elle revêt une certaine valeur dans le cadre du débat concernant la « fragmentation » car elle permet d'intégrer des obligations des États dérivant d'un traité spécifique au sein de leurs obligations plus larges, réduisant ainsi le risque d'incompatibilités. Un exemple important de cette pratique est l'arrêt rendu par la Cour européenne des droits de l'homme dans l'affaire Al-Adsani.[93] Dans le cadre de cette affaire, le Royaume-Uni argua qu'il disposait du pouvoir (implicite) de limiter le droit d'accès à un tribunal dont bénéficie (implicitement) une personne engageant une procédure civile au Royaume-Uni au titre de tortures commises par un autre État, de manière à donner effet aux règles d'immunité des États qui imposent au Royaume-Uni une obligation de ne pas permettre qu'ait lieu une telle action. La Cour de Strasbourg, affirmant que la Convention devait être interprétée « autant que faire se peut de manière à se concilier avec les autres règles de droit international » accepta ces arguments comme limite « raisonnable » du droit d'accès au titre de l'article 6, paragraphe 1 de la CEDH[94] et ce, en dépit de la forte valeur attachée par la Cour de Strasbourg à la protection effective des droits de l'homme (laquelle est la justification du droit implicite d'accès en lui-même).[95] La Cour affirma que la CEDH devait être interprétée dans son contexte juridique international. En l'occurrence, le fait de se fonder sur les règles de droit international contre le Royaume-Uni ne présentait pas de difficultés, ledit État les ayant introduits lui-même dans l'affaire (ni sans doute contre tous les autres États parties à la CEDH, dans la mesure où il est probable qu'ils partageaient le point de vue du Royaume-Uni sur l'immunité des États). Toutefois, là où existent plus de doutes au sujet des règles, en particulier là où existe un doute quant à son application à un État affecté par l'interprétation, un tribunal devrait avancer avec prudence. L'article 31, paragraphe 3, alinéa (c) ne renvoie qu'aux règles de droit international « applicables aux relations entre les parties ». L'importation à grande échelle d'éléments relevant des droits de l'homme ou du droit de l'environnement dans l'interprétation d'un traité, sans tenir compte

---

[92] Sentence, para. 58.

[93] *Al-Adsani c. Royaume-Uni* (2002), Requête no. 35763/97 (CEDH, Grande chambre).

[94] *Ibid.* aux paras. 55–56, 66.

[95] *Golder c. Royaume-Uni* (1975), Requête no. 4451/70 (CEDH, Plénière).

du caractère contraignant de ces règles sur les parties, ne peut pas être justifié par référence à l'article 31, paragraphe 3, alinéa (c).

Une approche analogue à celles adoptées pour l'interprétation des constitutions internationales et des traités relatifs aux droits de l'homme peut être trouvée dans l'arrêt de la CIJ relatif au droit de l'environnement rendu dans l'affaire *Gabčíkovo*.[96] Tout d'abord, la Cour n'était pas disposée à accepter l'argument de la Hongrie selon lequel le traité conclu avec la Tchécoslovaquie en 1977 relatif à l'aménagement du Danube était dépourvu de validité du fait d'un changement fondamental de circonstances, à savoir le développement des sciences et du droit de l'environnement. L'une des raisons pour laquelle de tels changements n'étaient pas imprévisibles, selon la CIJ, était que le traité de 1977 contenait des dispositions susceptibles d'être interprétées aux fins de tenir compte de changements dans le contexte environnemental.[97] Ainsi, s'agissant de l'interprétation du traité, la CIJ déclara :

Il est clair que les incidences du projet sur l'environnement et ses implications pour celui-ci seront nécessairement une question clef . . .

Aux fins de l'évaluation des risques écologiques, ce sont les normes actuelles qui doivent être prises en considération. Non seulement le libellé des articles 15 et 19 le permet, mais il le prescrit même dans la mesure où ces articles mettent à la charge des parties une obligation continue, et donc nécessairement évolutive, de maintenir la qualité de l'eau du Danube et de protéger la nature.

Ces normes nouvelles [en matière d'environnement] doivent être prises en considération et ces exigences nouvelles convenablement appréciées, non seulement lorsque des États envisagent de nouvelles activités, mais aussi lorsqu'ils poursuivent des activités qu'ils ont engagées dans le passé. Le concept de développement durable traduit bien cette nécessité de concilier développement économique et protection de l'environnement.[98]

---

[96] Affaire relative au projet Gabčíkovo-Nagymaros (Hongrie/Slovaquie), C.I.J. Recueil 1997 p. 7.

[97] *Ibid.* au para. 104.

[98] *Ibid.* au para. 140. Pour un commentaire de valeur sur les aspects intertemporaux de l'affaire, voir Afshin A-Khavari, *The Passage of Time in International Environmental Disputes*, 10 Murdoch University Electronic Journal of Law (Déc. 2003), paras. 32–66, disponible à <http://www.murdochedu.au/elaw/issues/v104/akhavari104_text. html>.

Il existe peu d'explication justifiant qu'une telle position soit prise : en effet, le statut de droit coutumier d'une règle sur le développement durable n'avait pas été établi explicitement, aucune raison n'avait été avancée quant au motif pour lequel les États n'auraient pas pu créer conventionnellement une *lex specialis*, y compris en présence d'une règle coutumière sur le développement durable. En fait, c'est la nature des termes utilisés dans le traité, dont il était jugé qu'elle créait des obligations de réévaluation constantes des activités du point de vue de la protection de l'environnement, qui fournissait la base de l'interprétation adoptée par la Cour. En l'absence de telles limites, il aurait pu être avancé après l'arrêt *Gabčíkovo* que toutes les obligations conventionnelles des États, dont l'exécution avait des conséquences suffisamment importantes, devraient être lues, si possible, comme prenant en compte le droit de l'environnement contemporain (au sens de contemporanéité « actuelle »). On entend ici l'écho de l'arbitrage *de l'Ile des Palmes* et de l'utilisation effective du droit intertemporel par l'arbitre unique. L'arbitre Huber avait en effet déterminé que même si le titre avait été licitement établi selon le droit contemporain « initial », il incombait à un État de maintenir ce titre en vigueur si le droit changeait et prescrivait davantage, non seulement pour établir un titre mais pour le maintenir.[99] Il fut critiqué pour avoir introduit un élément d'incertitude dans un domaine du droit où la stabilité était jusqu'alors une vertu cardinale,[100] mais une lecture attentive montre que ce n'était en réalité pas le cas. Si l'approche interprétative dans l'affaire *Gabčíkovo* devait ne pas être limitée aux dispositions auxquelles était confronté la Cour, une aura similaire d'incertitude serait introduite dans les relations conventionnelles, un besoin permanent d'apprécier ce que les accords entre États exigent au fur et à mesure du développement du droit international de l'environnement et de la progression des connaissances.

L'affaire Gabčíkovo laisse sans réponse la question de déterminer si le principe de contemporanéité « actuelle » est limité à certains catégories de traités, ces catégories comprenant désormais les accords en matière d'environnement, ou si le principe est applicable à tout exercice d'interprétation d'un traité. Les incertitudes résultant d'une telle position se résoudraient par une meilleure intégration des obligations internationales, ainsi qu'une réduction des effets de la « fragmentation ». Il pourrait également y avoir un

---

[99] *Supra* note 90.

[100] Philip Jessup, *The Palmas Arbitration*, 22 AMERICAN JOURNAL OF INTERNATIONAL LAW p. 735 (1928).

autre prix : dans sa note sur l'affaire des *Plates-formes pétrolières*, le professeur Franklin Berman a suggéré que les États étudieraient dorénavant attentivement les clauses de compétence dans leurs traités afin de voir à quels risques de litiges ils seraient maintenant exposés, même s'il ne s'attendait pas à de grands changements dans les pratiques de rédaction.[101]

XI.   LE TRAITÉ DE SÉPARATION DE 1839, L'ARTICLE XII ET LE DROIT INTERTEMPOREL

C'est le point auquel est parvenu le tribunal du Rhin de fer. L'article XII devait-il être interprété à la lumière, notamment, du droit de l'environnement moderne ? Le Traité de 1839 n'était toutefois pas un traité sur l'environnement. De même ne contenait-il pas de dispositions telles que celles qui étaient considérées comme imposant des obligations continues dans le traité de 1977 dans l'affaire *Gabčíkovo*. Le Tribunal a mis en avant l'article 31, paragraphe 3, alinéa (c) de la Convention de Vienne et indiqua que « le droit international de l'environnement est applicable aux relations entre les parties » mais observa qu'il y avait des « discussions considérables [qui] ont eu lieu en ce qui concerne ce qui, en matière du droit de l'environnement, constitue des « règles » ou des « principes », ce qui relève du droit non contraignant (« soft law »), et quel droit des traités en matière d'environnement ou principes a contribué au développement du droit international coutumier ».[102]

Bien que le Tribunal ne se soit pas étendu sur ce point, si lui-même ou tout autre tribunal devait se fonder sur l'article 31, paragraphe 3, alinéa (c), il doit identifier les « règles pertinentes de droit international » devant être prises en compte à des fins d'interprétation, et non se borner à renvoyer à un bric à brac de normes et d'aspirations non contraignantes.

La première question pour le Tribunal portait sur le fait de déterminer si la demande de la Belgique de réfection de la ligne du Rhin de fer était une demande de réactivation du modèle original ou s'il s'agissait d'un droit de passage entièrement nouveau, étant donné les modifications demandées. Le droit de passage de la Belgique concernait un tracé construit « d'après le même plan » que le tracé en Belgique. En envisageant l'article XII comme un tout, le

---

[101] *Supra* note 87, aux pp. 321–322.
[102] Sentence, para. 58.

Tribunal rejeta une solution littérale si celle-ci avait signifié que « plan » couvrait l'ensemble du projet dans toutes ses particularités. Les Pays-Bas jouissaient d'un « droit décisionnel »[103] du fait que la ligne belge serait prolongée sur le territoire néerlandais, sur lequel les Pays-Bas exercent un pouvoir souverain, sous réserve de ce qui est prévu par l'article XII. Quant à la question de savoir si un « nouveau » chemin de fer était envisagé, le Tribunal a plutôt éludé la question en la déplaçant sur celle de savoir à qui incombait le coût. Il établit une distinction entre « entretien » et « modernisation ». Les Traités n'abordaient pas la question de la responsabilité financière une fois la ligne construite. Les Pays-Bas avaient payé l'entretien de la ligne du Rhin de fer dans le passé et concédaient que remettre la ligne en état selon les normes précédentes – modestes – leur incombait. Le Tribunal fit appel à l'article 31, paragraphe 3, alinéa (c). La « règle intertemporelle » était l'une des règles de droit international qui s'appliquait entres les parties.[104] Ce qui était en jeu en l'occurrence était la différence entre le coût « limité et relativement modeste » du projet tel qu'il avait été envisagé en 1839 et les grandes avancées en matière de transport ferroviaire et les coûts associés qui ne « pouvaient pas avoir prévus par les parties ».[105] Le Tribunal indiqua qu'« il est en effet établi depuis longtemps que la compréhension des termes conceptuels ou génériques d'un traité peut être considérée comme « une question essentiellement relative qui dépend du développement des relations internationales »».[106]

Manifestement, il s'agit là d'une manière raisonnable et, en fait, nécessaire, de comprendre des termes juridiques tels que « nationalité » ou « plateau continental ». Mais comme l'a reconnu le Tribunal, sa mission ne consistait pas à déterminer le sens d'un terme générique mais à adapter la formulation d'un ancien traité aux développements techniques intervenus au fils des ans dans la construction et l'exploitation ferroviaires. Là également le Tribunal a décidé « qu'une interprétation évolutive … [est] préférable à une application stricte de la règle intertemporelle ».[107] Il ne s'agissait pas là de se fonder sur l'article 31, paragraphe 3, alinéa (c) mais cette décision était justifiée par le Tribunal car cela assurerait que le Traité soit appliqué d'une manière efficace pour répondre à son objet et à son but. Le Tribunal a fait allusion à l'affaire *Gabčíkovo* sans faire référence à, ni encore moins reconnaître une quelconque différence entre

---

[103] Sentence, para. 67.
[104] Sentence, para. 79.
[105] Sentence, para. 79.
[106] Sentence, para. 79.
[107] Sentence, para. 80.

les traités en jeu dans les deux affaires. Il convient également de répéter qu'une approche « évolutive » ou « dynamique » de l'interprétation n'est pas exactement la même chose qu'appliquer l'article 31, paragraphe 3, alinéa (c) pour tenir compte du droit international contemporain. Selon la Cour européenne des droits de l'homme par exemple, une approche « évolutive » vise tout d'abord à permettre à la Cour de prendre en compte les modifications pertinentes intervenues dans les éléments factuels d'une affaire, à l'époque où ils sont intervenus et à l'époque où ils sont appréciés par la Cour (les modifications intervenues dans le droit étant des « faits » à cette fin).[108]

Les considérations que nous venons d'évoquer ont affecté la compréhension des traités comme suit :

(a) Le Traité du Rhin de fer n'était pas destiné à avoir une durée déterminée.[109]

(b) Le but et l'objet de l'article XII étaient de fournir une « communication commerciale » entre la Belgique et l'Allemagne, traversant le territoire des Pays-Bas, de sorte que ce qui était nécessaire pour garantir une voie commerciale contemporaine « actuelle » évoluerait avec le temps.[110]

(c) « [U]ne interprétation compatible avec le principe d'effet utile amène le Tribunal à penser que l'article XII ... est toujours applicable à la mise à niveau et aux améliorations » et donc, faire application de « cette approche dynamique et évolutive » signifie que la réactivation de la ligne selon des spécifications considérablement plus exigeantes ne doit pas être considérée comme une demande de « nouvelle ligne ».[111]

(d) A la lumière du point (c) ci-dessus, il pourrait s'avérer nécessaire de voir dans l'article XII des éléments de droit international « tels qu'ils s'appliquent aujourd'hui » aux questions de répartition des coûts.[112]

---

[108] Par exemple, *Christine Goodwin c. Royaume-Uni* (2002), Requete no. 28957/95 (CEDH, Grande chambre).

[109] Sentence, para. 82.

[110] Sentence, para. 83.

[111] Sentence, para. 84.

[112] Sentence, para. 84.

Le Tribunal a abordé ensuite la situation juridique précise du chemin de fer qui comprenait les moyens de l'exercice du droit de passage de la Belgique. L'article XII prévoyait que sa construction était « sans préjudice des droits exclusifs de souveraineté [des Pays-Bas] sur le territoire qui serait traversé par la route ou le canal en question », depuis lors devenu un chemin de fer en vertu du Traité de 1873. Bien que le « sens ordinaire » de « sans préjudice » puisse suggérer sans aucune intrusion dans la souveraineté des Pays-Bas, le Tribunal indiqua que l'expression devait être lue de bonne foi et à la lumière du contexte, de l'objet et du but du Traité.[113]

Le contexte de l'article XII établissait que la souveraineté des Pays-Bas faisait l'objet d'une dérogation dans la mesure nécessaire aux fins d'interpréter le droit de passage mais que les Pays-Bas conservaient les « pouvoirs de police » sur cette partie du tracé, y compris notamment, le pouvoir de fixer des normes en matière d'environnement.[114] Constatant que le but et l'objet du Traité de 1839 visaient en premier lieu à garantir la séparation entre les Pays-Bas et la Belgique dans des conditions satisfaisantes, le Tribunal a conclu qu'appliqué à l'article XII, ceci exigeait « un délicat équilibre entre les droits accordés à chaque Partie ».[115] Le désaccord entre les Parties au sujet des questions environnementales tournait plus précisément autour de la demande de la Belgique selon laquelle, bien que les Pays-Bas conservent leur pouvoir de réglementation en matière d'environnement, ils ne pouvaient exercer celui-ci qu'en concertation avec la Belgique.[116] Les Pays-Bas restaient quant à eux sur leur position selon laquelle, dans la mesure où les questions d'environnement et, plus spécifiquement, le classement du site du Meinweg ne faisaient pas obstacle au droit de passage effectif, ils étaient en droit de prendre des mesures de manière unilatérale.[117] Bien que le Tribunal ait penché en faveur des Pays-Bas, il constata que les mesures prises par les Pays-Bas n'étaient pas nécessairement sans conséquence financière pour le droit de passage de la Belgique.[118]

Le Tribunal a ensuite abordé la question de l'application de sa compréhension du sens de l'article XII. Sa conclusion fut que les obligations

---

[113] Sentence, para. 85.
[114] Sentence, paras 89 et 202–206.
[115] Sentence, para. 91.
[116] MB, para. 82.
[117] CMPB, paras. 3.3.5.5. et 3.3.6.3.
[118] Sentence, para. 96.

des Pays-Bas au titre de l'article XII ne prescrivaient pas l'application de leur droit national et de leur politique à la réactivation du Rhin de fer d'une quelconque façon qui soit plus favorable pour la Belgique qu'aux autres chemins de fer du système néerlandais, à moins que ceci ne puisse être assimilé à un déni du droit de passage de la Belgique ou ne rende l'exercice de ce droit déraisonnablement difficile ce qui, selon le Tribunal, n'était pas le cas des mesures actuelles.[119]

Restait la question de la répartition des coûts de la réactivation, elle-même ayant un effet sur la nature raisonnable ou non de la réglementation néerlandaise.[120] La Belgique avait adopté une position très directe sur ce point, arguant que la réactivation n'était pas assimilable à une « nouvelle route » mais consistait au contraire en la modification nécessaire du tracé historique de manière à maintenir son caractère compétitif dans les conditions actuelles. En conséquence, tous les coûts incombaient aux Pays-Bas.[121] Les Pays-Bas, soutenant que la réactivation représentait en fait un « nouveau » chemin de fer, affirmaient que celle-ci devait être entièrement à la charge de la Belgique et devait également être conforme aux régimes réglementaires des Pays-Bas. Le Tribunal a rejeté ces deux positions. La réponse devait se trouver à l'article XII et dans les règles de droit international pertinentes. Sauf disposition contraire de l'article XII, les Pays-Bas conservaient leur souveraineté mais, dans la mesure où une adaptation et une modernisation étaient nécessaires, ils devaient tenir compte des règles de droit international, lesquelles comprenaient le droit de l'environnement. Ceci permit au tribunal de structurer quelque peu l'équilibre entre l'exercice du droit de passage de la Belgique et le pouvoir règlementaire des Pays-Bas.

Le droit de passage de la Belgique était désormais exprimé comme un droit de passage « correspondant à ses besoins économiques actuels », interprétant ainsi les droits de la Belgique dans un contexte actuel, ce contexte étant en l'espèce factuel.[122] Le besoin des Pays-Bas d'imposer des mesures en matière

---

[119] Sentence, paras. 204–205.

[120] Le Tribunal indiqua que la question du risque financier lié au projet était un point ne relevait pas du tout des termes du Traité et des considérations des Parties. Il jugea que le risque financier serait assumé par la Partie responsable du coût de chacune des parties du projet. Sentence, para. 209.

[121] En fait, la Belgique avait fait une concession en proposant de concourir aux coûts de la réaction. Sentence, para. 215.

[122] Sentence, para. 221 – une interprétation « évolutive », plutôt que le recours à l'article 31(3)(c) de la Convention de Vienne.

de protection de l'environnement en réaction à la modernisation était « légitime », en prenant en compte le développement du droit de l'environnement, et un élément de contemporanéité « actuelle » fut donc introduit dans leur demande.[123] Le Tribunal procéda par analogie partant de l'obligation des États de mener leurs activités de manière à respecter l'environnement des autres États pour arriver au Rhin de fer, dans le cadre duquel un État utilisant un droit conventionnel sur le territoire d'un autre était tenu de respecter l'environnement de l'État territorial. Ainsi « la réactivation de la ligne du Rhin de fer ne peut pas être envisagée comme dissociée des mesures de protection de l'environnement nécessaires à l'utilisation envisagée de la ligne de chemin de fer. Ces mesures doivent être totalement intégrées au projet et à ses coûts ».[124]

La responsabilité de la Belgique pour les coûts des mesures environnementales découlait du fait que ces dernières étaient indispensables à l'exploitation du chemin de fer telle qu'envisagée par la réactivation.[125] L'exception était le tunnel dans le site du Meinweg. Le Tribunal estimait en effet que les deux États étaient partiellement responsables de la situation à laquelle ils étaient parvenus, la Belgique du fait qu'elle n'avait pas tenu les Pays-Bas informés en temps utile de l'ampleur de ses projets de réactivation du Rhin de fer ; et les Pays-Bas du fait qu'ils n'avaient pas tenu compte du fait que le tracé historique du chemin de fer traversait la zone classée du Meinweg. Le Tribunal jugea que les coûts du tunnel devraient être partagés.[126] La position de la Belgique selon laquelle les questions environnementales auraient pu être résolues par des moyens moins onéreux que la construction du tunnel n'est pas prise en considération. La raison est que le tribunal était d'avis que les Pays-Bas n'avaient pas d'obligation d'efficacité en terme de coûts (c'est-à-dire « choisir le moins cher ») dans leur sélection de mesures de protection de l'environnement. La limitation de pourvoir des Pays-Bas était d'ordre général, ils ne pouvaient avoir d'exigence qui aurait entravé de façon déraisonnable le droit de passage de la Belgique et le Tribunal était d'avis que les coûts du tunnel ne le faisaient pas rentrer dans cette catégorie. Ces parties de la sentence, bien que claires dans ce qu'elles exigent, sont opaques quant aux motifs des

---

[123] Sentence, para. 221 – pas expressément mais il s'agit d'un recours à l'article 31(3)(c) de la Convention de Vienne.
[124] Sentence, para. 223.
[125] Sentence, para. 226.
[126] Sentence, para. 234.

conséquences tirées. Le problème est qu'il n'y avait que peu a déduire au sujet de la responsabilité de mesures environnementales née de l'exploitation du chemin de fer, à partir d'une analogie avec les obligations de droit coutumier en matière de dommages extraterritoriaux à l'environnement. Le recours à la réglementation spécifique qui aurait pu être utile, la Directive communautaire Habitats, avait été exclue de manière à permettre au Tribunal d'écarter toute objection en matière de compétence qui aurait pu être soulevée sur le fondement de l'article 292 du Traité CE si le Tribunal avait appliqué la Directive Habitats. Bien que ce ne soit pas formulé explicitement dans la sentence, le résultat est que le mécanisme de répartition des coûts est dicté par l'exercice de la souveraineté résiduelle. Tant que les Pays-Bas restaient au sein des pouvoirs que leur laissait l'article XII, la Belgique était tenue de payer le coût des mesures exigées par les Pays-Bas, sauf si celles-ci bénéficiaient également aux Pays-Bas, essentiellement du fait de l'utilisation partagée des voies et, s'agissant du tunnel, si les Pays-Bas portaient une part de responsabilité d'une situation exigeant une solution particulièrement onéreuse.

La sentence est sous-tendue par une méthodologie cohérente, à savoir l'interprétation des traités en fonction de leur but et de leur objet, ainsi que de leur contexte juridique. En outre, lorsque la Belgique disposait d'un droit, celui-ci devait être effectif. Le Tribunal a trouvé un moyen d'intégrer les changements tant dans les règles de droit international que dans la notion de caractère commercial, lui permettant de parvenir à une compréhension du Traité de Séparation conservant son utilité en tant que cadre pour l'exploitation d'un chemin de fer dans des conditions contemporaines (et, si cela devrait s'avérer nécessaire, dans les conditions à venir). Toutefois, en dépit de l'attention particulière prêtée aux principes d'interprétation, l'élément le plus important de la sentence est en définitive que l'objet et le but du Traité de Séparation sont atteints en trouvant un équilibre entre le droit de passage de la Belgique et le pouvoir réglementaire des Pays-Bas. Le fait d'invoquer le « caractère raisonnable » en tant que guide en ce qui concerne le niveau auquel l'équilibre devrait être atteint, un procédé très juridique (et, pour lever toute ambiguïté, procédé que je ne désapprouve pas) évite la possibilité de *non liquet* résultant du manquement des parties à prévoir ce qu'elles n'auraient absolument pas pu prévoir. Il me semble que ce que font les principes détaillés d'interprétation est de conditionner les limites du caractère raisonnable, réduisant ainsi la marge d'appréciation du Tribunal, mais ne la supprimant en définitive pas.

XII.   CONCLUSION

La sentence est loin d'être directement applicable. Les Parties ont annoncé qu'elles avaient l'intention de constituer le comité d'experts indépendants pour fournir les informations nécessaires afin de procéder à la répartition des coûts pour les tronçons partagés de la ligne.[127] Il sera important pour ce comité que la sentence lui fournisse suffisamment d'indications pour mener à bien sa mission. Les États, entre-temps, se sont préoccupés de constituer des provisions afin d'assurer le financement de l'ensemble du projet à long terme. Ce qui a divisé les deux États était en fin de compte une question financière. La sentence fournit un moyen de résoudre cette question qui a un fondement juridique et n'est pas simplement une décision rendue *ex aequo et bono* (quand bien même le résultat effectif pourrait-il correspondre à une proportion « équitable » autonome).

Si le Rhin de fer est réactivé, les Parties penseront sans aucun doute que le Tribunal a rempli son rôle. Cette sentence sera aussi intéressante pour d'autres États que la Belgique et les Pays-Bas. Du point de vue des juristes internationaux, l'aspect le plus important de la sentence est l'affirmation d'un principe d'interprétation des anciens traités à la lumière du droit international actuel et de leur contexte factuel. Bien que le Tribunal renvoie fréquemment à l'article 31, paragraphe 3, alinéa (c) de la Convention de Vienne comme élément d'explication de la raison pour laquelle il convient d'appliquer ce principe, l'adaptation des changements de circonstances ne peut être ramenée au sein de cette seule disposition, qui ne parle en effet que des règles de droit international. La sentence représente plutôt également une extension de procédés jusqu'alors confinés à certaines catégories de traités dont il est dit qu'ils exigent une interprétation « constitutionnelle » ou « dynamique », ou encore « évolutive ». Il est possible d'expliquer ces phénomènes en soutenant que maintenir à jour ces traités est l'intention des parties. Le Traité de 1839 et le Traité du Rhin de fer n'appartiennent à aucune catégorie établie de traités à laquelle une telle approche a été appliquée jusqu'alors. Le Tribunal fait valoir

---

[127] Sentence, para. 235. La sentence préconisait que le comité soit constitué dans les quatre mois suivant la sentence. L'annonce de l'intention des Parties d'y procéder eut lieu plus de douze mois après la publication de le sentence. Communiqué de presse conjoint, Ministère des Transports des Pays-Bas, Secrétaire d'État de Belgique, 6 juillet 2006. Je remercie ici Belinda Macmahon de la CPA pour la traduction anglaise du communiqué de presse et d'autres informations au sujet du Rhin de fer.

l'objet et le but des traités comme justifiant l'extension du principe. Ce faisant, il soulève une perspective intéressante : tout traité, dont l'application a des conséquences pour d'autres obligations des parties – les droits de l'homme, la protection de l'environnement, la paix et la sécurité internationales, etc., devrait être interprété à la lumière de ces règles de « contexte », y compris lorsque ces dernières sont nées depuis la conclusion du traité dont le sens est recherché. Tel peut bien être le cas – l'interprétation du Traité CE visant à tenir compte des droits de l'homme avant même leur mention spécifique dans le Traité lui-même peut être considérée comme un exemple antérieur. A la lumière de ce mouvement contre la « fragmentation », la protection des États qui pourraient avoir des réserves au sujet de ces développements, devrait être double :

(a) en ce qui concerne les règles en cours de développement, un tribunal devrait s'efforcer de démontrer quelle est la règle qui lie les États respectifs et que l'application de cette règle vient soutenir le sens de la sentence ;

(b) en ce qui concerne le changement de circonstances, un tribunal devrait indiquer la preuve sur laquelle est fondée sa conclusion qu'un changement de circonstances est intervenu, tout en observant que sur bien d'autres points, il peut exister une certaine marge pour des désaccords considérables entre les États.

Dans tous les cas, le tribunal devrait également être conscient qu'il peut y avoir d'autres instances chargées de l'interprétation du droit applicable ou qui ont traité des mêmes demandes de changements de circonstances. Il peut ne pas y avoir d'obligation contraignant un tribunal à s'incliner devant la décision d'un autre mais le développement d'une culture de respect entre les tribunaux pourrait alléger quelques uns des problèmes nés de la « fragmentation » procédurale. D'autres États peuvent avoir en jeu des intérêts importants ou même un intérêt juridique : par exemple, lorsqu'un traité multilatéral auquel ils sont parties constitue « l'autre règle de droit international ». La sentence du Rhin de fer fait partie d'un processus qui pourrait et devrait, peut-être, voir les tribunaux internationaux se considérer comme des acteurs au sein du système juridique international dotés d'une responsabilité de développement cohérent, en plus d'être des mécanismes de règlement des différends entre des parties à un litige. Ce que démontre par-dessus tout l'affaire du Rhin de fer, c'est que les litiges internationaux ne vont pas aller en se simplifiant. Les États doivent être conscients non seulement des détails précis de chaque différend, mais de tout le contexte que le Tribunal pourrait estimer devoir prendre en compte afin de parvenir à une sentence appropriée.

Enfin, je renvoie au rapport du Groupe d'études de la Commission du droit international. Le Rapport a deux prémisses – tout d'abord que le droit international est un système juridique et non un recueil aléatoire de normes et, en deuxième lieu, qu'il est un principe généralement admis que lorsque plusieurs normes affectent une question unique, elles devraient, autant que faire se peut, être interprétées pour donner lieu à un ensemble unique d'obligations compatibles.[128] Le Rapport fait état d'un certain nombre de techniques pour tenter de parvenir à l'objectif d'harmonisation, bien qu'il ne fournisse aucune explication quant à l'interaction de ces techniques. Dans son analyse, la CDI ne s'intéressait qu'à la « fragmentation » au fond et n'abordait donc pas le sujet des conflits juridictionnels de la nature de celui apparu dans l'affaire du Rhin de fer. Toutefois, en principe comme en pratique, il existe une indication dans la sentence selon laquelle la compétence exclusive de la CJCE en vertu de l'article 292 du Traité CE est hiérarchiquement supérieure, au moins dans la mesure où toutes les parties au différend sont également membres de la Communauté. Identifier s'il existe ou non un conflit juridictionnel peut s'avérer dans de nombreuses affaires, comme l'affirme le Dr Lavranos au sujet du Rhin de fer,[129] être une question beaucoup plus difficile à résoudre qu'elle ne le semble à première vue. La question centrale de « fragmentation » sur le fond pour le Tribunal du Rhin de fer était celle de l'application (ou non) de la règle intertemporelle aux Traités. La CDI renvoie à l'article 31, paragraphe 3, alinéa (c) de la Convention de Vienne comme à un élément important pour intégrer les particularités d'obligations en vertu d'un traité avec des obligations plus larges des parties en vertu du droit international. Le droit international, affirme la CDI, est un système juridique « dynamique ». En conséquence, le sens d'une disposition d'un traité « pourrait être affecté » par des développements ultérieurs du droit.[130] J'aurais aimé que le besoin de démontrer les changements du droit et leur effet contraignant sur les États concernés soit davantage mis en avant. La CDI va au-delà de l'article 31, paragraphe 3, alinéa (c) afin d'avaliser une approche évolutive de

---

[128] Rapport de la CDI, *supra* note 24, para. 14(1 & 2).
[129] *Supra* note 34.
[130] Rapport de la CDI, *supra* note 24 au para. 14(22).

l'interprétation des traités pour prendre en compte notamment « des évolutions techniques, économiques ou juridiques ultérieures », citant la sentence du Rhin de fer en exemple.[131] Ainsi que le note le Professeur McClachlan dans son article, l'article 31, paragraphe 3, alinéa (c) n'est pas la panacée pour résoudre les dilemmes de « fragmentation » dans le contexte de traités (et en fait ne peut le faire en présence d'une incompatibilité véritable des obligations).[132] Il s'agit là d'une tache appartenant aux politiques mais il y a d'abord du travail à faire en matière de droit international, afin de tenter d'éviter ces conflits par une utilisation subtile des techniques énoncées par la CDI. Il peut s'agir de politiques judiciaires, mais c'est une tache qui revient aux juges.

*****

---

[131] Rapport de la CDI, *supra* note 24, au para. 14(23), renvoyant aux paras. 82 et 83 de la Sentence.

[132] *Supra* note 86, au p. 318.

ENTRE :

LE ROYAUME DE BELGIQUE

- ET -

LE ROYAUME DES PAYS-BAS

SENTENCE DU TRIBUNAL ARBITRAL

Le Tribunal Arbitral :

Madame le Juge Rosalyn Higgins, Président

Monsieur le Professeur Guy Schrans

Monsieur le Juge Bruno Simma

Monsieur le Professeur Alfred H.A. Soons

Monsieur le Juge Peter Tomka

La Haye, 24 mai 2005

TABLE DES MATIERES

SENTENCE DU TRIBUNAL ARBITRAL

CHAPITRE I - HISTORIQUE DE LA PROCEDURE, CONTEXTE ET SOUMISSIONS DES PARTIES

A. Historique de la procédure

1. La présente sentence est rendue en vertu d'un compromis d'arbitrage (le « Compromis d'arbitrage ») conclu entre le Royaume de Belgique (la « Belgique ») et le Royaume des Pays-Bas (les « Pays-Bas ») (les « Parties ») dont les termes avaient fait l'objet d'un accord dans le cadre d'un échange de notes diplomatiques datées des 22 et 23 juillet 2003, prévoyant que le Compromis d'arbitrage serait provisoirement appliqué dans l'attente de l'achèvement des formalités constitutionnelles dans ces deux pays.

2. En vertu du Compromis d'arbitrage, les Parties convenaient de « soumettre [le] différend [qui les oppose] à propos de la réactivation du Rhin de fer à un tribunal arbitral qu'elles [devaient] constituer sous les auspices de la Cour permanente d'arbitrage de La Haye » ; ainsi que « de mettre en œuvre la décision du Tribunal arbitral dès que possible ».

3. Le Compromis d'arbitrage soumettait en outre des Questions spécifiques au Tribunal Arbitral :

> 1. Dans quelle mesure le droit néerlandais relatif à l'utilisation, la réfection, l'adaptation et la modernisation des lignes de chemin de fer sur le territoire néerlandais, et le pouvoir décisionnel qui en découle, s'appliquent-ils, de la même manière, à l'utilisation, la réfection, l'adaptation et la modernisation du tracé historique du Rhin de fer sur le territoire néerlandais ?
>
> 2. Dans quelle mesure la Belgique a-t-elle le droit d'exécuter ou de faire exécuter des travaux en vue de l'utilisation, de la réfection, de l'adaptation et de la modernisation du tracé historique du Rhin de fer sur le territoire néerlandais et d'arrêter tous plans, caractéristiques et procédures y afférents en vertu du droit belge et du pouvoir décisionnel qui en découle ? Convient-il d'établir une distinction entre les exigences, les normes, les plans, les caractéristiques et les procédures en rapport, d'une part, avec les possibilités d'utilisation de l'infrastructure ferroviaire proprement dite et, d'autre part, l'aménagement du territoire et l'intégration dans celui-ci de cette infrastructure ferroviaire et, dans l'affirmative, quelles en sont les conséquences ? Les Pays-Bas peuvent-ils imposer unilatéralement la construction de tunnels, de tranchées couvertes, de déviations et toute autre mesure similaire,

ainsi que les normes proposées de construction et de sécurité y afférentes ?

3. Dans quelle proportion, au vu des réponses aux questions précédentes, le coût et les risques financiers liés à l'utilisation, la réfection, l'adaptation et la modernisation du tracé historique du Rhin de fer sur le territoire néerlandais devraient-ils être supportés par la Belgique ou par les Pays-Bas ? La Belgique est-elle tenue de financer des investissements supérieurs à ceux qui sont nécessaires aux possibilités d'utilisation du tracé historique de la ligne de chemin de fer ?

4. Dans le Compromis d'arbitrage, les Parties demandaient au Tribunal arbitral de « se prononcer sur le fondement du droit international, y compris du droit communautaire le cas échéant, en tenant compte des obligations des Parties en vertu de l'Article 292 du Traité CE ».

5. Conformément au Compromis d'arbitrage, les Parties sont ensuite convenues d'un règlement de procédure pour l'arbitrage (le « Règlement de Procédure »),[1] fondé sur le « Règlement Facultatif de la CPA pour l'arbitrage des différends entre deux États ».

6. Conformément à l'Article 5, paragraphe 1, du Règlement de Procédure, la Belgique a désigné Monsieur le Professeur Guy Schrans et Monsieur le Juge Bruno Simma comme arbitres, et les Pays-Bas ont désigné pour leur part Monsieur le Professeur Alfred H.A. Soons et Monsieur le Juge Peter Tomka. Les quatre arbitres se sont réunis le 22 septembre 2003 et, conformément à l'Article 5, paragraphe 2, du Règlement de Procédure, ont désigné Madame le Juge Rosalyn Higgins en qualité de Président du Tribunal arbitral (le « Tribunal »).

7. Conformément au Compromis d'arbitrage et à la désignation de la Cour permanente d'arbitrage (la « CPA ») en qualité de Greffe en vertu de l'Article 1, paragraphe 3, du Règlement de Procédure, le Secrétaire général de la CPA a nommé Madame Anne Joyce, Directrice juridique adjointe, aux fins d'agir en qualité de greffière auprès du Tribunal.

8. Par lettres respectivement datées des 3 et 9 septembre 2003, les Pays-Bas et la Belgique ont, chacun pour leur part, désigné leur agent. L'agent nommé par les Pays-Bas était

---

[1] Le Règlement de Procédure, ainsi que d'autres documents relatifs à l'arbitrage, sont disponibles sur le site http://www.pca-cpa.org.

Monsieur le Professeur Johan G. Lammers et l'agent nommé par la Belgique était Monsieur Jan Devadder.

9. Le Tribunal s'est réuni avec les Agents le 29 septembre 2003. Lors de cette réunion, le Tribunal et les Agents sont parvenus à certains accords en ce qui concerne l'application du Règlement de Procédure et ont discuté d'autres questions pratiques relatives à la procédure d'arbitrage. Le Règlement de Procédure prévoyait la possibilité de procédures orales uniquement dans le cas d'une demande spécifique émanant de l'une des Parties (Article 13). Il fut toutefois convenu que si le Tribunal devait chercher à obtenir des informations supplémentaires auprès des Parties après avoir reçu les plaidoiries écrites, le Tribunal en notifierait les Parties et les consulterait afin de déterminer si ces informations pourraient être obtenues dans de meilleures conditions dans le cadre de plaidoiries écrites supplémentaires ou dans celui d'une procédure orale. Il fut convenu en outre que, dans le cas d'une audience ou d'un jeu supplémentaire de soumissions écrites, les délais pour rendre la sentence commenceraient à courir le jour suivant celui de la dernière soumission ou celui de la clôture de l'audience, selon le cas.

10. Les Parties ont déposé leurs plaidoiries écrites conformément au calendrier figurant dans le Règlement de Procédure. Les plaidoiries étaient constituées du Mémoire de la Belgique déposé le 1er octobre 2003 (« MB »), du Contre-Mémoire des Pays-Bas déposé le 30 janvier 2004 (« CMPB »), de la Réplique de la Belgique déposée le 30 mars 2004 (« RB ») et de la Duplique des Pays-Bas déposée le 1er juin 2004 (« DPB »).

11. Ni les Parties ni le Tribunal n'ont demandé d'audience de plaidoirie.

12. En juin 2004, le Tribunal constata que l'approbation du Compromis d'arbitrage par le Parlement des Pays-Bas prenait davantage de temps que prévu et qu'il était peu probable que sa ratification intervienne avant la date envisagée à l'Article 18 du Règlement de Procédure (soit le 29 septembre 2004) pour la remise de la sentence du Tribunal. Au vu de ces développements, le Tribunal décida qu'il ne rendrait pas sa sentence avant l'achèvement, par les deux Parties, de leurs procédures constitutionnelles respectives nécessaires à l'entrée en vigueur du Compromis d'arbitrage. Les 6 et 13 juillet 2004, le Tribunal reçut de la Belgique des copies des documents pertinents faisant état du fait que les procédures constitutionnelles nécessaires en Belgique pour l'entrée en vigueur du Compromis d'arbitrage étaient achevées. Le 20 mai 2005, les Pays-Bas notifièrent au

Tribunal que les procédures constitutionnelles requises aux Pays-Bas pour l'entrée en vigueur du Compromis d'arbitrage étaient achevées et des copies des documents pertinents furent fournis au Tribunal. Le 20 mai 2005, les Parties informèrent le Tribunal que, bien que le Compromis d'arbitrage, selon ses termes, n'entrerait pas en vigueur avant le 1er juillet 2005, les procédures de ratification nécessaires dans chacun des pays, ainsi que la notification mutuelle de celles-ci, étaient achevées. Elles souhaitaient toutes deux demander au Tribunal de rendre sa sentence « dès que possible avant son entrée en vigueur formelle ». Le Tribunal accéda au souhait des Parties et la sentence fut rendue en conséquence.

* * *

13.   Aucune des Parties n'a contesté la compétence du Tribunal pour connaître du différend. La Belgique, dans une partie de sa Réplique intitulée « Compétence » cite toutefois le principe découlant de l'Article 292 du Traité instituant la Communauté européenne (Journal officiel des Communautés européennes (« JOCE »), 1997, C 340 p. 3) (« Traité CE ») selon lequel « [l]es États membres s'engagent à ne pas soumettre un différend relatif à l'interprétation ou à l'application du présent traité à un mode de règlement autre que ceux prévus par celui-ci » et indique que, bien que la Belgique et les Pays-Bas aient fait référence au droit communautaire dans leurs plaidoiries, ces références ne constituent pas un motif suffisant pour en conclure que l'Article 292 avait été violé (RB, pp. 2, 4, paras. 3, 5).

14.   Afin d'étayer sa position, la Belgique distingue la présente affaire de celle de l'Usine *MOX*,[2] en cours actuellement, dans le cadre de laquelle l'Irlande a intenté une action à l'encontre du Royaume-Uni devant un tribunal arbitral constitué conformément à l'Annexe VII de la Convention des Nations-Unies sur le droit de la mer (procédure suspendue par ce tribunal) et à l'occasion de laquelle la Commission des communautés européennes (la « Commission européenne ») a intenté une action à l'encontre de l'Irlande devant la Cour de justice des Communautés européennes (la « CJCE ») au titre d'une violation alléguée de l'Article 292 du Traité CE. La Belgique indique que, contrairement au Royaume-Uni dans l'affaire de l'Usine *MOX*, les Pays-Bas n'ont pas présenté d'objection aux références de la Belgique au droit communautaire dans son

---

[2] Pour une description de cette affaire et autres informations y afférentes, voir http://www.pca-cpa.org (« l'affaire de l'Usine *MOX* »).

202

Mémoire. La Belgique avance en outre qu'aucune des deux Parties n'a prétendu que l'autre avait violé le droit communautaire. Enfin, la Belgique déclare que « les questions où intervient le droit communautaire dans cette affaire ne se rapportent en fait qu'à la répartition des coûts, ce qui ne relève pas du droit communautaire » (RB, p. 4, para. 6).

15. Les Parties ont ensuite développé leurs arguments concernant le droit applicable et ses relations avec le droit communautaire dans un courrier adressé au Secrétaire général de la Commission européenne, en date du 26 août 2003, dont une copie fut adressée à la CPA. Dans ce courrier, les Parties indiquaient :

> Pour les deux parties, le cœur du différend concerne l'interprétation du Traité bilatéral de séparation de 1839 et l'interprétation des obligations énoncées dans ce traité, c'est-à-dire des questions de droit international.

Le courrier se concluait ainsi :

> Si l'éventualité de l'application ou de l'interprétation du droit communautaire devait se présenter dans le cadre de la procédure, le Royaume de Belgique et le Royaume des Pays-Bas s'engagent à prendre toutes mesures nécessaires aux fins de se conformer aux obligations qui leur incombent en vertu du Traité CE et, en particulier, de son Article 292.

B. Contexte

16. Le Rhin de fer, ou « *IJzeren Rijn* » en néerlandais, est une ligne de chemin de fer reliant le port d'Anvers, en Belgique, au bassin de la Ruhr en Allemagne et traversant les provinces du Nord Brabant et du Limbourg aux Pays-Bas.[3] L'origine du Rhin de fer remonte aux négociations relatives à la séparation de la Belgique et des Pays-Bas dans les années 1830 et, en particulier, au Traité entre la Belgique et les Pays-Bas relatif à la Séparation de leurs Territoires Respectifs (le « Traité de Séparation de 1839 ») (Série des Traités Consolidés (« C.T.S. »), 1838–1839, Vol. 88, p. 427).

17. Parmi les différents points prévus par le Traité de Séparation de 1839 figurait la question d'une liaison de communication entre Anvers et l'Allemagne. À cet égard, l'Article XII du Traité de Séparation prévoyait ce qui suit :

---

[3] Voir la carte de la ligne de chemin de fer du Rhin de fer fournie conjointement par les Parties dans l'Annexe.

> Dans le cas où il aurait été construit en Belgique une nouvelle route, ou creusé un nouveau canal, qui aboutirait à la Meuse vis-à-vis le canton néerlandais de Sittard, alors il serait loisible à la Belgique de demander à la Hollande, qui ne s'y refuserait pas dans cette supposition, que la dite route ou le dit canal fussent prolongés d'après le même plan, entièrement aux frais et dépens de la Belgique, par le canton de Sittard, jusqu'aux frontières de l'Allemagne.[4] Cette route ou ce canal, qui ne pourraient servir que de communication commerciale, seraient construits, au choix de la Hollande, soit par des ingénieurs et ouvriers que la Belgique obtiendrait l'autorisation d'employer à cet effet dans le canton de Sittard, soit par des ingénieurs et ouvriers que la Hollande fournirait, et qui exécuteraient, aux frais de la Belgique, les travaux convenus, le tout sans charge aucune pour la Hollande, et sans préjudice de ses droits de souveraineté exclusifs sur le territoire que traverserait la route ou le canal en question. Les deux parties fixeraient, d'un commun accord, le montant et le mode de perception des droits et péages qui seraient prélevés sur cette même route ou canal.[5]

18. Le droit de passage conféré à la Belgique par l'Article XII du Traité de Séparation de 1839 était en outre spécifié dans des traités conclus au dix-neuvième siècle, parachevés par la Convention de 1873 entre la Belgique et les Pays-Bas relative au paiement de la dette belge, à l'abolition de la surtaxe sur les eaux de vie néerlandaises et au passage d'une ligne de chemin de fer entre Anvers et l'Allemagne à travers le Duché de Limbourg (le « Traité du Rhin de fer ») (C.T.S., 1872–1873, Vol. 145, p. 447), en vertu de laquelle la ligne de chemin de fer du Rhin de fer fut construite sur le territoire néerlandais. Elle fut achevée en 1879.

19. De 1879 à la Première Guerre Mondiale, la ligne du Rhin de fer fut en service de manière permanente. Au cours de cette période, le statut juridique de la ligne du Rhin de fer ne fut, pour l'essentiel, pas modifié, à l'unique exception de la propriété des voies ferrées qui fut transférée du concessionnaire belge « *Grand Central belge* » au Gouvernement de Belgique, puis au Gouvernement des Pays-Bas en vertu de la Convention sur les chemins de fer entre la Belgique et les Pays-Bas du 23 avril 1897 (la « Convention sur les chemins de fer de 1897 ») (C.T.S., 1896–1897, Vol. 184, p. 374). L'intensité d'utilisation de la ligne a varié au cours de la période 1914–1991. Chacun s'accorde toutefois sur le fait que

---

[4] Le Tribunal constate que l'Article XII parle de « *l'Allemagne* » alors même qu'en 1839, l'Allemagne n'existait pas selon le droit international en tant qu'État, mais en tant que simple confédération (« *Deutscher Bund* »). La nouvelle route ou le nouveau canal envisagé par le Traité aurait par conséquent atteint les frontières de la Prusse. Au moment de la conclusion du Traité du Rhin de fer en 1873 (*voir* paragraphe 18), la Prusse et les autres États germaniques avaient été unifiés dans l'Empire Germanique.

[5] *Voir* au paragraphe 32 ci-après la traduction [anglaise] de l'Article XII effectuée par le Tribunal. Le texte du Traité de Séparation de 1839 fourni par les Pays-Bas au Tribunal utilise, dans les versions française et anglaise, les chiffres romains ; le texte fourni par la Belgique utilise les chiffres romains dans la version anglaise et les chiffres arabes dans la version française. Le Tribunal utilise les chiffres romains lorsqu'il se réfère au Traité de Séparation de 1839.

tout trafic de marchandises fut stoppé au cours de la Première Guerre Mondiale. La Belgique indique qu'ensuite « douze trains de marchandises internationaux voyageaient chaque jour dans les deux directions entre Anvers et la zone de la Ruhr, entre Rotterdam et la zone de la Ruhr » (MB, p. 22, para. 18) ; tandis que les Pays-Bas indiquent que la ligne était peu utilisée, avec huit trains de marchandises par période de 24 heures en 1920, neuf en 1921 et depuis 1922, seulement un ou deux par période de 24 heures (et rarement sur l'intégralité de la ligne) (CMPB, p. 19, para. 2.11; DPB, p. 29, paras. 115–117). Les Pays-Bas expliquent ce fait par l'accès dont disposait la Belgique à la ligne récemment construite de Hasselt-Montzen-Aken et ses avantages économiques. Les deux pays conviennent du fait qu'au cours de la Seconde Guerre Mondiale, la voie du Rhin de fer fut détruite et qu'il fut nécessaire de la reconstruire. Pendant la période qui suivit, elle fut utilisée pour des transports militaires. En revanche, au cours des quarante années qui ont suivi, la ligne ne fut que très peu utilisée. Depuis 1991, la ligne du Rhin de fer n'a pas été utilisée pour du trafic transitant entre la Belgique et l'Allemagne, bien que certaines parties de la ligne aux Pays-Bas aient continué à être exploitées (cette dernière utilisation n'étant pas un point de désaccord entre les Parties).

20. Au cours des années 1990, un certain nombre de mesures juridiques ont été prises par le Gouvernement des Pays-Bas relativement au classement de réserves naturelles dans les provinces du Nord-Brabant et du Limbourg, dont certaines sont situées sur le tracé de la ligne du Rhin de fer. En 1987 et pendant les années 1990 (débutant ainsi même avant la cessation du trafic de transit en 1991), un certain nombre de communications eurent lieu, à la fois écrites et orales, entre des représentants officiels des Gouvernements de Belgique et des Pays-Bas au sujet d'une éventuelle réactivation de la ligne du Rhin de fer.

21. Des discussions formelles entre Gouvernements sur la question de l'utilisation, la réfection, l'adaptation et la modernisation de la ligne du Rhin de fer ont été initiées par le Premier ministre belge le 12 juin 1998 (le terme « réactivation » sera utilisé ci-après pour désigner les opérations mentionnées ci-dessus). Ces discussions ont débouché sur l'adoption, le 28 mars 2000, d'un Protocole d'accord (le « Protocole de mars 2000 ») conclu entre les deux Gouvernements qui prévoyait notamment la réalisation de certaines études d'impact environnemental concernant la réactivation, ainsi qu'un calendrier pour remettre progressivement la ligne en service.

22.   Les études d'impact environnemental envisagées dans le Protocole de mars 2000 furent achevées en mai 2001. La mise en œuvre du Protocole de mars 2000 achoppa toutefois, en particulier s'agissant des projets concernant ce qui a été appelé « l'utilisation temporaire » de la ligne du Rhin de fer, sur des désaccords entre les Parties au sujet des conditions dont devait être assortie une telle utilisation et sur la répartition des coûts nécessaires pour rendre la ligne adaptée à une utilisation à long terme, comme demandé par la Belgique. Les Parties n'étaient en outre pas d'accord sur le fait de déterminer si cette utilisation temporaire pouvait avoir lieu en l'absence d'un accord sur une utilisation à long terme. Les discussions entre les Parties s'orientèrent alors vers la possibilité de soumettre leur différend à un arbitrage et conduisirent au Compromis d'arbitrage conclu entre les Parties en juillet 2003.

23.   De manière générale, la Belgique considère que l'exercice de la compétence des Pays-Bas sur la ligne du Rhin de fer est limité par les obligations des Pays-Bas en vertu du droit international et, en particulier, par les obligations de bonne foi et de caractère raisonnable. Tel qu'appliqué au droit de passage concédé en vertu du Traité de Séparation de 1839, la Belgique soutient que les Pays-Bas sont tenus d'autoriser au minimum une utilisation immédiate, quoique modeste, « temporaire » de la voie historique et, à long terme, une réactivation majeure de la voie. L'exercice de ses droits, soutient la Belgique, ne doit pas être rendu « anormalement difficile » du fait notamment des mesures de protection environnementales « très onéreuses » que les Pays-Bas cherchent à imposer dans le cadre de cette réactivation.

24.   La Belgique soutient également, à titre subsidiaire, que si de telles mesures devaient néanmoins être imposées, les Pays-Bas devraient s'assurer que les travaux de construction résultant de ces mesures n'aient pas de conséquences négatives sur l'utilisation par la Belgique de la ligne du Rhin de fer et que les Pays-Bas devraient en supporter le coût et les risques financiers. À l'appui de son argument, la Belgique souligne que son obligation de supporter le coût en vertu de l'Article XII porte sur la *construction* de la route ou du canal, et non sur l'exercice du droit de passage de la Belgique (RB, p. 98, para. 104). La Belgique renvoie également à la formulation de l'Article XI du Traité de Séparation de 1839 – et notamment au mot « entretien » qui y figure – et avance en outre que les Pays-Bas ont une responsabilité d'entretien des voies de la ligne de chemin de fer du Rhin de fer afin que celles-ci soient « en bon état et propres à faciliter le commerce ». Selon la

Belgique, il convient d'envisager la question de ce signifie « entretenues en bon état et propres à faciliter le commerce » au vu des circonstances actuelles et de ce qui est considéré comme commercialement viable (RB, p. 113, para. 122). Si le Tribunal établit que la Belgique devrait supporter une quelconque partie du coût, celle-ci devrait, selon la Belgique, être limitée à ce qui est nécessaire pour satisfaire aux prescriptions minimales du droit néerlandais, par exemple en matière d'atténuation des nuisances sonores. Qui plus est, si la Belgique devait en définitive supporter le coût de mesures résultant d'autres obligations internationales (tel que le droit communautaire), les Pays-Bas ne devraient pouvoir demander que les options les moins onéreuses dont ils disposent pour satisfaire à ces obligations.

25. De manière générale, les Pays-Bas soutiennent quant à eux que bien qu'ils ne contestent pas le droit de passage de la Belgique sur le territoire néerlandais, ce droit est circonscrit par les dispositions énoncées à l'Article XII du Traité de Séparation de 1839 et que, dans la mesure où il représente une limitation de la souveraineté territoriale des Pays-Bas, ce droit de passage doit être interprété de manière restrictive. Les Pays-Bas citent en particulier la clause de réserve de leur souveraineté énoncée à l'Article XII et la disposition prévoyant que la Belgique supporte le coût des « *travaux* » envisagés par cet article. Les mesures environnementales et autres prescriptions imposées de manière putative par les Pays-Bas dans le cadre de la réactivation de la ligne du Rhin de fer constituent, selon les Pays-Bas, l'exercice légitime de leur souveraineté en vertu de l'Article XII, maintenant intacte l'obligation de la Belgique de payer le coût du respect des prescriptions néerlandaises. En outre, toujours selon les Pays-Bas, aucune disposition de l'Article XI du Traité de Séparation de 1839, ni de la Convention sur les Voies Ferrées de 1897, ou encore la pratique ultérieure des Parties n'aboutissent à une conclusion différente (CMPB, p. 57, paras. 3.3.8.2–3.3.8.4; DPB, pp. 33–35, paras. 133–139). La Belgique utilise une définition trop large du terme « entretien » affirment les Pays-Bas, et celle-ci ne peut pas être étendue aux fins de couvrir les coûts liés à la réactivation (DPB, p. 33, para. 135).

C. Soumissions Finales des Parties

1. <u>Belgique</u>

26. Les conclusions de la Belgique, figurant dans la Réplique, étaient les suivantes :

EN RÉPONSE À LA QUESTION 1

Le droit néerlandais relatif à l'utilisation, la réfection, l'adaptation et la modernisation des lignes de chemin de fer sur le territoire néerlandais et le pouvoir décisionnel qui en découle, ne s'appliquent pas de la même manière à l'utilisation, la réfection, l'adaptation et à la modernisation du tracé historique du Rhin de fer qui traverse le territoire néerlandais en ce que :

- Les Pays-Bas devront, si la Belgique décide de construire une « *nouvelle route ou de creuser un nouveau canal* » sur le territoire belge, comme décrit à l'Article XII du Traité de Séparation du 19 avril 1839, autoriser le prolongement de cette route ou de ce canal sur le territoire néerlandais « d'après *le même plan* » que sur le territoire belge, sans l'assentiment des Pays-Bas en ce qui concerne le plan.

- Si, dans l'hypothèse figurant ci-dessus, les Pays-Bas retiennent l'option d'exécuter les travaux eux-mêmes, ces travaux ne peuvent être effectués aux frais de la Belgique que s'ils ont fait l'objet d'un accord entre les deux Gouvernements. En revanche, si les Pays-Bas décident que ces travaux doivent être exécutés par la Belgique, aucun accord n'est nécessaire entre les parties en ce qui concerne les travaux. Dans cette dernière hypothèse, la Belgique est en droit de bénéficier d'un traitement au moins aussi favorable que celui qui est accordé à d'autres opérateurs à cet égard.

- Sans préjudice du droit communautaire, les Pays-Bas ont une obligation d'autoriser l'utilisation du tracé du Rhin de fer sous réserve que celui-ci « *ne serve que comme communication commerciale* » et de prendre toutes mesures nécessaires aux fins de permettre cette utilisation.

- Le niveau et les modalités de perception des droits de péage feront l'objet d'un accord entre les Pays-Bas et la Belgique. Un tel accord doit être conclu en conformité avec le droit international et le droit communautaire.

- Aucun changement de parcours déviant du tracé historique ne sera décidé par les Pays-Bas sans l'accord de la Belgique.

- Les Pays-Bas sont soumis à l'obligation d'exercer leurs pouvoirs législatif et décisionnel de bonne foi, raisonnablement et de manière à ne pas priver la Belgique de son droit à voir le Rhin de fer prolongé sur le territoire néerlandais « d'après le même plan » que sur le territoire belge en utilisant le tracé historique du Rhin de fer et, ainsi, de ne pas rendre l'exercice de ces droits anormalement difficile. Les Pays-Bas prendront toutes mesures nécessaires aux fins de permettre une telle utilisation.

- Si les Pays-Bas disposent de plusieurs possibilités pour se conformer à une obligation internationale, dont l'une leur permet de se conformer à leur obligation envers la Belgique en ce qui concerne le Rhin de fer, alors que les autres ne le leur permettent ou ne le leur permettaient pas, les Pays-Bas sont tenus de choisir la possibilité leur permettant de se conformer aux deux obligations.

- Si les Pays-Bas ont des obligations contradictoires en ce qui concerne la réactivation du Rhin de fer, ils devront en atténuer les effets en prenant les mesures qui sont les moins onéreuses pour la Belgique.

- Sans préjudice du droit de la Belgique à l'utilisation immédiate du tracé historique du Rhin de fer à pleine capacité et sur une base de long terme, si la Belgique demande le passage temporaire sur le tracé historique du Rhin de fer de 15 trains par jour civil (en prenant en compte le total des deux sens), y compris à vitesse limitée le soir, pour une période d'au moins 5 ans, les Pays-Bas accèderont immédiatement à cette demande et prendront immédiatement toutes les mesures nécessaires afin d'autoriser effectivement un tel passage dans le plus court délai de faisabilité matérielle possible, ce délai ne pouvant excéder un mois.

- Les Pays-Bas prendront toutes les mesures nécessaires aux fins de prévenir toute interruption de l'utilisation du Rhin de fer lors de la transition de l'usage « temporaire » à l'usage « à long terme » et de permettre effectivement cette dernière dans le délai le plus court possible.

- Sans préjudice de la position de la Belgique sur la Question 3, les mesures prévues dans le document ProRail « *IJzeren Rijn Concept Ontwerp-tracébesluit versie 1.4* » de juillet 2003 en ce qui concerne les tronçons A2, B et C de la voie ferrée, tels qu'identifiés dans ce document, pourraient ne pas être requises comme condition préalable de l'exercice des droits de la Belgique sur le Rhin de fer, à moins que de telles mesures ne rendent l'exercice du droit de la Belgique à l'utilisation du Rhin de fer anormalement difficile, et :

  o À titre principal, à moins que le coût et les risques financiers liés à ces mesures soient supportés en totalité par les Pays-Bas.

  o À titre subsidiaire, à moins que le coût et les risques financiers liés à ces mesures soient supportés par les Pays-Bas au moins dans la proportion de leurs prévisions d'utilisation de la ligne de chemin de fer d'ici 2020, ce qui représente au moins 77,889 pour cent, et par la Belgique dans une proportion maximale de 22,111 pour cent, sous la réserve supplémentaire que les Pays-Bas ne puissent pas imputer à la Belgique le coût qui est facturé aux usagers de la ligne conformément à l'Article XII du Traité de Séparation de 1839 et aux règles du droit communautaire, ni imputer à la Belgique des frais non liés à la réactivation, notamment les frais de réduction du bruit du trafic.

- Sans préjudice de la position de la Belgique sur la Question 3, les mesures de réduction des nuisances sonores prévues dans le document ProRail « *IJzeren Rijn Concept Ontwerp-tracébesluit versie 1.4* » de juillet 2003 qui ne sont pas nécessaires pour atteindre le seuil maximal autorisé de 70 dB(A) ou de 73 dB(A) prévu par la loi, [*mot(s) omi(s)*] à moins que de telles mesures ne rendent l'exercice du droit de la Belgique à l'utilisation du Rhin de fer anormalement difficile, et à moins que le coût et les risques financiers liés à ces mesures de réduction du bruit soient assumés en totalité par les Pays-Bas.

209

- Sans préjudice de la Question 3, les Pays-Bas ne peuvent pas exiger la construction d'un tunnel sur le site du Meinweg, ni d'autres mesures de protection de la vie sauvage et de la nature, y compris des mesures compensatoires dans des secteurs traversés par le tracé historique du Rhin de fer, à moins que de telles mesures ne rendent pas l'exercice du droit de la Belgique à l'utilisation du Rhin de fer anormalement difficile et à moins que les coûts et les risques financiers liés à ces mesures de réduction du bruit soient assumés en totalité par les Pays-Bas.

- A titre subsidiaire à la dernière soumission, si le Tribunal estime que le point précédent ne relève pas de sa compétence, les Pays-Bas ne peuvent pas exiger la construction d'un tunnel sur le site du Meinweg, ni d'autres mesures de protection de la vie sauvage et de la nature, y compris des mesures compensatoires dans des secteurs traversés par le tracé historique du Rhin de fer, à moins que cette exigence ne rende pas l'exercice du droit de la Belgique à l'utilisation du Rhin de fer anormalement difficile et que le coût et les risques financiers liés à ces mesures soient assumés en totalité par les Pays-Bas, sauf si les Pays-Bas n'avaient pas d'autre possibilité de respecter leurs obligations en vertu du droit communautaire et dans la mesure où les mesures requises constituent la manière la moins onéreuse de permettre aux Pays-Bas de se conformer à leurs obligations en vertu du droit communautaire.

SUR LA QUESTION 2

- La Belgique n'a pas le droit d'exécuter ou de faire exécuter des travaux en vue de l'utilisation, de la réfection, de l'adaptation et de la modernisation du tracé historique du Rhin de fer sur le territoire néerlandais, sauf si elle demande le prolongement d'une nouvelle route à partir du territoire belge « d'après le même plan » sur le territoire néerlandais et, si les Pays-Bas optent pour ce prolongement, d'après le nouveau plan établi par la Belgique conformément à l'Article XII du Traité de Séparation du 19 avril 1839.

- La Belgique est en droit, en vertu de l'Article XII du Traité de Séparation de 1839, de faire prolonger une nouvelle route construite sur son territoire sur le territoire néerlandais « d'après le même plan », sans préjudice des droits de souveraineté exclusifs des Pays-Bas, dans les limites énoncées à la Question 1. Le droit de la Belgique d'établir des plans, des caractéristiques et des procédures pour ces travaux, en vertu du droit belge et du pouvoir décisionnel qui en découle, est limité en conséquence.

- Le « plan » au sens où l'entend l'Article XII du Traité de Séparation de 1839 sera établi par la Belgique sans l'accord des Pays-Bas ; cependant, la Belgique informera et consultera les Pays-Bas conformément aux principes de bonne foi et de caractère raisonnable, tout ce qui précède étant entendu sans préjudice du droit communautaire.

- Le terme « plan », tel qu'il figure dans l'Article XII du Traité de Séparation doit être interprété sur la base de son acception ordinaire. Dans ce sens, il renvoie à toutes les caractéristiques techniques et particularités du chemin de fer.

- La demande de réactivation actuelle de la Belgique n'est pas une demande de « *nouvelle route ou ... canal* » au sens de l'Article XII du Traité de Séparation ayant pour conséquence de priver les Pays-Bas de l'option prévue à l'Article 12 du Traité de Séparation de 1839 d'exiger que la Belgique exécute des travaux sur le territoire néerlandais.

- Les travaux exécutés sur le territoire néerlandais par les Pays-Bas seront convenus d'un commun accord entre la Belgique et les Pays-Bas. Étant donné que la demande actuelle de réactivation du Rhin de fer par la Belgique ne constitue pas une demande de prolongement du Rhin de fer sur le territoire néerlandais « d'après le même plan » que sur le territoire belge, ladite limitation n'est pas applicable en l'espèce. Il en est de même du droit de la Belgique à bénéficier d'un traitement aussi favorable que celui accordé aux autres opérateurs des autres chemins de fer sur le territoire néerlandais, relativement à la liberté d'arrêter des plans, des caractéristiques et des procédures.

En outre, les pouvoirs règlementaires néerlandais d'établir des plans, des caractéristiques et des procédures demeurent limités par les principes définis à la Question 1.

- La distinction entre les exigences, les normes, les plans, les caractéristiques et les procédures liés, d'une part, aux possibilités d'utilisation de l'infrastructure ferroviaire proprement dite et, d'autre part, à l'aménagement du territoire et à l'intégration dans celui-ci de l'infrastructure ferroviaire, n'est pas pertinente en tant que telle, dans la mesure où la Belgique a le droit d'exécuter ou de faire exécuter des travaux sur le territoire néerlandais. De même, cette distinction n'est pas pertinente, en tant que telle, dans la mesure où la Belgique a le droit d'élaborer des plans, des caractéristiques et des procédures en vertu du droit belge et du pouvoir décisionnel qui en découle. Ceci n'a pas d'incidence sur la pertinence de la distinction visant le caractère raisonnable des exigences néerlandaises en matière de construction d'une infrastructure dont les coûts seraient assumés par la Belgique.

- Le droit des Pays-Bas à exiger unilatéralement la construction de tunnels et de tranchées couvertes, ainsi que les normes de construction et de sécurité qui y sont associées, est limité par les droits de la Belgique mentionnés ci-dessus si cette dernière demande un prolongement de la voie ferrée traversant le territoire néerlandais à partir du territoire belge d'après le même plan, ce qui n'est pas le cas en l'espèce. Il est en outre limité par l'obligation des Pays-Bas de coopérer avec la Belgique, ainsi que par les principes énoncés à la Question 1.

En conséquence, les Pays-Bas ne peuvent pas imposer la construction de tunnels et de tranchées couvertes aux frais de la Belgique, dès lors que cette exigence est contraire aux principes énoncés à la Question n° 1, et notamment aux principes de normalité et de proportionnalité, ainsi qu'à ceux d'absence de caractère arbitraire et de non discrimination.

Les Pays-Bas sont tenus d'informer la Belgique et de se concerter de bonne foi avec elle relativement à ces exigences, conformément à leur obligation de coopérer et aux principes de caractère raisonnable et de bonne foi.

La règle *'pacta sunt servanda'* et ses corollaires, les principes de bonne foi et de caractère raisonnable, s'appliquent également dans l'hypothèse où les Pays-Bas souhaitent construire sur le Rhin de fer, en territoire néerlandais, les tunnels et les tranchées couvertes mentionnés ci-dessus à leurs frais et non aux frais de la Belgique. En conséquence, les Pays-Bas ne peuvent notamment pas décider de construire un tunnel à leurs frais, si cette construction porte atteinte de manière déraisonnable au droit de passage conféré à la Belgique aux termes de l'Article XII du Traité de Séparation.

- Des déviations et autres mesures similaires ne peuvent pas être imposées unilatéralement par les Pays-Bas dans la mesure où elles exigent l'accord de la Belgique.

SUR LA QUESTION 3

À titre principal :

- qu'en application du régime conventionnel applicable au Rhin de fer, la Belgique n'assume les coûts et risques financiers liés au Rhin de fer sur le territoire néerlandais que si elle demande qu'un nouveau tracé à partir du territoire belge soit prolongé sur le territoire néerlandais d'après le même plan, et que les Pays-Bas décident alors de faire réaliser ce tracé par des ingénieurs et des ouvriers employés par les Pays-Bas, à condition, en outre, que les travaux fassent l'objet d'un accord mutuel.

- que la demande de réactivation du Rhin de fer présentée en l'espèce par la Belgique n'équivaut pas à une demande de prolongement d'un nouveau tracé sur le territoire néerlandais à partir du territoire belge d'après le même plan, étant précisé qu'une telle demande aurait pour conséquence de dégager la Belgique de son obligation d'assumer le coût et les risques financiers liés à cette réactivation.

- qu'en application du régime conventionnel applicable au Rhin de fer, les Pays-Bas assument la totalité des coûts et des risques financiers liés à la réfection, l'adaptation et la modernisation du tracé historique du Rhin de fer sur le territoire néerlandais, afin de le remettre en état et qu'il soit propre à faciliter le commerce.

- que la réactivation du Rhin de fer, telle qu'elle est envisagée à l'heure actuelle, n'aille pas au-delà de ce qui est nécessaire pour remettre la ligne en état et de nature à faciliter le commerce, ce qui aurait pour conséquence que les Pays-Bas assument la totalité des coûts et des risques financiers liés à la réfection, à l'adaptation et à la modernisation envisagées.

À titre subsidiaire :

- imputer aux Pays-Bas la totalité des coûts et des risques financiers liés à la réfection du tracé historique, suite au démantèlement, par les Pays-Bas, d'une partie de l'infrastructure du tracé historique le rendant impropre à l'utilisation, ou à l'absence d'entretien de cette voie.

- imputer aux Pays-Bas la totalité des coûts et des risques financiers liés (a) aux mesures relatives aux voies utilisées, actuellement ou à l'avenir, par les trains de marchandises néerlandais, (b) aux mesures nécessaires pour atteindre les objectifs susmentionnés conformément aux prescriptions législatives néerlandaises, (c) à la réalisation du contournement de Ruremonde, et (d) à la construction d'un tunnel dans la région du Meinweg et de tout autre dispositif de protection de l'environnement de nature similaire, et aux mesures compensatoires, dans les limites fixées par la Question 1.

2. **Les Pays-Bas**

27. Les conclusions des Pays-Bas, figurant dans la Duplique, étaient les suivantes :

SUR LA QUESTION 1

Les Pays-Bas estiment que dans la mesure où ils ont conservé leur droit d'exercer pleinement leur pouvoir législatif, exécutif et judiciaire sur la réactivation du Rhin de fer, le droit néerlandais relatif à la réfection, l'adaptation et la modernisation des lignes de chemin de fer sur le territoire néerlandais et le pouvoir décisionnel qui en découle, s'appliquent également à l'utilisation, la réfection, l'adaptation et la modernisation du tracé historique du Rhin de fer traversant le territoire néerlandais.

Hormis l'Article XII du Traité de Séparation, tel qu'amendé par le Traité du Rhin de fer, il n'existe aucune convention contraignant les Pays-Bas à autoriser la Belgique à utiliser, refaire, adapter et moderniser le Rhin de fer sur le territoire néerlandais.

L'Article XII du Traité de Séparation constitue quant à lui une convention spéciale. Il contient en effet une clause de réserve de souveraineté territoriale des Pays-Bas prévoyant que la Belgique a le droit d'utiliser, de refaire, d'adapter et de moderniser le Rhin de fer. Cependant, dans la mesure où il contient cette réserve de souveraineté territoriale des Pays-Bas, l'Article XII du Traité de Séparation devrait, conformément au droit international, être interprété de manière restrictive.

SUR LA QUESTION 2

Compte tenu de la réponse donnée à la Question 1, les Pays-Bas estiment que la Belgique n'a pas le droit d'exécuter ou de faire exécuter des travaux en vue de l'utilisation, de la réfection, de l'adaptation et de la modernisation du tracé

213

historique du Rhin de fer traversant le territoire néerlandais, ni d'arrêter des plans, caractéristiques et procédures relatifs à ces activités en vertu du droit belge et du pouvoir décisionnel qui en découle.

Quant au droit de la Belgique d'exécuter ou de faire exécuter des travaux en vue de l'utilisation, de la réfection, de l'adaptation et de la modernisation du Rhin de fer sur le territoire néerlandais, les Pays-Bas renvoient au texte de l'Article XII du Traité de Séparation, qui mentionne spécifiquement « *Cette route ... seraient construits,* au choix de la Hollande, *soit par des ingénieurs et ouvriers, que la Belgique obtiendrait l'autorisation d'employer à cet effet dans le canton de Sittard, soit par des ingénieurs et ouvriers, que la Hollande fournirait ...* ».

Il est impossible d'établir une distinction entre les exigences, les normes, les plans, les caractéristiques et les procédures liés d'une part, aux possibilités d'utilisation de l'infrastructure ferroviaire proprement dite et, d'autre part, à l'aménagement du territoire et à l'intégration dans celui-ci de l'infrastructure ferroviaire.

Les Pays-Bas sont en droit d'imposer unilatéralement la construction de tunnels, de tranchées couvertes et de déviations, etc., ainsi que les normes de construction et de sécurité qui y sont liées, tant que ceux-ci ne sont pas contraires aux règles de droit international en vigueur.

SUR LA QUESTION 3

Les Pays-Bas soutiennent que, conformément aux passages de l'Article XII du Traité de Séparation qui disposent « *entièrement aux frais et dépens de la Belgique* » et « *qui exécuteraient aux frais de la Belgique* », la totalité des coûts et des risques financiers liés à l'utilisation, la réfection, l'adaptation et la modernisation du tracé historique du Rhin de fer sur le territoire néerlandais, devrait être assumée par la Belgique, sous réserve des prescriptions du droit néerlandais et du pouvoir décisionnel qui en découle en ce qui concerne l'infrastructure ferroviaire et la protection des zones résidentielles et de l'environnement.

CHAPITRE II - FONDEMENT JURIDIQUE ET CONTENU DU DROIT DE PASSAGE BELGE

A. Dispositions juridiques applicables

28. Il a été demandé au Tribunal arbitral de rendre une sentence en répondant aux questions qui lui ont été posées par les deux Parties « sur le fondement du droit international, y compris du droit communautaire le cas échéant, en tenant compte des obligations des Parties en vertu de l'Article 292 du Traité CE ».

29. Divers traités sont pertinents dans le cadre de ce différend et ont été portés à l'attention du Tribunal par les Parties. Chacune des Parties a également invoqué divers principes et règles de droit international.

30. Comme mentionné ci-dessus (*voir* paragraphe 16), il existe un traité fondamental applicable à ce différend, à savoir le Traité de Séparation de 1839. Aux termes de ce Traité, la Belgique et les Pays-Bas ont réglé la question de la répartition de leur territoire respectif, entre autres questions. Ce Traité est l'aboutissement de longues négociations multilatérales diplomatiques entamées en 1830, au cours desquelles sont intervenues d'autres Puissances (la « Conférence de Londres »).

31. Le Traité de Séparation de 1839 délimitait donc le territoire de la Belgique et des Pays-Bas et précisait leurs frontières (Articles I, II et VI). Les Articles II et V traitaient de la cession, par Guillaume 1er, d'une partie du Grand Duché de Luxembourg. Les Articles III et IV attribuaient quant à eux une partie du Limbourg aux Pays-Bas et l'Article VII consacrait le maintien de la neutralité de la Belgique. L'Article XIII répartissait les dettes entre les deux pays. Divers droits de passage étaient garantis à la Belgique en vertu des Articles IX, X, XI et XII. C'est ce dernier Article XII qui a été le plus invoqué dans les plaidoiries des Parties dans le présent arbitrage.

32. Le Traité a été conclu en néerlandais et en français. Il n'existe pas de différend entre les Parties au sujet des légères variations existant entre les deux langues. Les Parties ont utilisé le texte français (Martens, *Nouveau Recueil des Traités*, Vol. XVI, p. 773) dans leurs plaidoiries. Chacune d'elles a fourni au Tribunal une traduction en anglais de certains articles particuliers et ces traductions diffèrent l'une de l'autre à plusieurs égards.

Pour ce motif et d'autres raisons techniques, le Tribunal a établi sa propre traduction [*en anglais*] de l'Article XII, dont la teneur est la suivante :

> *In the case that in Belgium a new road would have been built or a new canal dug, which would lead to the Maas facing the Dutch canton of Sittard, then Belgium would be at liberty to ask Holland, which in that hypothesis would not refuse it, that the said road, or the said canal be extended in accordance with the same plan, entirely at the cost and expense of Belgium, through the canton of Sittard, up to the borders of Germany. This road or canal, which could be used only for commercial communication, would be constructed, at the choice of Holland, either by engineers and workers whom Belgium would obtain authorization to employ for this purpose in the canton of Sittard, or by engineers and workers whom Holland would supply, and who would execute the agreed works at the expense of Belgium, all without any burden to Holland, and without prejudice to the exclusive rights of sovereignty over the territory which would be crossed by the road or canal in question.*

> *The two Parties would set, by common agreement, the amount and the method of collection of the duties and tolls which would be levied on the said road or canal.*

Le texte français, dont le texte qui précède est une traduction, est reproduit ci-dessus (*voir* paragraphe 17).

33. Le jour même où le Traité de Séparation de 1839 fut conclu, deux autres traités furent signés dans le cadre de la Conférence de Londres, l'un étant un traité conclu entre la Belgique, d'une part, et l'Autriche, la France, la Grande-Bretagne, la Prusse et la Russie, d'autre part, et l'autre un traité conclu entre les Pays-Bas et les mêmes parties (C.T.S., 1838–1839, Vol. 88, p. 411 et suivantes). Chacun de ces traités renvoyait aux dispositions du Traité de Séparation de 1839 dont les articles y étaient annexés et prévoyait que ces derniers « *sont considérés comme ayant la même force et valeur que s'ils étaient textuellement insérés dans le présent Acte, et qu'ils se trouvent ainsi placés sous la garantie de Leursdites Majestés* ».

34. Il était donc clair dès l'origine que les dispositions du Traité de Séparation de 1839, y compris de son Article XII, présentaient un intérêt plus que bilatéral. Cette situation a perduré jusqu'à présent. À notre époque, la Communauté européenne a démontré un certain intérêt pour la voie ferrée qui devait à terme être construite sur le fondement, notamment, de l'Article XII du Traité de Séparation de 1839. Cet intérêt et ses

implications juridiques pour le présent arbitrage, sont examinés plus en détail ci-après (*voir* paragraphes 145 et 146).

35. L'Article XII du Traité de Séparation de 1839 faisait référence à une route qui aurait pu être construite, ou à un canal qui aurait pu être creusé. En 1842, le Traité de limites entre la Belgique et les Pays-Bas fut conclu à La Haye (C.T.S., 1842–1843, Vol. 94, p. 37 et suivantes). Son but, tel qu'indiqué dans le préambule, était de clarifier un certain nombre de questions nées du Traité de Séparation de 1839. En particulier, l'Article III précisait que la construction de la route ou le creusement du canal traversant les Pays-Bas, mentionné à l'Article XII du Traité de Séparation de 1839, pouvait être confié à un concessionnaire. (En 1869, la Belgique avait en effet prévu une telle concession pour un chemin de fer (MB, p. 9, para. 9)). Le second paragraphe de l'Article III du Traité de limites envisageait la possibilité d'expropriation par les Pays-Bas, sur la base de leur droit et pour des raisons d'intérêt public, du terrain nécessaire au projet qui avait été envisagé par l'Article XII. La phrase « *et ce de la même manière que si le Gouvernement belge procédait par lui-même aux travaux d'exécution et d'exploitation de la route ou du canal* » a été immédiatement ajoutée à l'Article III du Traité de limites, maintenant ainsi entre les Parties l'équilibre soigneux qui avait été atteint dans l'Article XII du Traité de Séparation de 1839.

36. Néanmoins, le Traité de limites ne résolvait pas toutes les difficultés entre les Pays-Bas et la Belgique. Les Parties étaient en effet en désaccord sur le point de savoir si, aux fins du prolongement envisagé à l'Article XII du Traité de Séparation de 1839, la route aurait dû être construite, ou le canal creusé, ou simplement planifiés. Ce problème a été résolu depuis lors comme exposé plus loin (*voir* para. 62). Les Parties étaient également en désaccord sur le point de savoir si l'Article XII du Traité de Séparation de 1839 envisageait le prolongement d'une voie ferrée, par opposition à celui d'une route ou d'un canal. En définitive, les Pays-Bas sont convenus que la Belgique pourrait prolonger une ligne de chemin de fer par lettre datée du 12 août 1868 (MB, Pièce n° 15, Lettre du Gouvernement néerlandais à l'Ambassadeur de Belgique à La Haye, datée du 12 août 1868).

37. En 1873, la Belgique et les Pays-Bas conclurent un autre traité : le Traité du Rhin de fer. Aux termes de l'Article IV de ce Traité, les Pays-Bas reconnaissaient la *Compagnie du Nord de la Belgique* comme concessionnaire du chemin de fer sur le territoire

néerlandais. Il fut également convenu que le tronçon Anvers-Gladbach serait construit soit par cette société, soit par le *Grand Central belge*, selon des conditions reflétant les dispositions de l'Article XII du Traité de Séparation de 1839, à savoir « *sans charge aucune pour le Gouvernement des Pays-Bas, et sans préjudice de ses droits de souveraineté sur le territoire traversé* ». Un accord fut également conclu sur les questions relatives au pont que les Pays-Bas avaient, en 1873, accepté de voir construire sur la Meuse, près de Ruremonde.

38.   Un point important dans le contexte de cet arbitrage est que la modification du tracé d'origine prévu dans le Traité de Séparation de 1839 avait également été convenue dans le Traité du Rhin de fer : il ne passerait désormais plus par Sittard. L'Article IV, para. 4[6] dispose ce qui suit (dans la traduction *anglaise* du Tribunal) :

> *The line will enter the territory of the Duchy of Limbourg passing to the south of Hamont (Belgium); it will head towards Weert, pass to the south of that locality as well as of Haelen, traverse the Maas on a fixed bridge in the right part upstream of the bend at Buggenum, between the markers 83 and 84, rejoin the Maastricht line to Venlo north of the station of Ruremonde, follow part of this line, leave it south of that station to go to reach the Prussian frontier in a direction to be agreed upon with the Government of the German Empire.*

39.   Ainsi les Parties ont-elles modifié la disposition de l'Article XII du Traité de Séparation de 1839 qui prévoyait que la route ou le canal devait passer par Sittard. Pour signifier clairement que cette modification n'équivalait pas à une ligne supplémentaire s'ajoutant à celle envisagée en 1839, les représentants belges et néerlandais confirmaient conjointement, dans un document annexé au Traité au moment de la ratification que, comme prévu dans les déclarations des deux Gouvernements devant leurs Parlements respectifs :

> la concession de l'établissement d'un chemin de fer d'Anvers à Gladbach par le Duché de Limbourg, en passant à Ruremonde, comme elle est stipulée par le Traité du 13 janvier, 1873, constitue l'exécution pleine et entière de l'Article XII du Traité du 19 avril, 1839 [C.T.S., 1872–1873, Vol. 145, p. 447].

---

[6] Les Pays-Bas utilisent les chiffres arabes dans le texte néerlandais fourni au Tribunal et la Belgique utilise les chiffres romains par référence au texte français du Traité du Rhin de fer. Le Tribunal utilise les chiffres romains.

Rien ne suggérait, au cours de ces procédures de ratification, que l' « *exécution pleine* » devait être comprise comme signifiant que le droit de passage avait expiré ou que les droits de la Belgique à l'égard de ce qui est désigné actuellement par « tracé historique » étaient devenus caducs. Au contraire, l'intention était de faire état d'une modification convenue pour l'emplacement de la voie, qui avait été à l'origine indiqué comme étant Sittard ; le droit de passage de la Belgique s'exercerait désormais le long d'une voie qui incorpore actuellement la modification convenue à l'Article IV, paragraphe 4, du Traité du Rhin de fer (le « tracé historique »). La déclaration convenue précisait clairement qu'il s'agissait d'une décision définitive au sens où aucune demande à venir émanant de la Belgique relative à un canal, une route ou une voie ferrée passant par Sittard ne serait désormais prise en compte.

40.   Bien entendu, affirmer qu'un « tracé historique » et les droits belges y afférents perdurent ne répond pas à la question de savoir si les demandes actuelles de la Belgique équivalent bien à une « nouvelle voie » *supplémentaire* ou, si tel n'est pas le cas, si l'Article XII a un quelconque rôle à jouer. Ces questions, qui sont d'une grande importance pour le présent arbitrage, sont des questions distinctes qui seront traitées plus loin par le Tribunal (*voir* paras. 74 et suivants).

41.   L'utilisation du Rhin de fer, sur le tracé modifié prévu à l'Article IV, para. 4 du Traité du Rhin de fer, a débuté en 1879, le concessionnaire pour les territoires de Belgique et des Pays-Bas étant en l'occurrence le *Grand Central belge*.

42.   À la fin du dix-neuvième siècle, les lignes de chemin de fer sur le territoire belge furent nationalisées par le Gouvernement. Les Pays-Bas se portèrent acquéreurs des intérêts relatifs au chemin de fer du *Grand Central belge* présents sur leur propre territoire, en vertu d'une convention aux termes de laquelle la Belgique était autorisée en premier lieu à acheter au *Grand Central belge* la concession « *[d']Anvers à la frontière Prussienne vers Gladbach* », puis à la revendre aux Pays-Bas (Convention sur les chemins de fer de 1897). Un autre accord fut conclu entre le Gouvernement des Pays-Bas et le *Maatschappij tot Exploitatie van Staatsspoorwegen* (« *Maatschappij tot Exploitatie* ») pour faire passer sur le territoire néerlandais les lignes de chemin de fer qui avaient été cédées aux Pays-Bas en vertu de la Convention sur les chemins de fer de 1897. Cette Convention de 1897, qui comprenait des stipulations financières détaillées applicables entre *Maatschappij tot Exploitatie* et le Gouvernement, fut annexée à la législation des

Pays-Bas, le 2 avril 1898, en application de la Convention sur les chemins de fer de 1897 (MB, Pièce n° 25, Convention du 29 octobre 1897 entre l'État néerlandais et le *Maatschappij tot Exploitatie*, annexée à la Loi du 2 avril 1898 approuvant la Convention sur les chemins de fer du 23 avril 1897). Elle prévoyait, entre autres choses, que les stipulations d'une convention antérieure entre le Gouvernement des Pays-Bas et le *Maatschappij tot Exploitatie* concernant l'entretien étaient applicables aux cessions récemment intervenues.

43. Comme exposé ci-dessus (*voir* paragraphes 16 à 22), un différend est né entre la Belgique et les Pays-Bas dans le contexte d'une option relativement longue et d'un certain niveau d'utilisation de la ligne du Rhin de fer et de l'intérêt de la Belgique pour sa réactivation, telle qu'initiée et élaborée entre 1987 et 2003, différend portant sur leurs droits et obligations juridiques relatifs à la ligne du Rhin de fer, donnant lieu à des propositions belges et des contre-propositions néerlandaises. Le Tribunal devra à la fois interpréter certaines dispositions des traités susmentionnés et commenter la signification juridique de certains termes.

B. Principes d'interprétation que le Tribunal doit appliquer

44. Il est clair que pour répondre aux Questions qui lui sont posées par les Parties, le Tribunal doit interpréter différentes dispositions des instruments fondamentaux tout en appliquant les règles du droit international pertinentes.

45. La Belgique et les Pays-Bas sont tous deux parties à la Convention de Vienne sur le Droit des Traités du 23 mai 1969 (la « Convention de Vienne ») (Recueil des Traités des Nations-Unies (« R.T.N.U. »), Vol. 1155, p. 331). C'est précisément parce que certains des termes de cette Convention reflètent le droit coutumier et que certains étaient nouveaux, que l'Article 4 a prévu d'une manière générale la non-rétroactivité de la Convention, mais « sans préjudice de l'application de toutes règles énoncées dans la présente Convention auxquelles les traités seraient soumis en vertu du droit international indépendamment de ladite Convention ». Il est bien établi désormais que les dispositions relatives à l'interprétation des traités figurant aux Articles 31 et 32 de la Convention reflètent le droit international coutumier préexistant et peuvent donc (sauf indications contraires particulières) s'appliquer aux traités conclus avant l'entrée en vigueur de la Convention de Vienne de 1980. La Cour internationale de justice a appliqué les règles

coutumières d'interprétation, désormais reprises dans les Articles 31 et 32 de la Convention de Vienne, à un traité conclu en 1955 (*Litige Territorial (Jamahiriya arabe libyenne/Tchad), Recueil C.I.J. 1994*, p. 6 à p. 21–22, para. 41) ; et à un traité conclu en 1890, portant sur les droits des États qui, le jour de l'arrêt, n'étaient pas encore parties à la Convention de Vienne (*Arrêt Kasikili/Sedudu Island (Botswana/Namibie), Recueil C.I.J. 1999 (II)*, p. 1045 à p. 1059, para. 18). Dans l'affaire sur la Souveraineté sur *Pulau Ligitan et Pulau Sipadan*, le Tribunal a constaté que bien que l'Indonésie n'ait pas été partie à la Convention de Vienne, elle avait néanmoins appliqué à un traité conclu en 1891 les règles formulées aux Articles 31 and 32 de cette Convention. L'Indonésie n'a pas contesté le caractère applicable des règles codifiées dans ces Articles (*Souveraineté sur Pulau Ligitan et Pulau Sipadan (Indonésie/Malaisie), Recueil C.I.J. 2002*, p. 625 à p. 645–646, para. 37 à 38). Il n'existe aucune affaire après l'adoption de la Convention de Vienne en 1969 dans laquelle la Cour internationale de justice ou tout autre tribunal éminent n'ait pas agi ainsi.

46.   Ces articles disposent ce qui suit :

Article 31 Règle générale d'interprétation

1.   Un traité doit être interprété de bonne foi suivant le sens ordinaire à attribuer aux termes du traité dans leur contexte et à la lumière de son objet et de son but.

2.   Aux fins de l'interprétation d'un traité, le contexte comprend, outre le texte, préambule et annexes inclus :
   a)   tout accord ayant rapport au traité et qui est intervenu entre toutes les parties à l'occasion de la conclusion du traité ;
   b)   tout instrument établi par une ou plusieurs parties à l'occasion de la conclusion du traité et accepté par les autres parties en tant qu'instrument ayant rapport au traité.

3.   Il sera tenu compte, en même temps que du contexte :
   a)   de tout accord ultérieur intervenu entre les parties au sujet de l'interprétation du traité ou de l'application de ses dispositions ;
   b)   de toute pratique ultérieurement suivie dans l'application du traité par laquelle est établi l'accord des parties à l'égard de l'interprétation du traité ;
   c)   de toute règle pertinente de droit international applicable dans les relations entre les parties.

4.   Un terme sera entendu dans un sens particulier s'il est établi que telle était l'intention des parties.

Article 32 Moyens complémentaires d'interprétation

Il peut être fait appel à des moyens complémentaires d'interprétation, et notamment aux travaux préparatoires et aux circonstances dans lesquelles le traité a été conclu, en vue, soit de confirmer le sens résultant de l'application de l'Article 31, soit de déterminer le sens lorsque l'interprétation donnée conformément à l'Article 31 :
a)   laisse le sens ambigu ou obscur ; ou
b)   conduit à un résultat qui est manifestement absurde ou déraisonnable.

47.   Bien qu'aucune hiérarchie ne soit prévue entre les clauses de l'Article 31, il est clair que le point de départ pour l'interprétation est la signification ordinaire à attribuer aux termes pris dans leur contexte, compte tenu de l'objet et de l'intention du traité. Le Tribunal attachera une attention particulière à ces facteurs lors de son interprétation, ainsi qu'aux autres principes pertinents d'interprétation. Son analyse de l'application des différents principes d'interprétation sera effectuée dans les paragraphes traitant des différentes phrases contenues dans l'Article XII du Traité de Séparation de 1839 dont la signification est contestée.

48.   En parallèle, il convient que le Tribunal fasse, à titre liminaire, certaines observations d'ordre plus général. Bien que les parties lui aient fourni des extraits des longues négociations diplomatiques ayant abouti à la conclusion du Traité de Séparation de 1839, le Tribunal considère que ces extraits ne présentent pas le caractère de *travaux préparatoires* sur lesquels il pourrait se fonder en toute sécurité comme moyen complémentaire d'interprétation conformément aux dispositions de l'Article 32 de la Convention de Vienne. Ces extraits peuvent être des indications des souhaits ou de la compréhension de l'une ou l'autre des Parties à des moments particuliers au cours des longues négociations, mais ils n'ont pas pour effet de mettre à jour une compréhension commune de la signification des différentes dispositions de l'Article XII. Cette observation porte en particulier sur la question de savoir si le droit de passage accordé à la Belgique doit être compris comme une contrepartie de l'accord selon lequel, à l'issue de la séparation, le territoire qui constitue désormais la province néerlandaise du Limbourg devait faire partie des Pays-Bas (point de vue de la Belgique) ou bien si l'obtention du Limbourg par les Pays-Bas était une contrepartie de l'obtention par la Belgique d'une partie du Luxembourg (point de vue des Pays-Bas). En l'absence de *travaux préparatoires* reflétant une compréhension commune, la réponse ne peut être catégorique, mais le Tribunal estime que de très nombreux éléments (et non pas seulement l'un ou

l'autre de ces éléments) ont contribué à l'équilibre atteint dans le texte de l'Article XII. Par ailleurs, le Tribunal sera attentif aux circonstances entourant la conclusion de chacun des traités applicables, comme l'exige l'Article 32 de la Convention de Vienne. Le Tribunal note également que la bonne foi est à la fois un élément spécifique de l'Article 31, paragraphe 1 de la Convention de Vienne et un principe général du droit international régissant la conduite des parties vis-à-vis l'une de l'autre.

49. Le Tribunal observe en outre qu'il existe d'autres principes bien établis applicables au processus d'interprétation. Le principe d'effet utile a une importance particulière : *ut res magis valeat quam pereat*. La pertinence de l'effet utile porte sur l'objet et l'intention d'un traité ; pour autant, celui-ci n'autorise pas un tribunal à réviser un traité.

50. Les Pays-Bas ont souligné le fait que le droit de passage d'un pays sur le territoire d'un autre doit obligatoirement faire l'objet d'un accord spécifique. Cet argument est incontestablement correct et n'est d'ailleurs pas contesté par la Belgique. Les Pays-Bas soutiennent en outre que le droit de passage en tant que tel doit être interprété de manière restrictive et cite plusieurs affaires à l'appui de son opinion. Cette dernière proposition *est* contestée par la Belgique.

51. Dans l'affaire *des Zones franches de la Haute-Savoie et du Pays de Gex* (*C.P.J.I., Série A/B, n° 46 (1932)* p. 166), la Cour permanente de justice internationale (« Cour permanente ») a déclaré, au sujet des droits mentionnés dans l'affaire, que la « souveraineté de la France… doit être respectée dans la mesure où elle n'est pas limitée par ses obligations internationales et … par ses obligations en vertu des traités… » et que « aucune restriction dépassant celles résultant de ces instruments ne peut être imposée à la France sans son accord ». Dans l'affaire de l'*Interprétation du Statut du Territoire de Memel* (*C.P.J.I., Série A/B, n° 49 (1932)* à pp. 313–314), la Cour permanente a indiqué qu'en l'absence dans le traité de dispositions prévoyant l'autonomie de Memel, « les droits résultant de la souveraineté de la Lituanie doivent s'appliquer ». Il n'est pas douteux en l'espèce qu'au-delà des droits de la Belgique prévus à l'Article XII du Traité de Séparation de 1839, la souveraineté des Pays-Bas demeure intacte.

52. Il est vrai que dans l'affaire des *Zones Franches* et *l'affaire du S.S. Wimbledon* (*C.P.J.I. Série A, n° 1 (1923)* p. 24) la Cour permanente a estimé qu'en cas de doute au sujet de la limite de souveraineté, cette limite doit être interprétée dans un sens restrictif. Dans la

dernière affaire, la Cour permanente a prudemment déclaré qu'elle se sentirait néanmoins « tenue de s'arrêter au point où l'interprétation dite restrictive serait contraire aux termes sans ambiguïté de l'Article et contredirait ce qui a été clairement accordé ».

53.   La doctrine de l'interprétation restrictive n'a jamais eu de suprématie hiérarchique, mais constituait néanmoins une technique permettant d'assurer un bon équilibre de répartition des droits au sein d'un système de traités. Le principe d'interprétation restrictive, selon lequel les traités doivent être interprétés en faveur de la souveraineté de l'État en cas de doute, n'est effectivement pas mentionné dans les dispositions de la Convention de Vienne. L'objet et l'intention d'un traité, ainsi que l'intention des Parties, sont les éléments d'interprétation qui prévalent. En effet, la doctrine précise qu'une application trop rigoureuse du principe d'interprétation restrictive pourrait s'avérer incompatible avec le but essentiel du traité (*voir* Jennings and Watts, *Oppenheim's International Law*, 9ème édition (1992), p. 1279). Ainsi, l'interprétation restrictive joue-t-elle un rôle insignifiant dans certaines catégories de traités tels que, par exemple, les traités concernant les Droits de l'Homme. En fait, certains auteurs notent que le principe n'a guère été appliqué dans la jurisprudence récente des cours et tribunaux internationaux et que sa pertinence actuelle peut être mise en doute (Bernhardt « *Evolutive Treaty Interpretation, Especially of the European Convention on Human Rights* » 42 *German Yearbook of International Law* (1999), p. 11, à p. 14).

54.   La sentence rendue dans l'Arbitrage du *Lac Lanoux* (R.S.A., vol. XII, p. 301) demeure à ce jour un guide très utile dans le cadre de la présente affaire en ce qui concerne le type de tensions inévitables entre les droits accordés sur son propre territoire, en vertu d'un traité, et les réserves de souveraineté. La clause pertinente dans la disposition du traité pour l'utilisation des eaux du lac Lanoux portait sur la souveraineté territoriale « sauf modifications convenues entre les deux Gouvernements » (p. 120). L'Article XII du Traité de Séparation de 1839 a une structure inverse, les droits de la Belgique étant spécifiés, puis suivis de la réserve générale concernant la souveraineté. Le Tribunal estime que ceci ne change rien ; chaque terme est un équilibre entre les droits spéciaux accordés par un État à un autre sur son propre territoire et une affirmation générale de la souveraineté territoriale. Le Tribunal a statué comme suit dans l'affaire du *Lac Lanoux* :

    [il] a été soutenu devant le Tribunal que ces modifications doivent être interprétées de manière stricte car elles constituent une dérogation à la

souveraineté. Le Tribunal ne peut pas admettre une règle d'interprétation aussi absolue. La souveraineté territoriale se présume. Elle doit s'incliner devant toutes les obligations internationales, quelle que soit leur origine, mais uniquement devant ces obligations [*Ibid.*].

Le tribunal de l'affaire du *Lac Lanoux* a observé qu'en application de cette observation « la question consiste donc à déterminer les obligations du Gouvernement français dans cette affaire ... ». (*Ibid.*).

55. C'est précisément de la même manière que la souveraineté garantie aux Pays-Bas en vertu de l'Article XII du Traité de Séparation de 1839 ne peut être comprise qu'après avoir déterminé les droits de la Belgique et les obligations des Pays-Bas à cet égard. Ceci ne peut pas être effectué en invoquant le principe d'interprétation restrictive, mais plutôt en examinant (à l'aide des règles normales d'interprétation précisées aux Articles 31 et 32 de la Convention de Vienne) quels sont exactement les droits qui ont été concédés à la Belgique. Tout le reste relève de la souveraineté des Pays-Bas. Et en fait, le bien-fondé de cette méthodologie semble en définitive être reconnu par les Pays-Bas (DPB, p. 7, para. 24).

56. En d'autres termes, les Pays-Bas peuvent exercer leur droit de souveraineté sur le territoire sur lequel passe la ligne du Rhin de fer, sauf si l'exercice de ce droit est en contradiction avec les droits accordés à la Belgique par le Traité ou avec les droits dont la Belgique pourrait jouir en vertu du droit international général ou des contraintes imposées par le droit communautaire.

57. Enfin, le Tribunal souhaite souligner un point qui lui paraît avoir une grande importance dans cette affaire : le problème de l'intemporalité de l'interprétation des dispositions d'un traité. Cette idée aura une pertinence considérable dans l'interprétation qui suit de certaines phrases figurant à l'Article XII du Traité de Séparation de 1839.

58. Il convient de rappeler que l'Article 31, paragraphe 3, alinéa (c) de la Convention de Vienne sur le Droit des Traités renvoie à « toute règle pertinente de droit international applicable dans les relations entre les parties ». Pour cette raison, ainsi que pour des raisons relatives à sa propre juridiction, le Tribunal a examiné toutes les dispositions du droit communautaire qui pourraient être considérées comme éventuellement pertinentes en l'espèce (*voir* Chapitre III ci-après). Les dispositions du droit international général sont

également applicables aux relations entre les Parties et par conséquent, doivent être prises en compte aux fins de l'interprétation de l'Article XII du Traité de Séparation de 1839 et de l'Article IV du Traité du Rhin de fer. En outre, le droit international de l'environnement est applicable aux relations entre les Parties. Des discussions considérables ont eu lieu en ce qui concerne ce qui, en matière de droit de l'environnement, constitue des « règles » ou des « principes », ce qui relève du droit non contraignant (« *soft law* »), et quel droit conventionnel ou principes en matière d'environnement a contribué au développement du droit international coutumier. Sans entrer plus avant dans ces controverses, le Tribunal remarque que dans toutes ces catégories, le terme « environnement » englobe l'air, l'eau, la terre, la faune et la flore, les écosystèmes et les sites naturels, la santé et la sécurité humaine, ainsi que le climat. Les principes qui en résultent, quel que soit leur statut actuel, font référence à la préservation, à la gestion, aux notions de prévention et de développement durable et à la protection des générations futures.

59. Depuis la Conférence de Stockholm sur l'Environnement de 1972, le droit international relatif à la protection de l'environnement a connu un essor notoire. Aujourd'hui, le droit international et le droit communautaire exigent l'intégration de mesures de protection de l'environnement appropriées dans la conception et la mise en œuvre des activités de développement économique. Le principe 4 de la Déclaration de Rio sur l'environnement et le développement adoptée en 1992 (*RGDIP*, 1992, p. 975), qui reflète cette tendance, prévoit que « la protection de l'environnement doit faire partie intégrante du processus de développement et ne peut être considérée isolément ». Le point important est que ces principes émergents intègrent désormais la protection de l'environnement au processus de développement. Le droit de l'environnement et le droit applicable au développement ne constituent pas des alternatives, mais des concepts intégrés se renforçant mutuellement ; ainsi, lorsque le développement risque de porter atteinte de manière significative à l'environnement, doit exister une obligation d'empêcher, ou au moins d'atténuer, cette pollution (*voir* paragraphe 222). Le Tribunal estime que ce devoir est désormais devenu un principe du droit international général. Ce principe s'applique non seulement aux activités autonomes, mais également aux activités entreprises pour mettre en œuvre des traités spécifiques conclus entre les Parties. Le Tribunal rappelle l'observation de la Cour internationale de justice dans l'affaire *Gabčíkovo-Nagymaros* selon laquelle « le concept de développement durable traduit bien cette nécessité de concilier développement

économique et protection de l'environnement » (*Gabčíkovo-Nagymaros (Hongrie/Slovaquie), Arrêt, Recueil C.I.J. 1997, p. 7, à p. 78, para. 140)*. Dans ce contexte, la Cour a clairement précisé que « ces normes nouvelles doivent être prises en considération et ... ces exigences nouvelles convenablement appréciées, non seulement lorsque des États envisagent de nouvelles activités, mais aussi lorsqu'ils poursuivent des activités qu'ils ont engagées dans le passé » (*Ibid*). Le Tribunal estime que cet argument s'applique également à la ligne de chemin de fer du Rhin de fer.

60. Il va de soi que la simple évocation de ces questions n'apporte pas les réponses dans le présent arbitrage concernant ce qui peut ou ne peut pas être fait, ou par qui et à quel prix. Néanmoins, le Tribunal considère que, en ce qui concerne les questions qui lui sont posées, aucune des Parties ne conteste que les normes de protection de l'environnement soient applicables aux relations entre les Parties. Dans cette mesure, elles peuvent s'avérer pertinentes pour l'interprétation des traités dans lesquels les réponses aux questions peuvent être recherchées en premier lieu.

61. Le Tribunal va maintenant examiner l'application des principes d'interprétation aux dispositions pertinentes du Traité.

C. L'interprétation des éléments litigieux de l'Article XII du Traité de Séparation de 1839

1. « Il aurait été construit »

62. Dès 1864, des différends sont survenus sur la signification de « [I]l aurait été construit », et ces différends n'ont pas cessé avec l'accord de 1873 visant à remplacer les références à « route » et « canal » par « voie ferrée » dans le Traité de Séparation de 1839. En effet, les Pays-Bas informèrent la Belgique en 1864 que ce qui avait été convenu dans le Traité de Séparation de 1839 était le prolongement d'une ligne qui avait déjà été construite en Belgique, et non le prolongement d'une ligne qui en était encore au stade de projet (MB, Pièce n° 13, Lettre du Gouvernement néerlandais à l'Ambassadeur de Belgique à La Haye, datée du 7 mars 1864). En 1868, un prolongement vers une ligne en projet fut convenu « *en principe* » à des fins « *de[s] bonnes et cordiales relations* » (MB, Pièce n° 15, Lettre adressée le 12 août 1868 par le Gouvernement néerlandais à l'Ambassadeur de Belgique à La Haye). Les questions juridiques concernant l'expression « *aurait été*

227

construit » n'ont pas été résolues, mais n'ont plus d'importance. L'Article IV du Traité du Rhin de fer de 1873 prévoyait que la *Compagnie du Nord de la Belgique*, qui était le concessionnaire de la ligne de chemin de fer d'Anvers à Gladbach deviendrait concessionnaire « *de cette même ligne qui est située sur le territoire du Duché de Limbourg* ». Nonobstant l'utilisation du temps présent, ce tronçon restait à construire. L'Article IV prévoyait toutefois que le tronçon néerlandais soit « construit et exploité » soit par la *Compagnie du Nord de la Belgique* soit par le *Grand Central belge*.

2. « <u>Que ladite route ou ledit canal fussent prolongés d'après le même plan</u> »

63. Le différend entre les Parties quant à la signification du terme « plan » est facile à comprendre. Selon les Pays-Bas, le terme « plan » renvoie aux travaux qui permettraient physiquement un passage transfrontières pour qu'une ligne de chemin de fer soit « prolongée » en partant de la Belgique et en traversant les Pays-Bas (DPB, p. 31, para. 126). La Belgique, invoquant le « sens évident » de ce terme, ainsi que la signification à lui donner dans le contexte des projets de travaux publics, insiste sur le fait que « plan » doit être compris comme s'appliquant aux propositions et descriptifs du projet dans sa totalité.

64. Les Parties sont également en désaccord s'agissant des droits découlant, pour chacune d'elles, de ces différents points de vue sur le sens de « d'après le même plan ». La position des Pays-Bas est très nette. Ils estiment en effet que la demande de la Belgique équivaut à exiger une « nouvelle ligne de chemin de fer » qui, en conséquence, doit être prolongée « d'après le même plan ». La réserve de « droits exclusifs de souveraineté sur le territoire qui serait traversé » indique, selon les Pays-Bas, que « le même plan » ne peut pas donner lieu à des spécifications pour l'ensemble du projet. Tout au plus peut-elle être une référence à une possibilité d'utilisation transfrontière. Le « même plan » se réfère à la continuité physique que les Pays-Bas sont tenus d'assurer, mais pas davantage. Le point de vue des Pays-Bas s'appuie, selon eux, sur la référence, dans l'Article XII, à l'exécution des « travaux convenus », cette expression affirmant qu'un plan pour la ligne de chemin de fer dans son ensemble ne peut donc pas être unilatéralement imposé par la Belgique. Les Pays-Bas soutiennent également que l'Article V du Traité du Rhin de fer, pris conjointement avec l'Article 3 de la Convention de 1867 entre la Belgique et les Pays-Bas « *pour la jonction de quatre chemins de fer* » (Convention entre la Belgique et les Pays-

Bas pour la jonction des chemins de fer, La Haye, 9 novembre 1967, C.T.S. 1866 à 1867, Vol. 135, p. 467) suggère que le « plan » doit nécessairement faire l'objet d'un accord.

65. La Belgique considère quant à elle que ces dernières dispositions ne sont pas pertinentes. Elle soutient en effet qu'aucune demande de prolongement de la ligne de chemin de fer au titre de l'Article XII n'existe ; elle considère toutefois le développement et la modernisation du chemin de fer comme également soumis à la disposition « selon le même plan » de l'Article XII. Dans la mesure où le « même plan » fait référence au plan que seule la Belgique était en droit de faire réaliser sur le territoire belge, il ne peut pas faire l'objet de négociations pour son application au territoire des Pays-Bas. La détermination unilatérale du plan est donc aux yeux de la Belgique un « corollaire logique du fait que conformément à l'Article XII du Traité, les coûts de construction de la nouvelle ligne aux Pays-Bas seraient supportés par la Belgique » (RB, p. 77, para. 77). Prenant acte du fait que les Pays-Bas ont le droit d'exercer leur juridiction sur leur propre territoire (en citant l'exemple de la création de passages à niveau), la Belgique soutient qu'elle ne peut pas le faire d'une manière qui ne tienne pas compte des droits belges reconnus par le droit international. Elle établit toutefois une distinction entre le droit, qu'elle revendique unilatéralement, d'établir le plan lorsque c'est *elle* qui doit exécuter les travaux, et la disposition qui prévoit le cas où les Pays-Bas choisissent d'exécuter les travaux. Dans la première hypothèse, un accord peut être souhaitable, mais selon la Belgique, il n'est pas nécessaire d'un point de vue juridique ; la Belgique admet en revanche que dans la dernière hypothèse, l'accord des Pays-Bas pour les *travaux** est juridiquement nécessaire (RB, p. 82, para. 81).

66. Le Tribunal considère que les possibilités d'utilisation du prolongement de la ligne en Belgique, en passant par les Pays-Bas, doivent être conformes aux spécifications de la voie, dont la dimension et la nature peuvent effectivement avoir été décidées par la Belgique. Toutefois, tant en ce qui concerne le prolongement que la réactivation, le plan général de la ligne doit faire l'objet d'un accord mutuel. Les travaux qui en résultent sont des « travaux convenus ». Bien entendu, cet accord ne saurait être refusé par les Pays-Bas si cela équivalait à un déni du droit de passage de la Belgique. Le Tribunal ne voit aucune disposition de l'Article XII du Traité de Séparation de 1839, ni du Traité du Rhin de fer, qui établisse une distinction à cet égard entre les travaux qui peuvent être exécutés

---

* Le texte en italique est une correction apportée à la sentence par le Tribunal arbitral en septembre 2005, après une Requête en Correction de la Sentence déposée par la Belgique, à laquelle les Pays-Bas avaient consenti.

légalement par la Belgique et les travaux que les Pays-Bas feront exécuter. Le Tribunal ne peut accepter les arguments de la Belgique sur ce point.

67. L'expression « d'après le même plan » doit être lue de manière à permettre une interprétation qui concilie les droits spécifiques de la Belgique et la préservation de la souveraineté des Pays-Bas. Bien que le terme « plan » soit couramment compris dans le secteur des travaux publics et dans certains dictionnaires comme le descriptif de l'ensemble du projet, diverses dispositions de l'Article XII suggèrent que ce n'est pas la signification qui doit lui être imputée en l'espèce. En particulier, la référence à des « travaux convenus », ainsi que la préservation de la souveraineté des Pays-Bas tendent à lui donner un autre sens : la préservation de la souveraineté des Pays-Bas lui assure en effet que, hormis les éléments spécifiés en faveur de la Belgique, aucune autre limitation de souveraineté n'est impliquée. Toutefois, la préservation de la souveraineté ne peut pas être invoquée en parallèle pour porter atteinte aux droits concédés à la Belgique par l'Article XII. Compte tenu de ces observations, le Tribunal note que le plan mentionné dans l'expression « d'après le même plan » dans la mesure où il se rapporte à la continuité à la frontière, relève de la compétence de la Belgique. Ceci résulte du fait que, selon l'Article XII, une ligne belge aura été construite et pourrait, ou pourrait ne pas, faire l'objet d'une demande ultérieure de prolongement. Au-delà, les spécifications d'utilisation de la totalité de la ligne doivent être convenues conjointement. Les questions relevant uniquement de la souveraineté des Pays-Bas, et sur lesquelles ces derniers ont le droit de décision, comprennent notamment tous les éléments de sécurité de l'ensemble de l'ouvrage, ainsi que les conditions de sécurité dans lesquelles les travaux sont exécutés.

3. **« que la dite route ou le dit canal fussent prolongés … entièrement aux frais et dépens de la Belgique …. »**
« des ingénieurs et ouvriers … qui exécuteraient, aux frais de la Belgique, les travaux convenus, le tout sans charge aucune pour la Hollande …. »

68. Le Tribunal observe tout d'abord que l'introduction de l'adjectif « convenu » après le terme « travaux » suggère clairement, dans son acception ordinaire, que les deux Parties envisageaient, bien que les Pays-Bas ne puissent pas refuser une demande de prolongement d'une ligne de chemin de fer sur son territoire, que les travaux

230

concerneraient les deux pays. Ainsi, les droits de souveraineté des Pays-Bas et le droit de passage de la Belgique pourraient-ils être conciliés.

69. Outre cette question, il est clair que les travaux d'une ligne de chemin de fer devant être prolongée depuis la Belgique jusqu'aux frontières de l'Allemagne étaient bien à la charge exclusive de la Belgique.

70. Le différend qui concerne la question de savoir si la demande spécifique de la Belgique de modernisation et de réfection de la ligne au-delà de sa capacité précédente est « un prolongement » au sens de l'Article XII (question commentée par le Tribunal aux paragraphes 82 à 84 ci-après) ; et plus particulièrement, si les « frais et dépens » à mettre à la charge de la Belgique doivent comprendre les « frais et dépens » encourus si les travaux finalement convenus prévoient les mesures de protection de l'environnement requises par le droit néerlandais. La Belgique conteste une telle obligation au motif que ces mesures ne sont pas nécessaires au prolongement physique de la ligne, mais sont des mesures imposées unilatéralement par les Pays-Bas dans le cadre de l'exercice de leur souveraineté ; la Belgique soutient en outre qu'elle aurait dû être consultée avant que les diverses zones soient classées en réserve naturelle protégée. Elle observe que les Pays-Bas ont affirmé (DPB, p. 23, para. 93) que ces mesures spécifiques ne sont pas celles qui lui sont imposées par le droit communautaire. En outre, la Belgique soutient que les mesures proposées pour la protection contre les nuisances sonores, et notamment le creusement d'un tunnel, ne sont pas la solution de protection de l'environnement la moins onéreuse.

71. Les Pays-Bas soutiennent qu'ils jouissent du droit souverain d'évaluer les moyens appropriés aux fins de protéger l'environnement conformément aux prescriptions communautaires et à leurs propres normes nationales ; qu'ils ont cherché à identifier objectivement ces moyens par le biais de rapports d'experts et que ces mesures n'auraient pas été nécessaires en l'absence de la demande de la Belgique de réfection et de modernisation significatives de la capacité de la ligne ferroviaire du Rhin de fer.

72. Les deux arguments sont bien fondés. Le Tribunal estime nécessaire, aux fins de répondre à cette question, de s'assurer tout d'abord que le projet est susceptible de relever de la disposition prévoyant la répartition des coûts prévue à l'Article XII et ensuite, dans

l'affirmative, de vérifier si les « frais et dépens » des mesures envisagées par les Pays-Bas font partie intégrante du prolongement de la ligne du Rhin de fer.

73. Le Tribunal reviendra plus loin sur ces questions.

4. Une « nouvelle route » ou un « nouveau canal » à « prolonger » ?

74. La demande de réactivation de la Belgique est à la fois immédiate et à long terme. Il est entendu que la Belgique souhaite, d'ici 2020, faire circuler tous les jours sur la ligne et dans les deux sens, 43 trains de 700 mètres de long roulant à 100 kilomètres / heure. Les travaux nécessaires sont, selon les Pays-Bas, si importants qu'« ils équivalent ... à une demande, au sens de l'Article XII, de prolongement d'une ligne de chemin de fer du territoire belge sur le territoire néerlandais. Ce chemin de fer est *nouveau* dans la mesure où il exige des travaux considérables d'adaptation et de modernisation à de nombreux égards pour parvenir à l'utilisation souhaitée » (CMPB, para. 3.3.4.5). En conséquence, selon les Pays-Bas, les dispositions de l'Article XII concernant les coûts (outre le rétablissement du niveau d'entretien de 1991, dont ils supporteront le coût) sont applicables. Ce nouvel ouvrage doit, en ce qui concerne ses possibilités d'utilisation, être « entièrement aux frais et dépens de la Belgique » et « sans charge aucune pour la Hollande ». La Belgique affirme pour sa part que sa demande de réactivation n'est pas une demande de « prolongement » – « [le] Rhin de fer a été prolongé sur le territoire néerlandais dans les années 1870 et existe encore à l'heure actuelle ». Dans ce sens, la Belgique estime que ses demandes actuelles ne relèvent pas de l'Article XII du Traité de Séparation de 1839.

75. La question se pose donc de savoir si la demande de la Belgique porte sur une nouvelle route, un nouveau canal ou encore une ligne de chemin de fer traversant les Pays-Bas au sens de l'Article XII ; ou bien s'il s'agit d'une demande d'adaptation d'un droit de passage qui existait déjà en vertu de l'Article XII. Il est demandé au Tribunal de dire si les coûts de la réactivation doivent être supportés ou non par la Belgique. Dans ce contexte, le Tribunal note que les positions adoptées par les Parties ne sont pas entièrement identiques à ce que chacune d'elles était disposée à envisager lors des négociations, avant de recourir à l'arbitrage. La Belgique assimile sa demande à l'entretien d'une ligne existante dont le coût doit être supporté par les Pays-Bas. Elle invoque à cet effet l'Article XI du Traité de Séparation de 1839. Les Pays-Bas pour leur

part assimilent la demande de la Belgique à une demande de nouvelle ligne de chemin de fer, dont la totalité du coût doit être à la charge de la Belgique. En tout état de cause, aucune des Parties n'exclut totalement la pertinence de l'Article XII. Toutefois, chacune de ces possibilités comporte ses propres difficultés.

76. Le Tribunal constate que l'Article XII du Traité de Séparation de 1839 ne traite ni de la question de l'entretien, ni de celle de « l'adaptation et la modernisation » (le descriptif convenu conjointement dans les Questions posées au Tribunal par les Parties). La première question a été résolue par la pratique néerlandaise d'assumer la responsabilité physique et financière de l'entretien (que les Pays-Bas perçoivent sans aucun doute comme un élément de leur souveraineté territoriale) et est acceptée par les deux Parties. Ni l'Article XII, ni les conventions financières détaillées, élaborées dans le cadre de la Convention ferroviaire de 1897, ne prévoyaient spécifiquement les frais d'entretien des lignes sur le territoire néerlandais (y compris de la ligne du Rhin de fer) appartenant actuellement aux Pays-Bas. L'Article IX de la Convention ferroviaire de 1897 parlait d'accords futurs pour l' « *exploitation internationale des chemins de fer rachetés* », mais semble n'avoir jamais été appliqué à la question de l'entretien. L'accord qui lui est lié conclu entre les Pays-Bas et le *Maatschappij tot Exploitatie* (selon lequel cette société néerlandaise devait désormais exploiter la ligne du Rhin de fer sur le territoire néerlandais) présuppose clairement que la responsabilité des réparations et des rénovations incombe au Gouvernement néerlandais (MB, Pièce n° 25, Convention entre l'État des Pays-Bas et le *Maatschappij tot Exploitatie*, 29 octobre 1897, annexée à la Loi du 2 avril 1898 approuvant la Convention ferroviaire du 23 avril 1897, Articles 2 et 8). La déclaration explicative, associée à la ratification par les Pays-Bas de la Convention ferroviaire de 1897, mentionne que « l'État a l'obligation d'assurer, à ses propres frais, un niveau d'entretien suffisant pour que les chemins de fer puissent être repris par Exploitatie-Maatschappij » (MB, Pièce n° 22, Ratification de la convention entre les Pays-Bas et la Belgique, signée à Bruxelles le 23 avril 1897 – Déclaration explicative, p. 12 à 13). Ceci ne permet pas nécessairement de conclure que la « rénovation », au titre de la demande belge actuelle, nécessaire aux fins de respecter les normes de niveaux d'activité qui n'étaient pas prévus auparavant, fait partie de ce fait de l'obligation d'entretien et de rénovation assumée par les Pays-Bas à la fin du XIXème siècle. Le Tribunal considère que les Pays-Bas (ce que ceux-ci acceptent) sont tenus de ramener la ligne du Rhin de fer au niveau qu'elle avait atteint lors de l'utilisation régulière (quoique

233

réduite) de la ligne avant l'interruption de cette utilisation en 1991 ; mais ces obligations d'entretien et de réparation ne couvrent pas les coûts de modernisation significatifs impliqués par la demande actuelle de la Belgique. Que ces coûts doivent ou non être assumés par la Belgique en vertu de l'Article XII du Traité de Séparation de 1839 dépend d'autres questions.

77.   La question de l'adaptation significative et de la modernisation est un problème plus complexe qui n'a pas encore été exploré. L'application des principes du droit international à l'interprétation des traités peut toutefois aider à la résoudre.

78.   La disposition selon laquelle la Belgique supportera tous les « frais et dépens » de la « nouvelle route » ou du « nouveau canal » (chemin de fer) est claire, et a un « sens évident ». Toutefois, pour décider ce qui est ou n'est pas une « nouvelle route » ou un « nouveau canal » (chemin de fer), mais plutôt la réactivation d'une route ou d'un canal ou d'une ligne de chemin de fer existant et décider en conséquence si l'Article XII est applicable et dans quelle mesure, il convient de recourir à d'autres principes d'interprétation.

79.   L'Article 31, paragraphe 3, alinéa (c) de la Convention de Vienne exige également que soit prise en compte « toute règle pertinente de droit international applicable dans les relations entre les parties ». La règle intemporelle semble bien être une telle « règle pertinente ». À cet égard, il convient de tenir compte, dans l'interprétation de l'Article XII, de la situation juridique telle qu'elle existait en 1839. En particulier, il est certain qu'en 1839, il était envisagé que les coûts de tout prolongement d'une nouvelle route ou d'un nouveau canal que la Belgique pourrait demander seraient relativement modestes et d'un montant limité. Les progrès considérables qui ont été réalisés par la suite en matière d'électrification, de conception et de spécifications des voies, d'importance du fret, etc. et leur coût concomitant, ne pouvaient pas être prévus par les Parties. Pour autant, cette règle n'exige pas que le Tribunal ignore ni des faits ultérieurs concernant l'application effective du Traité, ni tous les développements juridiques ultérieurs. Il est en effet établi depuis longtemps que la compréhension des termes conceptuels ou génériques d'un traité peut être considérée comme « une question essentiellement relative qui dépend du développement des relations internationales » (*Décrets sur la Nationalité établis à Tunis et au Maroc, C.P.J.I. Série B, n° 4 (1923)*, p. 24). Certains termes sont « non pas statiques, mais par définition, évolutifs .... Les Parties à la Convention doivent en

234

conséquence être réputées les avoir acceptés en tant que tels » (*Namibie (Sud-Ouest Africain), Avis consultatif, Recueil C.I.J. 1971*, p. 16 à p. 31). Lorsqu'un terme peut être considéré comme générique « on présume nécessairement que sa signification est destinée à suivre l'évolution du droit et à correspondre à la signification attachée à l'expression par le droit en vigueur à un moment donné » (*Plateau Continental de la Mer Égée (Grèce/Turquie), Arrêt, Recueil de la C.I.J. 1978*, p. 3 à p. 32, para. 77). Une constatation similaire a été faite par l'instance d'appel de l'OMC lorsqu'elle a eu à interpréter le terme « ressources naturelles » de l'Article XX, paragraphe (g) de l'Accord sur l'OMC (« États-Unis - Prohibition à l'importation de certaines crevettes et de certains produits à base de crevettes » (WT/DS58/AB/R) adopté le 12 octobre 1998, para. 130).

80.   En l'espèce, il n'est pas question ici d'un terme conceptuel ou générique, mais plutôt de développements techniques nouveaux, relatifs à l'exploitation et à la capacité du chemin de fer. Toutefois, là aussi, il semble qu'une interprétation évolutive, qui permettrait une application du Traité efficace en termes d'objet et de but, soit préférable à une application stricte de la règle intemporelle. Ainsi, dans l'affaire *Gabčíkovo-Nagymaros*, la Cour internationale était prête à accepter, dans l'interprétation d'un Traité antérieur à certaines normes récentes du droit de l'environnement, que « le traité n'est pas un instrument figé et est susceptible de s'adapter à de nouvelles normes du droit international ». (*Recueil C.I.J. 1997*, p. 7 à pp. 67 et 68, para. 112). Le tribunal d'instance néerlandais de Rotterdam a été confronté à la question de savoir si une disposition portant sur des câbles télégraphiques pourrait être interprétée de manière à inclure les câbles téléphoniques, bien que ceux-ci n'aient pas encore été mis au point au moment de la conclusion de la Convention de 1884 sur la protection des câbles sous-marins. Le Tribunal a estimé qu'il était « raisonnable » d'inclure les câbles téléphoniques ultérieurs dans l'interprétation de ce qui était protégé par la Convention (*The Netherlands (PTT) and the Post Office (London) v. Ned Lloyd*, 74 *International Law Reports*, p. 212).

81.   Enfin, le Tribunal constate qu'une interprétation évolutive des traités recueille à l'heure actuelle le suffrage des principaux auteurs. Ainsi, les éditeurs de la 9ème édition de *Oppenheim* conviennent que, nonobstant la règle intertemporelle, « à certains égards l'interprétation des dispositions d'un traité ne peut pas être isolée des développements du droit intervenus après leur adoption ... les concepts incorporés dans un traité peuvent ne pas être figés, mais évolutifs ... » (Jennings and Watts, *Oppenheim's International Law*,

Vol. 1, p. 1282). *Voir également* Jiménez de Aréchaga « *International Law in the Past Third of a Century* » (le Droit international dans le dernier tiers d'un siècle) » 159 *Recueil des Cours* (1978-1), p. 49). Rudolf Bernhardt l'explique de la manière suivante : « L'objet et le but d'un traité jouent ... un rôle central dans son interprétation. Cette référence à l'objet et au but peut être comprise comme une introduction dans un certain dynamisme. Si le but d'un traité est de créer des relations durables et solides entre les parties ... , il n'est guère compatible avec ce but d'éliminer les nouveaux développements intervenus dans le processus de l'interprétation du traité » (42 *German Yearbook of International Law* (1999) pp. 16 et 17).

82. Le Traité du Rhin de fer n'a pas été conçu pour avoir une durée limitée ou fixe. Les Parties ne pensaient probablement qu'à un « prolongement » d'une voie ferrée belge à travers les Pays-Bas, qui serait effectué à un moment donné. Bien entendu, les déclarations faites par les Parties au moment de la ratification du Traité du Rhin de fer, lequel a notamment amendé l'Article XII du Traité de Séparation de 1839, prévoyaient que ceci « constitue l'exécution pleine et entière de l'Article XII du Traité du 19 avril 1839 ». Toutefois, le Tribunal estime qu'il serait incompatible avec l'objet et le but du traité antérieur d'interpréter ces déclarations dans le sens où de nouveaux travaux et de nouvelles demandes seraient considérés comme *en dehors* du champ de l'Article XII. Il convient de comprendre ces déclarations comme renvoyant plutôt à la modification du tracé de la ligne du Rhin de fer dont les parties étaient convenues.

83. Le but et l'objet du Traité de Séparation de 1839 étaient de résoudre plusieurs problèmes épineux qui compliquaient l'instauration d'une séparation stable entre la Belgique et les Pays-Bas : ceux de l'Article XII étaient de prévoir des liaisons de transport ferroviaire entre la Belgique et l'Allemagne, sur un tracé prévu par le Traité de limites de 1842. Cet objet n'avait aucune durée fixe et son but était « la communication commerciale ». Il en résulte nécessairement, même si ce n'est pas formulé de manière spécifique, que ces travaux, qui vont au-delà de la simple restauration des possibilités d'utilisation précédentes, et qui seraient nécessaires ou souhaitables pour s'adapter au commerce actuel, seraient indissociables du droit de passage que la Belgique pourrait demander. Ceci étant, l'Article XII dans son ensemble, qui équilibre soigneusement les droits et obligations des Parties, reste en principe applicable à l'adaptation et à la modernisation demandées par la Belgique.

84. Il est également raisonnable d'interpréter l'Article XII comme envisageant l'éventualité de travaux futurs sur la ligne, outre ceux nécessaires dans le cadre de l'entretien. L'Article XII ne prévoit aucune disposition distincte en ce qui concerne la répartition des futurs coûts et des droits sur la ligne et le territoire qu'elle traverserait, mais une interprétation compatible avec le principe d'effet utile amène le Tribunal à penser que l'Article XII du Traité de Séparation de 1839 est toujours applicable à la mise à niveau et aux améliorations (sauf en ce qui concerne le tracé, qui est toujours régi par les avenants au Traité du Rhin de fer). Si l'on applique cette approche dynamique et évolutive à un traité qui était censé garantir un droit de passage commercial dans la durée, le Tribunal conclut qu'une demande de réactivation d'une ligne depuis longtemps en sommeil, avec une capacité de fret et les moyens de réaliser cette réactivation dépassant de loin ce qui a existé auparavant, pendant près de 130 années, ne doit pas être considérée comme une demande de « nouvelle ligne ». Pour autant, les conditions liées à cette demande (à savoir, la réfection, une mise à niveau et une modernisation considérables d'un « prolongement » existant) sont toujours régies par les dispositions de l'Article XII du Traité de Séparation de 1839. Il convient de reconnaître que la rédaction, telle que formulée, visait la construction d'une nouvelle route, le creusement d'un nouveau canal ou la construction d'une nouvelle voie ferrée plutôt qu'une mise à niveau régulière inhérente à un droit de passage commercial. En conséquence, il peut s'avérer nécessaire d'intégrer à l'Article XII, en ce qui concerne l'attribution des coûts actuels de remise à niveau, les dispositions du droit international telles qu'elles s'appliquent aujourd'hui (*voir* paragraphe 59). Le Tribunal considérera le concept de caractère raisonnable à la lumière de toutes les circonstances, ainsi que de l'équité et de l'équilibre contenus dans l'Article XII.

5. « et sans préjudice de ses droits de souveraineté exclusifs sur le territoire que traverserait la route ou le canal en question ».

85. Si l'on applique ce point à l'Article 31, paragraphe 1, de la Convention de Vienne, qui stipule qu'un traité doit être interprété de bonne foi suivant le sens ordinaire à attribuer à ses termes, on pourrait penser que l'expression « sans préjudice » suggère que toute ingérence dans la souveraineté des Pays-Bas, autre que l'acceptation du prolongement d'une nouvelle voie ferrée traversant le Limbourg, est contraire à l'Article XII. Toutefois, l'Article 31, paragraphe 1, exige que ce « sens ordinaire » ne soit pas seulement interprété

de bonne foi, mais également dans son contexte et à la lumière de l'objet et du but du traité.

86.   Dans leurs plaidoiries, les Parties ont contesté que la bonne foi constitue une source distincte du droit international. La Belgique fait allusion à une absence de bonne foi dans une série d'actes et d'omissions des Pays-Bas, tandis que ceux-ci font allusion à un abus de droit relativement à diverses demandes faites par la Belgique au sujet de la réactivation de la ligne du Rhin de fer. Le Tribunal pense pour sa part qu'il y a eu d'importantes différences de perception des Parties en ce qui concerne l'étendue de leurs droits et obligations respectifs en matière de droit international et notamment en ce qui concerne l'Article XII du Traité de Séparation de 1839, et que ce sont ces différences de perception qui sont à l'origine des affirmations d'absence de bonne foi et d'abus de droit. Il incombe donc au Tribunal de clarifier les droits et obligations de chaque Partie, pour pouvoir ensuite répondre aux Questions que ces dernières lui ont posées conjointement.

87.   En ce qui concerne l'injonction de l'Article 31, paragraphe 1, de la Convention de Vienne de replacer un terme « dans son contexte » pour pouvoir l'interpréter correctement, le Tribunal remarque que le contexte pertinent de la phrase « *sans préjudice de ses droits de souveraineté exclusifs* » réside dans l'insertion de celle-ci au sein d'un paragraphe qui traite également des droits consentis à la Belgique. Les Pays-Bas ont déjà nécessairement dérogé à leur souveraineté territoriale en autorisant la construction d'une voie ferrée sur leur territoire, à la demande d'un autre État. La souveraineté faisant l'objet d'une réserve concerne le territoire que traverse la voie ferrée. Les Pays-Bas n'ont pas abandonné plus de souveraineté que ce qui était nécessaire pour la construction de la voie afin de relier commercialement la Belgique et l'Allemagne à travers le Limbourg. Ils conservent donc les pouvoirs de police sur le secteur concerné, le pouvoir de définir des normes d'hygiène et de sécurité pour les travaux effectués sur la voie, ainsi que le pouvoir de définir des normes de protection de l'environnement dans ce secteur.

88.   Dans ce contexte, le Tribunal constate que le droit néerlandais prévoit que le niveau d'entretien des voies ferrées n'est pas un niveau fixe, mais varie plutôt en fonction du trafic existant à un moment donné. Lorsque la ligne du Rhin de fer est tombée en désuétude après 1991, l'entretien a été minimal. En 1996, les passages à niveau du tronçon Ruremonde-Vlodrop ont été supprimés. Conformément au droit néerlandais également, et de manière plus générale, les feux clignotants ont également été supprimés.

Il a été expliqué au Tribunal que « cette politique vise à empêcher les utilisateurs de la route de s'habituer à des passages à niveau qui ne fonctionnent plus, afin d'éviter le risque qu'ils ne s'attendent plus au passage de trains à des passages à niveau encore opérationnels » (CMPB, p. 10, para 2.5.4).

89. Le Tribunal estime que cette politique, et l'abaissement des niveaux d'entretien en vertu de celle-ci, ne violent pas les droits conférés à la Belgique par l'Article XII du Traité de Séparation de 1839 et relèvent de la réserve de souveraineté des Pays-Bas figurant audit Article XII. Et ce, d'autant plus que les Pays-Bas acceptent pleinement leur obligation de remettre la ligne au niveau d'entretien et de sécurité de 1991, à leurs frais, en cas de demande de réactivation de la Belgique.

90. On pourrait dire que les Pays-Bas n'agiraient pas conformément aux dispositions de l'Article XII uniquement dans le cas où la réserve de souveraineté s'exercerait d'une manière incompatible avec le droit de la Belgique de prolonger la voie ferrée à travers le Limbourg, ou en violation d'autres obligations internationales. Le Tribunal examinera ci-après (*voir* paragraphes 202–206) si tel est le cas.

91. L'Article 31, paragraphe 1, de la Convention de Vienne dispose également que les termes d'un traité doivent être interprétés « à la lumière de son objet et de son but ». On peut se demander en l'espèce si l'application de ce principe très important sera éclairante, car l'objet et le but du Traité de Séparation de 1839 étaient très vastes – à savoir la séparation de la Belgique et des Pays-Bas dans des conditions satisfaisant les participants à la Conférence de Londres. Il est clair que la revendication de la Belgique sur ce qui est maintenant la province néerlandaise du Limbourg a été rejetée et que, par ailleurs, la proximité commerciale dont la Belgique aurait pu autrement bénéficier avec l'Allemagne a été préservée par les dispositions relatives au prolongement de la route et du canal. De cette manière, entre autres, l'objet et le but général du Traité de 1839 furent atteints. Ce que l'on peut incontestablement affirmer est que cet objet et ce but exigent un délicat équilibre entre les droits accordés à chaque Partie au titre de l'Article XII.

92. Il convient également de se demander si la clause de réserve de la souveraineté néerlandaise exigeait ou non une concertation avec la Belgique avant de classer en réserve naturelle le territoire traversé par le tracé historique de la ligne.

93.   La Belgique n'a pas contesté le droit souverain des Pays-Bas à classer certains espaces en zones naturelles, mais cela impliquait (MB, p. 42, para. 31) que la nature du droit de passage dont elle bénéficiait en vertu du Traité de Séparation de 1839 et du traité du Rhin de fer obligeait les Pays-Bas à la consulter avant de classer ainsi le site du Meinweg (*voir* paragraphe 189). La Belgique rappelle également l'Article 9 du Traité du 21 décembre 1996 relatif à la construction d'une liaison ferroviaire pour trains à grande vitesse entre Rotterdam et Anvers, qui fait référence à la ligne de chemin de fer du Rhin de fer :

> Les dossiers concernant la prolongation de la ligne de marchandises 11 vers la ligne de chemin de fer entre Goes et Bergen-op-Zoom et le désenclavement du port d'Anvers par l' « IJzeren Rijn » [Rhin de fer] vers l'Allemagne seront évalués selon leurs propres mérites, en bonne concertation et comme il convient entre bons voisins. Dans le premier dossier, on s'efforcera de faire un choix de tracé avant le 1er janvier 2000. Dans le deuxième dossier, les Pays-Bas collaboreront activement à l'étude de faisabilité, en ce compris le développement de variantes de tracés à la hauteur de Ruremonde et de la frontière entre les Pays-Bas et l'Allemagne. En fonction des résultats de cette étude, les Parties se concerteront conjointement avec les instances compétentes de la République Fédérale d'Allemagne [R.T.N.U. vol. 2054 p. 293 (1999)].

94.   Le 12 juin 1998, Le Premier ministre belge a fait part sans ambiguïté au Premier ministre néerlandais de la préférence de la Belgique pour le tracé historique de la ligne du Rhin de fer, en se prévalant « d'un droit relevant du droit public international sur ce tracé historique ». Des déviations étaient soit trop longues, soit ne « pourraient être réalisées que sur le long terme » (MB, Pièce n° 67, Lettre du Premier ministre belge M. Dehaene à M. Kok, ministre-Président des Pays-Bas, datée du 12 juin 1998). Les septième et huitième paragraphes du Protocole d'accord de mars 2000 (*voir également* le paragraphe 155 de la présente sentence) prévoyaient ce qui suit :

> S'il est décidé que le tracé définitif sera différent de celui traversant le Meinweg (ce que les Pays-Bas présument, contrairement à la Belgique), ce [dernier] tracé sera considéré comme satisfaisant pleinement les obligations de droit public international découlant du Traité de Séparation de 1839 et du Traité du Rhin de fer conclu en 1873 entre la Belgique et les Pays-Bas. Ces accords feront l'objet d'un Traité.

> Jusqu'à la sélection du tracé définitif, la Belgique réserve l'intégralité de ses droits en vertu du Traité de Séparation de 1839 et du Traité Néerlando-belge du Rhin de fer de 1873.[7]

95. Le Tribunal constate qu'à différentes reprises, les Pays-Bas ont reconnu que la Belgique disposait d'un droit de passage en vertu du droit international (MB, p. 46, para. 34). Ce droit de passage n'est pas affecté en soi par le classement du site du Meinweg en réserve naturelle : le rapport entre le droit de passage de la Belgique et les droits de souveraineté des Pays-Bas est resté équilibré comme le prévoyait l'Article XII. Si les Pays-Bas avaient supposé, au moment de classer le site du Meinweg, que la Belgique était sur le point de proposer un programme de réactivation de grande envergure, il aurait probablement été souhaitable, sur la base de « bons rapports de voisinage » de se concerter avec elle avant de procéder au classement du site. Les mesures relatives au site du Meinweg ont été prises en 1994, c'est-à-dire après la communication belge de 1987. Or, si l'on tient compte du contexte d'utilisation minimale – et d'une période récente de non utilisation totale – de la ligne par la Belgique, et du fait que son droit de passage n'avait fait l'objet de réserves que périodiquement, il n'était pas déraisonnable pour les Pays-Bas de présumer que cette situation pourrait perdurer dans un avenir prévisible. En tout état de cause, le classement du site du Meinweg ne constituant pas en théorie une restriction du droit de passage, les Pays-Bas n'étaient pas légalement tenus de consulter la Belgique. Le fait qu'ultérieurement, le classement du site du Meinweg en réserve naturelle risquait d'avoir des implications en cas de demandes imprévues de réactivation à un niveau inconnu jusqu'alors est un problème différent, qui aurait clairement dû être résolu à l'origine par des concertations entre les Parties. En conséquence, sur ce point précis, le Tribunal penche en faveur des arguments des Pays-Bas.

96. Cela étant, l'exercice légitime, par les Pays-Bas, de leur droit souverain de classer le site du Meinweg en réserve naturelle, dans le contexte particulier décrit ci-dessus, ne va pas nécessairement sans conséquences financières, dans la mesure où est concerné l'exercice par la Belgique de son droit de passage.

---

[7] Les Pays-Bas et la Belgique proposent des traductions en anglais légèrement différentes de ces dispositions (MB, para. 34 ; CMPB, para. 2.12.1). Ici, le Tribunal utilise la version néerlandaise.

CHAPITRE III - RÔLE DU DROIT COMMUNAUTAIRE DANS LE PRÉSENT ARBITRAGE

A. Obligations découlant de l'Article 292 du Traité CE

97.   Le Compromis d'arbitrage entre les Parties demande au Tribunal « de se prononcer sur le fondement du droit international, y compris du droit communautaire le cas échéant, en tenant compte des obligations des Parties en vertu de l'Article 292 du Traité CE » (italiques ajoutées).

98.   Le Tribunal a déjà évoqué (voir paragraphe 15 ci-dessus) la lettre envoyée par les Parties à la Commission européenne le 26 août 2003, dans laquelle elles mentionnaient leur position commune, à savoir que, bien que les questions au cœur du présent différend relèvent davantage du droit international que du droit communautaire, elles prendraient, si nécessaire, toutes les mesures leur permettant de satisfaire à leurs obligations dans le cadre du droit communautaire, et notamment de l'Article 292 du Traité CE.

99.   Conformément à l'Article 292 du Traité CE, « [L]es États membres s'engagent à ne pas soumettre un différend relatif à l'interprétation ou à l'application du présent traité à un mode de règlement autre que ceux prévus par celui-ci » (voir paragraphe 13 ci-dessus).

100.   Cette disposition doit être considérée au regard des articles 227 et 239 du Traité CE. Conformément à l'Article 227, chacun des États membres peut saisir la CJCE s'il estime qu'un autre État membre a manqué à l'une quelconque des obligations lui incombant en vertu du Traité CE, tandis que l'Article 239 prévoit que les États membres peuvent soumettre tout différend en connexité avec l'objet du Traité CE à la CJCE si ce différend lui est soumis en vertu d'un compromis.

101.   L'effet combiné des articles susmentionnés du Traité CE (ainsi que de l'Article 234 sur les décisions prises à titre préjudiciel, voir paragraphe 102 ci-après) vise à établir que la CJCE est seule compétente « pour assurer le respect du droit dans l'interprétation et l'application du présent Traité » (Article 220 du Traité CE). En conséquence, au sein du système juridique communautaire, suite à une répartition des compétences entre les tribunaux des États membres et la CJCE, seule cette dernière a le pouvoir de statuer en dernier recours sur les questions d'interprétation ou d'application du droit

communautaire. Si les États membres saisissent un tribunal autre qu'un « tribunal communautaire » d'un différend juridique pour lui demander d'interpréter ou d'appliquer des dispositions du droit communautaire, la Commission peut les poursuivre pour violation de l'Article 292 du Traité CE.[8]

102. Concernant l'obligation de soumettre les questions relatives au droit communautaire à la décision autoritaire de la CJCE, le Traité CE évoque expressément les juridictions des États membres à l'Article 234. Aux termes de cet article, une juridiction nationale confrontée à l'interprétation du droit communautaire peut, et dans certains cas, doit,[9] saisir la Cour à titre préjudiciel « si [elle] estime qu'une décision sur ce point [interprétation du droit communautaire] est nécessaire pour rendre son jugement ». Conformément à la jurisprudence constante de la CJCE (voir, par exemple, *Maso, Gazzetta et al. c. Istituto Nazionale della Previdenza Sociale (INPS)*, C-373/95, arrêt du 10 juillet 1997, para. 26),

> il appartient aux seules juridictions nationales, qui sont saisies d'un litige et doivent assumer la responsabilité de la décision judiciaire à intervenir, d'apprécier, au regard des particularités de chaque affaire, tant la nécessité d'une décision préjudicielle pour être en mesure de rendre leur jugement que la pertinence des questions qu'elles posent à la Cour.

La Cour a également considéré qu'« une demande formée par une juridiction nationale n'est possible que s'il apparaît de manière manifeste que l'interprétation du droit communautaire … demandée par cette juridiction, n'a aucun rapport avec la réalité ou l'objet du litige au principal » (*Durighello c. Istituto Nazionale della Previdenza Sociale (INPS)*, C-186/90, arrêt du 28 novembre 1991, para. 9).

103. Pour rendre sa sentence, le Tribunal a soigneusement pris en compte ces éléments. Le Tribunal estime qu'il se trouve dans une situation analogue à celle d'une juridiction nationale d'un État membre, décrite aux paragraphes précédents, en ce qui concerne les limites fixées à sa compétence dans le Compromis d'arbitrage, par renvoi à l'Article 292 du Traité CE. En d'autres termes, si le Tribunal parvenait à la conclusion qu'il lui est impossible de statuer sur l'affaire qui lui est soumise sans devoir interpréter les règles du droit communautaire qui ne constituent ni des *actes clairs* ni des *actes éclairés*, cela

---

[8] *Cf.* Requête de la Commission européenne à la CJCE contre l'Irlande dans l'affaire de *l'Usine Mox* (RB, Pièce n°. 1, pp. 1 et suivantes).
[9] La distinction entre un tribunal étatique ayant un droit ou un devoir de renvoi n'est pas pertinente dans le présent contexte, comme les autres éléments de la demande mentionnés à l'Article 234.

déclencherait les obligations des Parties au titre de l'Article 292 dans le sens où elles seraient tenues de saisir la CJCE des questions pertinentes relevant du droit communautaire (en l'espèce, non au sens de l'Article 234 mais probablement au sens de l'Article 239 du Traité CE).

104. Quant à la nécessité ou non pour le Tribunal de statuer sur des questions de droit communautaire pour pouvoir rendre sa sentence, les critères élaborés en application de l'Article 234 du Traité CE par les tribunaux étatiques et la CJCE s'appliquent également par analogie. À cet égard, toute référence au droit communautaire n'implique pas une obligation de renvoi préjudiciel. La CJCE a clarifié ce point dans l'affaire *Srl CILFIT et Lanificio di Gavardo SpA c. Ministero della Sanità*, C-283/81, *Rec.* 1982, p. 3415 (« Affaire *CILFIT* ») en déclarant que les juridictions nationales confrontées à l'interprétation du droit communautaire et tenues de soumettre cette question à la CJCE conformément à l'Article 234 du Traité CE,

> jouissent du même pouvoir d'appréciation que toutes autres juridictions nationales en ce qui concerne le point de savoir si une décision sur un point de droit communautaire est nécessaire pour leur permettre de rendre leur décision. Ces juridictions ne sont, dès lors, pas tenues de renvoyer une question d'interprétation de droit communautaire soulevée devant elles si la question n'est pas pertinente, c'est-à-dire dans les cas où la réponse à cette question, quelle qu'elle soit, ne pourrait avoir aucune influence sur la solution du litige.

> Par contre, si elles constatent que le recours au droit communautaire est nécessaire en vue d'aboutir à la solution d'un litige dont elles se trouvent saisies, l'Article 177 [qui est devenu l'Article 234] leur impose l'obligation de saisir la Cour de justice de toute question d'interprétation qui se pose. [Affaire *CILFIT*, 3429, paragraphes 10–11].

105. En ce qui concerne la juridiction nationale, le même point a été expliqué avec la lucidité qui le caractérise par Lord Denning dans l'affaire opposant *H.P. Bulmer Ltd. à J. Bollinger SA*, [1974] 2 C.M.L.R. 91, [1974] 2 All E.R. 1226. Comme il l'a souligné,

> *Le point doit être déterminant.*

> La juridiction [nationale] doit apprécier si une « décision sur ce point est *nécessaire* pour lui permettre de rendre un *jugement* ». Ce jugement s'appliquant à l'affaire même soumise au tribunal. Le juge doit être parvenu au stade où il se pose la question suivante : « cette clause du Traité est susceptible d'être interprétée de plusieurs manières. Si elle signifie *ceci*, je me prononce en faveur du demandeur. Si elle signifie *cela*, je me prononce en

faveur du défendeur ». En bref, quelle que soit la manière de le trancher, le point doit être décisif pour l'affaire. Ne reste alors plus qu'à prononcer le jugement...

106. C'est en se fondant sur ce qui précède que le Tribunal examinera les points de droit communautaire avancés par les Parties. Dans leurs mémoires, les Parties renvoient de manière répétée aux dispositions de droit communautaire dérivé applicables à deux secteurs, à savoir celui des réseaux ferrés transeuropéens et celui de la protection de l'environnent (*voir* paragraphes 121 à 137 ci-après). La Belgique fait également état de l'Article 10 du Traité CE, tout en déclarant qu'il n'est pas déterminant. Le Tribunal va maintenant décider si ces références sont suffisamment concluantes, ou pertinentes, au sens du paragraphe précédent pour impliquer que le différend entre les Parties requière une « interprétation » du droit communautaire.

B. Questions relatives aux Réseaux Transeuropéens

107. Ainsi que le signalent les deux Parties, la ligne de chemin de fer du Rhin de fer figure comme projet prioritaire au sein du système des réseaux ferroviaires transeuropéens prévu par les articles 154 à 156 du Traité CE. Même s'il ne semble en fait y avoir aucun différend entre les Parties relativement à « l'interprétation ou l'application » des dispositions pertinentes du droit communautaire (et qu'il semble donc, à cet égard, qu'il n'existe aucun « différend » au sens de l'Article 292 du Traité CE, il est nécessaire d'examiner brièvement les dispositions du Traité CE relatives au système des réseaux ferroviaires transeuropéens et le droit dérivé communautaire pertinent, ainsi que les arguments respectifs des Parties.

108. Conformément à l'Article 154 du Traité CE, la Communauté « contribue à l'établissement et au développement de réseaux transeuropéens dans les secteurs des infrastructures du transport, des télécommunications et de l'énergie » (paragraphe 1). L'action de la Communauté « vise à favoriser l'interconnexion et l'interopérabilité des réseaux nationaux ainsi que l'accès à ces réseaux » (paragraphe 2).

109. Afin de réaliser ces objectifs, l'Article 155 prévoit l'établissement « d'un ensemble d'orientations couvrant les objectifs, les priorités ainsi que les grandes lignes des actions envisagées dans le domaine des réseaux transeuropéens ». Ces orientations identifient des projets d'intérêt commun. L'article 155 prévoit en outre la mise en œuvre de toute action

qui peut s'avérer nécessaire pour assurer l'interopérabilité des réseaux, autorise la Communauté à soutenir des projets d'intérêt commun définis dans le cadre des orientations relatives au Réseau ferroviaire transeuropéen, et mentionne la possibilité de contribuer, par le biais du Fonds de cohésion, au financement de projets spécifiques en matière d'infrastructure des transports (paragraphe 1). L'article 155 dispose ensuite que les États membres sont tenus de coordonner entre eux les politiques menées au niveau national qui peuvent avoir un impact significatif sur la réalisation des objectifs liés au réseau ferroviaire transeuropéen (paragraphe 2).

110. L'article 156 contient des prescriptions de forme selon lesquelles les orientations et autres mesures visées au paragraphe 1 de l'Article 155 sont arrêtées par le Conseil, statuant conformément à la procédure [de position commune] visée à l'Article 251, tout en prévoyant que les orientations et projets d'intérêt commun qui concernent le territoire d'un État membre requièrent l'approbation de l'État membre concerné.

111. Le programme défini aux articles 154 et 155 a été mis en œuvre par divers textes de droit communautaire, notamment la Décision n° 1692/96/CE du 23 juillet 1996 (« Décision 1692/96 ») (JOCE 1996, L 228 p. 1) du Parlement européen et du Conseil sur les orientations communautaires pour le développement du réseau transeuropéen de transport. La Décision 1692/96 a pour but de définir les orientations mentionnées dans le titre comme « un cadre général de référence destiné à encourager les actions des États membres et, le cas échéant, de la Communauté visant à réaliser des projets d'intérêt commun » (Article 1, paragraphe 2). L'article 3 de la Décision 1692/96 est consacré au développement d'un réseau ferroviaire transeuropéen constitué à la fois du réseau ferroviaire à grande vitesse et du réseau ferroviaire conventionnel. Il a été concrétisé par un certain nombre d'autres textes législatifs de nature plus technique. Relativement au coût de développement des projets du réseau ferroviaire transeuropéen, l'Article 155 du Traité CE a été mis en œuvre par un Règlement du Conseil (CE) n° 2236/95 du 18 septembre 1995 (JOCE 1995, L 228 p. 1), substantiellement amendé par le Règlement (CE) n° 807/2004 du Parlement européen et du Conseil du 21 avril 2004 (JOCE 2004, L 143 p. 46), qui fixe les règles pour l'octroi d'un concours financier communautaire dans le domaine des réseaux transeuropéens, en règle générale à hauteur de 10 % du coût d'investissement total.

112. L'annexe II à la Décision n° 884/2004/CE du Parlement européen et du Conseil du 29 avril 2004 (JOCE 2004, L 167 p. 1), qui modifie la Décision 1692/96, énumère les « projets prioritaires dont les travaux devraient commencer avant 2010 », y compris le « tronçon transfrontalier 'Rhin de fer' Rheidt-Antwerpen » (qui fait partie du projet n° 24).

113. C'est à ce domaine du droit communautaire, dans la mesure où il est consacré au développement d'un réseau ferroviaire transeuropéen, que les Parties renvoient dans leurs plaidoiries, chacune parvenant toutefois à des conclusions différentes et recourant à différents degrés d'emphase.

114. La Belgique estime que la réactivation de la ligne du Rhin de fer est régie non seulement par l'Article XII du Traité de Séparation de 1839 mais également par le droit communautaire (RB, p. 23, para. 25), c'est-à-dire tant le Réseau ferroviaire transeuropéen qui vient d'être décrit que le droit communautaire de l'environnement sur lequel le Tribunal se penchera ultérieurement (*voir* paragraphes 121 à 137 ci-après). Plus spécifiquement, en ce qui concerne le réseau ferroviaire transeuropéen, la Belgique souligne « la haute valeur ajoutée européenne » que constitue l'inclusion de la ligne de chemin de fer du Rhin de fer parmi les projets prioritaires du réseau ferroviaire transeuropéen sur tous les tronçons dont les travaux doivent commencer au plus tard en 2010 pour être opérationnels au plus tard en 2020 (MB, p. 29, para. 22). La Belgique considère également que la mise à niveau de la ligne du Rhin de fer est une étape importante vers la réalisation de la politique dite du « transfert modal » du transport routier au transport ferroviaire prôné par la Communauté et, par voie de conséquence, vers un développement durable. Selon la Belgique, la nécessité de ce transfert modal, qui permettra de réduire les émissions de gaz à effet de serre, est reconnue et soutenue par plusieurs textes officiels de la Communauté, ainsi que par des déclarations du Gouvernement néerlandais lui-même (MB, p. 26, para. 20). La Belgique renvoie à sa position, exprimée dans une note établie conjointement par les administrations belge, néerlandaise et allemande le 20 août 2001, dans laquelle les trois pays indiquaient leurs points de vue respectifs sur la répartition des coûts pour le tracé définitif de la ligne du Rhin de fer. Selon la Belgique, les obligations découlant de la Décision 1692/96 « impliquent que la responsabilité de la réalisation de l'infrastructure requise sur son territoire incombe à chaque État membre … lequel assume le financement des travaux sur

son territoire » (MB, p. 64, para. 47).[10] Toutefois, le Tribunal constate que dans sa Réplique, la dernière fois qu'elle se réfère à l'ensemble des textes communautaires concernant le Réseau ferroviaire transeuropéen, la Belgique déclare qu'elle

> ne se fonde pas... sur ces dispositions aux fins d'interpréter le régime conventionnel du Rhin de fer à la lumière du droit communautaire ou autrement, mais seulement pour attirer l'attention du Tribunal sur l'existence de règles communautaires européennes dans le domaine en discussion à des fins juridictionnelles [RB, p. 112, para. 119].

115. Avec cette conclusion, le point de vue belge sur le rapport entre le Réseau ferroviaire transeuropéen et le droit communautaire dans la présente affaire semble pour l'essentiel rejoindre celui des Pays-Bas. En conséquence, considérant que la Belgique fonde ses arguments en faveur de la réactivation de la ligne du Rhin de fer sur son inclusion en tant que projet prioritaire au sein du Réseau ferroviaire transeuropéen, les Pays-Bas déclarent :

> Cette classification signifie que l'Union européenne accorde de l'importance à la liaison ferroviaire considérée et que toutes les améliorations qui y sont apportées seront en principe éligibles pour un cofinancement limité de l'Union européenne (10 pour cent de l'investissement au maximum). En dehors de cela, elle n'a aucune signification ou effet spécifique [CMPB, p. 17, para. 2.9.3].

116. Les Pays-Bas citent également l'Article 8 de la Décision 1692/96 en vertu duquel les projets du Réseau ferroviaire transeuropéen doivent prendre en compte la protection de l'environnement. Concernant les avantages pour l'environnement, cités par la Belgique, du transfert modal (*voir également* le paragraphe 114 ci-dessus), les Pays-Bas soutiennent que l'impact des avantages du transfert modal est controversé, et qu'en tout état de cause « les Pays-Bas ne s'orientent pas activement vers une politique de transfert modal » (DPB, p. 25, para. 105). En outre, selon les Pays-Bas, la Belgique n'a pas fait état des conséquences spécifiques en termes d'émissions [de gaz à effet de serre] de la réactivation de la ligne du Rhin de fer sur les régions nécessitant une protection environnementale le long de la ligne de chemin de fer du Rhin de fer (CMPB, p. 15, para.2.9.1).

---

[10] Le fait que l'adoption des décisions relatives à la mise à niveau de la ligne du Rhin de fer ait été approuvée par les Pays-Bas semble suggérer qu'ils ne pensaient pas avoir à financer intégralement le développement sur le territoire néerlandais de la ligne du Rhin de fer dans le cadre du réseau ferroviaire transeuropéen.

117. Le Tribunal est d'accord avec l'argument des Pays-Bas selon lequel le Réseau ferroviaire transeuropéen a un rapport très limité avec l'affaire en cause. L'opinion de la Belgique selon laquelle la réactivation de la ligne du Rhin de fer n'est pas simplement régie par le Traité de Séparation de 1839, mais également par le droit communautaire (et notamment le droit communautaire dérivé sur le Réseau ferroviaire transeuropéen) est, en principe, correcte. Cependant, à aucun moment la Belgique ne soutient que l'inclusion de la ligne de chemin de fer du Rhin de fer dans le Réseau ferroviaire transeuropéen entraîne en sa faveur des droits allant au-delà du droit de passage qu'elle revendique sur le fondement de l'Article XII du Traité de Séparation de 1839. Au contraire, l'objectif de la Belgique lorsqu'elle invoque le droit communautaire comme base légale du Réseau ferroviaire transeuropéen semble être simplement de souligner l'intérêt général d'une réfection de la ligne du Rhin de fer dans la double perspective de stimuler la politique communautaire en matière de transports et le transfert modal du transport routier au transport ferroviaire. Sur les points spécifiques opposant actuellement la Belgique et les Pays-Bas, le développement de la ligne du Rhin de fer au sein du Réseau ferroviaire transeuropéen dans le cadre du droit communautaire n'offre rien de plus que le contexte politique et juridique dans le cadre duquel le Tribunal doit interpréter l'Article XII du Traité de Séparation de 1839. À cet égard, dans le contexte spécifique de la présente affaire, seule la programmation du Réseau ferroviaire transeuropéen est pertinente. L'inclusion de la ligne du Rhin de fer dans la liste des projets prioritaires de la Communauté en matière de réseaux de transports transeuropéens est un fait dont le Tribunal reconnaît l'existence, mais qui n'a aucune conséquence légale dans le cadre du présent arbitrage.

118. Bien que les Pays-Bas aient un avis différent sur la politique de transfert modal à laquelle la Belgique adhère, ils ne contestent pas le droit de passage de la Belgique découlant (exclusivement selon eux) de l'Article XII du Traité de Séparation de 1839, et ce, y compris au sens que la Belgique donne à cet Article XII dans ses plaidoiries. Toutefois, les Pays-Bas subordonnent l'exercice de ce droit à ce qu'ils estiment être des mesures de protection de l'environnement, adéquates selon le droit communautaire et prescrites par leur propre droit sur leur territoire, et affectées par la réactivation de la ligne du Rhin de fer. Or, ces exigences ne génèrent aucun conflit avec le Réseau ferroviaire transeuropéen qui respecte expressément les impératifs de protection de l'environnement, conformément à la teneur de l'Article 8, paragraphe 1 de la Décision 1692/96 :

« Lors du développement et de la réalisation des projets, les États membres doivent tenir compte de la protection de l'environnement en réalisant des évaluations de l'impact sur l'environnement des projets d'intérêt commun devant être mis en œuvre, conformément à la directive 85/337/CEE et en appliquant la directive 92/43/CEE ».

(Le Tribunal reviendra sur les Directives mentionnées ; *voir* paragraphe 123 ci-après).

119. En résumé, l'inclusion de la ligne du Rhin de fer dans la liste des projets communautaires prioritaires dans le cadre du Réseau ferroviaire transeuropéen n'entraîne pas la nécessité, pour le Tribunal, d'interpréter le droit communautaire (c'est-à-dire le réseau ferroviaire transeuropéen) dans le sens défini ci-dessus (*voir* paragraphes 99 à 105), car cette inclusion n'a créé pour les Parties aucun droit ni obligation outre ceux que l'Article XII du Traité de Séparation de 1839 prévoyait déjà. Ainsi, les points de droit communautaire mis en avant par les Parties ne sont-ils pas déterminants pour la mission du Tribunal.

120. Même si le droit communautaire applicable au Réseau ferroviaire transeuropéen avait offert à la Belgique un droit à une ligne de chemin de fer du Rhin de fer réhabilitée et modernisée, cela n'aurait aucun effet déterminant sur la décision du Tribunal. Dans le cadre de la mission qui a été confiée au Tribunal, il suffit en effet que ce droit découle de l'Article XII du Traité de Séparation de 1839, point sur lequel les Parties sont d'accord. En conséquence, pour utiliser les termes de l'Article 234 du Traité CE, dans le contexte du Réseau ferroviaire transeuropéen, il n'est pas nécessaire que le Tribunal se prononce sur une question d'interprétation du droit communautaire. Par conséquent, l'obligation découlant de l'Article 292 du Traité CE ne s'applique pas.

C. Questions concernant le droit communautaire de l'environnement

121. Les Parties ont également débattu des conséquences juridiques de la réactivation de la ligne du Rhin de fer, en particulier en ce qui concerne la répartition des coûts que celle-ci implique, notamment en conséquence de la soumission de certaines zones le long du tracé historique au régime de la Directive du Conseil 92/43/CEE du 21 mai 1992 concernant la conservation des habitats naturels ainsi que de la faune et de la flore sauvages (JOCE 1992, L 206 p. 7) (la « Directive Habitats »). Si l'on se place du point de vue de l'Article 292 du Traité CE, le Tribunal se trouve confronté à la même question que celle soulevée par le Réseau ferroviaire transeuropéen : le Tribunal doit-il interpréter la Directive

Habitats pour pouvoir statuer sur la question de la réactivation de la ligne du Rhin de fer et de son coût ?

122. Pour pouvoir répondre à cette question, le Tribunal procèdera de la même manière que pour la question liée au Réseau ferroviaire transeuropéen. Il décrira brièvement le régime juridique de la Directive Habitats. Ensuite, il exposera les arguments des Parties relativement à cette Directive, avant de se prononcer sur la pertinence et le rôle déterminant des questions de droit communautaire sur sa propre décision.

123. Le Tribunal constate que dans leurs plaidoiries, les Parties renvoient non seulement à la Directive Habitats, mais également à un texte antérieur du droit communautaire dans un domaine plus restreint, à savoir la Directive du Conseil 79/409/CEE du 2 avril 1979 relative à la préservation des oiseaux sauvages (JOCE 1979, L 103 p. 1) (la « Directive Oiseaux »). Toutefois, comme l'énoncent clairement son préambule et son Article 7, la Directive Habitats a annulé et remplacé aux fins de la présente affaire le régime établi 13 ans auparavant par la Directive Oiseaux. En conséquence, le Tribunal estime inutile d'aborder la Directive Oiseaux séparément, ses constatations sur la question de la nature concluante ou non de la Directive Habitats s'appliquant également au droit communautaire antérieur.

124. La Directive Habitats se fonde juridiquement sur les articles 174 et 175 du Traité CE qui définissent la politique communautaire en matière de protection de l'environnement et qui ont été introduits à l'origine par l'Acte unique européen de 1986 (JOCE 1987, L 169 p. 1). Alors que l'Article 174 énonce l'objectif et les principes de base de la politique communautaire en matière d'environnement, l'Article 175 règlemente les prises de décision et la procédure d'adoption législative dans ce domaine. Plus récemment, le Traité d'Amsterdam (JOCE 1997, C 340 p. 1) a modifié le Traité CE en introduisant un nouvel Article 6, qui intègre les considérations communautaires environnementales à la définition et à la mise en œuvre de toutes les politiques et actions de la communauté.

125. En conséquence, les dispositions du Traité CE ainsi mentionnées sont complétées par celles de l'Article 176, aux termes duquel, et sous réserve de certaines conditions, les mesures de protection adoptées conformément à l'Article 175 « ne font pas obstacle au maintien et à l'établissement, par chaque État membre, de mesures de protection renforcées ».

251

126. La Directive Habitats vise à concilier maintien de la diversité biologique et développement durable en créant un réseau écologique communautaire cohérent (« Natura 2000 ») qui classe des zones protégées en « sites d'importance communautaire », conformément à un calendrier spécifié. Les sites susceptibles d'obtenir cette classification sont proposés par les États membres (Article 4). À titre exceptionnel, et après concertation avec l'État membre concerné, la Commission européenne pourra proposer au Conseil de sélectionner des sites supplémentaires. Les zones ainsi choisies sont soumises à un régime de conservation élaboré assurant un niveau élevé de protection (*voir* article 174, paragraphe 2, sous-paragraphe 1 du Traité CE), dont le maintien est supervisé par la Commission européenne.

127. Les dispositions de la Directive Habitats les plus fréquemment invoquées par les Parties sont les paragraphes 2 à 4 de l'Article 6, qui prévoient ce qui suit :

> 2. Les Etats membres prennent les mesures appropriées pour éviter, dans les zones spéciales de conservation, la détérioration des habitats naturels et des habitats d'espèces ainsi que les perturbations touchant les espèces pour lesquelles les zones ont été désignées, pour autant que ces perturbations soient susceptibles d'avoir un effet significatif eu égard aux objectifs de la présente directive.

> 3. Tout plan ou projet non directement lié ou nécessaire à la gestion du site mais susceptible d'affecter ce site de manière significative, individuellement ou en conjugaison avec d'autres plans et projets, fait l'objet d'une évaluation appropriée de ses incidences sur le site eu égard aux objectifs de conservation de ce site. Compte tenu des conclusions de l'évaluation des incidences sur le site et sous réserve des dispositions du paragraphe 4, les autorités nationales compétentes ne marquent leur accord sur ce plan ou projet qu'après s'être assurées qu'il ne portera pas atteinte à l'intégrité du site concerné et après avoir pris, le cas échéant, l'avis du public.

> 4. Si, en dépit de conclusions négatives de l'évaluation des incidences sur le site et en l'absence de solutions alternatives, un plan ou projet doit néanmoins être réalisé pour des raisons impératives d'intérêt public majeur, y compris de nature sociale ou économique, l'état membre prend toute mesure compensatoire nécessaire pour assurer que la cohérence globale de Natura 2000 est protégée. L'état membre informe la Commission des mesures compensatoires adoptées.

> Lorsque le site concerné est un site abritant un type d'habitat naturel et/ou une espèce prioritaires, seules peuvent être évoquées des considérations liées à la santé de l'homme et à la sécurité publique ou à des conséquences bénéfiques primordiales pour l'environnement ou,

après avis de la Commission, à d'autres raisons impératives d'intérêt public majeur.

128. En l'espèce, le deuxième aspect de droit communautaire porte sur le fait que les Pays-Bas ont classé le secteur du Meinweg, que traverse le tracé historique de la ligne du Rhin de fer, comme zone spéciale de conservation conformément à la Directive Habitats, et l'ont en outre classé comme parc national et « Zone de Silence » conformément à leur législation nationale (*voir* paragraphe 189 ci-après). En 1994, les Pays-Bas ont également classé le site du Meinweg en zone spéciale de protection conformément à la Directive Oiseaux mentionnée au paragraphe 123 ci-dessus, mais, comme mentionné ci-dessus, les dispositions de la Directive Oiseaux applicables au présent différend ont été amendées et remplacées, à toutes fins pratiques, par celles de la Directive Habitats.

129. Quant aux arguments des Parties sur les questions de droit communautaire en matière d'environnement décrites ci-dessus, la position de la Belgique en ce qui concerne la soumission du site du Meinweg au régime de la Directive Habitats en soi n'est pas très claire. Toutefois, la Belgique soutient que les Pays-Bas auraient dû (et devraient encore) faire davantage aux fins d'harmoniser leurs obligations résultant d'une part, du droit communautaire et, d'autre part, de l'Article XII du Traité de Séparation de 1839 (RB, pp. 64–65, para. 67). Selon la Belgique, cette harmonisation serait possible car les Pays-Bas jouissent d'une certaine latitude en ce qui concerne l'étendue du classement du site du Meinweg et les conséquences qui en résultent. Par exemple, selon la Belgique, les Pays-Bas auraient dû, pour le site du Meinweg, suivre l'approche adoptée par la CJCE dans l'affaire dite du *Marais Poitevin* (*Commission c. République française,* arrêt du 25 novembre 1999, C-96/98), dans laquelle la bande de territoire destinée à la construction d'une autoroute devait être considérée comme étant exclue de la Zone de Protection Spéciale (MB, pp. 85 et suivantes, paras. 70 et suivants ; RB, pp. 65–66, para. 68). La Belgique soutient également que les Pays-Bas ont conservé une certaine latitude pour déterminer le type de protection requis conformément au droit communautaire. En particulier, les Pays-Bas auraient pu envisager la possibilité de mesures compensatoires conformément à l'Article 6, paragraphe 4 de la Directive Habitats, aux termes duquel ces mesures doivent être adoptées dans les zones classées si un projet, même s'il est en conflit avec le régime de préservation établi conformément à la Directive Habitats, doit néanmoins être mis en œuvre « pour des raisons impératives d'intérêt public majeur » (MB, p. 87, para. 72). En tout état de cause, la Belgique n'est pas convaincue que les

253

mesures de protection de l'environnement envisagées par les Pays-Bas dans la zone classée conformément à la Directive Habitats, et notamment la construction d'un tunnel sous le site du Meinweg, soient les options les moins onéreuses susceptibles d'être retenues compte tenu des obligations des Pays-Bas en vertu du droit communautaire. De surcroît, la Belgique estime que, même si les mesures extrêmement coûteuses envisagées par les Pays-Bas pour protéger l'environnement du site du Meinweg étaient les seuls moyens dont disposaient les Pays-Bas pour respecter leurs obligations en vertu du droit communautaire, cela n'impliquerait nullement, au sens de ce droit, que ces mesures doivent être financées par la Belgique (MB, p. 88, para. 75). La Belgique insiste sur le fait qu'en tout état de cause, il n'est pas possible que le creusement d'un tunnel sous le site du Meinweg soit le seul et unique moyen à la disposition des Pays-Bas aux fins de respecter leurs obligations en matière d'environnement (MB, p. 87, para. 73 ; RB, pp. 61–62, para. 62).

130. La Belgique renvoie également à une discussion qui eut lieu en juillet 2001 entre les Pays-Bas, la Belgique et l'Allemagne, d'une part, et la Commission européenne, d'autre part. À l'issue de celle-ci, la Commission européenne a précisé que la valeur de conservation de référence selon la Directive Habitats était fondée sur la situation de l'environnement prévalant en 1994, au moment où, selon la Commission européenne, le site du Meinweg était encore traversé par du trafic ferroviaire[11] (la référence utilisée précédemment dans la Directive Oiseaux, renvoyait, quant à elle, à la situation de 1981) (MB, pp. 52–56, paras. 39–42). La Belgique rappelle également au Tribunal que la Commission estimait en 2001 que le transfert modal du transport routier vers le transport ferroviaire, dans lequel la ligne du Rhin de fer jouera un rôle, pourrait avoir des conséquences positives majeures sur l'environnement au sens de l'Article 6 de la Directive Habitats (MB, pp. 54–56, para. 42).

131. Toutefois, dans d'autres parties de ses plaidoiries, la Belgique elle-même minimise l'importance de la Directive Habitats dans la présente affaire en renvoyant (sans les contester de quelque manière que ce soit) aux déclarations des Pays-Bas (*voir* paragraphes 132 à 136 ci-après) confirmant que le classement du site du Meinweg et les mesures qui en résultent ont été décidés de leur propre initiative par les Pays-Bas, plutôt que pour satisfaire à leurs obligations en vertu du droit communautaire dans le sens où ces

---

[11] Le Tribunal prend acte du fait que les Parties conviennent qu'en ce qui concerne le trafic transfrontalier entre la Belgique et l'Allemagne à travers le Limbourg, l'utilisation de la ligne du Rhin de fer a cessé après 1991.

mesures auraient été le seul moyen possible pour les Pays-Bas de satisfaire à leurs obligations imposées par la Directive Habitats. En conséquence, la Belgique fait remarquer que les décisions prises par les Pays-Bas en matière d'environnement sont reconnues nécessaires non au sens du droit communautaire, mais en vertu des normes nationales des Pays-Bas régissant le statut des zones naturelles protégées que les Pays-Bas ont décidé de créer dans les secteurs traversés par le tracé historique de la ligne du Rhin de fer (MB, p. 87, para. 73; RB, p. 51, para. 56). En outre, la Belgique ne suggère pas que ces mesures des Pays-Bas sont incompatibles avec les obligations imposées aux Pays-Bas par le droit communautaire.

132. L'analyse des soumissions des Pays-Bas relativement à la pertinence de la Directive Habitats dans la présente affaire confirme que la Belgique a fait une lecture correcte de ces arguments.

133. Les Pays-Bas sont prêts à débattre des arguments avancés par la Belgique quant à l'impact que peut avoir la Directive Habitats sur les mesures qu'ils ont adoptées relativement au milieu naturel traversé par le tracé de la ligne du Rhin de fer. Ainsi, ils contestent l'affirmation belge concernant la latitude qui leur a été laissée relativement au choix du site du Meinweg comme zone classée ; en fait, selon les Pays-Bas, les classements effectués conformément aux Directive(s)[12] doivent être fondés sur des critères écologiques qui laissent très peu de marge aux États membres (DPB, p. 23, paras. 95 à 97) et ces classements ont été effectués après concertation avec la Commission européenne.

134. En outre, selon les Pays-Bas, la jurisprudence de l'affaire du *Marais Poitevin* n'est pas applicable à la ligne du Rhin de fer (DPB, pp. 24–25, para. 102). Selon eux, une distinction existe entre les faits de cette affaire et la situation de la présente affaire et ils soutiennent qu'une approche analogue appliquée à la ligne du Rhin de fer est inappropriée et ne serait admise ni par les tribunaux néerlandais, ni par la Commission européenne.

135. En ce qui concerne les mesures pertinentes consécutives au classement, la Belgique maintient qu'il aurait été possible de prendre des mesures compensatoires conformément à l'Article 6, paragraphe 4, de la Directive Habitats. Les Pays-Bas estiment toutefois que

---

[12] Le site du Meinweg a d'abord été classé en zone de protection spéciale conformément à la Directive Oiseaux avant d'être soumis, plus récemment, au régime de la Directive Habitats ; *cf.* MB, pp. 38-40, para. 29.

255

ces mesures n'auraient pu être prises que s'il avait été impossible de minimiser un impact négatif significatif sur l'environnement, et de trouver des solutions alternatives et uniquement dans cette mesure (CMPB, p. 51, para. 3.3.5.6). Les Pays-Bas considèrent la construction d'un tunnel sous le site du Meinweg précisément comme une mesure permettant de minimiser cet impact et en conséquence, la nécessité de prendre des mesures compensatoires au sens de l'Article 6, paragraphe 4 de la Directive Habitats ne s'impose pas. Les Pays-Bas soutiennent également qu'il est peu probable que leurs tribunaux nationaux ou la CJCE admettent que l'obligation imposée aux Pays-Bas par le droit de passage de la Belgique constitue une « raison impérative d'intérêt public majeur » au sens de l'Article 6, paragraphe 4 (CMPB, p. 51, para. 3.3.5.6). En tout état de cause, les Pays-Bas soutiennent que le classement du site du Meinweg en zone protégée conformément aux Directive(s)[13] est intervenu conformément à la jurisprudence communautaire et selon des critères objectifs (DPB, p. 26, para. 107).

136. Toutefois, ce qui est en fin de compte plus significatif dans le présent contexte, c'est l'affirmation, sans équivoque et répétée, des Pays-Bas selon laquelle, bien qu'ils aient tenu pleinement compte du droit communautaire,

> il n'est pas nécessaire – au regard du pouvoir législatif fondé sur la souveraineté territoriale exclusive des Pays-Bas – que les mesures prescrites par le droit néerlandais en matière de protection de la nature et de l'environnement soient fondées sur les Directives Oiseaux ou Habitats, ou justifiées par l'une ou l'autre de ces directives, tant que ces mesures ne sont pas contraires au droit communautaire [CMPB, p. 49, para. 3.3.5.6].

En conséquence, les décisions prises par les Pays-Bas concernant les mesures appropriées de protection de l'environnement dans le cadre de la réactivation de la ligne du Rhin de fer l'ont été en se référant au droit de l'environnement et aux procédures administratives néerlandaises et ce, d'une manière compatible avec les directives communautaires pertinentes.

Les Pays-Bas poursuivent :

> Les Pays-Bas ne disent *pas* : « La Commission européenne nous impose de construire un tunnel sur le site du Meinweg, parce que c'est une conséquence automatique de la Directive Habitats [*sic*] ».

---

[13] *Voir* note précédente.

> Les Pays-Bas ont décidé *de leur propre initiative,* en se fondant sur la Loi de protection de la Faune et de Flore (*Flora en Faunawet*) et les valeurs écologiques qu'ils défendent, que la construction d'un tunnel était nécessaire pour protéger les valeurs écologiques du site du Meinweg parce qu'ils estiment que c'est le seul moyen de protéger ces valeurs de la manière qui convient [CMPB, p. 49, para. 3.3.5.6].

En conclusion, les Pays-Bas renvoient au principe contenu dans l'Article 176 du Traité CE, selon lequel les États membres ont le droit d'imposer des conditions cadres et des mesures de protection de l'environnement plus strictes que celles prescrites par les directives communautaires. En résumé, selon les Pays-Bas, l'application de ces directives « n'est pas un facteur décisif pour la construction d'un tunnel sur le site du Meinweg » (DPB, p. 23, para. 93). En revanche, est déterminant le droit néerlandais en matière d'environnement, tant qu'il est conforme au droit communautaire. Les Pays-Bas estiment qu'ils étaient parfaitement en droit de prendre ces mesures, non seulement en vertu du droit communautaire mais également en vertu des dispositions de l'Article XII du Traité de Séparation de 1839, du fait de la réserve de souveraineté que celui-ci contient. En conséquence, les Pays-Bas considèrent qu'il s'ensuit nécessairement qu'il appartient à la Belgique d'assumer les coûts impliqués.

137. C'est précisément sur ce point que le Tribunal devra se prononcer. Il devra toutefois décider au préalable s'il doit interpréter la Directive Habitats aux fins de rendre sa sentence. En se fondant sur les principes énoncés aux paragraphes 102 à 105 ci-dessus, le Tribunal s'est demandé s'il parviendrait à des conclusions différentes concernant l'application de l'Article XII au projet du tunnel du Meinweg et à ses coûts dans l'hypothèse où la Directive Habitats n'existerait pas. Le Tribunal répond à cette question par la négative, car sa décision serait la même s'il se fondait uniquement sur l'Article XII et le droit néerlandais de l'environnement. En conséquence, les questions de droit communautaire débattues par les Parties ne sont pas significatives, ni concluantes pour le Tribunal ; il n'est pas nécessaire que le Tribunal interprète la Directive Habitats pour rendre sa sentence. En conséquence, comme dans le cas du Réseau ferroviaire transeuropéen, les questions de droit communautaire impliquées dans cette affaire n'entraînent aucune obligation au sens de l'Article 292 du Traité CE.

D. Article 10 du Traité CE

138. Conformément à l'Article 10 du Traité CE,

Les États membres prennent toutes mesures générales ou particulières propres à assurer l'exécution des obligations découlant du présent traité ou résultant des actes des institutions de la Communauté. Ils facilitent à celle-ci l'accomplissement de sa mission.

Ils s'abstiennent de toutes mesures susceptibles de mettre en péril la réalisation des buts du présent traité.

139. La Belgique se réfère à ce principe de base du droit communautaire pour argumenter que l'Article 10 du Traité CE la place dans l'obligation de faciliter l'application des règles communautaires de protection de l'environnement évoquées ci-dessus et, à cette fin, d'aider les Pays-Bas qui sont tenus d'appliquer ces règles sur leur territoire (MB, p. 90, para. 75). Or, la Belgique estime que ses obligations au titre de l'Article 10 ne pourraient en aucun cas aller jusqu'à l'obliger à financer la mise en œuvre des mesures communautaires sur le territoire néerlandais. La Belgique rappelle ensuite divers aspects de la position qu'elle a adoptée au cours des années au sujet de la modernisation de la ligne du Rhin de fer et souhaite qu'ils soient interprétés comme des actes d'assistance aux Pays-Bas pour leur permettre de se conformer à l'Article 10.

140. De leur côté, à aucun moment dans leurs plaidoiries, les Pays-Bas ne contestent ce point. Par conséquent, il n'existe aucun différend entre les Parties en ce qui concerne l'Article 10.

141. En conséquence, le Tribunal estime qu'il n'a pas à statuer sur la question des obligations découlant de l'Article 10 dans le contexte du différend concernant la ligne du Rhin de fer car cette question n'est ni concluante, ni déterminante pour que l'Article 292 du Traité CE trouve à s'appliquer.

CHAPITRE IV - LA DEMANDE DE RÉACTIVATION DE LA BELGIQUE ET LE
PROTOCOLE D'ACCORD DE MARS 2000

142. Le 28 mars 2000, le ministre des Transports belge et son homologue néerlandais signèrent
un Protocole d'accord relatif à la ligne du Rhin de fer conformément aux accords
intervenus entre les ministres le 29 février 2000 (le « Protocole d'accord de mars 2000 »).
Les principaux aspects de cet acte ont été confirmés lors d'une rencontre tripartite
réunissant les ministres des Transports belge et néerlandais, ainsi que le Secrétaire d'État
allemand aux transports, le 5 avril 2001 (MB, Pièce n° 86, Procès-verbal des discussions
entre les ministres belge et néerlandais et le Secrétaire d'État allemand aux transports
portant sur la réactivation de la ligne de chemin de fer du Rhin de fer, qui ont eu lieu à
Luxembourg le 5 avril 2001). Normalement, un Protocole d'accord (« *Memorandum of
understanding* ») est « un instrument conclu entre des États qui ne les lie pas
juridiquement » (A. Aust, *Modern Treaty Law and Practice*, Cambridge University Press
(2000), p. 26, à p. 31). Le facteur clé qui permet de distinguer un « instrument qui ne lie
pas juridiquement » d'un Traité est l'intention des Parties. Pour s'assurer de cette
intention, le Tribunal commencera par examiner les événements qui ont précédé la
signature du Protocole d'accord de mars 2000. Ensuite, il exposera le contenu et la
signification juridique de cet instrument particulier. Enfin, il résumera les circonstances
qui ont suivi la signature du Protocole d'accord de mars 2000 et ont abouti au présent
arbitrage entre les Parties.

A. Les circonstances qui ont précédé la signature du Protocole d'accord

143. Comme mentionné au paragraphe 19 ci-dessus, l'utilisation de la ligne du Rhin de fer a
beaucoup varié au cours de la période allant de 1914 à 1991. Les Parties sont d'accord sur
le fait que l'utilisation de la ligne du Rhin de fer entre la Belgique et l'Allemagne a été
interrompue après le 31 mai 1991 (MB, p. 23, para. 18 ; CMPB, pp. 9 à 10, para. 2.5.4).

144. Il convient de relever un fait intéressant pour le présent arbitrage, à savoir que, même
avant mai 1991, plusieurs instances officielles belges avaient manifesté l'intérêt de la
Belgique pour une future utilisation de la ligne du Rhin de fer (MB, pp. 32–38, paras. 24–
28). L'expression la plus frappante de cet intérêt est la lettre que le ministre belge des
Transports adressa à son homologue des Pays-Bas le 23 février 1987 (version originale en
néerlandais dans MB, Pièce n° 59, lettre du ministre belge des Transports au ministre

néerlandais des Transports et Waterstaat, datée du 23 février 1987 ; traduction libre [en anglais] dans MB, p. 33, para. 24). Cette lettre anticipait déjà les difficultés de concilier l'utilisation future du chemin de fer du Rhin de fer et la protection de l'environnement. Le Tribunal reproduit ci-après la traduction de certains passages de la lettre du ministre belge :

> J'ai l'honneur d'attirer votre attention sur la ligne de chemin de fer transfrontières Anvers-Ruremonde-Mönchen Gladbach, connue également sous le nom de Rhin de fer.
>
> Certains milieux belges,[14] montrent un vif intérêt pour une ligne de chemin de fer moderne reliant directement Anvers à la région de la Ruhr ; en conséquence, j'estime nécessaire de réaliser une analyse approfondie des coûts et des avantages de cette liaison ferroviaire.
>
> J'ai donné pour instruction à la SNCB [Société Nationale des chemins de fer belge] d'étudier cette question, mais cette étude ne peut être finalisée sans la coopération de la NS [Société nationale des chemins de fer néerlandaise] et de la DB [Société nationale des chemins de fer allemande].[15]
>
> Je vous serais extrêmement obligé de bien vouloir demander à la NS de coopérer avec la SNCB à cette étude.
>
> [...]
>
> En conclusion, je renvoie au projet existant aux Pays-Bas de créer un parc naturel entre Ruremonde et Erkenbosch le long du Rhin de fer, qui limiterait l'utilisation du chemin de fer sur cette ligne.
>
> J'estime qu'une telle limitation irait à l'encontre des droits accordés à la Belgique par l'Article 12 du Traité de Londres conclu le 19 avril 1839 entre la Belgique et les Pays-Bas, qui a été exécuté jusqu'au Traité du 13 janvier 1873 règlementant le passage de la ligne de chemin de fer Anvers-Gladbach à travers le territoire du Limbourg.
>
> Dans ce contexte, il ne fait aucun doute que la Belgique va défendre fermement ses droits à la liberté du transport sur le Rhin de fer.

Dans sa réponse du 26 octobre 1987, le ministre des Transports des Pays-Bas n'évoque pas de lien entre la ligne du Rhin de fer et le classement en réserve naturelle d'une zone

---

[14] Le Tribunal constate que les Pays-Bas, dans leur Contre-Mémoire, mentionnent que la traduction anglaise correcte de « in sommige Belgische middens » est « in certain Belgian circles » (voir CMPB, p. 12, para. 2.7.1.2. et note 19). Le Tribunal interprète cette phrase de la manière suivante : « in some Belgian circles ».

[15] Voir également la lettre que le ministre belge des Transports adresse le 9 novembre 1987 à son homologue allemand : MB, Pièce n°. 60, lettre adressée le 9 novembre 1987 par le ministre belge des Transports au ministre allemand des transports.

contiguë à la ligne du chemin de fer, mais se contente de reconnaître le droit de passage de la Belgique.

145. En mai 1991 fut publiée une étude économique commandée par la Commission européenne. Cette étude recommandait de conserver le tracé existant de la ligne du Rhin de fer et concluait que « la réfection du Rhin de fer aurait une incidence économique généralement positive » (MB, Pièce n° S2, Prognos, *The Iron Rhine Railway Link between Antwerp and the Rhine-Ruhr Area*, Rapport final, mai 1991). Il fut débattu de cette étude lors de la réunion de la Commission des Transports de l'Union économique du Benelux le 11 décembre 1991. Au cours de cette réunion, le représentant belge déclara que « la réactivation éventuelle du Rhin de fer doit rester garantie au vu de l'augmentation des transports à l'avenir » (MB, Pièce n° 63, Union économique du Benelux, Commission des Transports, Sous-commission « Transports Ferroviaires » Rapport de la réunion organisée à Luxembourg le 11 décembre 1991). Une déclaration similaire fut faite lors de la réunion de la Commission des Transports de l'Union Économique du Benelux du 20 avril 1993 (MB, Pièce n° 64, Union économique du Benelux, Commission des Transports, Sous-commission « Transports ferroviaires », Rapport de la réunion organisée à La Haye le 20 avril 1993).

146. En 1994, la Commission européenne approuva la demande de la Belgique de financement d'une étude de faisabilité sur la modernisation de la ligne du Rhin de fer. Cette étude fut par la suite envisagée au titre de l'Article 9 du Traité relatif à la construction d'une ligne de chemin de fer pour les trains à grande vitesse entre Rotterdam et Anvers en 1996. L'étude (le Rapport Tractebel), commencée en décembre 1996, fut achevée en janvier – février 1997.

147. Le 12 juin 1998, le Premier ministre belge écrivit ce qui suit à son homologue, le Premier ministre néerlandais (MB, Pièce n° 67, lettre adressée le 12 juin 1998 par M. Dehaene, Premier ministre belge à M. Kok, ministre-Président des Pays-Bas, traduction libre : MB, p. 38, para. 28) :

> J'accorde une grande importance à une réalisation rapide du Rhin de fer. C'est pourquoi la préférence est donnée au tracé historique existant actuellement, plus plat, plus court et plus économique. La Belgique peut également se prévaloir d'un droit relevant du droit international public sur ce tracé historique. Des alternatives (le tracé du Brabant, la déviation via Venlo) soit

constituent un tracé trop détourné, soit nécessitent l'installation de nouvelles lignes qui ne peuvent être réalisées qu'à longue échéance.

148. Il convient maintenant d'examiner si l'interruption de la ligne en 1991 a entraîné des conséquences sur le plan juridique.

149. Du point de vue des Pays-Bas, cet historique démontre que la Belgique n'a pas toujours eu la même position sur la réactivation de la ligne du Rhin de fer.

150. Quoi qu'il en soit, le Tribunal estime que les Pays-Bas savaient qu'il était possible, nonobstant ce qui s'était passé auparavant, qu'une demande officielle de réactivation à un niveau d'utilisation significativement supérieur intervienne dans un proche avenir. Et la Belgique avait réservé son droit de « libre passage » – que les Pays-Bas avaient reconnu et continuent à reconnaître.

151. Le Tribunal constate que la réaction des Pays-Bas à ces développements a toujours été fondée sur deux principes : (i) les Pays-Bas ne contestent pas le droit de passage de la Belgique en ce qui concerne la ligne du Rhin de fer ; et (ii) eu égard à la souveraineté des Pays-Bas sur leur territoire, toute réactivation de la ligne du Rhin de fer doit se conformer au droit néerlandais, notamment en ce qui concerne la protection de l'environnement. Ceci apparaît clairement notamment dans la réponse adressée le 10 juillet 1998 par le Premier ministre des Pays-Bas à la lettre du Premier ministre belge, citée ci-dessus:

> [Les Pays-Bas participeront aux concertations dans un esprit de bon voisinage, comme ils l'ont déclaré à plusieurs reprises. Il va sans dire que la réactivation de la ligne historique, ou de toute autre ligne, sur le territoire néerlandais, relève du droit néerlandais en matière d'environnement et du droit communautaire sur la préservation des habitats naturels (Directive Habitats) [CMPB, Pièce n° 19, Lettre adressée le 10 juillet 1998 par M. Wim Kok, Premier ministre des Pays-Bas à M. Jean-Luc Dehaene, Premier ministre belge].

152. À la même période, les Pays-Bas établirent un inventaire de leur droit national relatif à la réactivation de la ligne du Rhin de fer (*voir* CMPB, p. 21, para. 2.12.2). Sur la base de cet inventaire, la Belgique accepta la proposition des Pays-Bas de soumettre la totalité de la ligne de chemin de fer à la procédure fixée par le droit néerlandais sur l'infrastructure des transports (Procédures de Planification). En outre, le site du Meinweg fut classé par les Pays-Bas le 20 mai 1994 « zone de protection spéciale » au sens de la Directive Oiseaux,

ultérieurement remplacée par la Directive Habitats. Au cours des années 1994-1995, les Pays-Bas ont également classé le site du Meinweg parc national et « Zone de silence » en vertu de leur droit national (*voir* discussion ci-après au paragraphe 189).

153.	Il devint rapidement évident que l'harmonisation de la réactivation de la ligne du Rhin de fer avec le droit de l'environnement prévalant aux Pays-Bas entraînerait des coûts d'infrastructure substantiels (notamment le projet de tunnel sur le site du Meinweg). Lors d'une réunion entre les ministres belge et néerlandais des Transports et le secrétaire d'État allemand aux Transports, qui eut lieu à Bruxelles le 9 décembre 1999, il fut impossible de parvenir à un accord global sur la répartition des coûts entre les pays concernés. Alors qu'il était convenu que les coûts de la réactivation temporaire du tracé historique seraient assumés par la Belgique, il semble qu'il ait été impossible de parvenir à un accord sur la répartition des coûts dans le cadre d'une solution définitive. La Belgique et l'Allemagne fondaient leur argumentation sur le principe de territorialité : chaque pays assume les investissements d'infrastructure sur son propre territoire, tandis que les Pays-Bas se fondaient sur l'Article XII du Traité de Séparation de 1839 pour soutenir que ces coûts sur le territoire néerlandais devaient être assumés par la Belgique (MB, Pièce n° 96, Rapport sur la réunion entre les ministres belge et néerlandais et le secrétaire d'État allemand aux Transports sur la réactivation du Rhin de fer, organisée à Bruxelles le 9 décembre 1999).

### B.	Contenu et portée juridique du Protocole d'accord

154.	Le Protocole d'accord du 28 mars 2000 entre le ministre Durant et le ministre Netelenbos concernant le Rhin de fer prévoit ce qui suit :[16]

> La Belgique et les Pays-Bas soulignent à quel point il est important dans un marché intérieur en constante expansion de pouvoir rapidement transporter des marchandises par rail depuis les ports belges et néerlandais vers l'intérieur, et inversement. Toutes les sociétés de chemins de fer auront accès à l'infrastructure disponible à cette fin.
>
> Les deux pays œuvreront en étroite collaboration avec l'Allemagne à une étude internationale de l'impact positif et négatif de la réactivation du Rhin de fer et des éventuelles alternatives de tracés. Cette étude évaluera la situation

---

[16] Pour le texte néerlandais original du protocole d'accord de mars 2000, voir MB, Pièce n°. 82 et CMPB, Pièce n°. 22. Des traductions libres en anglais de certains paragraphes ont été reproduites dans le MB, pp. 44–47, para. 34 et CMPB, pp. 20–21, para. 2.12.1. Sauf indication contraire, c'est la traduction néerlandaise qui est reproduite ici.

« comme s'il n'y avait pas de frontière ». Les résultats de cette étude seront disponibles en mars 2001, pour permettre au processus décisionnel international d'avoir alors lieu.

Étant donné le lien existant entre l'étude internationale et l'EIE néerlandaise,[17] les Pays-Bas mettront tout en œuvre pour que les résultats de l'EIE relatifs au tronçon du Rhin de fer situé sur le territoire néerlandais, soient prêts en mars 2001. L'EIE étudiera les points suivants :

- À court terme, l'éventuelle[18] réactivation temporaire limitée de la totalité du tracé historique, cette réactivation temporaire prenant fin dès que le tracé définitif sera mis en service.

- En ce qui concerne la solution définitive, étude de tous les tracés possibles ; les possibilités relatives aux transports de voyageurs seront également étudiées.

Les Pays-Bas et la Belgique proposeront à l'Allemagne des réunions tripartites régulières afin de discuter de l'avancement de l'EIE. Les Pays-Bas inviteront la Belgique à désigner un responsable chargé de surveiller l'avancement quotidien de l'EIE.

Les décisions concernant l'usage temporaire et le tracé définitif seront prises simultanément.

Si, au moment de la prise des décisions concernant l'usage temporaire et le tracé définitif, au plus tard au milieu de l'année 2001, l'EIE conclut qu'un usage temporaire limité n'entraînera pas une dégradation irréversible de l'environnement, dès la fin de 2001, quelques trains pourront circuler à vitesse réduite sur le tracé historique tous les jours, entre 7 h et 19 heures. Dans les mêmes conditions (décisions prises en temps opportun et absence de dégradation irréversible de l'environnement), dès la fin de 2002, il pourra circuler temporairement, à vitesse réduite, quinze trains au maximum (dans les deux sens) par période de 24 heures, sur l'ensemble du tracé historique le soir et pendant la nuit. Le cas échéant, la dégradation écologique fera l'objet d'indemnisations.

S'il est décidé que le tracé définitif passera par un autre itinéraire que celui traversant le site du Meinweg (ce que les Pays-Bas envisagent, mais non la Belgique), ce tracé sera réputé satisfaire intégralement les obligations de droit public international résultant du Traité de Séparation de 1839 et du Traité belgo-néerlandais du Rhin de fer de 1873. Ces accords feront l'objet d'un Traité.

Jusqu'à ce que le tracé définitif ait été retenu, la Belgique réserve tous ses droits en vertu du Traité de Séparation de 1839 et du Traité belgo-néerlandais du Rhin de fer de 1873.

---

[17] EIE = Évaluation de l'Impact Environnemental.
[18] Le Tribunal utilise ici le terme « éventuelle » (de la traduction belge) plutôt que le terme « éventualité », qui figure dans la version néerlandaise.

Le coût de l'utilisation temporaire du tracé historique sera assumé par la Belgique.

Si la Société Nationale des Chemins de Fer belge (la SNCB) le souhaite, elle pourra entreprendre ces travaux elle-même ou les confier à un tiers, en tenant compte des règles européennes des marchés publics et des prescriptions légales néerlandaises en vertu desquelles ces travaux devront être effectués par un entrepreneur agréé par les Pays-Bas. L'entrepreneur pourra être de nationalité belge.[19]

En ce qui concerne la construction du tracé définitif, les Pays-Bas sont disposés à prendre à leur charge une partie des coûts qui y sont associés. Des accords à cet égard seront pris ultérieurement lorsque le tracé définitif aura été choisi.

155. Le Tribunal observe qu'il est possible de résumer de la manière suivante les intentions énoncées au Protocole d'accord de mars 2000 :

(1) Réalisation, conjointement avec l'Allemagne, d'une « étude internationale » portant sur les conséquences de la réactivation de la ligne du Rhin de fer. Les résultats de cette étude doivent être disponibles en mars 2001.

(2) Les Pays-Bas « mettront tout en oeuvre » pour que soient prêts, également en mars 2001, les résultats de leur Procédure d'Évaluation de l'Impact Environnemental (« EIE ») pour le tronçon de la ligne du Rhin de fer situé sur le territoire néerlandais. La procédure d'EIE contiendra une étude tant de l'usage temporaire de la ligne du Rhin de fer que des différents tracés possibles pour la solution définitive.

(3) Les décisions relatives à l'usage temporaire et au tracé définitif doivent être prises simultanément (la « double décision »), au plus tard au milieu de l'année 2001. La décision concernant l'usage temporaire est subordonnée à la décision concernant l'utilisation à long terme pour garantir que cet usage soit effectivement temporaire.

(4) Au cours des négociations entre les Parties, plusieurs significations ont été avancées en ce qui concerne la notion « d'usage temporaire » de la ligne de chemin de fer du Rhin de fer. Selon les termes du Protocole d'accord, l'utilisation temporaire désigne « une réactivation limitée de l'ensemble du tracé historique » jusqu'à la mise en service du tracé définitif (si le tracé définitif coïncide avec le tracé historique, on peut s'attendre à ce que la réfection du tracé historique ait des conséquences négatives sur l'usage temporaire du tracé). Bien que le Protocole d'accord n'évoque

---

[19] La traduction [*anglaise*] de ce paragraphe a été effectuée par le Tribunal (aucune des Parties n'en ayant fourni de traduction).

pas cette question, ses termes semblent suggérer qu'un accord sur l'utilisation définitive pourrait ne pas suivre intégralement le tracé historique. L'usage temporaire doit être autorisé si, au moment où les Parties adoptent la double décision, la procédure d'EIE conclut qu'un usage temporaire limité ne causera aucun dommage irréversible à l'environnement. Si tel est bien le cas, à compter de la fin de l'année 2001, un nombre limité de trains pourra circuler tous les jours à vitesse réduite sur l'ensemble du tracé historique, entre 7 heures et 19 heures. À compter de la fin de l'année 2002, les trains pourront, dans les mêmes conditions, circuler à vitesse réduite sur l'ensemble du tracé historique, le soir et la nuit, à raison de 15 trains par période de 24 heures et ce, au total et dans les deux directions. Le coût de l'usage temporaire du tracé historique serait assumé par la Belgique.

(5) En ce qui concerne la solution définitive, tous les tracés possibles seront envisagés. Jusqu'à ce que le tracé définitif ait été choisi, la Belgique réserve tous ses droits découlant du Traité de Séparation de 1839 et du Traité du Rhin de fer de 1873. S'il est décidé que le tracé définitif ne passera pas par le Meinweg, cet autre tracé sera réputé satisfaire pleinement aux dispositions de l'Article XII du Traité de Séparation de 1839 et du Traité du Rhin de fer de 1873 et les accords à cet égard feront l'objet d'un traité. Les Pays-Bas seraient prêts à participer au coût de construction du tracé définitif.

156. Les Parties conviennent que, selon le droit international, le Protocole d'accord de mars 2000 n'est pas un acte juridique qui les lie (RB, p. 29, para. 32; DPB, p. 7, para. 26). Toutefois, il est clair qu'il n'a pas été considéré pour autant comme dénué de pertinence juridique. Les Parties ont en effet mis en œuvre un certain nombre de dispositions du Protocole d'accord de mars 2000 (*voir* paragraphe 159 ci-après). La Belgique évoque également sa « caducité » si la double décision n'est pas adoptée à la date prévue « au milieu de l'année 2001 au plus tard ». La Belgique conclut qu'en conséquence, « l'engagement de la Belgique de financer les coûts de l'usage temporaire est également caduc ».

157. Le Tribunal constate que, dans les arguments avancés par les Parties relativement à certaines des Questions qui lui sont posées, le Protocole d'accord de mars 2000 n'est pas non plus traité comme un document doté de pertinence juridique. Les principes de bonne

266

foi et de caractère raisonnable amènent à conclure que les principes et procédures définis dans le Protocole d'accord de mars 2000 doivent encore être interprétés et mis en œuvre de bonne foi et qu'ils fournissent des indications utiles sur ce que les Parties sont prêtes à considérer comme compatible avec les droits que leur confèrent l'Article XII du Traité de Séparation de 1839 et le Traité du Rhin de fer. La répartition des coûts de l'usage temporaire ne dépend pas des engagements pris dans le Protocole d'accord de mars 2000, mais d'autres considérations juridiques (y compris de ce que les Parties ont jugé raisonnable au cours de leurs négociations relatives au Protocole d'accord de mars 2000). Le tracé définitif putatif – dans la mesure où il risque d'impliquer un léger écart par rapport au tracé historique – exige un accord ; et le Protocole d'accord de mars 2000 suggère que les Parties n'ont pas considéré cette option comme déraisonnable en soi.

158. Le Tribunal constate également que l'adoption simultanée de la décision à court terme et de la décision définitive est toujours d'actualité. Tout comme il n'est pas possible d'affirmer que la Belgique ait convenu de financer la solution temporaire en l'absence d'accord sur une solution définitive, il n'est également pas possible de considérer que les Pays-Bas aient approuvé la mise en œuvre immédiate de la solution à court terme, en l'absence d'accord sur une solution définitive. En outre, alors qu'à aucun moment le droit de passage de la Belgique n'est devenu caduc, la longue période d'utilisation minimale, voire d'interruption totale, associée à la complexité technique de la réactivation de la ligne du Rhin de fer suggèrent que l'usage à court terme souhaité par la Belgique n'aura pas lieu dans un avenir immédiat. Les Pays-Bas ont clairement déclaré qu'ils préféraient qu'il n'y ait pas d'usage temporaire, tout en concédant qu'un usage temporaire éventuel ne devrait pas durer plus de cinq ans (CMPB p. 25, para. 2.12.4 ; DPB p. 9, para. 35).

C. Mesures prises après l'adoption du Protocole d'accord

159. L'étude internationale mentionnée dans le Protocole d'accord de mars 2000 est parue en mai 2001 (MB, Pièce n° S3, Arcadis, *Comparative Cross-Border Study on the Iron Rhine*, Rapport final, 14 mai 2001). Ce même mois, les Pays-Bas publièrent les résultats de leur procédure d'EIE, dans un rapport intitulé « Évaluation du tracé/Rapport d'impact sur l'environnement » (« RIE » ou « Déclaration d'impact sur l'environnement » (DIE)), (MB, Pièce n° S4, *Railinfrabeheer/Directoraat-Generaal Rijkswaterstaat, Trajectnota /MER*). Tant l'étude internationale que l'Évaluation du tracé (DIE) néerlandaise contiennent un examen détaillé de différentes options de tracés pour la ligne du Rhin de

267

fer réactivée, ayant pour même origine le point de pénétration historique dans les Pays-Bas à la frontière avec la Belgique. Une série d'options fait passer le tracé par Venlo ; l'autre série par Ruremonde ou à proximité de cette ville. Ces derniers tracés englobent le tracé historique, avec plusieurs variations. Toutes les options, et les travaux requis, ont été évalués sur la base de critères exhaustifs et notamment de leur coût et de leurs effets sur l'environnement. Les deux études concluent que l'option privilégiée serait le tracé historique. Le rapport d'Évaluation du Tracé/DIE qualifie cette option de « moins dommageable pour l'environnement » avec des modifications qui incluent un tunnel dans le Meinweg et le contournement de Ruremonde. Le 21 septembre 2001, les ministres des Transports belge, néerlandais et allemand ont décidé de prendre une décision globale, incluant la double décision relative à l'usage temporaire et à l'utilisation à long terme (*voir* paragraphe 155, alinéa 4 ci-dessus), ainsi qu'une décision sur la répartition des coûts (MB, Pièce n° 89, Mémo des discussions informelles entre les ministres des Transports belge, néerlandais et allemand concernant la réactivation du Rhin de fer qui ont eu lieu à La Haye le 21 septembre 2001). Pendant cette même période, les trois pays concernés ont rencontré la Direction générale de l'environnement de la Commission européenne. Cette rencontre a abouti à une déclaration provisoire et définitive de la Commission sur les questions d'interprétation de la Directive Habitats. Lorsqu'il est devenu évident que les seules négociations ne permettraient pas de réaliser la réactivation de la ligne du Rhin de fer, les Parties sont convenues de résoudre un certain nombre de problèmes dans le cadre d'une procédure d'arbitrage.

CHAPITRE V - MESURES ENVISAGÉES PAR LES PAYS-BAS À LA LUMIÈRE DE L'ARTICLE XII DU TRAITÉ DE SÉPARATION DE 1839

A. Introduction

160. Le Tribunal a conclu (*voir* paragraphe 56) que, du fait de la réserve de souveraineté prévue à l'Article XII du Traité de Séparation de 1839, les Pays-Bas peuvent exercer leur souveraineté sur le territoire traversé par la ligne du Rhin de fer sauf si cela entre en conflit avec les droits concédés à la Belgique en vertu du Traité, ou avec ceux dont elle dispose en vertu du droit international général, ou encore avec les contraintes imposées par le droit communautaire.

161. La question des contraintes imposées par le droit communautaire est évoquée séparément, au Chapitre III ci-dessus et au paragraphe 206 ci-après.

162. Selon la Belgique, les restrictions imposées par l'Article XII impliquent que les Pays-Bas sont tenus d'exercer leur pouvoir législatif et leur pouvoir décisionnel de manière raisonnable et de bonne foi, afin de ne pas vider le droit de passage de la Belgique de sa substance ou d'en rendre l'exercice anormalement difficile (RB, p. 69, para. 70). Les Pays-Bas ne contestent pas ces restrictions, mais soutiennent que les actions qu'ils ont entreprises satisfont pleinement à ces exigences.

163. Selon le Tribunal, la première restriction évidente découlant de l'Article XII est que le droit des Pays-Bas d'appliquer leur droit national à la réactivation du Rhin de fer ne peut pas avoir pour conséquence un déni du droit de passage de la Belgique sur le tracé historique. La seconde restriction découle des principes généralement admis de bonne foi et de caractère raisonnable : toutes les mesures devant être prescrites par les Pays-Bas sur le fondement de leur droit national pour la réactivation de la ligne du Rhin de fer ne doivent pas rendre anormalement difficile l'exercice du droit de passage de la Belgique.

164. Dans ce contexte, le Tribunal relève que la Belgique considère que les travaux jugés nécessaires par les Pays-Bas pour réactiver le Rhin de fer « ne restreignent pas les droits intrinsèques de la Belgique en eux-mêmes, sous réserve que des mesures soient prises pour garantir l'utilisation sans interruption de la ligne de chemin de fer pendant ces travaux et en dépit de ceux-ci, de manière à ce que (1) l'usage temporaire soit directement

suivi d'une exploitation à long terme [*voir* paragraphe 155, alinéas 3 et 4 ci-dessus] et (2) qu'aucun de ces 'régimes' ne soit affecté par les travaux de construction » (RB, p. 34, para. 37).

165. La Belgique déclare que les exigences des Pays-Bas relativement à ces travaux ne constituent pas en elles-mêmes un exercice déraisonnable de leurs droits. Néanmoins, lorsque ces exigences sont associées à la demande insistante que ces travaux soient financés par la Belgique, et non par les Pays-Bas, elles deviennent alors, selon la Belgique, un tel exercice déraisonnable de leurs droits. Ainsi, la Belgique considère-t-elle que l'imposition d'obligations financières serait susceptible de constituer un déni de son droit de passage (RB, p. 34, para. 37). Les mesures prescrites pour la réactivation de la ligne du Rhin de fer et la répartition des coûts de celles-ci sont des problèmes étroitement liés qui sont traités dans le présent chapitre et au chapitre VI, respectivement.

166. Dans le présent chapitre, le Tribunal examinera les mesures envisagées par les Pays-Bas pour réactiver la ligne du Rhin de fer à la lumière de leur compatibilité avec les obligations imposées aux Pays-Bas en vertu du Traité. À cette fin, il est nécessaire en premier lieu de s'intéresser au droit néerlandais sur lequel se fondent les mesures envisagées.

B. Droit applicable et procédures décisionnelles des Pays-Bas

167. Dans leurs écritures, les Pays-Bas ont établi une distinction entre deux catégories de droit applicables à la réactivation de la ligne du Rhin de fer : d'une part, le droit dit « sectoriel spécifique » et, d'autre part, les règles générales de droit administratif. Les Pays-Bas n'ont fourni que des informations parcellaires sur la teneur de leur droit national et la Belgique n'a, quant à elle, commenté que certains points spécifiques. Le Tribunal estime néanmoins utile de donner un aperçu des informations fournies par les Parties.

1. Droit sectoriel spécifique

168. Plusieurs lois ou règlements néerlandais s'appliquent à la réactivation de la ligne de chemin de fer du Rhin de fer. Ceux concernant les problèmes techniques et la sécurité sont particulièrement importants, tels que les spécifications des voies et des passages à niveau et ceux traitant des questions environnementales (aménagement du territoire,

protection de la santé et des sols et préservation de la nature). Les questions techniques et de sécurité sont couvertes pour l'essentiel par la loi sur les chemins de fer (*Spoorwegwet*). Le différend entre les Parties relativement aux conséquences de l'application du droit néerlandais se concentre particulièrement sur le droit de l'environnement. Le droit que les Parties considèrent comme particulièrement pertinent dans leurs plaidoiries comprend les lois suivantes.

169. La loi sur la réduction des nuisances sonores (*Wet Geluidhinder*) définit les normes des niveaux de bruit admissibles applicables à diverses catégories de bâtiments et d'activités. Dans le cas de zones d'habitation et autres lieux similaires, il existe une distinction entre le seuil maximum dérogatoire et ce qu'on appelle le « niveau sonore préférentiel ». Le niveau sonore maximal autorisé sur une ligne de chemin de fer modifiée est de 73 dB(A) ; pour une nouvelle ligne, il est de 70 dB(A). Le niveau préférentiel est, quant à lui, de 57 dB(A). L'article 106, paragraphe (d), alinéa (4) de la loi prescrit les mesures à adopter en cas de dépassement du niveau préférentiel. Ces mesures doivent être prises dans l'ordre suivant : (1) mesures prises à la source (par exemple, en utilisant une infrastructure et/ou des trains plus silencieux) ; (2) mesures liées à la propagation du son (par exemple, barrières antibruit) et (3) mesures prises au point d'impact (par exemple, isolation des façades). Lorsque ces mesures ne sont pas suffisantes pour garantir que le bruit ne dépassera pas le niveau préférentiel, une dérogation peut être accordée dans certaines conditions. Lorsque la nuisance sonore dépasse le seuil maximum dérogatoire, les habitations concernées perdent leur fonction résidentielle (ce qui peut aboutir à une expropriation faisant l'objet d'une indemnisation) (RB, pp. 44–46, paras. 48–50; DPB, pp. 18–19, paras. 74–77).

170. L'arrêté de réduction du bruit des lignes ferroviaires (*Besluit Geluidhinder Spoorwegen*) fournit les bases nécessaires pour imposer des prescriptions (afin d'atténuer le bruit dû à l'utilisation des voies ferrées) :

> sur la nature, la composition ou le mode de construction et la modification d'une ligne de chemin de fer. Le terme « modification » renvoie notamment à une augmentation significative du nombre de trains et/ou de leur vitesse de passage. Certaines mesures sont requises dans ce cas. La société chargée de la gestion de la ligne de chemin de fer doit présenter ces mesures aux municipalités concernées. Une construction ou une adaptation ne peuvent être entamées que lorsqu'une décision définitive a été prise [CMPB, p. 21, n. 44].

271

171. La Loi sur la Faune et la Flore (*Flora en Fauna Wet*) protège les espèces végétales et animales. Elle implique :

> l'interdiction de détruire ou de perturber les espèces protégées, ainsi que leurs nids, leur reproduction, leur repos et leur habitat. Les termes des interdictions de la Loi sur la Faune et la Flore ne contiennent pas le mot « significatif ». En conséquence, *toute* perturbation et/ou destruction résultant de la pose de la voie représente une violation de ces dispositions. Pour les espèces touchées par la construction du tracé, la mise en œuvre d'un projet ne peut être entreprise que moyennant l'obtention d'une dérogation sur le fondement de l'Article 75 de la Loi sur la Faune et la Flore [CMPB, Annexe A, p. 1].

172. L'article 4, paragraphe 9 de la Loi de Gestion Environnementale (*Wet Milieubeheer*) exposée au paragraphe 82 de la Duplique des Pays-Bas dispose que les provinces :

> adopteront un Plan provincial quadriennal de gestion de l'environnement identifiant les zones qui exigent une protection spéciale afin de préserver l'environnement ou certains de ses aspects (tels que le silence). Une zone de silence désigne une zone où la nuisance sonore doit être si faible qu'elle y perturbe peu, voire pas du tout, les sons naturels (principe de « *stand still* »). Le niveau sonore préférentiel dans les zones de silence peut varier d'une province à l'autre, mais les Plans de gestion de l'environnement des provinces du Nord Brabant et du Limbourg appliquent un niveau de 40 dB(A) dans la journée.

173. L'arrêté relatif à l'Évaluation de l'Impact Environnemental (« EIE ») (*Besluit Milieueffect-rapportage*) exige l'élaboration d'un Rapport d'impact sur l'environnement pour l'adoption d'un projet relatif à une nouvelle ligne de chemin de fer ou à la réactivation d'une ligne de chemin de fer existante passant au moins sur cinq kilomètres dans une zone tampon ou une zone sensible délimitée dans le cadre d'un plan d'aménagement du territoire ou d'un plan régional (CMPB, p. 21, n. 45).

174. Les Pays-Bas appliquent également les lignes directrices internationales adoptées en 1969 concernant l'implantation des parcs nationaux dans le cadre de l'Union internationale pour la conservation de la nature (UICN). La définition d'un Parc National est la suivante :

> un territoire d'un seul tenant d'au moins 1000 hectares contenant des terrains, de l'eau et/ou des surfaces boisées, présentant des caractéristiques spéciales au niveau du paysage et des espèces végétales et animales. C'est un secteur qui présente de bonnes opportunités de loisirs. Un Parc National a pour vocation d'intensifier la préservation de la nature et sa mise en valeur,

d'encourager vivement l'initiation à la nature et à l'environnement et de promouvoir des formes de divertissements et de recherches orientées vers la nature [CMPB, Annexe A, p. 2].

175. Il existe au niveau provincial également un certain nombre de réglementations et de politiques pertinentes, qui mettent en œuvre la législation nationale. Outre le Plan provincial de politique environnementale prévu par la Loi sur la protection de l'environnement déjà mentionné au paragraphe 172, les provinces disposent de la possibilité de classer des zones dans le cadre de leur « Structure écologique provinciale » (Limbourg) ou de leur « Structure Verte Principale » (Nord-Brabant). Il s'agit de zones clés, de zones de développement écologique et de zones de liaison écologique auxquelles s'applique une politique de protection spécifique. Le Plan de politique environnementale de la Province du Limbourg prévoit également le classement de sites en fonction de leur intérêt paysager (CMPB, Annexe A, pp. 1–2).

176. Enfin, au niveau provincial, le Plan de politique environnementale de la Province du Limbourg prévoit la possibilité de classer des secteurs en « Zone de silence ». Cette réglementation provinciale inclut une disposition de protection générale pour les zones de protection écologique, y compris les « Zones de silence » (Article 5.4) dont la teneur est la suivante :

> Toute personne se livrant à des activités dans une zone de protection de l'environnement, qui sait ou devrait raisonnablement savoir que ces activités risquent de dégrader ce secteur qui a une importance particulière justifiant son classement en zone protégée, doit prendre toutes les mesures raisonnablement nécessaires pour éviter cette dégradation ou, si elle se produit, pour limiter les dommages et neutraliser les conséquences des activités susmentionnées dans toute la mesure du possible.

Le Plan provincial de politique environnementale ne définit aucune norme quantitative de bruit pour les « Zones de silence », mais le Plan de politique environnementale de la Province du Limbourg prévoit un niveau maximal de 40 dB(A) et la Province a l'intention d'introduire ce plafond dans le Plan provincial de politique environnementale (CMPB, Annexe A, p. 3).

2. **Règles générales de droit administratif**

177. Dans le cadre de l'application du droit sectoriel spécifique, le Gouvernement des Pays-Bas doit également se conformer aux principes administratifs généraux et, notamment, aux principes généraux de saine administration codifiés dans la Loi générale d'administration (*Algemene Wet Bestuursrecht*). Les Pays-Bas renvoient notamment aux « principes généraux de saine administration », codifiés dans les articles 3.2 et 3.4 de la Loi générale d'administration, qui disposent ce qui suit :

> Lorsqu'elle prépare un acte administratif, une administration recueillera toutes les informations nécessaires relatives aux faits concernés et aux intérêts en jeu.
>
> L'administration évaluera les intérêts impliqués directement dans la mesure où ce droit n'est pas restreint par une réglementation obligatoire ou par la nature du pouvoir exercé [DPB, p.17, para. 69].

Selon les Pays-Bas, ces principes peuvent avoir une influence sur l'interprétation et l'application des dispositions légales, ainsi que sur la mise en œuvre de la politique, et peuvent également servir de politique administrative lorsqu'une réglementation accorde une certaine marge de manœuvre, ou encore en cas de vide juridique. Les Pays-Bas expliquent que ces principes seront appliqués dans le cadre de toute procédure de contrôle de légalité (DPB, p. 17, paras. 69–70).

3. **Loi sur la Planification des infrastructures de transport (Procédures de planification)**

178. En principe, chaque loi sectorielle spécifique comprend ses propres procédures décisionnelles (y compris en ce qui concerne le contrôle de légalité) permettant ainsi la mise en application du droit positif. Les projets importants d'infrastructure de transport font l'objet d'une loi distincte qui remplace les procédures décisionnelles spécifiques du secteur, à savoir la Loi sur la planification des infrastructures de transport (*Tracéwet*) (CMPB, p. 21, para. 2.12.2). Cette procédure comprend des études de conformité avec l'ensemble du droit spécifique pertinent, ainsi qu'une Etude d'impact sur l'environnement (EIE). Seule l'ordonnance procédurale de planification finale rendue dans le cadre de cette procédure pourra faire l'objet d'un contrôle de légalité. Les Pays-Bas expliquent que la loi sur la planification des infrastructures de transport doit s'appliquer à la réactivation

du tronçon du Rhin de fer entre Ruremonde et la frontière allemande (CMPB, p. 21, para 2.12.2). Les Pays-Bas, avec l'accord de la Belgique, ont décidé d'appliquer ladite Loi aux fins de la réactivation de la totalité de la ligne du Rhin de fer.

179. La procédure décisionnelle prévue par la loi sur la planification des infrastructures de transport (y compris l'EIE) se déroule en six étapes décrites dans le Contre-Mémoire néerlandais (p. 22, para. 2.12.3.1) de la manière suivante (à l'exclusion des notes de bas de page) :

1. Une *Notification d'Intention* (*Startnotitie*) marque le lancement officiel de la procédure. Elle mentionne les projets de l'auteur, les alternatives à l'activité envisagée et les conséquences potentielles sur l'environnement attachées à chaque option.

2. Les résultats de l'étude des alternatives et de leurs conséquences sont consignés dans *l'Évaluation du tracé/RIE* (*Trajectnota/MER*), en tenant compte des résultats de l'enquête publique relative à la Notification d'Intention. Le but de l'Évaluation du tracé/RIE est de décrire les effets prévus sur l'environnement, de manière à ce que l'environnement reçoive l'attention qui lui est due au cours de la procédure décisionnelle relative à l'activité envisagée.

3. Sur la base de l'Évaluation du Tracé/RIE et compte tenu des résultats de l'enquête publique et de l'avis consultatif du Comité indépendant d'évaluation de l'impact sur l'environnement constitué conformément à la loi, les autorités compétentes sélectionnent une alternative préférentielle et la publient dans une *Position Officielle* (*Standpuntbepaling*).

4. L'alternative préférentielle fait l'objet d'une étude approfondie (qui implique les spécifications relatives au tracé de la ligne de chemin de fer précis au mètre près) dont les résultats sont consignés dans un *Projet d'ordonnance procédurale de planification* (*Ontwerp-Tracébesluit*) qui est publié.

5. Après consultation publique sur le Projet d'ordonnance procédurale de planification, les ministres compétents adoptent une *Ordonnance Procédurale de Planification* (*Tracébesluit*), qui permettra d'établir les permis de construire, de procéder aux expropriations, etc. Une Ordonnance procédurale de planification peut faire l'objet de recours administratifs pouvant aboutir, le cas échéant, à l'annulation de tout ou partie de cette Ordonnance.

6. Dès lors que l'Ordonnance procédurale de planification est adoptée définitivement, l'étape de construction du projet peut être lancée.

180. L'étape 1 (La Notification d'Intention) s'est achevée en novembre 1999. L'étape 2 (Évaluation du tracé/RIE) s'est achevée en 2001. Ce document analysait et évaluait une série d'options pour la réactivation de la ligne du Rhin de fer. Simultanément, l'étude internationale (commanditée par les trois Gouvernements impliqués dans la planification de la réactivation de la ligne du Rhin de fer, c'est-à-dire l'Allemagne, la Belgique et les Pays-Bas) s'est achevée (*voir* paragraphe 159 ci-dessus). En conclusion, les Gouvernements concernés se sont accordés en faveur de l'option préférentielle du tracé historique (avec le contournement de Ruremonde).

181. L'Étape 3 de la procédure décisionnelle (communication de la Position officielle) n'a pas pu avoir lieu car il a été impossible de parvenir à un accord avec la Belgique au cours des négociations concernant le coût de l'option préférentielle et sa répartition. Déclarant que son intention était d'éviter que la mise en œuvre du projet prenne du retard, le Gouvernement des Pays-Bas a décidé de poursuivre la procédure de manière informelle (CMPB, p. 23, para. 2.12.3.2). Le Gouvernement a ainsi approuvé une Position officielle préliminaire en novembre 2001 (laquelle n'a pas été publiée) et, en se fondant sur cette position, Prorail, l'organisme public néerlandais chargé de la gestion de l'infrastructure, a finalisé une version préliminaire du Projet d'ordonnance procédurale de planification (*IJzeren Rijn, Concept ontwerp-tracébesluit*) en juillet 2003. Cette version préliminaire a été transmise officieusement à la Société nationale des chemins de fer belges, SNCB, et la Belgique l'a utilisée pour préparer sa Réplique (les Pays-Bas ont émis une objection (DPB, p.13, para. 52)).

182. Les Pays-Bas estiment que l'application de leur droit aboutirait à la série de mesures nécessaires pour réactiver à long terme la ligne du Rhin de fer de la manière décrite dans la version préliminaire du Projet d'ordonnance procédurale de planification. Le Tribunal note que ce document est officieux et provisoire, comme indiqué au paragraphe 181 ci-dessus. Les Pays-Bas ont observé, que d'un point de vue formel, les mesures proposées dans cette version préliminaire ne peuvent pas être considérées comme les mesures définitives devant être mises en œuvre. En effet, même après la parution de la version définitive de l'Ordonnance, une possibilité de contrôle de légalité existera toujours. En conséquence, une certaine incertitude demeure quant aux mesures exactes à prescrire pour la réactivation de la ligne du Rhin de fer sur le territoire néerlandais. Néanmoins, puisque les Parties ont centré leurs arguments sur les mesures proposées dans la version

préliminaire, le Tribunal s'y consacrera de manière plus exhaustive. Le Tribunal relève que la Belgique, dans sa Réplique (p. 35, para. 38), indique que lorsqu'elle se réfère à ce document, cela n'implique pas qu'elle ait approuvé le contenu de celui-ci.

C. Les mesures envisagées dans la version préliminaire du Projet d'ordonnance procédurale de planification

183. Le Tribunal constate que les Pays-Bas ont fondé la version préliminaire de l'Ordonnance procédurale de planification sur le postulat que la Belgique souhaitait réactiver la ligne du Rhin de fer de manière à pouvoir y faire circuler, en 2020, 43 trains (total combiné dans les deux sens) par jour ouvrable (DPB, p. 14, para. 54). Le Tribunal relève que la Belgique, dans ses plaidoiries, n'a pas remis en cause ce postulat.

184. Le tracé de la ligne du Rhin de fer sur le territoire néerlandais est divisé en quatre tronçons (de A à D, d'ouest en est). L'article 3 de la version préliminaire du Projet d'Ordonnance procédurale de planification décrit ces tronçons de la manière suivante (RB, pp. 35–38, para. 40) :

(1) Le tronçon A traverse les municipalités de Cranendonck et Weert et suit le tracé historique de la ligne du Rhin de fer depuis la frontière belge, située à proximité de Budel, jusqu'à la limite orientale de Weert. La version préliminaire de l'Ordonnance procédurale de planification fait une distinction supplémentaire entre deux parties du tronçon A. La première partie, désignée « A1 », va de la frontière belgo-néerlandaise à l'embranchement de la ligne de chemin de fer Eindhoven-Weert. Cette partie, qui traverse la zone protégée « Weerter-en Budelerbergen » est décrite de la manière suivante :

> La ligne de chemin de fer est (et reste) à une seule voie de la frontière belgo-néerlandaise à l'embranchement de la ligne de chemin de fer Eindhoven-Weert. Cette voie n'est pas électrifiée. Actuellement, il y circule deux trains de marchandises par période de 24 heures, dans les deux sens. La réactivation du Rhin de fer implique une intensification du trafic ferroviaire jusqu'à 45 trains de marchandises par période de 24 heures dans les deux sens.
>
> Les normes applicables sont celles qui existent déjà. La sécurité aux passages à niveau est assurée selon le risque de collision moyen national. Les risques de collision sur la voie ne doivent pas dépasser la moyenne nationale après la réactivation.

La seconde partie du tronçon A, ou tronçon A2, part de l'est de l'embranchement de la ligne de chemin de fer Eindhoven-Weert. Elle est décrite de la manière suivante :

À l'est de l'embranchement, la ligne existante est (et reste) à double voie et est électrifiée. Actuellement, il y circule 104 trains par période de 24 heures dans les deux sens, dont 92 trains de voyageurs. Il s'agit à la fois de trains de marchandises et de trains de voyageurs. En 2020, les 43 trains « Rhin de fer » viendront s'ajouter à ce trafic. Si l'on inclut le développement autonome du transport ferroviaire, il est prévu de faire circuler 199 trains par période de 24 heures dans les deux sens, dont 152 trains de voyageurs. Les normes applicables correspondent également aux normes existantes. En ce qui concerne les risques de collision, cela signifie qu'il est fait application du principe de *stand still*. Les risques d'incident resteront ainsi au-dessous de la moyenne nationale.

(2)   Le tronçon B traverse les municipalités de Nederweert, Heythuysen et Haelen. Il longe la zone protégée « Leudal » et sa description est la suivante :

Cette partie de la ligne de chemin de fer suit la voie qui existe déjà et qui est en service, qui va de Weert (et des accès orientaux) aux ponts sur la Meuse à proximité de Ruremonde. Cette voie, comme le tronçon A2, fait partie de la ligne de chemin de fer qui relie Eindhoven à Ruremonde en passant par Weert. Le tronçon B, électrifié, est (et reste) à double voie. Il y circule 92 trains par période de 24 heures dans les deux sens. Il s'agit tant de trains de marchandises que de trains de voyageurs.

La norme applicable est la même que celle du tronçon A2, c'est-à-dire une augmentation du trafic existant qui devrait passer à 199 trains par période de 24 heures dans les deux sens.

(3)   Le tronçon C, qui traverse les municipalités de Ruremonde et Swalmen, est décrit de la manière suivante :

Ce tronçon exige la réalisation d'une nouvelle ligne de chemin de fer, qui va de l'est de la Meuse aux environs de Ruremonde. Cette ligne contourne Ruremonde au nord et à l'est. À proximité de Herkenbosch, elle rejoint la partie du tracé historique désaffectée qui va de la gare de Ruremonde à la frontière allemande, près de Vlodrop. Dans la mesure du possible, la nouvelle ligne sera reliée à la Route Nationale 73. Il s'agit d'une ligne à une seule voie, non électrifiée. Les normes applicables à cette partie de la voie se fondent sur le fait qu'il s'agit d'une nouvelle situation créée localement.

(4)   Le tronçon D traverse la municipalité de Roerdalen et est décrit de la manière suivante :

Cette partie de la ligne suit le tracé historique, désaffecté depuis 1991. Le tronçon D va de l'Asenrayerweg à la frontière germano-néerlandaise près de

Vlodrop. Le tracé traverse la zone protégée du Meinweg. Aux fins de la réactivation du Rhin de fer, la ligne traversant le De Meinweg sera réalisée en partie dans un tunnel et en partie sur un remblai. Cette ligne est actuellement désaffectée. La définition des normes du tronçon D est fondée sur la création d'une nouvelle situation résultant de la réactivation du Rhin de fer.

185. Pour ces différents tronçons de voies, la version préliminaire du Projet d'ordonnance procédurale de planification décrit en détail toutes les mesures à prendre pour la réactivation à long terme de la ligne du Rhin de fer. Les principales sources de désaccord entre les Parties portent sur les mesures de réduction du bruit et de protection du milieu naturel. Le Tribunal va maintenant faire le point sur ces mesures.

1. Mesures de réduction du bruit concernant les zones d'habitation et lieux similaires

186. Pour l'ensemble de la voie, des mesures significatives sont envisagées pour protéger les habitants des zones situées à proximité de la voie ferrée de l'augmentation du niveau sonore résultant de la réactivation envisagée de la ligne du Rhin de fer. Ces mesures, exigées par la loi sur la réduction des nuisances sonores, prévoient en outre des expropriations faisant l'objet d'indemnisations visant des logements pour lesquels les mesures d'atténuation du bruit sont insuffisantes pour que celui-ci reste au-dessous du seuil maximum dérogatoire.

187. La Belgique considère que les Pays-Bas n'appliquent pas le seuil maximum dérogatoire prévu par la Loi sur l'atténuation des nuisances sonores, mais uniquement le seuil préférentiel, lequel est plus strict. S'il était fait application du seuil maximum dérogatoire, les mesures nécessaires seraient moins importantes. Sur cette question et ses implications financières, la Belgique conclut que :

> il serait contraire aux principes de bonne foi et de caractère raisonnable de subordonner la réactivation du Rhin de fer à l'adoption de mesures de réduction du bruit prévues par le Concept [la version préliminaire du Projet d'Ordonnance procédurale de planification] qui ne sont pas nécessaires pour atteindre le seuil dérogatoire de 70 dB(A) (ou 73 dB(A)), si ces mesures doivent être financées par la Belgique ou rendent de toute autre manière l'exercice du droit de la Belgique sur le Rhin de fer anormalement difficile.

La Belgique estime que cela constituerait une ingérence inutile dans son droit de passage (RB, p. 44–46, paras. 48 à 50).

279

188. Les Pays-Bas reconnaissent que la version préliminaire du Projet d'Ordonnance procédurale de planification applique effectivement le seuil préférentiel, mais soutiennent que la législation en matière d'atténuation du niveau sonore, y compris le critère de seuil préférentiel, est appliquée de la même manière que pour d'autres lignes de chemin de fer, et ne voient donc aucune raison de s'écarter de cette politique générale au détriment de l'intérêt des parties concernées. Dans ce contexte, les Pays-Bas évoquent également les principes de saine gestion sur lesquels se fondent également les mesures envisagées (DPB, pp. 18–19, paras. 74–78).

2. Tunnel du site du Meinweg

189. Le site du Meinweg est une zone d'environ 1.600 hectares située à proximité de la partie orientale du tronçon D. Le 18 février 1994, la Province du Limbourg l'a classée « Zone de silence ». Un arrêté ministériel du 20 mai 1994 a classé le site du Meinweg en zone de protection spéciale en vertu de l'Article 4, paragraphe 1 de la Directive Oiseaux. Le 1er juin 1995, la zone a été déclarée parc national par le ministre de l'agriculture, de la protection de l'environnement et de la Pêche. Le 18 février 2003, le Gouvernement des Pays-Bas a inclus le site du Meinweg dans la liste proposée des zones de protection spéciale prévues par la Directive Habitats. La Commission européenne a ratifié cette proposition en juillet 2003. La Belgique déclare n'avoir été consultée à aucune de ces occasions. Les Pays-Bas répondent qu'ils n'étaient pas tenus de la consulter.

190. Selon la Belgique, les Pays-Bas étaient tenus d'éviter tout classement, autre que ceux découlant de leurs obligations au titre des Directives communautaires, susceptible d'entraîner des mesures supplémentaires de réduction des nuisances sonores et de protection de la nature.

191. Pour le passage de la ligne du Rhin de fer suivant le tracé historique dans le secteur du Meinweg, la version préliminaire du Projet d'Ordonnance procédurale de planification envisage la construction d'un tunnel de 6,5 kilomètres de long, avec un aqueduc et un remblai.

192. Selon les Pays-Bas, ces mesures sont la conséquence du classement du secteur du Meinweg en parc national et en « Zone de silence » et non une conséquence de son classement en vertu des Directives communautaires, lesquelles exigent uniquement la

construction de barrières antibruit. Le droit communautaire autorise en effet les Pays-Bas à appliquer des normes de protection de l'environnement plus rigoureuses que celles prescrites par les Directives communautaires pertinentes. Le classement du secteur en parc national et « Zone de silence » résulte de l'application du droit néerlandais et de la politique nationale qui, selon les Pays-Bas, se fondent sur des critères objectifs. Les mesures envisagées sont le résultat d'études approfondies et de la prise en compte des diverses options dans le cadre des procédures décisionnelles applicables, y compris d'une EIE (CMPB, p. 49, para. 3.3.5.6; DPB, p. 23, paras. 93 et suivants).

193. Sur le principe, la Belgique conteste non pas le droit des Pays-Bas d'effectuer ces classements, mais leur implication financière pour les Parties.

3. <u>Weerter-en Budelerbergen</u>

194. Le Weerter-en Budelerbergen est une zone protégée située sur le tronçon A1. Cette zone fut classée en zone de protection spéciale au titre de la Directive Oiseaux le 24 mars 2000 (ce qu'affirment les deux Parties, mais la Belgique ne fait pas état de cette zone dans la Pièce 77 de son Mémoire – Pays-Bas, arrêté ministériel du 24 mars 2000), et en « Zone de silence » par la province du Limbourg le 18 février 1994 (à la même date que le De Meinweg) et, semble-t-il, également par la province de Noord-Brabant.

195. La version préliminaire du Projet d'Ordonnance procédurale de planification envisage un certain nombre de mesures pour le secteur de Weerter-en Budelerbergen. Ces mesures comprennent la construction de barrières antibruit, un enfouissement partiel de la voie et la construction d'un corridor écologique. En outre, les expropriations doivent également faire l'objet d'une indemnisation.

196. Selon les Pays-Bas, ces mesures résultent de l'application de la législation et de la politique nationales et sont une conséquence de leur classement en « Zone de silence » et en zone de protection spéciale au titre de la Directive Oiseaux.

197. La Belgique ne conteste pas ce point, mais ses conséquences financières pour les Parties.

4. Contournement de Ruremonde

198. Le projet de tronçon C implique de dérouter la ligne du Rhin de fer de son tracé historique en lui faisant contourner la ville de Ruremonde à l'est et au nord sur une nouvelle voie. C'est l'option privilégiée par le Gouvernement néerlandais pour cette partie du tronçon. Il serait possible de conserver le tracé historique, mais les exigences actuelles en matière de sécurité et de réduction du bruit entraîneraient des mesures supplémentaires importantes, mesures qui ne seraient pas nécessaires en cas de déroutement du tracé hors du centre ville. En outre, compte tenu du développement croissant des normes de sécurité en matière de transport de produits dangereux qui interdiront à l'avenir qu'un grand nombre de trains de marchandises traverse la ville de Ruremonde, les Pays-Bas estiment que cette solution est préférable (CMPB, pp. 28–29, para. 2.13.2).

199. La Belgique insiste sur le fait que les Pays-Bas ne peuvent pas décider de s'écarter du tracé historique en l'absence de son accord (RB, p. 69, para. 70).

200. Les Pays-Bas sont d'accord en substance avec cette position. Ils sont également disposés à assumer les frais supplémentaires de cette déviation (DPB, p. 21, para. 85).

201. Le Tribunal en conclut que les Parties conviennent que toute décision des Pays-Bas relative au détournement de la ligne du Rhin de fer exige l'accord de la Belgique. Il note également qu'en principe, cet accord interviendra bientôt.

D. Conclusions

202. Relativement aux mesures envisagées par les Pays-Bas et décrites ci-dessus, la Belgique affirme que les Pays-Bas sont tenus d'appliquer leur droit de la manière la moins défavorable possible pour la Belgique. En n'agissant pas ainsi, les Pays-Bas agiraient à l'encontre aux principes de bonne foi et de caractère raisonnable. Or, la Belgique considère que certaines des mesures envisagées constituent une atteinte inutile à son droit de passage, ainsi qu'une violation par les Pays-Bas de leurs obligations envers la Belgique (RB, pp. 32–33, 46, et 68–71, paras. 37, 50 et 70).

203. Les Pays-Bas soutiennent qu'ils appliquent à la réactivation de la ligne du Rhin de fer le même traitement qu'à toutes les autres lignes de chemins de fer néerlandaises. Ils

acceptent le droit de la Belgique à la réactivation, mais ne voient aucun motif de faire bénéficier la ligne du Rhin de fer d'un régime plus favorable que les lignes néerlandaises régulières. Les Pays-Bas affirment donc agir raisonnablement et de bonne foi en demandant les mesures envisagées pour la réactivation. Leurs actions ne constituent pas un abus de droit et ne sont ni arbitraires, ni discriminatoires. En fait, ils soutiennent que leur législation est appliquée de la manière la plus favorable qui soit à la Belgique (DPB, pp. 40–42, paras. 158–170).

204. Le Tribunal estime que les obligations imposées aux Pays-Bas par l'Article XII du Traité de Séparation de 1839 n'exigent pas qu'ils appliquent leur législation et leur politique nationales à la réactivation de la ligne du Rhin de fer d'une manière plus favorable que pour les autres lignes de chemins de fer néerlandaises, sauf si une telle application non discriminatoire devait aboutir à un déni du droit de passage de la Belgique ou devait en rendre l'exercice anormalement difficile.

205. Le Tribunal conclut que les mesures envisagées actuellement par les Pays-Bas ne peuvent pas être considérées comme un déni du droit de passage de la Belgique et qu'elles ne rendent pas anormalement difficile l'exercice de ce droit. La question liée à ce point, mais qui en est toutefois distincte, selon laquelle le coût de ces mesures aboutirait à un déni du droit de passage de la Belgique ou rendrait l'exercice de ce droit anormalement difficile sera traitée par le Tribunal au Chapitre VI.

206. Dans la mesure où les Pays-Bas insistent sur le fait que les mesures envisagées découlent exclusivement de l'application de leur droit national, ce que la Belgique ne conteste pas, le Tribunal juge inutile d'examiner le problème des contraintes imposées par le droit communautaire (*voir* Chapitre III des présentes).

CHAPITRE VI - RÉPARTITION DES COÛTS

207. Le Tribunal va maintenant aborder la question de la répartition des coûts qui fait l'objet de la troisième Question posée conjointement par les Parties au Tribunal. Elle est formulée dans ces termes :

> Dans quelle proportion, au vu des réponses aux questions précédentes, le coût et les risques financiers liés à l'utilisation, la réfection, l'adaptation et la modernisation du tracé historique du Rhin de fer sur le territoire néerlandais devraient-ils être supportés par la Belgique ou par les Pays-Bas ? La Belgique est-elle tenue de financer des investissements supérieurs à ceux qui sont nécessaires aux possibilités d'utilisation du tracé historique de la ligne de chemin de fer ?

208. Le Tribunal constate que le Compromis d'arbitrage l'invite à se prononcer en se fondant sur le droit international, ce qui inclut, le cas échéant, le droit communautaire. Il n'est en revanche pas autorisé à statuer sur ces questions en qualité d'amiable compositeur. La rédaction de l'introduction de la troisième Question indique clairement que le Tribunal doit fonder sa décision relative à la répartition des coûts sur ses réponses aux deux Questions précédentes. Le Tribunal abordera donc la question des coûts en se fondant sur le raisonnement adopté au cours des chapitres précédents.

209. Le Tribunal observe que le Traité de Séparation de 1839 ne mentionne pas le terme de « risques financiers ». Les Parties utilisent néanmoins ce terme dans les Questions qu'elles ont conjointement posées au Tribunal, sans préciser davantage le sens qu'elles lui attribuent, pas plus qu'elles n'exposent dans leurs plaidoiries la compréhension qu'elles en ont. Le Tribunal comprend que dans le contexte d'un projet d'infrastructure, ce terme renvoie à la couverture du montant du financement dépassant les coûts budgétés pour ledit projet en raison de différents facteurs, tels qu'une inflation supérieure à celle qui avait été prévue, une sous-estimation des coûts, des impondérables, de l'augmentation du coût des matériaux utilisés ou encore des frais de main-d'œuvre. Le Tribunal constate que, quelle que soit la position respective des Parties quant à la répartition des risques et des coûts qu'elles ont peut-être adoptée à un moment ou à un autre au cours de leurs négociations, les Parties ne font aucune distinction dans leurs plaidoiries entre les coûts de réactivation et les risques financiers liés à celle-ci, ni ne suggèrent que les risques financiers devraient être à la charge d'une Partie autre que celle qui assumerait le coût proprement dit. Le Tribunal estime qu'il ne convient pas de distinguer les risques

284

financiers des coûts. En conséquence, la Partie qui assume le coût devra également assumer les risques financiers et lorsque le Tribunal fera référence aux coûts dans le présent Chapitre, ceux-ci devront être compris comme incluant également les risques financiers.

A. Arguments des Parties

210. Le Tribunal note en outre que les deux Parties déclarent que la répartition des coûts relève du régime conventionnel de la ligne du Rhin de fer. Elles diffèrent toutefois quant aux dispositions concernées et à leur interprétation.

211. L'Article XII du Traité de Séparation de 1839 prévoit d'exécuter les « travaux convenus » « aux frais de la Belgique, sans charge aucune pour la Hollande ».

212. La Belgique soutient toutefois que son obligation de supporter les frais prévue à l'Article XII concernait la construction d'une ligne de chemin de fer sur le territoire néerlandais venant prolonger une nouvelle ligne de chemin de fer sur le territoire belge, et non l'exercice du droit de passage de la Belgique (RB, p. 98, para. 104). La Belgique renvoie à l'Article XI du Traité de Séparation de 1839 et à ce qu'elle appelle les « *travaux préparatoires* » pour étayer son argumentation selon laquelle son obligation d'assumer les coûts concerne la construction d'une nouvelle ligne de chemin de fer prolongée sur le territoire néerlandais, et non l'exercice de son droit de passage (RB, pp. 99–100, para. 105). La Belgique considère que l'exercice du droit de passage n'est assujetti qu'à des droits de péage modérés, versés par les usagers de la ligne de chemin de fer du Rhin de fer aux fins de financer son entretien (RB, p. 99, para. 105).

213. La Belgique, en raison du fait qu'elle estime que sa demande actuelle de réactivation n'est pas une demande de « nouvelle route » au sens de l'Article XII du Traité de Séparation de 1839, soutient qu'elle n'est pas tenue d'assumer le coût et les risques financiers associés à la réactivation du Rhin de fer. Elle déclare en conséquence qu'en application du régime conventionnel du Rhin de fer, tous les postes de coûts et les risques financiers liés à l'utilisation, la réfection, l'adaptation et la modernisation du tracé historique de la ligne du Rhin de fer sur le territoire néerlandais incombent aux Pays-Bas et non à la Belgique (MB, p. 101, para. 86; RB, pp. 103 et suivants et p. 127, paras. 110 et suivants et Soumission sur la Question 3).

285

214. La Belgique soutient également que les Pays-Bas ont rendu impossible l'usage de la ligne de chemin de fer en démantelant une partie de son infrastructure, rendant celle-ci impropre à être utilisée, en ne l'entretenant pas et en décidant d'interrompre les travaux visant à ramener le tracé historique de la ligne à un niveau nécessaire pour un usage temporaire. Ainsi, selon la Belgique, les Pays-Bas ont contrevenu au droit de la Belgique d'utiliser le tracé historique de la ligne du Rhin de fer, ainsi qu'au principe de « *due diligence* ». La Belgique conclut qu'en conséquence le coût et les risques financiers liés à la réfection du tracé historique, lesquels n'existeraient pas si les Pays-Bas s'étaient acquittés de leurs obligations, doivent être assumés par les Pays-Bas (MB, p. 109, para. 96). Si le Tribunal devait rejeter la demande de la Belgique d'imputer l'ensemble des coûts et des risques financiers aux Pays-Bas, la Belgique soutient, à titre subsidiaire, qu'elle ne serait pour autant pas tenue d'assumer ces coûts et ces risques financiers dont la cause réside dans le non respect par les Pays-Bas de leurs obligations envers la Belgique. Selon la Belgique, cela serait une conséquence de l'obligation de réparer le préjudice causé par une violation du droit international et l'application du principe selon lequel nul ne peut tirer avantage de ses actes illégaux (*nullus commodum capere de sua injuria propria*) (MB, p. 107, para. 95).

215. La Belgique souligne donc le fait que tous les coûts relatifs à la réactivation, y compris ceux liés à la protection de l'environnement, incombent aux Pays-Bas. Toutefois, à titre « subsidiaire », elle soutient, relativement à l'usage à long terme du tracé historique de la ligne du Rhin de fer, que les Pays-Bas ne peuvent pas exiger qu'elle assume les éléments suivants : (1) les mesures relatives aux voies utilisées actuellement ou à l'avenir par les transports ferroviaires néerlandais ; (2) les mesures nécessaires pour atteindre des objectifs supérieurs à ceux fixés par les exigences législatives néerlandaises ; (3) le contournement de Ruremonde ; et (4) le tunnel sur le site du Meinweg et toutes structures de nature similaire, ainsi que toutes mesures compensatoires le long du tracé. La Belgique conclut que si les Pays-Bas imposent ces conditions, ils devront financer les mesures nécessaires pour assurer l'exercice du droit de passage de la Belgique (RB, pp. 118–119, para. 131).

216. Selon les Pays-Bas, la Belgique revendique le droit de passage mais n'est pas disposée à respecter les conditions et les obligations qui y sont inextricablement liées en vertu de l'Article XII du Traité de Séparation de 1839 (CMPB, p. 43, para. 3.3.4.4).

217. Les Pays-Bas soutiennent en outre que la demande belge de réactivation de la ligne du Rhin de fer équivaut à une demande, au sens de l'Article XII du Traité de Séparation de 1839, de prolongement d'une ligne de chemin de fer ayant son origine en Belgique sur le territoire néerlandais qu'elle traverse. Selon les Pays-Bas, cette ligne est nouvelle dans la mesure où l'usage envisagé implique une adaptation et une modernisation considérables (CMPB, p. 43, para. 3.3.4.5). En conséquence, les Pays-Bas soutiennent que les coûts mentionnés à l'Article XII doivent être intégralement assumés par la Belgique, renvoyant à l'Article XII et, notamment, aux passages suivants « entièrement aux frais et dépens de la Belgique » et « aux frais de la Belgique, sans charge aucune pour la Hollande », « sans préjudice de ses droits de souveraineté exclusifs sur le territoire que traverserait la route ou le canal en question » (CMPB, p. 56, para. 3.3.8.1).

218. En conséquence, selon les Pays-Bas, l'Article XII du Traité de Séparation de 1839 oblige la Belgique à assumer l'ensemble des coûts engagés pour sa demande d'adaptation et de modernisation de l'infrastructure existante, dont l'état actuel ne permet pas l'usage souhaité par la Belgique (CMPB, p. 57, para. 3.3.8.2).

B. Opinion du Tribunal

219. Que les Parties avancent les arguments ci-dessus exposés est parfaitement compréhensible. Ces positions trouvent toutefois chacune leur origine dans une lecture différente de l'Article XII du Traité de Séparation de 1839, dont aucune ne peut être soutenue. Le Tribunal a en effet expliqué plus haut (*voir* paragraphes 82 à 84) que bien que l'Article XII vise directement la construction du Rhin de fer et le régime applicable à celui-ci, le droit de passage qui y est prévu inclut également la réactivation de la ligne, ainsi que son exploitation dans le temps. Les dispositions financières spécifiques de l'Article XII ont été formulées pour la construction d'une nouvelle route ou ligne de chemin de fer ou le creusement d'un nouveau canal. Les vraies questions, en matière de répartition des coûts, sont les suivantes : quels sont les éléments de l'Article XII relatifs aux coûts qui s'appliquent à une réactivation qui, bien que n'étant pas une construction d'une nouvelle ligne de chemin de fer, n'en tombe pas moins dans le champ d'application de l'Article XII ? Quels sont les autres éléments dudit Article XII, interprété conformément aux principes juridiques exposés au chapitre II des présentes, susceptibles d'éclairer la répartition des coûts de la réactivation souhaitée par la Belgique et à laquelle elle a droit ?

287

220. Le Tribunal se trouve en présence de trois points de départ pour entreprendre son analyse de ces questions. Le premier est que, pour des sujets autres que ceux spécifiquement prévus dans le cadre de la construction d'une nouvelle ligne, les Pays-Bas conservent leur souveraineté. Le deuxième point est qu'à l'heure actuelle, les mesures de protection de l'environnement sont nécessairement l'une des composantes à part entière d'un projet majeur d'adaptation et de modernisation. Il a été démontré aux paragraphes 58 et 59 que les règles de droit international relatives à la protection de l'environnement font partie du droit applicable aux relations des Parties pour l'interprétation du régime conventionnel de la ligne du Rhin de fer. Troisièmement, le Tribunal gardera à l'esprit que la charge financière liée à la réactivation ne doit pas peser d'une manière qui interdise, ou rende anormalement difficile, l'exercice du droit de passage de la Belgique en vertu de l'Article XII du Traité de Séparation de 1839. L'ensemble de ces éléments suggère que les coûts ne doivent pas être assumés exclusivement par la Belgique comme s'il s'agissait d'une « nouvelle route » mais ne doivent pas non plus être assumés exclusivement par les Pays-Bas. En conséquence, les obligations financières des Parties doivent être soigneusement équilibrées, ce qui exige que l'on prenne en compte un nombre important de facteurs. Les Parties ne considèrent pas cet équilibre comme déraisonnable si l'on en juge par leurs offres, au cours des négociations, de contribuer aux frais de la réactivation : les Pays-Bas ont proposé, en octobre 2001, de prendre à leur charge 25% (140 millions d'euros) de l'estimation du coût d'alors (DPB, p. 15, para. 60) et de verser une somme supplémentaire de 40 millions d'euros si la Belgique renonçait à l'usage temporaire de la ligne (DPB, p. 16, para. 65). Quant à la Belgique, elle s'est déclarée disposée à verser 100 millions d'euros (MB, pp. 66–67, para. 48).

221. Le Tribunal considère que la Belgique peut, en principe, exercer son droit de passage d'une manière correspondant à ses besoins économiques actuels. Par ailleurs, les préoccupations des Pays-Bas en matière d'environnement et celles concernant les effets sur l'environnement de l'utilisation envisagée, beaucoup plus intensive, de la ligne de chemin de fer, sont parfaitement légitimes. Il convient de concilier, dans toute la mesure du possible, l'exercice du droit de passage de la Belgique et les préoccupations légitimes des Pays-Bas en ce qui concerne leur environnement. Le Tribunal relève que cette conciliation des droits peut être mise en parallèle avec l'équilibre des intérêts reflété par l'Article XII du Traité de Séparation de 1839. Le Tribunal estime que la réfection et la modernisation de la ligne demandées par la Belgique doivent donc être analysées en se

référant à l'Article XII du Traité de Séparation de 1839, non parce que cela équivaut à une « nouvelle ligne » (selon les Pays-Bas), mais plutôt parce que l'objet et le but du Traité suggèrent une interprétation impliquant, dans le cadre de l'équilibre qui y est atteint, de nouveaux besoins et développements relatifs à son exploitation et à sa capacité (*voir* paragraphe 84 ci-dessus). Ainsi que le Tribunal l'a noté ci-dessus (*voir* paragraphe 59), il convient de concilier croissance économique et protection de l'environnent et, ce faisant, de prendre en considération de nouvelles règles, y compris lorsque des activités commencées dans le passé sont étendues et modernisées.

222. L'utilisation de la ligne du Rhin de fer remonte à quelque 120 ans et la Belgique envisage et demande à présent l'augmentation de celle-ci et son intensification à un niveau beaucoup plus élevé. Or, cette nouvelle utilisation risque d'avoir un impact négatif sur l'environnement et de le dégrader. Actuellement, le droit international de l'environnement met de plus en plus l'accent sur le devoir de prévention. Une grande partie de ce droit international de l'environnement a été élaboré en fonction de l'impact que les activités d'un territoire sont susceptibles d'avoir sur le territoire d'un autre. La Cour internationale de justice a exprimé l'avis que « l'obligation générale qu'ont les États de veiller à ce que les activités exercées dans les limites de leur juridiction ou sous leur contrôle respectent l'environnement dans d'autres États ou dans des zones ne relevant d'aucune juridiction nationale fait maintenant partie du corps de règles du droit international de l'environnement » (*Licéité de la menace ou de l'emploi des armes nucléaires, avis consultatif, Recueil C.I.J. 1996 (I)*, p. 226 à pp. 241–242, para. 29).

223. Appliquant les principes du droit international de l'environnement, le Tribunal constate qu'il est confronté, dans la présente affaire, non à une situation où l'activité économique transfrontalière du territoire d'un État a des conséquences sur le territoire d'un autre État, mais aux conséquences de l'exercice des droits d'un État, garantis par un traité, sur le territoire d'un autre État et à l'impact éventuel de l'exercice de ce droit sur le territoire de ce dernier. Le Tribunal estime, par analogie, que lorsqu'un État exerce un droit relevant du droit international sur le territoire d'un autre État, les considérations relatives à la protection de l'environnement doivent également être prises en compte. En conséquence, telle que la demande de la Belgique est formulée, l'exercice de son droit de passage pourrait bien exiger que les Pays-Bas prennent des mesures pour protéger l'environnement, mesures auxquelles la Belgique devra participer car elles font partie

intégrante de sa demande. La réactivation de la ligne du Rhin de fer ne peut pas être envisagée comme dissociée des mesures de protection de l'environnement nécessaires à l'utilisation envisagée de la ligne de chemin de fer. Ces mesures doivent être totalement intégrées au projet et à ses coûts.

224. Il n'a pas été demandé au Tribunal, qui aurait d'ailleurs été dans l'impossibilité de le faire, de déterminer les mesures à adopter spécifiquement. Il lui est en revanche demandé de se prononcer sur la répartition des coûts relatifs aux mesures à prendre. Le Tribunal note que le Protocole d'accord de mars 2000 prévoyait que ces mesures seraient énoncées dans le cadre d'un traité. Le Tribunal ne précisera pas la répartition des coûts en termes financiers mais, sur la base du droit applicable en la matière, indiquera les critères et principes pertinents que les Parties devraient appliquer à cette répartition.

225. Le Tribunal rappelle qu'il incombe aux Pays-Bas de restaurer à leurs frais la ligne du Rhin de fer dans l'état où celle-ci se trouvait en 1991 (*voir* paragraphes 76 et 89 ci-dessus). Tel est le cas pour la totalité du tracé historique. Cette conclusion s'entend indépendamment de toute violation des Pays-Bas de leurs obligations en matière d'entretien de la ligne depuis le début des années 90. Le Tribunal rappelle également que les Pays-Bas ont reconnu qu'ils seront responsables de l'entretien d'une ligne réactivée (DPB, p. 34, para. 136).

226. L'obligation de la Belgique de financer l'aspect environnemental de l'ensemble des coûts de la réactivation est inhérente à l'exercice de son droit de passage. Par ailleurs, une interprétation des dispositions financières de l'Article XII fondée sur le caractère raisonnable exige également la reconnaissance de l'usage par les Pays-Bas de certaines parties de la ligne. S'agissant de ces tronçons, il convient de prendre en considération tant les frais imputables au développement autonome que les avantages qu'en retireront les Pays-Bas et ceci d'autant plus que la ligne sera adaptée et modernisée. Sur les tronçons de voie où circuleront à la fois les trains du Rhin de fer et les trains néerlandais, la Belgique n'aura à financer que les frais liés aux mesures imputables à l'usage de la ligne par les trains du Rhin de fer. Les Pays-Bas assumeront quant à eux le coût total dans la mesure où ils en obtiennent des avantages particuliers et quantifiables.

227. L'application de ces principes dépendra des informations fournies au Tribunal relativement à chaque tronçon de la ligne. Ces tronçons et leur future utilisation sont

décrits au paragraphe 184 ci-dessus. Les informations pertinentes ont été fournies par les Parties, qui n'ont établi aucune distinction entre les trains de marchandises et les trains de voyageurs en ce qui concerne les mesures que requiert leur utilisation.

228. Le tronçon A comprend deux parties. Sur la première partie (ou tronçon A1), qui va de la frontière belgo-néerlandaise à l'embranchement de la ligne de chemin de fer Eindhoven-Weert (*voir* paragraphe 184 ci-dessus), ne circulent actuellement que deux trains par période de 24 heures. Il s'agit de trains régionaux qui ne doivent pas être pris en compte dans le cadre de l'exercice du droit de passage de la Belgique sur le Rhin de fer. Le Tribunal estime que les coûts des travaux nécessaires à la réactivation (c'est-à-dire l'utilisation, la réfection, l'adaptation et la modernisation, ainsi que les mesures nécessaires pour la protection de l'environnement) de cette partie du tracé sont dus à la demande belge de permettre à l'avenir la circulation de 43 trains de marchandises supplémentaires par période de 24 heures. En conséquence, le Tribunal conclut que les coûts de réactivation de cette partie du tronçon A doivent être supportés par la Belgique.

229. La seconde partie du tronçon A (ou tronçon A2) (*voir* paragraphe 184) se situe entre l'est de l'embranchement de la ligne de chemin de fer Eindhoven-Weert et la municipalité de Nederweert. Actuellement, il y circule 104 trains par période de 24 heures. La version préliminaire du Projet d'Ordonnance Procédurale de Planification prévoit qu'en 2020, il y circulera 199 trains, dont les 43 du Rhin de fer. On ne peut pas exclure le fait que le développement des transports ferroviaires des Pays-Bas (le « développement autonome ») envisagé pour 2020, à savoir l'ajout de 52 trains au niveau d'usage actuel de 104 trains par période de 24 heures, entraînera sans doute également certains frais. En conséquence, le Tribunal estime que les coûts de réactivation de ce tronçon A2 doivent être répartis entre les Parties : l'obligation de la Belgique de financer les coûts associés à la réactivation sera minorée d'un facteur financier incluant les coûts qui auraient été nécessaires au développement autonome si le Rhin de fer n'avait pas été réactivé, tant en ce qui concerne la ligne que les aspects environnementaux. Le Tribunal renvoie à cet égard au projet de développement autonome dont les Pays-Bas eux-mêmes ont tenu compte lors de l'élaboration de la version préliminaire du Projet d'Ordonnance Procédurale de Planification.

230. Bien que l'obligation générale, en termes de financement, demeure celle de la Belgique, le Tribunal considère également qu'il convient de tenir compte de tout élément

291

susceptible de représenter un avantage quantifiable particulier pour les Pays-Bas – résultant notamment d'une amélioration de la circulation et de la sécurité routière, d'une réduction du niveau sonore et d'un potentiel, supérieur au développement envisagé actuellement, d'utilisation supplémentaire de la ligne par les trains néerlandais – lors de la répartition des coûts entre les Parties. En fait, au cours des négociations tripartites avec la Belgique et l'Allemagne au début de 1999, les Pays-Bas ont soutenu que la répartition des avantages (tant économiques que socio-économiques) devait être le point de départ pour répartir les coûts de la réactivation entre les Parties (MB, Pièce 78, Groupe de Pilotage Administratif flamand-néerlandais, Projet de rapport sur le « Rhin de fer » pour les ministres des Transports de Belgique, des Pays-Bas et d'Allemagne, p. 25).

231. Le tronçon B (*voir* paragraphe 184) couvre la ligne qui va de Nederweert à Haelen. L'usage actuel et l'usage prévu de ce tronçon ressemblent à ceux du tronçon A2, sauf qu'il y circule actuellement, par période de 24 heures, 92 trains et non 104 (néanmoins, d'ici 2020, c'est le même nombre de 199 trains par période de 24 heures qui est prévu). En conséquence, le Tribunal estime que les coûts de réactivation de la ligne de chemin de fer doivent être répartis entre les Parties selon le principe énoncé aux paragraphes 229 et 230.

232. Le tronçon C (*voir* paragraphe 184) dessert les municipalités de Swalmen et de Ruremonde. Au vu des éléments en sa possession, le Tribunal comprend que ce tronçon ne sera utilisé que comme liaison ferroviaire entre la Belgique et l'Allemagne (RB, Pièce n° 10 corrigée, version préliminaire 1.4 du Projet d'Ordonnance Procédurale de Planification, p. 98, para. 6.1 et suivants). Le tracé envisagé contourne Ruremonde au nord et à l'est, selon la proposition des Pays-Bas, lesquels ont, au cours des négociations, exprimé leur intention d'assumer le coût supplémentaire de cette déviation autour de Ruremonde. Ce contournement s'écarte du tracé convenu à l'Article IV du Traité du Rhin de fer. Cette déviation ne peut être exécutée sans l'accord de la Belgique, ce qui signifie qu'elle doit faire l'objet d'un accord, modifiant ainsi le tracé historique convenu. La Belgique est donc en droit de demander aux Pays-Bas d'assumer le coût financier supplémentaire de cette déviation qui dépasse le coût qui aurait été nécessaire pour une adaptation et une modernisation du tracé historique traversant Ruremonde. Par ailleurs, si les Pays-Bas sont disposés à prendre à leur charge ce coût supplémentaire, la Belgique ne peut pas raisonnablement refuser d'approuver cette déviation. Si le contournement de

292

Ruremonde est approuvé, les coûts seraient répartis entre les Parties de la manière suivante : la Belgique serait tenue d'assumer le financement qui aurait été nécessaire pour réactiver le tracé historique existant actuellement, tandis que les Pays-Bas assumeraient les coûts supplémentaires dus au déplacement de la ligne au nord et à l'est de Ruremonde.

233. Le tronçon D (*voir* paragraphe 184) traverse la municipalité de Roerdalen. Il va de l'Asenrayerweg jusqu'à la frontière germano-néerlandaise. La ligne de chemin de fer sur ce tronçon n'est plus utilisée depuis 1991 et le Tribunal comprend qu'à l'avenir, ce tronçon ne sera utilisé que pour la liaison entre la Belgique et l'Allemagne (RB, Pièce n° 10 corrigée, Version préliminaire 1.4 du Projet d'Ordonnance Procédurale de Planification, p. 117, para. 7.1 et suivants). La réactivation est demandée par la Belgique. Pour les raisons exposées ci-dessus, la Belgique assumera le coût de réactivation de la voie.

234. De manière spécifique, la Belgique devra assumer le coût des barrières antibruit érigées à proximité des zones d'habitation et des mesures compensatoires de préservation sur ce tronçon. Le Tribunal est conscient du fait que le principal facteur de coût non seulement pour ce tronçon, mais pour l'ensemble du projet de réactivation du Rhin de fer est le projet de construction d'un tunnel sur le site du Meinweg. La Belgique a soutenu que le coût des diverses mesures de protection de l'environnement, et notamment du tunnel dans le De Meinweg, était « trop élevé » (MB, p. 82, para. 66), « très onéreux » (MB, p. 88, para. 74), voire « prohibitif » (MB, p. 81, para. 66). La construction de ce tunnel est envisagée en raison du fait que le tracé traverse la zone du Meinweg, classée parc national par le Ministère de l'Agriculture, de la Protection de l'environnement et de la Pêche le 1er juin 1995, et « Zone de silence » par la Province du Limbourg. Lorsque les Pays-Bas ont pris cette décision, ils savaient déjà que le tracé historique traversait ce secteur et que la Belgique, bien que n'exerçant pas son droit de passage depuis 1991, avait réservé son droit à utiliser la ligne à l'avenir. Le Tribunal estime que la décision des Pays-Bas de classer le site du Meinweg parc national dans un secteur sur lequel la Belgique jouissait d'un droit de passage aux termes d'un traité, ne peut rester sans conséquences financières pour les Pays-Bas, même s'il s'agit d'une décision souveraine permise aux Pays-Bas. Par ailleurs, le Gouvernement belge n'avait réservé son droit qu'en termes abstraits, sans préciser les paramètres d'une future utilisation de la ligne, avant que ces décisions ne soient adoptées par les Pays-Bas. La construction du tunnel est requise non seulement du

fait de l'utilisation intensive envisagée par la Belgique, dont les Pays-Bas n'ont d'ailleurs pas été informés pleinement en temps opportun, mais également du fait de la décision des Pays-Bas d'établir un parc national dans une zone déjà traversée par le tracé historique. Le Tribunal considère que les deux Parties ont contribué à l'émergence de la situation qui exige désormais l'adoption de mesures plus onéreuses. En conséquence, il estime que le coût du tunnel dans le Meinweg doit être réparti équitablement entre les Parties.

235. Le Tribunal a défini aux paragraphes 228 à 234 les principes de répartition des coûts qu'il estime découler des dispositions de l'Article XII du Traité de Séparation de 1839, tout en prenant en compte les dispositions applicables du droit international. Il n'a pas été demandé au Tribunal de calculer avec exactitude le coût total de la réactivation, le coût du développement autonome, ni les bénéfices que retireraient les Pays-Bas de la ligne de chemin de fer réactivée du Rhin de fer. En outre, il constate que le Projet d'Ordonnance Procédurale de Planification est une version préliminaire et est donc susceptible d'être modifiée ultérieurement. La mission du Tribunal ne consiste pas davantage à examiner des questions d'une grande complexité scientifique portant sur le fait de savoir si les mesures adoptées seront suffisantes aux fins d'assurer le respect des niveaux prescrits de protection de l'environnement. Ces questions relèvent du domaine de l'expertise technique et, à cet effet, le Tribunal recommande aux Parties de prendre dans les plus brefs délais et, en tout état de cause, au plus tard quatre mois après la date de la présente sentence, les mesures nécessaires pour constituer une commission d'experts indépendants dans le même délai, sauf si les Parties en conviennent autrement, dont la mission consisterait à déterminer :

1. le coût de la réactivation de la ligne du Rhin de fer ;

2. le coût du développement autonome ; et

3. les avantages particuliers, quantifiables – en termes financiers – de la réactivation pour les Pays-Bas résultant notamment de l'amélioration du trafic routier et de la sécurité routière, de la réduction des nuisances sonores et du potentiel de développement autonome supérieur aux prévisions actuelles, découlant de l'utilisation supplémentaire de la ligne par les trains néerlandais.

Cette commission d'experts indépendants devra rendre ses conclusions dès que possible et en aucun cas pas plus de six mois après la date de sa constitution.

Les Parties devront utiliser les conclusions de la commission d'experts indépendants pour déterminer leur part respective des coûts et risques liés à l'amélioration de la ligne du Rhin de fer sur les tronçons A2 et B. Les Pays-Bas devront participer aux coûts et aux risques financiers liés à la réactivation du Rhin de fer sur les tronçons A2 et B à hauteur d'un montant englobant le coût du développement autonome (point 2 ci-dessus) et de l'équivalent financier des bénéfices qu'ils en retirent (point 3), tels que déterminés par la commission d'experts indépendants. La Belgique assumera les autres coûts et risques financiers liés à la réactivation du Rhin de fer sur les tronçons A2 et B.

236. Le Tribunal conclut ainsi que les coûts et les risques financiers liés à l'utilisation à long terme de la ligne du Rhin de fer doivent être assumés par les Parties de la manière suivante :

1. la Belgique sera tenue d'assumer seule le coût et les risques financiers liés à la réactivation du tronçon A1 et du tronçon D, à l'exception du tunnel sur le site du Meinweg ;

2. la Belgique et les Pays-Bas se répartiront le coût et les risques financiers liés à la réactivation des tronçons A2, B et C et du tunnel du Meinweg du tronçon D selon les formules exposées aux paragraphes 229 à 231 (pour les tronçons A2 et B), 232 (pour le tronçon C) et 234 (pour le tunnel sur le site du Meinweg).

237. Dans les soumissions des Parties, le débat ne portait pas uniquement sur la distinction entre l'usage temporaire et un accord sur une utilisation à long terme, mais également sur la durée éventuelle d'un usage temporaire, sur le fait de savoir si celui-ci pourrait être interrompu par les travaux relatifs à la réactivation à long terme, ainsi que sur le financement de cet usage temporaire. Dans le Protocole d'accord de mars 2000, les Parties étaient convenues que la Belgique assumerait le coût de cet usage temporaire, mais depuis lors, la Belgique a affirmé que ses engagements étaient devenus caducs du fait d'un défaut d'accord en temps opportun sur le financement de l'utilisation à long terme. Le Tribunal constate que le financement de l'usage temporaire ne fait pas partie des Questions qui lui ont été posées officiellement. Le Tribunal ne considère pas non plus

que les Questions qui lui ont été posées relativement à « l'utilisation, à la réfection, à l'adaptation et à la modernisation du tracé historique » sont liées aux questions mentionnées ci-dessus concernant l'usage temporaire.

CHAPITRE VII - RÉPONSE DU TRIBUNAL AUX QUESTIONS POSÉES PAR LES PARTIES

A. Question 1

238. La première Question spécifique posée au Tribunal arbitral dans le Compromis d'arbitrage est la suivante :

> Dans quelle mesure le droit néerlandais relatif à l'utilisation, la réfection, l'adaptation et la modernisation des lignes de chemin de fer sur le territoire néerlandais, et le pouvoir décisionnel qui en découle, s'appliquent-ils, de la même manière, à l'utilisation, la réfection, l'adaptation et la modernisation du tracé historique du Rhin de fer sur le territoire néerlandais ?

239. Réponse du Tribunal :

(a) Le Tribunal comprend l'expression « de la même manière » comme signifiant que le droit néerlandais et le pouvoir décisionnel qui en découle s'appliquent de la même manière à l'utilisation, la réfection, l'adaptation et à la modernisation du tracé historique du Rhin de fer et à l'utilisation, la réfection, l'adaptation et la modernisation de n'importe quelle autre ligne de chemin de fer traversant le territoire néerlandais.[20]

(b) Le droit néerlandais relatif à l'utilisation, la réfection, l'adaptation et la modernisation des lignes ferroviaires sur le territoire néerlandais et le pouvoir décisionnel qui en découle s'appliquent de la même manière à l'utilisation, la réfection, l'adaptation et la modernisation du tracé historique du Rhin de fer dans la mesure décrite aux alinéas (c) et (d) suivants.

(c) Il ne peut y avoir conflit entre l'application du droit néerlandais et du pouvoir décisionnel qui en découle, et les droits concédés par traité à la Belgique, ou les droits et obligations des Parties en vertu du droit international général ou les contraintes imposées par le droit communautaire (*voir* paragraphe 56). En conséquence, l'application du droit néerlandais et du pouvoir décisionnel qui en

---

[20] Le Tribunal a utilisé le terme officiel « Pays-Bas » dans toute la [NdT : *version originale anglaise de la*] sentence, mais utilise l'adjectif « néerlandais » dans toutes les réponses aux Questions, car c'est la terminologie utilisée par les Parties.

découle ne peut pas aboutir à dénier le droit de passage à la Belgique (*voir* paragraphe 66), ni à rendre anormalement difficile l'exercice à ce droit par la Belgique (*voir* paragraphe 163).

(d)   Le Tribunal juge également que :

(i)   Le droit néerlandais et le pouvoir décisionnel qui en découle ne peuvent être appliqués de manière unilatérale aux fins de décider d'une déviation par rapport au tracé historique ;

(ii)   l'application du droit néerlandais et du pouvoir décisionnel qui en découle n'est pas subordonnée au fait que les travaux correspondants soient exécutés par les Pays-Bas eux-mêmes ou par la Belgique ;

(iii)   le droit néerlandais et le pouvoir décisionnel qui en découle ne permettent pas de fixer unilatéralement le niveau, ni le barème de perception des droits de péage ; et

(iv)   les mesures résultant de l'application du droit néerlandais et du pouvoir décisionnel qui en découle doivent permettre la réactivation de la ligne de chemin de fer du Rhin de fer d'après « le même plan » (compris dans le sens de possibilités d'utilisation : *voir* paragraphe 67).

B. Question 2

240. La deuxième Question spécifique posée au Tribunal arbitral dans le cadre du Compromis d'arbitrage est la suivante :

Dans quelle mesure la Belgique a-t-elle le droit d'exécuter ou de faire exécuter des travaux en vue de l'utilisation, de la réfection, de l'adaptation et de la modernisation du tracé historique du Rhin de fer sur le territoire néerlandais et d'arrêter tous plans, caractéristiques et procédures y afférents en vertu du droit belge et du pouvoir décisionnel qui en découle ? Convient-il d'établir une distinction entre les exigences, les normes, les plans, les caractéristiques et les procédures en rapport, d'une part, avec les possibilités d'utilisation de l'infrastructure ferroviaire proprement dite et, d'autre part, l'aménagement du territoire et l'intégration dans celui-ci de cette infrastructure ferroviaire et, dans l'affirmative, quelles en sont les conséquences ? Les Pays-Bas peuvent-ils imposer unilatéralement la construction de tunnels, de tranchées couvertes, de déviations et toute autre mesure similaire, ainsi que les normes proposées de construction et de sécurité y afférentes ?

241. Réponse du Tribunal :

(a)   La Belgique a le droit d'arrêter un plan fixant les spécifications du tracé pertinentes pour les possibilités d'utilisation du prolongement de la ligne traversant les Pays-Bas. Les travaux résultant de l'utilisation, de la réfection, de l'adaptation et de la modernisation du tracé historique du Rhin de fer demandées doivent être des « travaux convenus ». La Belgique ne peut exécuter sur le territoire néerlandais des travaux qui n'ont pas fait l'objet d'un accord préalable. Les Pays-Bas ne peuvent refuser d'approuver une proposition de la Belgique si ce refus équivaut à lui dénier ses droits de passage, ou à rendre l'exercice de ces droits anormalement difficile.

(b)   Tel est le cas que les Pays-Bas décident d'exécuter eux-mêmes les travaux convenus sur leur territoire, ou qu'ils demandent à la Belgique de s'en charger.

(c)   Le Tribunal observe toutefois que les Pays-Bas ne peuvent pas imposer unilatéralement une déviation par rapport au tracé historique.

(d)   Les Pays-Bas étaient en droit de classer des secteurs le long du tracé historique en zones protégées car cette décision ne constitue pas en soi une restriction du droit de passage de la Belgique et les circonstances examinées par le Tribunal n'indiquent pas qu'existait une obligation légale de consulter préalablement la Belgique.

(e)   Les Pays-Bas ont en principe le droit d'imposer unilatéralement la construction de tunnels souterrains, de tranchées couvertes « et toute autre mesure similaire ». Néanmoins, quelles que soient les mesures imposées, elles ne doivent pas aboutir à dénier à la Belgique son droit de passage sur le tracé historique, ni à rendre l'exercice de ce droit anormalement difficile.

C. Question 3

242. La troisième Question spécifique posée au Tribunal arbitral dans le cadre du Compromis d'arbitrage est la suivante :

Dans quelle proportion, au vu des réponses aux questions précédentes, le coût et les risques financiers liés à l'utilisation, la réfection, l'adaptation et la modernisation du tracé historique du Rhin de fer sur le territoire néerlandais devraient-ils être supportés par la Belgique ou par les Pays-Bas ? La Belgique est-elle tenue de financer des investissements supérieurs à ceux qui sont nécessaires aux possibilités d'utilisation du tracé historique de la ligne de chemin de fer ?

243. Ce à quoi le Tribunal répond, en commençant par le second élément de la Question :

Le Tribunal rappelle que les obligations de la Belgique, autres que celles liées aux possibilités d'utilisation, découlent du fait que la réactivation demandée représente un développement économique sur le territoire des Pays-Bas, auquel il convient d'intégrer les mesures de prévention et de réduction des atteintes à l'environnement. Le Tribunal a également estimé qu'il est impossible de dissocier le coût des mesures de protection de l'environnement (et d'autres mesures de sécurité) des coûts nécessaires aux possibilités d'utilisation du tracé historique. Le coût et les risques financiers liés au droit de passage sur lequel la Belgique fonde sa demande d'utilisation, de réfection, d'adaptation et de modernisation (« réactivation ») doivent refléter l'équilibre entre les Parties inhérent à l'Article XII du Traité de Séparation de 1839, interprété par référence aux principes applicables du droit international. En conséquence, les obligations de la Belgique de financer les investissements ne sont pas limitées aux investissements nécessaires aux possibilités d'utilisation du tracé historique de la ligne de chemin de fer.

244. Le Tribunal estime également que les postes de coûts et les risques financiers liés à la réactivation du tracé historique du Rhin de fer sur le territoire néerlandais sont les suivants :

(a) Les coûts du tronçon reliant la frontière belgo-néerlandaise à l'embranchement avec la ligne de chemin de fer Eindhoven-Weert (« tronçon A1 ») sont à la charge de la Belgique.

(b) En ce qui concerne le tronçon qui va de l'est de l'embranchement de la ligne de chemin de fer Eindhoven-Weert à la municipalité de Nederweert (tronçon A2), les coûts seront répartis entre les Parties de la manière suivante : l'obligation de la Belgique d'assumer le coût et les risques financiers associés à la réactivation sera minorée d'un facteur financier représentant le coût du développement autonome des transports ferroviaires néerlandais prévu pour 2020 en l'absence de la réactivation du Rhin de fer. L'obligation restante de la Belgique doit en outre être minorée d'un facteur financier correspondant aux avantages particuliers, quantifiables, qu'en retirent les Pays-Bas (en dehors de ce qui concerne le développement autonome) et notamment à une amélioration de la circulation et de la sécurité routières, à une réduction des nuisances sonores et à une optimisation du potentiel dépassant les prévisions de développement autonome.

(c)   Quant au tronçon reliant la municipalité de Nederweert à celle de Haelen (« tronçon B »), les coûts seront répartis entre les Parties de la manière suivante : l'obligation de la Belgique de financer les coûts associés à la réactivation sera minorée d'un facteur financier correspondant au développement autonome des transports ferroviaires néerlandais, prévu pour 2020, en l'absence de réactivation du Rhin de fer. L'obligation restante de la Belgique doit également être minorée d'un facteur financier correspondant aux avantages particuliers et quantifiables qu'en retirent les Pays-Bas (en dehors de ce qui concerne le développement autonome) résultant, notamment, d'une amélioration de la circulation et de la sécurité routières, d'une réduction des nuisances sonores et d'une optimisation du potentiel dépassant les prévisions de développement autonome.

(d)   Les coûts relatifs au tronçon couvrant les municipalités de Swalmen et de Ruremonde (« tronçon C »), seront répartis entre les Parties de la manière suivante : si le contournement de Ruremonde fait l'objet d'un accord, la Belgique sera tenue d'assumer les coûts et les risques financiers liés à la réactivation du tracé historique tel qu'il existe actuellement, tandis que les Pays-Bas seront tenus de supporter le coût et les risques supplémentaires liés au fait de détourner la ligne au nord et à l'est de Ruremonde, détournement qui aura fait l'objet d'un accord.

(e)   Les coûts relatifs au tronçon traversant la municipalité de Roerdalen (« tronçon D ») seront répartis entre les Parties de la manière suivante : la Belgique sera tenue d'assumer le coût et les risques financiers liés à la réactivation de la ligne de chemin de fer qui ne doit être utilisée que comme liaison entre la Belgique et l'Allemagne, incluant le coût et les risques financiers liés aux barrières antibruit érigées à proximité des habitations et aux mesures compensatoires de préservation sur ce tronçon. Toutefois, en ce qui concerne tout tunnel éventuellement construit dans le secteur du Meinweg, classé parc national par le ministre néerlandais de l'Agriculture, de la Protection de l'environnement et de la Pêche le 1er juin 1995 et « Zone de silence » par la Province du Limbourg, la nécessité de ce tunnel étant imputable à la conduite passée des deux Parties, elles partageront à part égale l'obligation d'assumer le coût et les risques financiers qui y sont liés.

LA LIGNE DE CHEMIN DE FER DU RHIN DE FER *

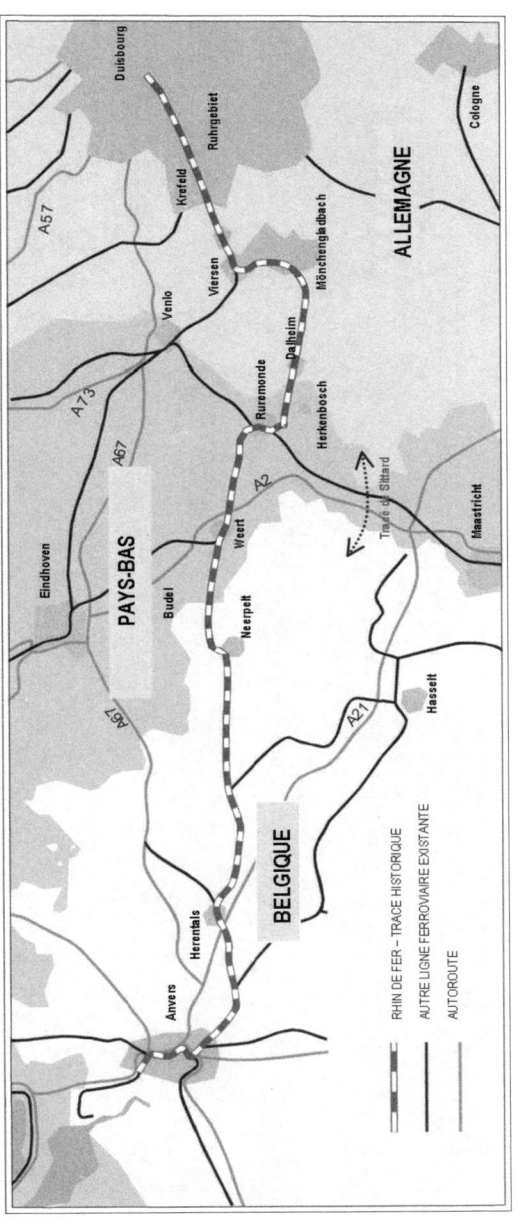

RHIN DE FER - TRACE HISTORIQUE

AUTRE LIGNE FERROVIAIRE EXISTANTE

AUTOROUTE

* Pour une version en couleur de cette carte voir page 314.

DANS LE CADRE DE L'ARBITRAGE RELATIF

A LA LIGNE DU RHIN DE FER (« IJZEREN RIJN »)

ENTRE :

LE ROYAUME DE BELGIQUE

- ET -

LE ROYAUME DES PAYS-BAS

INTERPRÉTATION DE LA SENTENCE DU TRIBUNAL ARBITRAL

Le Tribunal Arbitral :

Madame le Juge Rosalyn Higgins, Président
Monsieur le Professeur Guy Schrans
Monsieur le Juge Bruno Simma
Monsieur le Professeur Alfred H.A. Soons
Monsieur le Juge Peter Tomka

La Haye, 20 septembre 2005

305

INTERPRÉTATION DE LA SENTENCE DU TRIBUNAL ARBITRAL

1. Le 25 juillet 2005, la Belgique, en vertu de l'article 23(1) du Règlement de procédure régissant l'arbitrage concernant le chemin de fer dénommé le Rhin de fer (« Ijzeren Rijn ») entre le Royaume de Belgique et le Royaume des Pays-Bas, déposa une demande visant à obtenir une Interprétation de la Sentence rendue par le Tribunal arbitral le 24 mai 2005.

2. La demande de la Belgique comprenait trois Requêtes, chacune d'elles étant accompagnée d'explications et d'arguments, ainsi que de pièces.

3. Par un courrier en date du 25 juillet 2005, les Pays-Bas furent invités à commenter les Requêtes de la Belgique. Les commentaires des Pays-Bas sur chacune des Requêtes d'interprétation de la Belgique furent reçus par le Tribunal le 15 août 2005.

4. Le Tribunal a soigneusement étudié les arguments de chaque Partie. Par ailleurs, il note qu'il appartient au Tribunal d'interpréter la manière dont la Sentence doit être comprise à la lumière de ses propres intentions au moment où il a rendu sa Sentence. Ainsi, les paragraphes qui suivent ne répondent-ils pas aux différentes observations et commentaires des Parties mais constituent plutôt une interprétation par le Tribunal de sa Sentence ayant autorité en vertu de l'article 23(1) des Règles de Procédure.

*   *   *

5. Première Requête :

> La Sentence devrait-elle être interprétée comme signifiant que les Pays-Bas sont soumis à l'obligation de ramener, à leurs frais, la ligne du Rhin de fer à un niveau permettant l'utilisation du Rhin de fer comparable à celui qui existait lors de l'utilisation, quoique réduite, de la ligne avant l'interruption d'une telle utilisation en 1991 ?

6. Le Tribunal répond ce qui suit.

7. Au paragraphe 76, la Sentence indique que : « [l]e Tribunal considère que les Pays-Bas (ce que ceux-ci acceptent) sont tenus de ramener la ligne du Rhin de fer au niveau qu'elle avait atteint lors de l'utilisation régulière (quoique réduite) de la ligne avant l'interruption de cette utilisation en 1991 ; mais ces obligations d'entretien et de réparation ne couvrent pas les coûts de modernisation significatifs impliqués par la demande actuelle de la Belgique ».

8. Au paragraphe 89, le Tribunal a jugé que la loi néerlandaise qui prévoyait l'entretien des chemins de fer par référence à un niveau de trafic existant à un moment donné ne violait pas les droits de la Belgique au titre de l'article XII du Traité de Séparation de 1839. Le Tribunal ajoutait « et ce, d'autant plus que les Pays-Bas acceptent pleinement leur obligation de ramener la ligne au niveau d'entretien et de sécurité de 1991, à leurs frais, en cas de demande de réactivation de la Belgique ».

9. Dans la partie de la Sentence traitant de la répartition des frais (cf. paragraphe 225), le Tribunal rappelait « qu'il incombe aux Pays-Bas de restaurer à leurs frais la ligne du Rhin de fer dans l'état où celle-ci se trouvait en 1991 (*voir* paragraphes 76 et 89 ci-dessus). Tel est le cas pour la totalité du tracé historique ».

10. Bien que cette décision ne soit pas répétée dans les Réponses du Tribunal (aux paragraphes 238 à 244 de la Sentence) aux Questions spécifiques qui lui avaient été posées, ladite décision constituait toutefois une étape nécessaire pour parvenir à la formulation de ces Réponses.

11. Le Tribunal observe tout d'abord que la référence à l'obligation des Pays-Bas de remettre la ligne dans l'état dans lequel elle se trouvait en 1991 doit être comprise comme renvoyant à des obligations financières (plutôt que comme une obligation en matière de construction) incombant aux Pays-Bas en ce qui concerne l'entretien restant à réaliser dans le cas d'une réactivation de la ligne. Ceci est clair au vu de la

référence à la répartition des coûts dans chacun des paragraphes de la Sentence cité ci-dessus.

12. Si les Parties décident de réactiver le Rhin de fer et si elles sont convenues des modalités d'utilisation future, la répartition des coûts de sa réactivation (comme précisé dans la Sentence dans la Réponse à la Question 3) devra inclure l'élément constitué par l'obligation des Pays-Bas de supporter cette partie des coûts qui représente les frais qui auraient été encourus pour l'entretien de la voie restant à réaliser, y compris de ses caractéristiques de sécurité, afin de permettre un usage comparable à celui qui existait en 1991. Le Tribunal rappelait au paragraphe 225 de sa Sentence que les Pays-Bas avaient reconnu qu'ils seraient « responsables de l'entretien d'une ligne réactivée ».

13. Les décisions du Tribunal citées ci-dessus doivent être comprises comme signifiant que les obligations financières des Pays-Bas (nées de l'éventualité décrite au paragraphe précédent) porteraient sur les normes de sécurité (en tant qu'éléments de l'entretien) telles que le droit néerlandais les prescriraient et non telles qu'elles ont pu être applicables en 1991.

*   *   *

14. Deuxième Requête :

> La Sentence devrait-elle être interprétée comme signifiant que la Belgique n'a aucun droit à une utilisation temporaire de la ligne du Rhin de fer ?

> La décision selon laquelle les exigences des Pays-Bas peuvent ne pas équivaloir à un déni du droit de passage de la Belgique, ni rendre l'exercice de ce droit par la Belgique déraisonnablement difficile (§§ 239(c) et 241(e)) devrait-elle être interprétée comme s'appliquant à la question de l'utilisation temporaire du Rhin de fer, ainsi que la décision du Tribunal sur les principes et les procédures énoncés dans le Protocole de mars 2000, figurant aux paragraphes 157 et 158 de la Sentence ?

15.   Dans sa Requête, la Belgique indique qu' « il ne fait aucun doute que le Tribunal a décidé de ne pas retenir les arguments de la Belgique » en ce qui concerne la circulation immédiate et provisoire et qu' « [i]l ne fait également aucun doute que le Tribunal n'a pas statué sur les questions relatives à l'utilisation temporaire ». La Belgique poursuit : « toutefois, ceci ne veut pas dire pas qu'il est possible d'interpréter la Sentence comme signifiant que la Belgique n'a aucun droit à une utilisation temporaire, ni que cette utilisation temporaire n'est pas régie par des principes énoncés dans la Sentence, en particulier les principes de caractère raisonnable et de bonne foi auxquels il est fait référence aux paragraphes 239(c), 241(e) et 157 ». La Belgique demande une interprétation sur ces points.

16.   Les Pays-Bas ont fait remarquer au Tribunal « qu'ils estiment que le pouvoir décisionnel concernant une éventuelle utilisation effective du Rhin de fer appartient aux Parties ».

17.   Le Tribunal répond ce qui suit.

18.   La Sentence ne peut pas être interprétée comme signifiant que la Belgique n'a aucun droit à une utilisation temporaire. Elle ne peut pas davantage être interprétée comme comprenant une quelconque déclaration du Tribunal quant aux circonstances dans lesquelles un tel droit peut être exercé.

19.   Au paragraphe 237 de sa Sentence, le Tribunal observait « que le financement de l'usage temporaire ne fait pas partie des Questions qui lui ont été posées officiellement ». En conséquence, les Réponses aux Questions n'incluaient aucune décision relative à la répartition des coûts d'une éventuelle utilisation temporaire.

20.   Le Tribunal n'a pas statué sur le caractère légal ou l'interprétation correcte du Protocole d'accord, signé le 28 par les Ministres belge et néerlandais des transports, dans la mesure où cela ne lui a pas été demandé dans le cadre des Questions qui lui

310

ont été posées. Le Tribunal s'est limité à déclarer que « les principes et procédures définis dans le Protocole d'accord de mars 2000 ... fournissent des indications utiles sur ce que les Parties sont prêtes à considérer comme compatible avec les droits que leur confèrent l'Article XII du Traité de Séparation de 1839 et le Traité du Rhin de fer (cf. Sentence, paragraphe 157).

21.   Le Tribunal a jugé que l'application du droit néerlandais et les pouvoirs décisionnels découlant de celui-ci pouvaient ne pas équivaloir à un déni du droit de passage de la Belgique sur le tracé historique, ni rendre déraisonnablement difficile l'exercice de ce droit par la Belgique. Ces décisions, de même que l'ensemble de la Sentence, sont applicables à toute utilisation du Rhin de fer.

                        *   *   *

22.   Troisième Requête :

> La décision du Tribunal sur la répartition des coûts concernant le tronçon C, si un contournement de Ruremonde fait l'objet d'un accord, devrait-elle être interprétée comme faisant supporter à la Belgique le coût de la réactivation du tracé historique traversant Ruremonde, alors que ce coût résulte de mesures demandées par les Pays-Bas après que la Sentence ait été rendue, outre le coût compris dans les chiffres présentés au Tribunal, le droit néerlandais d'application générale demeurant inchangé ?

23.   Le Tribunal répond ce qui suit.

24.   Les soumissions des Parties et leurs annexes suggéraient que les deux Parties envisageaient qu'une éventuelle réactivation du Rhin de fer entraînerait vraisemblablement une déviation du tracé historique par le biais d'un contournement de la ville de Ruremonde. Aucune alternative n'a donc été présentée au Tribunal en ce qui concerne le tronçon C.

25.   Le Tribunal, lorsqu'il a rédigé ses Réponses à la Question 3, au paragraphe 244(d), ainsi que les principes qui y sont énoncés, ne présumait pas que les montants estimés

qui lui avaient été présentés pour les travaux envisagés demeureraient figés dans le temps. Par ailleurs, le Tribunal a clairement signifié dans sa Sentence que l'application du droit néerlandais et du pouvoir décisionnel qui en découle ne pouvaient pas être assimilés à un déni du droit de passage de la Belgique sur le tracé historique de la ligne, ni rendre déraisonnablement difficile l'exercice de ce droit par la Belgique.

26. La décision du Tribunal relative à la répartition des coûts pour le tronçon C, si un contournement autour de Ruremonde fait l'objet d'un accord, doit être interprétée comme applicable au scenario qui lui a été présenté à l'exclusion de toute alternative hypothétique.

THE IRON RHINE RAILWAY

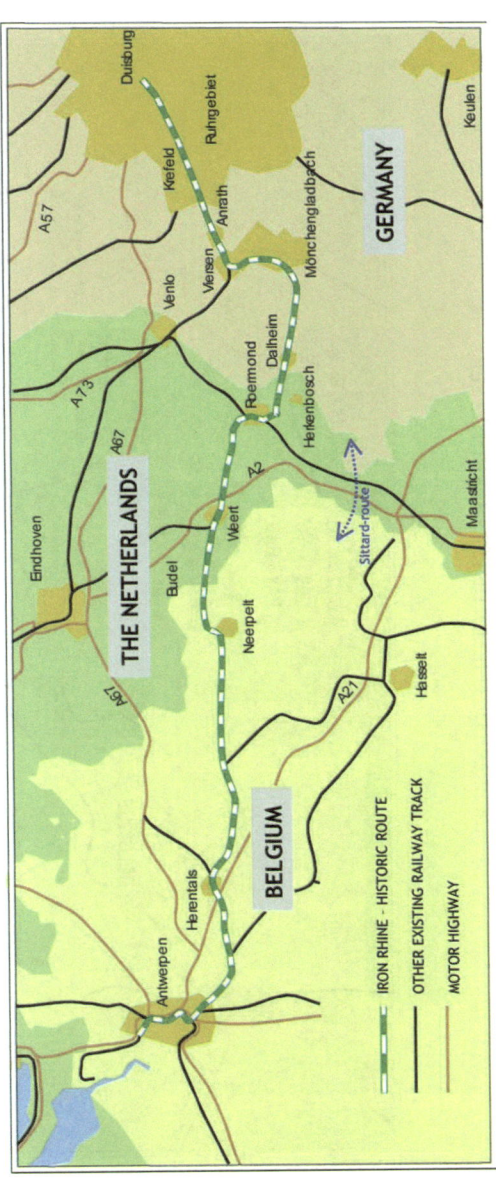

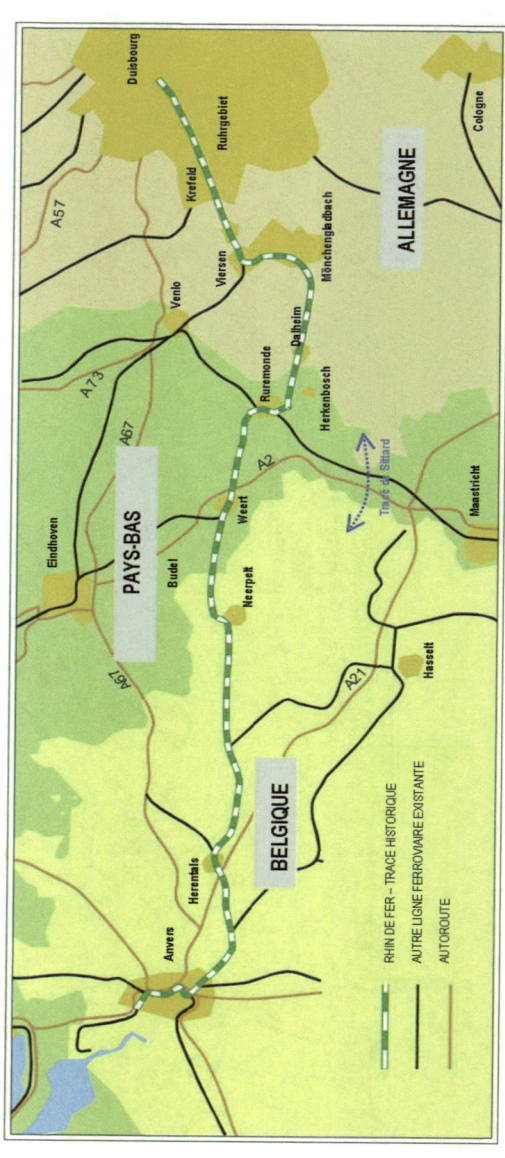

LA LIGNE DE CHEMIN DE FER DU RHIN DE FER